The Daily Telegraph

CASTLES & ANCIENT MONUMENTS OF ENGLAND

The Daily Telegraph

CASTLES
& ANCIENT
MONUMENTS
OF ENGLAND

BY DAMIEN NOONAN

AURUM PRESS

To Olivia, with love

Thanks to: Dilys and Terry Noonan, Mark, Gaynor and Amy, Sean, Allie and Ellie, John, Lydia, Nicola Jane (and Steve), Martin, Philippa, Marcus and Barnaby, Paul and Jonty, Tass, Simon, Isabelle and Harry, and Mel for all her help

Illustrations

Cover: *Dunstanburgh Castle, Northumberland*

Frontispiece: *Orford Castle, Suffolk*

This page: *The motte at Pickering Castle, Yorks*

Opposite: *Lower Brockhampton, Hereford & Worcester*

Page 6: *Launceston Castle, Cornwall*

Page 8: *Scotney Castle, Kent*

Graphics by Stephen Lockett and Nina Belluomo

Base maps supplied by Perrott Cartographics, Machynlleth, Wales

First published 1999 by Aurum Press Limited, 25 Bedford Avenue, London WC1B 3AT

A catalogue record for this book is available from the British Library.

ISBN 1 85410 621 X (paperback)
ISBN 1 85410 636 8 (hardback)

Printed and bound in Italy by Printer Trento srl

10   9   8   7   6   5   4   3   2

2003   2002   2001   2000

Contents

WELCOME TO THIS BOOK. There isn't anything complicated about it, but I've found when I've explained the idea to people that they always have a few questions to ask, so I thought we might try to get some of the answers out of the way first.

As is so often the case with things like this, the reason I wanted to write this book was that I've spent ages looking in the shops for something like it, only to find that nothing similar exists.

The basic idea was to provide a fully illustrated guide, in colour, with a photograph of every place mentioned. It's only recently that colour printing has become cheap enough for a publisher to consider doing this, and as far as I'm aware, this is the first time it has been attempted.

The other aim was to be reasonably comprehensive. There are traces of hundreds of minor castles in England, so of course we couldn't mention them all – and there are many thousands of archaeological sites. But what we have tried to do is to cover all the major castles that are regularly open to the public, and to include all the most important, exciting or attractive ancient monuments. If it's not in the book, then, it's probably the sort of thing that will only appeal to archaeologists or historians (though this also means there's plenty more to find if you get keen).

In Elizabethan times, the sort of wealthy people who lived in castles wanted to live in a nice, modern house instead, with big, modern windows and the latest thing in fireplaces. Many houses built after this date are called 'Castle Such-and-such', but they won't be in the book. After the time of Henry VIII, the major fortifications of England were artillery forts, and a number of these – from Tudor to Victorian times – are included.

So the line-up is pretty much like this: prehistoric ancient monuments, from neolithic tombs and stone circles to iron age hillforts; Roman remains; castles from Norman to Tudor times; and forts right up to the end of the last century. Also included, for their beauty as well as their historical interest, are ruined abbeys. And there's a smattering of whatever else caught my eye, too.

Most importantly, though, the idea of the book is to suggest attractive and interesting places to visit, perhaps for a pleasant drive in the country at the weekend, or maybe while you're on holiday. Visiting historic sites should be fun, and I've tried to give a flavour of the enjoyment to be had as you explore the nooks and crannies of a ruin, or just sit back and enjoy the scenery. Inevitably this means that personal opinions come into it in quite a big way. Generally, I hope you'll find this helpful; but if you really feel I've got it wrong, I would be glad to hear from you. (Write care of the publisher.)

Finally, we have done our best to ensure that all information is correct and reliable, but if you find any mistakes or omissions, please get in touch.

DAMIEN NOONAN

Alphabetical Index of Counties

INTRODUCTION: FROM BOXGROVE MAN TO THE ROMAN EMPIRE

Prehistoric England

KNOWLTON CHURCH, DORSET

A Norman church, now ruined, was built inside a huge henge monument which was already some 3000 years old when work on the church first started. Perhaps the henge was still seen as a sacred place by local people in medieval times, though any memory of the sort of ceremony that might have taken place there must surely have been long forgotten.

THE OLD STONE AGE

THE OLDEST TRACES OF MANKIND IN BRITAIN are a leg bone and a tooth about half a million years old. They were found quite recently, along with stone tools and the bones of hunted animals, in a gravel pit at Boxgrove in Sussex. Quarrying for stone at Westbury sub Mendip in Somerset uncovered a cave used by people over 450,000 years ago, but the only traces they left behind were flint tools.

These first people in Britain were not modern humans but a different species, known as *Homo erectus* ('upright man'). With huge jaws and prominent ridges of bone across their brows, these people would have looked primitive by our standards, but they were the first upright apes intelligent enough to be classified as '*homo*' – mankind. *Homo erectus* originated in Africa and reached the Mediterranean shores of Europe as much as one and a half million years ago.

What we known of the story of human evolution is pieced together from genetic evidence and a few scattered fossils, so frankly there's a lot of guesswork involved, but it seems that people and apes both developed from a common ancestor between five and eight million years ago. The earliest known fossils of a man-like species (or 'hominid') are the Australopithecines ('southern apes') from about four million

10

years ago. They were small, about the size of a modern twelve-year-old, and had ape-like skulls, but they walked upright, and the evidence suggests that they were cleverer than modern chimpanzees. Several varieties of Australopithecine still lived in southern Africa as recently as 200,000 years ago, but by this time *Homo erectus* was thriving in North Africa, Asia and Europe.

We are not, however, direct descendants of the first inhabitants of Britain. Although 'archaic' *Homo sapiens* ('clever man') appeared as much as 400,000 years ago, our own direct ancestors are much more recent. Genetic evidence shows that all modern humans are very closely related, from the Arctic to Australia, and the same evidence also suggests that about 65,000 years ago our ancestors were an endangered species, reduced to a small population of perhaps ten thousand, possibly because of global cooling caused by a volcano in Sumatra. They survived, the theory goes, by becoming the most inventive species on the planet, creating an explosion of technology, art and culture around 50,000 years ago known as the Great Leap Forward (or, more soberly, the Upper Palaeolithic transition; 'palaeolithic' means 'the old stone age' while 'upper' simply means 'the more recent part of'). It was the European descendants of these Upper Palaeolithic people (often called 'Cromagnon man' after a burial uncovered near the village of Cromagnon in the Dordogne, France) who created the famous cave paintings of southern France and northern Spain.

These modern people arrived in Europe some 40,000 years ago and, over the next 10,000 years, completely took over from the European Neanderthals who already lived in the region. (And who, incidentally, were not the drooling idiots they're generally thought to be. They may have looked primitive, but their brains were larger, on average, than those of Europeans today.)

DURING THE FIRST HALF A MILLION YEARS of British history, the outstanding topic is, naturally enough, the weather. There were at least four major ice ages (as well as lots of minor ones) during which the polar ice cap expanded to cover most of Britain and arctic tundra covered the rest. When the climate warmed up again, woodland grew back (scattered pine and birch trees at first, then oak forests) and in the warmest periods, though it was only two or three degrees warmer than today, exotic animals like elephants and rhinoceros roamed the river valleys of southern England.

The earliest people in Britain camped by rivers and lakes (and occasionally in caves) and used wooden spears and crude flint choppers to hunt and butcher animals like deer, bison, wild horses and oxen, while

STONE, BRONZE, IRON: THE 'THREE-AGE SYSTEM'

The 'Three-Age System' was created in Victorian times by a Danish museum curator as a way of classifying objects made by prehistoric people. What lay behind it was the vague idea that technology improved through time, and civilisation presumably improved with it; so stone tools and weapons could safely be said to have been made and used before copper or bronze ones, by less developed societies. The most recent tools were undoubtedly the ones made of hard, technologically advanced iron.

The system became widely used, and grew into a convenient way of labelling the different kinds of society that existed in different periods of prehistory. It is now regarded rather sniffily by archaeologists, who are aware that its broad stereotypes can often be confusing rather than helpful, but it remains in widespread use as a very convenient shorthand.

Broadly, in modern use, the system works like this. You do have to be aware that Britain has its own unique pattern of development, so the exact periods covered by its 'ages' will be quite different from, say, the rest of Europe.

The Stone Age has been divided into three sub-sections. The Old Stone Age (or palaeolithic) covers all species of early man from the time they first started using tools. Middle Stone Age (mesolithic) describes a specific phase of modern man (*Homo Sapiens*) when more advanced flint tools were made and used. The story of people in Britain really starts in the mesolithic, in about 10,000 BC, when the last great ice age was over and hunter-gatherers made their way across from Europe to live here. The New Stone Age (or neolithic) is when it starts getting really interesting, however. This label is specifically applied to the phase after 4000 BC when people took up farming and settled permanently on the land, with pottery being the most notable of the new skills that they developed.

The Bronze Age is a less useful label as far as the specific history of Britain is concerned, and is generally blurred into a phase of slow change from the late neolithic onwards. Basically, the use of metals such as gold and bronze seems to coincide with a more organised society with distinct leaders, and there's a sense of prestige separating certain people in society. It is in this phase, after about 2200 BC, that round barrows appear and most stone circles were built.

The iron age is probably the simplest: iron was introduce into Britain about 700 BC, was in widespread use by about 500 BC, and by 300 BC is clearly associated with the culture we know as Celtic.

trying to avoid predators such as lions, jaguars, wolves and sabre-tooth tigers.

It's very difficult to get a meaningful picture of these early people. Undoubtedly their technology developed over time: the earliest, crudely hacked flint choppers (known as Clactonian, because they were found in large quantities at Clacton-on-Sea in Essex) were later replaced by much more carefully worked hand-axes (a type known as early Acheulian). These later, finer tools suggest that the makers took pride in craftsmanship and treasured the tools as possessions. Yet the exact same design of hand-axe was in use for more than a million years in Africa: it's impossible to imagine that these people were like us if they had no sense of technological innovation. Similarly, they have left no kind of art; and though it's assumed that they must have had all kinds of crafts (woodworking, basketry, leatherwork) it is also known that the Neanderthals, who lived much more recently, had not managed to invent sewing, even though they wore clothes made of skins.

From 400,000 years ago, with the first great ice age over, there was a slow improvement in man's control of his environment. Technology improved, with better hand-axes (a type known as late Acheulian) made using soft hammers of bone or wood to give a fine finish. Parts of a skull more than 300,000 years old from a gravel pit near Swanscombe, Kent, seem to be from yet another intermediate species of human, an early type of *Homo sapiens*. There is some evidence that people deliberately cleared patches of forest by burning them, perhaps to attract particular animals to graze on the regrowth. At Stoke Newington in London, traces were found of a man-made shelter more than 200,000 years old which had left impressions in the mud of post-holes and a bed of ferns. Human remains of a similar age found in a cave at Pontnewydd in North Wales might be early Neanderthals, and at about the same time, a new type of flintworking emerges (known as 'Levallois') in which tools are made from flakes of flint chipped from a prepared core.

Around 200,000 years ago, another great ice age kicked in; but even after it faded, there is scant evidence of human occupation of Britain before the first 'modern' people arrived between 26,000 and 20,000 years ago – by which time the climate was already deteriorating towards the last ice age. The 15 or 20 sites of human occupation known from this era are nearly all caves – such as Kent's Cavern in Devon and Badger's Hole in the

WAYLAND'S SMITHY, WILTSHIRE

The long barrow tombs of northern Europe are often described as 'the oldest style of traditional architecture in Europe', which is as good as saying 'the oldest buildings in the world'. The most outstanding examples are the great megalithic tombs, which came into fashion after 2800 BC but these were often built to replace earlier, simpler types of monument, as has been revealed by excavations here at Wayland's Smithy.

Mendips – where the distinctive flint blades and leaf-shaped points made by Upper Palaeolithic man were found alongside the bones of hunted animals (horse, woolly rhino, deer, bison and great Irish elk).

In one such cave, at Paviland in Wales, was found the earliest human burial known in Britain (somewhere between 24,000 BC and 16,500 BC). A young man was buried in a shallow grave and sprinkled with red ochre; with him were perforated sea shells, mammoth-ivory rods, and a necklace and bracelets made from wolf and reindeer teeth.

AFTER THE ICE:
THE MIDDLE STONE AGE

BY 18,000 BC, THE ICE COVERED ENGLAND as far south as the Bristol channel, but eventually the glaciers of the last ice age withdrew and by about 10,000 BC people were settling in England once again. New types of stone blades were now in use, as well as tools and weapons of antler and bone (including barbed harpoons for hunting fish, and bone awls and needles). The first crude British art appears – scratchy representations, on bone, of a horse and a man, found in the caves of *Creswell Crags, Derbyshire*.

Around 8000 BC much of post-glacial Britain was covered with 'wildwoods', home to smaller animals such as wild ox, roe deer, red deer and wild pig. The Mesolithic people (middle stone age) used tools made from tiny, carefully engineered flakes of flint known as 'microliths', set in resin to make arrows and spears. Plenty of evidence has been found to show that these people lived in highly developed hunter-gatherer societies, armed with lots of clever strategies for making a living from the natural resources all around them, and going about their daily lives with the support of a complex system of spiritual beliefs. An amazing picture has been built up from excavations at Star Carr in Yorkshire of one such tribe living in the area in about 7000 BC. Their favoured source of food was deer, and they wore the fronts of deer skulls complete with antlers, either during some kind of ritual or as a hunting disguise.

By 6000 BC Britain was again an island, cut off by the rising sea and accessible only by boat. But this didn't mean it was isolated from the next great movement sweeping across Europe – the arrival of farming.

MODERN TIMES:
THE NEOLITHIC

BY ABOUT 4000 BC THE FIRST settled farming communities of Europe were living in wooden houses in small villages along the valleys of major rivers, where the soil was good. They grew barley and wheat, and they herded domesticated cattle; they used new tools, such as flint sickles for harvesting grain and querns (grindstones) for grinding it into flour; and they made pottery. Agriculture quickly spread to Britain, ushering in a new era (the neolithic, or new stone age) in which settled farming societies would create the first great stone monuments – the chambered tombs.

Not so long ago, it was commonly accepted in archaeology that new ideas, new technologies and new cultural habits (such as burial rites) were inevitably associated with new people, and so the history of England was seen as a series of great folk movements sweeping into the British Isles and pushing the old, inferior people with their old, inferior ways into the sea (or perhaps into Wales). Nowadays, however, it is thought that goods and ideas travel much more easily than people. Communication between neighbours led to the 'cultural transmission' of new techniques and beliefs, while the people generally stayed in the same place.

PIMPERNE LONG BARROW, DORSET

This is one of the largest earthen long barrows in England, 100m (330ft) long, and the ditches and low banks along each side are still clearly visible. Earthen long barrows are older even than those with stone chambers, having been widely built from about 3500 BC onwards. Originally, the white chalk of the barrows would have gleamed in the sun, and the sides of the barrow would have been supported by rows of timber posts, so it would have looked far more like a building.

New farming techniques were imported to Britain from the other side of the Channel along with seeds of domesticated crops and breeding stock of domesticated cattle. (This also suggests, incidentally, that people must have been crossing the sea in boats from the very earliest times.) That's not to imply, though, that the hunter-gatherers of Britain took up farming after 4000 BC in slavish imitation of their Continental cousins. Probably the pioneers of agriculture started work much earlier than that: in some areas of southern England, it seems that crops were being tried out as early as 5000 BC. And in any case, the change from a nomadic hunter-gatherer lifestyle to a settled agricultural one must have been a very, very gradual process. After all, it's not such a big step from 'managing' herds of wild animals and harvesting wild herbs, vegetables and fruit to keeping cattle and planting crops.

By 3500 BC, pottery – one of the defining innovations of the neolithic age – and agricultural tools were being made and used right across Britain. From impressions of seeds in the clay of pots, it is possible to identify the exact varieties of crop that were grown – two kinds of wheat and one kind of barley – and by measuring the size of the grains, it's easy to show that wheat grown 5000 years ago on the chalklands of Wessex was very nearly as healthy a crop as the modern stuff.

Animal bones show that cattle, sheep and pigs were kept in different proportions in different areas (more pigs in woodland, more sheep on the uplands). Advances in technology included delicate leaf-shaped flint arrowheads and top-quality stone axes, polished with sand to a fine finish and often distributed over wide areas, perhaps as gift exchanges between neighbouring communities.

Neolithic farmers were tied much more closely to a particular patch of land than their ancestors had been, and it seems quite possible that their spiritual beliefs would come to reflect this. The great monuments of the age, the chambered long barrows, seem to be an expression of the community's relationship with the land. The barrows are positioned as if they are territorial markers, each one related closely to a particular tract of farmland. The communal effort required for their construction would have been an expression of the individual's duty to the community. And the fact that important bones

MAYBURGH HENGE, CUMBRIA

The earth circles known as henges seem mostly to have developed into stone circles during the bronze age, but the few that survive in something more like their stone age form, as here, can be very impressive. Mayburgh, near Penrith, is probably the best of them all. Its huge circular bank, with just one entrance gap, encloses an area that seems very like an arena – very similar, in fact, to a Roman amphitheatre like the one at Cirencester. Mayburgh's bank is built from millions of football-sized boulders which had to be carried here from the nearby river.

CHAMBERED LONG BARROWS

These burial mounds are among the most dramatic of our ancient monuments, as well as being just about the oldest – though they were preceded by the earthen long barrows, in widespread use from about 3500 BC.

Earthen long barrows are generally built on top of some kind of wooden structure, a mortuary house or exposure platform, on or within which the bodies of the dead were exposed until the bones were weathered clean. Long barrows are communal tombs, so presumably on some sort of cue, like the death of an important person, the barrow would be built over the accumulated remains of an indefinite number of people. Generally it was disarticulated bones that were buried, but sometimes individuals were buried whole, and sometimes cremation took place. Grave goods – items of value buried to accompany the dead – are not very common.

Earthen barrows were generally built on (and therefore from) chalk, and must have looked very dramatic when new, gleaming white in the sun. They were usually wider at one end, faced eastwards, and had rows of timber posts supporting the sides. In certain parts of Britain (most notably Cornwall, in

the case of England) a lack of soil meant that stone cairns were built instead.

The chambered long barrows – with passages or chambers built from huge stones, or 'megaliths' – developed after about 3000 BC, and both these and the earthen long barrows continued to be built for more than a thousand years. The big difference between these and the earthen barrows was that the chambered ones could be re-used, with more burials added later. (The biggest similarity between the two, incidentally, is that both were used for the communal burial of men, women and children alike – an egalitarian custom that is rare in the history of the world.)

These great monuments, their dark, mysterious chambers once filled with scattered bones, can seem pretty alien to us, but a good way to think of them is as ancient cathedrals. They are likely to have shared all the same functions – a centre for spiritual beliefs and worship, a burial place for the most important members of the community (not enough bones are found to suggest that everyone was buried in a chambered tomb) and perhaps also as a defining marker for territory, marking a tract of farmland in the same way that a church marks a parish.

WEST KENNETT LONG BARROW, WILTSHIRE

Set on open land near Silbury Hill and Avebury, this is the finest chambered barrow in England. It's also a good example of how these barrows were treated at the end of their working lives. Some time before 2000 BC, when the barrow had been in use for about a thousand years, the chambers were filled to the roof with earth and stones and the entrance was permanently blocked with huge upright stones.

THE BEST CHAMBERED LONG BARROWS

West Kennett, Wiltshire

Wayland's Smithy, Oxfordshire

Stoney Littleton, Somerset (when it's open)

Hetty Pegler's Tump, Gloucestershire

Belas Knap, Gloucestershire

Coldrum, Kent

like thigh bones and skulls were selected and arranged in the chambers seem to point towards worship of ancestors, which would inevitably give the barrow-builders a sense of being rooted in a specific place.

The few houses of the era known from excavations are mostly individual farmsteads – small, rectangular houses built from wooden planks supported by a post at each corner – but in Scotland there is one exceptional example of a neolithic village. The stone-built houses of Skara Brae, on the Mainland of Orkney, date back to about 3100 BC. They're not big, but they are perfectly habitable, even fitted out with stone furniture.

Some of the most remarkable pieces of work left behind by neolithic communities in England are in the Somerset levels, where the marshy country made getting around difficult. To avoid getting stuck, the people of the area built raised wooden pathways, and one such, the Sweet Track, has been tree-ring dated to the winter of 3807 to 3806 BC – the earliest date in English history.

Generally, the picture throughout the neolithic is of small, peaceful farming communities, but there is also some evidence of greater social organisation and even of conflict on a large scale. At *Hembury hillfort, Devon*, a village was protected by a rampart as early as 3300 BC. At Carn Brae hillfort near Redruth in Cornwall, hundreds of broken flint arrowheads were found scattered around a neolithic village that was attacked in about 2700 BC. And at *Hambledon Hill* in *Dorset*, ramparts built as early as 3500 BC were attacked and burned in about 3300 BC.

Hambledon Hill is also representative of the most mysterious of all neolithic monuments, the 'causewayed camp' (or, more simply,

'causewayed enclosure'). These enclosures are even more inexplicable than stone circles, and detailed excavations have not yet been able to come up with a satisfying explanation.

Basically, they were just large areas of open hilltop which were marked around by a rough circle of ditches. The ditches were in short sections with gaps, or causeways, in between – hence the name 'causewayed enclosures'. The digging of the ditches seems in itself to have been a ritual activity, and deposits varying from animal bones to human skulls are found at the bottom of them. There are some signs of feasting, suggesting that the enclosures were used for celebrations, but the favoured explanation at the moment is that these places were where the bodies of the dead were exposed before burial.

THE BRONZE AGE

The round barrow absolutely typifies the bronze age. Each one is a monument to an individual who stood out from the rest of the community in death as in life and was buried with prestige goods such as pottery, weapons and jewellery. What this buried treasure suggests is that after about 2200 BC society was developing in a way that was more highly structured, with high-status individuals separated from the rest by power and wealth. It was also around this time that stone circles really started to take off.

When you match up the manpower needed to build a monument like Stonehenge with the treasure found in nearby Bush Barrow (on display in the British Museum), you tend to be left with an image of gold-bedecked chieftains commanding lost civilisations in early Hollywood jungle movies.

Generally, though, the picture of bronze age life is far more pastoral. By about 1700 BC, more land was being cultivated than ever before, though around 1500 BC a change in the climate and the wearing out of poor soils meant that upland farms were abandoned and turned to moorland. *Dartmoor (Devon)* has preserved a snapshot of bronze age agriculture, with small, enclosed villages of round houses set among well-defined field systems. In more fertile areas, similar bronze age fields remained in use until Roman times and were still visible, known as 'Celtic fields', until modern deep ploughing started to destroy them within the last 30 years.

KINGSTON RUSSELL
STONE CIRCLE, DORSET

One of the smaller stone circles typical of the later bronze age. By about 1300 BC stone circles were no longer being built.

HENGES AND STONE CIRCLES

The henge is a uniquely British invention. It's a circular bank, enclosing a large area like an arena, often with a ditch inside the bank (the opposite of the arrangement of an earthwork built for defence, where the ditch would be on the outside). Not many henges survive in good, clean condition: the one at *Mayburgh, near Penrith, Cumbria* is particularly good, and there are also good ones to be seen at Thornborough in Yorkshire (*see page 231*) and at *Arbor Low* in *Derbyshire*, where a stone circle was later built inside the henge. Early henges tended to have a single entrance, but later ones often had two (at Avebury, there were four).

Henges were built in the later neolithic era, after about 2800 BC, but they remained in use right into the bronze age and were continually updated, principally by the addition of stone circles. Later in the bronze age, smaller stone circles were also built which must have performed similar functions to the larger henge circles.

Nobody seems to doubt that stone circles were religious monuments, or that they stood in their own right (that is, they weren't part of some kind of building). The simple

astronomical alignments shown by many are also self-evident. It's easy to see how the builders of the circles could line up stones to mark the midsummer sunrise; and it's easy to understand why these farmers would want to celebrate such events as the longest day of summer and the shortest day of winter. More complicatedly, some circles (Stonehenge is one) also seem to mark the extreme rising and setting points of the moon.

Many other features associated with henges and stone circles are beginning to be re-evaluated as new sites are explored with modern methods. In particular, the circular arrangements of post-holes found at places like Woodhenge (near Stonehenge) in Wiltshire were not generally thought to represent buildings, but that possibility is now being explored more actively. Certainly, a modern parallel exists: the Cherokee indians of North America built large roundhouses which they used for ceremonial gatherings and for feasting.

Surprisingly, there are quite a few large stone circles and henges that have not been excavated in detail (*Stanton Drew* in *Somerset* is probably the most important) and it is possible that more answers are waiting to be found.

STANTON DREW, SOMERSET

The Great Circle here is the largest stone circle in Britain after Avebury, and there are two smaller circles nearby. Recent surveys of the site have revealed the traces of a large henge-style bank around the Great Circle and post-holes arranged in concentric circles inside it.

THE BEST STONE CIRCLES

Avebury, Wiltshire

Stonehenge, Wiltshire

Stanton Drew, Somerset

Castlerigg, Cumbria

Long Meg and her Daughters, Cumbria

The Hurlers, Cornwall

The Merry Maidens, Cornwall

Arbor Low, Derbyshire

Rollright Stones, Oxfordshire

Kingston Russell, Dorset

THE IRON AGE: THE CELTS

BY THE TIME JULIUS CAESAR first attempted to conquer western Europe in about 50 BC, the term 'Celts' was generally applied to the native people of north-west Europe (though in France and northern Italy they tended to be called Gauls, and the British tribes were referred to as Britons). The Celts were seen as barbarians, admired for their bravery and their speedy lightweight chariots, mocked for their bristling moustaches and their habit of going naked ('sky-clad') into battle, and reviled for their custom of taking heads as trophies.

There is no reason to think that the Celts were outsiders who invaded Britain. Instead, the things we think of as 'Celtic' – styles of art, types of building (such as hillforts), methods of fighting and so on – are indicative of a Celtic culture that spread among the people of Western Europe during the iron age.

England has always been part of a western European community. The English Channel would always have been more of a link to Europe than a barrier, just as the great rivers were then the most important trade routes. Since before 3000 BC, the people of the Western Atlantic from Scotland down to Portugal had, culturally, a good deal in common: Neolithic chambered tombs were built throughout this region; in the bronze age, between 2000 BC and 1000 BC, commodities such as stone axes, gold, amber and faience (natural glass) were traded from one end of the region to the other; and the 'beaker' burial tradition spread across the same area. Probably, then, we all shared a common language and we all became Celts together.

There were two great phases of Celtic culture, both of which placed great emphasis on the conspicuous display of wealth. The first, known as Hallstatt, developed in central Europe before 600 BC. It valued the horse very highly, under the influence of the mounted tribes of the east, but 'civilised' goods and customs from the Mediterranean civilisations were also very important. The second phase, called La Tene, developed after 500 BC in northern and western Europe and probably owed a good deal to trading links to the Mediterranean through the Greek port of Marseille in the south of France. It's to the La Tene culture that the flowing, organic shapes so typical of Celtic art belong.

The use of iron started in Britain around 700 BC, but it became widespread only after 500 BC, as Celtic culture drifted over from the Continent and the building of hillforts started to take off. After about 300 BC, the La Tene culture was well established in Britain.

BADBURY RINGS, DORSET

A round hillfort with impressive ramparts, Badbury is typical of the way that Celtic hillforts continued to fascinate later generations: it is associated with the legendary King Arthur's great battle at Mount Badon, and Arthur is said to live on as a crow in the trees that top the fort.

THE IRON AGE: HILLFORTS

There are about 2000 iron age hillforts in England, nearly all in the south-western half of the country (draw a line from the top left of Shropshire to the top right of Kent, and they're below left of that line). Some seem to have been refuges in times of trouble and show no signs of having had buildings within the ramparts, but others were clearly major towns.

In the larger occupied hillforts, such as *Danebury* in *Hampshire* or *Hod Hill* in *Dorset*, groups of round huts are laid out along streets and there is often a building which seems to have been some kind of chief's house or town hall. Other common features found during excavations are deep pits used for storing grain, and small, rectangular structures mounted on four or six posts, which might be just about anything but are often reconstructed as looms, drying platforms or threshing floors.

Lots of trades and activities took place within these larger hillforts: at Danebury, for example, lots of pottery, grain and animal bones were found; there was evidence of weaving and iron-smelting; and shale seems to have been distributed as a raw material. Salt was also packaged in large quantities, as if for distribution. The theory is that these towns were run by a chief who owned the territory around the hillfort and who maintained his power and wealth by controlling the distribution and exchange of commodities in the area.

These hillfort-towns were often equated with the *oppida* which Caesar describes as being Celtic regional capitals, but nowadays the term *oppidum* is used only for the larger Celtic towns built later in the iron age on low-lying land next to rivers. These were much more easily integrated into the Roman idea of a city, as at Colchester in Essex, where the earthworks that defined the *oppidum* can still be seen.

The best thing about hillforts, of course, is that they are usually great places for a walk, with good views guaranteed. The ones that really impress, though, are the hillforts that have large ramparts, especially if they also feature complex gateways like those at *Maiden Castle, Dorset*.

The ramparts might look like big banks of earth, but there is often a good deal more work in them than you might think. Many are composed of rocks and stones rather than just soil; some are built like dry-stone walls, or at least supported by walls. Others are laced with criss-cross layers of timber to give them added strength. Some were faced with large stones (megaliths). Frequently, the ditches are cut deep into solid rock. The topmost rampart would have been equipped with a sturdy timber palisade. The entrances would have been closed with large wooden gates, and guard chambers stood on either side of the gate.

MAIDEN CASTLE, DORSET

Defended by the biggest ramparts and the most complex gateways of any Celtic hillfort, this is one of the most impressive architectural achievements in human history, though its defences didn't delay the Roman army for long.

THE BEST HILLFORTS

Hambledon Hill, Dorset

Maiden Castle, Dorset

Hod Hill, Dorset

Hembury, Devon

Danebury, Hampshire

Cissbury, Sussex

Chanctonbury, Sussex

Herefordshire Beacon, Hereford & Worcester

Old Oswestry, Shropshire

RICHBOROUGH CASTLE, KENT

The fort known traditionally as Richborough Castle has some of the most impressive Roman walls in England. The port of **Rutupiae** *was the gateway to Roman Britain, and one of the more remarkable features to be seen inside the fort is the foundation of a massive ceremonial archway which greeted visitors to* **Britannia.**

THE ROMAN INVASION

IN 55 BC, THE GLORY-SEEKING YOUNG GENERAL Julius Caesar – later to become the first Roman emperor – took his troops to Kent for a quick look round. Unfortunately for them, they went in September.

The trip started badly, with a difficult landing in storms and a fight with the locals on the beach. After setting up camp near the seashore, however, the Romans started to enjoy themselves, taking day trips into the countryside to steal corn and fight the natives.

What happened next was predictable enough for the seaside in September: there followed, as Caesar reported in his diary, "Several days of continuous bad weather which kept our men in camp and stopped the enemy from attacking." Reading the account more than 2000 years later, you can almost hear the sound of rain on canvas as bored soldiers play dice.

Caesar, depressed by the weather and by the natives' highly developed skills in running away ("Even if the enemy were beaten, their speed would enable them to escape," he wrote) decided to pack up and head back to France before a fortnight was out.

He and his men returned for a more purposeful expedition the following year, but in fact it seems that at no stage did he intend to make a full-scale invasion, and his two trips to Britain – although they might have had a hidden agenda, to do with personality politics among the Gaulish tribes – were basically intended to impress the folks back home.

Britain remained a tempting prize for the Romans for the next 100 years, valued all the more highly because it was seen as the northern extreme of the known earth. It wasn't until 43 AD, however, that an invasion was finally mounted. The immediate reason was that the Emperor Claudius, who had taken the reins of power after the death of Caligula two years before, was badly in need of a military success to boost his prestige.

An excuse was provided by the fact that the south-eastern tribe of the Catuvellauni, led by Caratacus, son of Cunobelin, had been pursuing a policy of aggressive expansion which had led the ruler of the pro-Roman tribe of the Atrebates, a man by the name of Verica, to flee to Rome in search of help. By this time, remember, the Gauls had been living as part of the Roman empire for almost a century, and so the British tribes had had plenty of time to align themselves with Rome if they were so inclined.

In the spring of 43 AD, therefore, some 40,000 Roman troops – four legions, plus infantry and cavalry auxiliaries – landed at the natural harbour of *Richborough* in *Kent*, later to become the Roman gateway to Britain. They first met Caratacus at a crossing of the River Medway, probably at Rochester, and after a hard-fought battle, the British were forced to drop back to the Thames. The Romans were able to travel steadily north, harassed from the forests and the marshes but not opposed in force, until they captured *Camulodunum* (Colchester), tribal capital of the Catuvellauni. Caratacus fled to Wales to raise support among the anti-Roman tribes of the region, while Claudius was summoned to enter the captured city at the head of his army, with a troupe of elephants joining the parade. A triumph was declared, and Claudius had achieved the propaganda victory he sought.

Claudius soon returned to Rome, but the invasion continued on three fronts. Vespasian led the 2nd Legion through the friendly territory of the Atrebates in Sussex and Hampshire before meeting considerable resistance from the tribe of the Durotriges in Dorset, but the well-equipped, well-drilled Roman legionaries were easily able to clean out Dorset's largest hillforts. The attack was pressed as far as Exeter. The 14th Legion, meanwhile, followed the line of the later Watling Street, which eventually ran from Richborough to Chester, as far as somewhere near Leicester, where the diagonal road known as the Fosse Way would give access to the more hostile regions of the Midlands. The third line of attack was followed by the 9th Legion, who headed north in flat country to somewhere near York, probably establishing themselves in a fort at Lincoln.

It seems that the Romans only planned at this stage to occupy lowland England, where in any case many of the people were sympathisers. By 47 AD, the Fosse Way had been established as a *limes* – not exactly a frontier in itself, but more the backbone for a frontier region that extended some way to the north-west. Meanwhile, however, Caratacus had succeeded in stirring up militancy among the Silures of south-east Wales and the mid-Welsh Ordovices. In response, legionary bases were established west of the Fosse Way line, at Gloucester and at *Wroxeter, Shropshire*.

COLLAPSED BASTION, BURGH CASTLE, NORFOLK

A Fort of the Saxon Shore of very similar design to Portchester in Hampshire (pictured on page 24), Burgh has only three sides of wall remaining. This bastion fell and rolled away from the wall when the ground beneath it subsided, showing clearly that the bastions were of solid construction. They were used as platforms on which light catapults were mounted.

In North Wales in 51 AD, Caratacus was finally able to gather together men from the anti-Roman tribes ready for all-out war, and a pitched battle followed. Caratacus was beaten and his family were captured, but he fled to the Brigantes in Yorkshire in the hope that he might be able to rouse the anti-Roman elements there, but instead he was handed over to his enemies by the tribe's pro-Roman queen, Cartimandua. He was shipped off to Rome and put on public display as a captive. There he is said to have asked the emperor: "Why do you, with all these grand possessions, still covet our poor huts?"

Actually, it's a good question. What did the Romans expect to get out of all this conquering they were doing? The military glory would be short-lived, and scarcely worth the enormous investment in roads, forts, aqueducts and cities that followed when a new province was pacified and developed. There seems almost to have been a moral crusade to bring the *Pax Romana* and the benefits of a civilised urban lifestyle to the barbarians of Europe. In the end, though, the investment paid off: not only in the taxation which was gathered by the officials in charge of the provinces, but also in the new markets opened up for exploitation by Roman manufacturers and merchants.

THE BRITISH RESISTANCE CONTINUED after the capture of Caratacus and was still centred on North Wales, so the Romans' next move was a concerted campaign in the area which by the late 50s AD had largely succeeded. The main base for the resistance movement was now the island of Anglesey, but in 61 AD this resistance was stamped out in bloody fashion by a short, swift, ruthless expedition across the Menai Straits. The Romans didn't get the chance to follow up their victory, however, because barely was it completed before news arrived of the rebellion of the Iceni of East Anglia led by their queen, Boudicca.

Romanised towns were rapidly developing in the tribal heartlands of the south-east – at Colchester, St Albans, London, Canterbury, Chelmsford and Chichester. But not all Britons were happy with the way things were going. Taxation was heavy, and the attitude of the local administrators was brutal.

In East Anglia, the final straw came when the tribal king Prasutagus died leaving no male heirs. Roman policy was to abolish native kingdoms whenever the opportunity presented itself, and so officials were sent to take control of royal property and to reduce the kingdom to the status of a province, which involved disarming the populace. For some reason, things got out of hand: the king's widow, Boudicca, was flogged and her daughters were raped.

The Iceni immediately rose in revolt and, joined by the neighbouring Trinovantes, fell on Colchester and destroyed it, slaughtering the population and burning the buildings. In the weeks that followed, as the Romans attempted to move troops back from the north, both St Albans and London suffered the same fate as Colchester. The Roman historian Tacitus recorded that as many as 70,000 men, women and children were killed.

Before long, though, the over-confident Iceni were defeated by a much smaller force of Roman soldiers, and tens of thousands of British warriors were killed. The Romans laid waste to East Anglia.

Although this was the most bitter episode in the history of the Roman occupation, in some ways it proved to be a turning point. A new man, called Classicianus, was put in charge of public administration. He used his influence to ensure that Suetonius Paulinus, who had been responsible for the previous policy of outright warfare in North Wales, was replaced by a new governor. He also reformed the tax system, making it fairer and more flexible. He was a true champion of the British people, and fragments of his tombstone are on display in the British Museum.

In 68 AD, following the death of Nero and a short period of civil war in Rome, Vespasian became emperor. By this time the Brigantes of northern England were in rebellion, the

HADRIAN'S WALL
AT WALLTOWN CRAGS

Impressive though the Wall is, striding off across craggy country, it is the forts along it that provide a unique picture of Roman military life between 100 and 200 AD. In the museum at Vindolanda, for example, you can see the 500 pieces of leather that went into a Roman army tent, or read a soldier's letter home about his need for clean underwear.

ROMAN ENGLAND: THE SITES TO SEE

Roman remains in England can be a little disappointing: you expect to see a villa, and all you find are a few low walls and some stacks of clay tiles which are supposed to be a hypocaust (an underfloor heating system). The rarity of Roman buildings is such that even the merest traces are sometimes put on permanent public display.

However… although England does not have any grand Roman remains to match the Colosseum in Rome or the famous aqueduct called the Pont du Garde in southern France, it does have a number of things which are far more exciting than just a few bits of low wall. Here are some of the best ones.

Incidentally, bear in mind that the label "Roman" does not necessarily mean built by actual Roman citizens from Rome. Military buildings, such as forts, were the work of army engineers who would have been citizens; but most of the villas scattered around the countryside were owned by native Britons who adopted Roman ways.

ROMAN FORTS

PORTCHESTER CASTLE, *Hampshire* – The full circuit of walls from a rectangular fort still stand to their full height, complete with round bastions used for mounting light catapults. Said to be the best-preserved Roman fort walls in northern Europe.

RICHBOROUGH CASTLE FORT, *Kent* – Although the circuit of walls is not as complete as Portchester's, the remaining fragments are a good deal higher. Also on the site are the foundations of a massive ceremonial archway – the gate to *Britannia* in the province's main port.

BURGH CASTLE, *Norfolk* – Very similar walls to Portchester, though not quite as well preserved, standing on three sides only.

HARDKNOTT FORT, *Cumbria* – Also has a complete circuit of stone walls, though they stand only a few feet high. In each corner are the remains of a square tower. The most memorable thing about this fort, though, is its superb scenic location.

ROMAN VILLAS

LULLINGSTONE, *Kent* – Full plan of a medium-sized country house complete with large mosaic. This is the clearest and most easily understood villa in England.

BRADING, *Isle of Wight* – Very similar to Lullingstone, in that it's a compact layout housed in a modern building. Has lots of mosaics, and there's a vast collection of odds and ends found at the site.

BIGNOR, *Sussex* – A very large villa indeed. It's not so easy to make sense of the ground plan, here, but the mosaic floors are the most remarkable in England.

OTHER ROMAN REMAINS

HADRIAN'S WALL – The most extraordinary Roman monument in England, which also encompasses many of Britain's finest Roman fort remains. *Housesteads fort, Chesters fort, Corbridge* and *Vindolanda* are all outstanding for one reason or another, as is the Temple of Mithras at *Brocolitia*. There is an entire chapter devoted to the Wall later in the book.

SILCHESTER, *Hampshire* – A very crumbly but complete circuit of Roman town walls now surrounding nothing but fields.

DOVER CASTLE ROMAN LIGHTHOUSE, *Kent* – One of a pair of lights either side of Dover harbour used to guide ships to the docks.

LULLINGSTONE ROMAN VILLA, KENT

With its excavated remains visible from a gallery at first-floor level, this is the most easily understood Roman villa in Britain. It was a decent-sized country house that stood at the centre of a large estate farm. The main crop was corn, stored in a large granary a short distance from the house.

anti-Roman factions in the tribe having got the upper hand led by Venutius, husband of their former queen, Cartimandua. Vespasian appointed a friend of his, Quintus Pettilius Cerialis, to the post of governor of Britain with the brief of stamping out this rebellion. Within two years he had succeeded; for details of how the Brigantes made their last stand, see *Stanwick Fortifications, Yorkshire*.

By 75 AD the frontier had been pushed into South Wales, with a new fort built at Caerleon to take over the front-line duties of Gloucester. A couple of years later, the legionary fort at Chester was established, similarly taking over the front-line role of Wroxeter. By 78 AD, when Agricola was appointed as the new governor, Wales was pretty much under control. When the Ordovices slaughtered a cavalry regiment, Agricola took it as his cue to finally stamp out the last vestiges of Welsh resistance.

Agricola later led expeditions that pushed the northern frontier of *Britannia* right back to the highlands of Scotland, and that story is told in the chapter on Hadrian's Wall.

THE MOST STRIKING MONUMENTS left behind by the Romans are nearly all military. This includes the roads, many of which are now buried under Tarmac but some of which can be seen preserved in their original state, with a raised bank (*agger*) designed to help water run off the road surface and drainage ditches on either side. Good examples are at Wheeldale on the North Yorkshire Moors and at *Cranborne Chase* in *Dorset*. The most important legionary forts, such as Chester and York, were buried as the cities developed, but in both cases there is something of the stonework of the Roman walls to be seen (and at York, there are also a couple of towers). At Lincoln, you can still walk (or, indeed, drive a car) through an arch from the gateway of the Roman fort.

The early forts which have survived best are those in the northern uplands, where they were less likely to be built over or robbed of their stone. The forts of *Hadrian's Wall* and the contemporary *Hardknott fort* in *Cumbria* are obvious examples. Perhaps the most outstanding Roman buildings in England, however, are the later Forts of the Saxon Shore in Hampshire, Sussex, Kent and Norfolk. We'll come to them in a moment.

The story of Roman England after the time of Hadrian is generally a tale of steady, peaceful integration and Romanisation. This process was helped along by an official policy of investment in cities, probably the best example of which is *Wroxeter, Shropshire*. Although the remains of the city aren't extensive, they include a vast public bath

PORTCHESTER CASTLE, HAMPSHIRE

The castle keep is Norman and the gateways are later medieval, but the walls and the round bastions (not towers) are from the Fort of the Saxon Shore known to the Romans as **Portus Adurni,** *built about 260 AD. The complete circuit of Roman walls still stands to practically its full height.*

house which amply demonstrates that large sums of money were being spent on improving civic amenities to encourage the native British to adopt the urban lifestyle of the Romans.

The final proof of the Romanisation of Britain is the country villa. These were big estate farms rather than mansions: they were built on the sites of earlier British farmsteads and were nearly always the property of native British landowners rather than Roman interlopers. Just about every villa you visit can be shown to have grown in size and splendour throughout the 200s and 300s as Britain grew fat from its Roman connections, and increasing amounts of money were spent on features like a large bath-house, or a fine mosaic on the floor of the dining room.

THE BEGINNING OF THE END for Roman Britain came not long after 250 AD, when a series of forts was built along the south coast of England from the Solent to try to prevent an increasing number of raids by 'barbarians' from northern Germany.

In fact, these Forts of the Saxon Shore seem to have been entirely successful in keeping the problem under control. In the early 300s Britain was more prosperous than ever, despite upheavals such as the rebellion by Carausius, a governor of Britain who declared himself Emperor and ruled his rebel empire from 286 to 293 AD.

By the mid-300s, however, Britain was being constantly harassed on all fronts; by Picts and Scots in the north and west, and by Saxons and Franks in the south and east. Worse, military resources were increasingly withdrawn to support the Roman empire in central Europe.

In 367, when a great 'barbarian conspiracy' threatened to destroy Britain, the emperor Valentinian sent a task force that swept away the raiders and restored order; but this kind of help could not be sustained. Throughout Europe, the Roman Empire was under more pressure than it could take. Eventually, in 409, the people of Britain were finally disowned by Rome, abandoned to defend themselves as best they could. In 410, Rome itself was sacked by Alaric the Goth.

Urban, civilised Britain had already been suffering from a huge economic decline, but now it more or less collapsed. Industries stopped producing, forts were abandoned and cities and villas were no longer maintained.

SAXON ENGLAND: AN OUTLINE

By the mid-400s, substantial numbers of Germanic tribesmen were crossing the North Sea and setting up home in eastern England. These were settlers, not raiders. They spread out in scattered hamlets and farmsteads, probably taking land that had not been farmed before or that had been abandoned during the post-Roman decline.

Before long, the many small Saxon tribes coalesced into regional kingdoms – Sussex, Wessex, East Anglia, Kent – and from as early as the late 400s there was a tradition that the king of the dominant region was looked on as a 'bretwalda' ('wide-ruler'), speaking for saxon England as a whole. In the mid-700s the kingdom of Mercia was dominant and Offa was bretwalda, and he was able to put the nation to work to build his famous dyke.

In the late 700s, the Viking raids began, and in the mid-800s the Vikings started to settle in Britain, gradually taking over the kingdoms of East Anglia and Northumbria and much of Mercia. By 878, Wessex stood alone.

Wessex – and with it Anglo-Saxon England – was saved more or less single-handedly by King Alfred, who created a new system defences. He established a network of fortified towns right across southern England, known as *burhs* (boroughs), laid out on a regular pattern and defended by walls and gates. Perhaps more importantly, he also established an administrative system unrivalled in Europe, run by monks (clerics, hence 'clerks') who could read and write; and whereas the *burhs* were soon replaced by Norman castles, the English civil service lived on.

SAXON CHURCH, BRADFORD ON AVON, WILTSHIRE

The Saxons haven't left much in the way of monuments, but nearly all the Saxon buildings that do survive are churches. This little church might be the oldest standing Anglo-Saxon building in England. The other notable Saxon legacy (apart from the basis of the English language, of course) is in the towns of southern England, just a few of which – such as Wareham in Dorset – still show the regular grid pattern of streets surrounded by a wall that reveal their origins as Saxon planned burhs.

A SHORT HISTORY OF CASTLES

ON SEPTEMBER 28TH 1066, the Norman army landed at Pevensey, Sussex, an excellent natural harbour guarded by a Roman fort whose stone walls still stood to an impressive height. The Norman invaders immediately built their first castle here, within the walls of the fort, using prefabricated timber sections which they had brought with them across the English Channel. (Similar prefabricated forts were later used by Henry II in Ireland and by Richard I in the Mediterranean.)

William the Conqueror was very aware of the importance of castle-building to secure his line of retreat. Just along the coast, on the cliff-top at Hastings, the Normans built their first new castle – probably an earthwork rampart with a timber palisade and gatehouse, possibly with a timber tower in the middle.

After victory in the Battle of Hastings on October 14th, 1066, the Normans advanced steadily on London, securing their rear at every stage. They spent eight days rebuilding what was apparently already a Norman-style castle at Dover, and they put up a new 'tower' at Canterbury. Before finally entering London, they also started work on a

Pickering Castle in Yorkshire retains the feel of an early motte and bailey castle despite its later stone walls.

castle next to the Thames crossing at Wallingford. William was crowned King of England on Christmas Day 1066, and his first task was to order a survey of the country which would help him to plan a programme of castle-building. This was the castle in its second role: not as a tactical weapon used in a military campaign, but as the tool of the invaders to enslave the people of a nation. By 1071 there were 33 Norman castles in England, and by the time of William's death in 1087 there were 86.

THE MOTTE AND BAILEY

Not all early Norman castles were of the type known as 'motte and bailey' – some were of a far simpler type called a 'ringwork', made up of a single circuit of earth ramparts with a timber palisade around the top – but this is the classic basic Norman castle.

The 'motte' was a large mound, where possible based on solid rock, but in any case made of something far more substantial than heaped-up earth. It provided a look-out post, with views over surrounding country, as well as adding tactically important height if the castle was attacked.

The 'bailey' was a large, level enclosed area beside the motte, surrounded by an earthwork bank and ditch and a timber palisade.

Other timber buildings would be put up inside the bailey, including a hall building (with the hall itself on

Pevensey, Sussex: the Normans built their first English castle inside the walls of the Roman fort here.

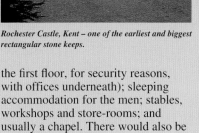

Rochester Castle, Kent – one of the earliest and biggest rectangular stone keeps.

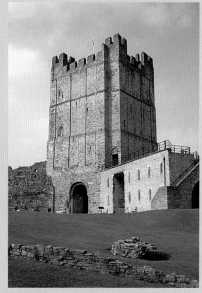

Richmond Castle, Yorkshire – The work of Henry II, who in the late 1100s built many fine keeps.

Orford Castle, Suffolk – Also the work of Henry II, but this time a more experimental cylindrical design.

the first floor, for security reasons, with offices underneath); sleeping accommodation for the men; stables, workshops and store-rooms; and usually a chapel. There would also be a kitchen and a well.

The function of the early castle was twofold. First, it acted as an administrative centre. Second, its main military role was as a base for cavalry (mounted knights, if you prefer) who could range over a wide area but could also withdraw behind the castle's defences if they were attacked by a large force.

The basic motte and bailey developed in a number of ways. Timber palisades and look-out towers were added on top of the mounds, while the mounds themselves became bigger and higher over the years. Access to the motte was made possibly only across a 'flying bridge' or walkway. Before long, the top of the motte had taken on all the defensive aspects of a keep.

There's an excellent account, written in northern France in about 1130 by a chap called Jean de Colmien, of castles of this kind. 'It is the custom of the nobles to make a mound of earth as high as they can and then dig about it as wide and deep as possible. The space on top of the mound is enclosed by a palisade of very strong hewn logs, strengthened at intervals by as many towers as their

means can provide. Inside the enclosure is a citadel or keep, which commands the whole circuit of defences. The entrance to the fortress is by means of a bridge which, arising from the outer side of the moat and supported on posts as it ascends, reaches the top of the mound.'

It is often easy to make out the layout of the original motte and bailey where a castle has been later rebuilt in stone. A particularly good example of this is *Pickering Castle* in *Yorkshire*, where the motte was later topped by a stone shell keep (see below) and the stone walls followed the line of the timber fences, giving the impression of the timber castle preserved in stone. *Berkhamstead Castle, Hertfordshire* is another interesting example.

Earthworks and timber palisades continued to be important long after castles were rebuilt in stone. There are many examples of castles that had a stone keep but never had stone walls (*Bowes Castle* in *County Durham* is one such). Frequently, stone walls would be put up where they were needed most, but timber fences would be retained where natural defences made a stone wall superfluous. A good example is *Richmond Castle, Yorkshire*: it was one of the first castles in England to have stone walls, but initially the timber palisade was retained on the edge of the steep cliff.

RECTANGULAR STONE KEEPS

In 1079, work started on the first great stone keep of Norman England, now known as the White Tower at the *Tower of London* (though some would argue that *Colchester Castle, Essex* was started earlier).

Stone keeps were not a new idea, and William already had one at his own castle in Rouen in France. In some cases, castles were built in stone right from the start (particularly if stone was easier to come by than wood, as was the case at *Launceston* in *Cornwall* and *Totnes* in *Devon*).

The main advantage of stone keeps was that they were to all intents and purposes fireproof, providing secure storage for money and documents as well as offering more comfortable accommodation for the nobles and providing a pretty formidable defence.

The great keeps were also an expression of the pride of the Norman rulers and their domination of the country around, so they were often carefully faced with dressed stone (ashlar) – much of it, in the early days, shipped in from the quarries at Caen in France – and decorated with details like arcading. (*Norwich Castle* and *Castle Rising*, both in *Norfolk*, have excellent arcaded decoration.)

The biggest keeps are all set on flat areas within a bailey, but if a keep was to be put on a motte there were certain structural considerations. The ideal foundation was a natural rock outcrop with an underground water supply that could be tapped by a well. Otherwise, an artificial mound would be strengthened with layers of rock or hard-beaten earth, or covered over with a thick layer of clay.

The classic Norman keep is the great rectangular tower. The Tower of London and Colchester Castle were the first, followed by the keep at *Canterbury, Kent,* which was modelled on Colchester but only half the size. Then came *Rochester* in *Kent,* the biggest of them all, which stood 35m (120ft) high and took 13 years to build (from the late 1120s to about 1130). This was followed by *Hedingham* in *Essex,* which was a three-quarters-size copy of Rochester.

England's great builder of keeps, however, was King Henry II, who built superb rectangular towers throughout the country. Probably the most impressive of all is his keep at *Dover Castle, Kent,* though the immensely tall tower at Richmond Castle is also pretty awesome.

Defensively, the greatest weakness of a stone keep was that it could be undermined: that is, attackers would dig a tunnel underneath the walls shored up by pit props, then burn out the props to collapse the tunnel and bring down the wall. There's an excellent record of this tactic being employed against Rochester Castle by King John. If a keep was built on solid rock, this tactic could not be used; but otherwise, the most obvious way to counteract it was with a water-filled moat, which meant that any tunnel would flood immediately. Such a moat would also in itself be a more effective deterrent than a dry ditch. Many of the most sophisticated castles had extensive systems of water defences, diverting water from nearby streams and rivers.

Another weak point in the defences was the access to the keep, which would originally have been by some kind of wooden ladder or stair to a door on the first floor. In later designs, a permanent stone stair was fitted, and this was protected inside a stone building known as a forebuilding. One of the best examples is at Dover Castle, where the main entrance stair

Arundel Castle, Norfolk – a good example of a shell keep, restored to something like its original condition.

leads direct to the second floor, where the king's principal reception rooms were located.

Certain aspects of keep design remained consistent throughout the years and in different types and sizes of keep. Entry was always to the first floor (or higher), with the main great hall at this level. The top floor (or floors) would be private chambers for the lord of the castle.

At ground-floor level was a basement used for storage and reached only by an internal stair; quite often this was where the well was located, though often (as at Dover or at *Newcastle-upon-Tyne*) access to the well was taken up to a higher level.

An alternative name for a keep – the word 'donjon' – came to be associated with similar windowless strong rooms in the basements of towers, and of course these are now known to us as 'dungeons'; but the basement of a keep would never have been used to hold prisoners, especially since this was where the food was stored and the water supply was located.

Square towers had certain weaknesses, particularly at the corners, where engineers working under cover of a siege engine could use crowbars to prise apart the stonework. Rounded towers were the obvious answer...

ROUND TOWERS
AND SHELL KEEPS

One version of the round tower approach was the cylindrical keep, but this was not widely used. A look inside the enormous buttressed keep at *Conisbrough Castle, Yorkshire* will suggest one of the main reasons why not: a round tower simply couldn't match a rectangular one for accommodation space inside. The cylindrical keep at *Orford, Suffolk* is rather more grand inside, but it doesn't really compare with Dover or Rochester for spaciousness.

Another approach was the shell keep. The idea here was to build a very tall circular wall around the top of a motte, and to place all the most important buildings of the castle up against the interior walls of the shell. (In fact, this was not a 'keep' as most of understand it, because it wasn't a building with floors.)

Far and away the best example of the shell keep is *Restormel Castle* in *Cornwall,* though *Totnes* in *Devon* also has an interesting one, and another has survived in pretty good condition at *Lewes Castle* in *Sussex.* There were also shell keeps at *Arundel Castle,* also in *Sussex,* where the shell is well preserved, and at *Windsor Castle* in *Berkshire,* where it has become the Round Tower. In both these cases, the keep was built on a motte that overlooked not one but two baileys, giving the castles a distinctive 'bow-tie' pattern when you see aerial photographs of them.

Alongside the shell keep came another major development in castle design: a more sophisticated kind of wall surrounding a large bailey.

This 'curtain' wall would be equipped with a number of towers, and the walkway along the top of the wall was broken at various points by gaps spanned by light bridges. These bridges could be pulled back or thrown down to separate off small sections of wall. This allowed for very flexible defence. If one part of the wall was captured, it could be isolated to stop the attack spreading.

This thinly spread type of castle was also better at resisting the attack of huge stone-throwing catapults which were in use at the time.

LATER CASTLE DESIGN

Curtain walls with projecting rectangular towers (so that the area in front of the walls could be shot at with arrows) were established as a standard, and in some cases became the only form of defence, with the keep omitted altogether. The most notable (and earliest) example of this is *Framlingham Castle, Suffolk*. Framlingham was also one of the first castles to be equipped with proper loopholes for use with crossbows.

As the emphasis was increasingly placed on the curtain walls, so too did the gatehouses become particularly important. The entrance was nearly always the weakest part of a castle, and bigger and better gatehouses were a natural response.

By the late 1200s, these ideas had come together in the classic medieval castle design known as the 'concentric' castle, in which the keep was replaced by a rectangular or polygonal curtain wall with towers; this wall was completely surrounded by an outer curtain wall, to give a second full line of defence; and a massive gatehouse, equipped with every possible defence, was placed on the castle's weakest side.

This design was widely employed by the most capable of English kings, Edward I, in his campaigns in Wales. Unfortunately for this book, that's where you'll find the best examples, though Edward made the Tower of London into something like a concentric castle by adding an outer moat, the outer bailey, three gates and a barbican.

The barbican was one of the most important developments in the defence of gateways, and it took several different forms. The simplest was just a long, walled passageway in front of the gate, which extended the opportunities offered to defenders to drop things on attackers from above and fire at them from the sides as they approached the gate and struggled with its doors and portcullises. The barbican gateway of Lewes Castle in Sussex is particularly memorable. Another type of barbican was a fortified 'island' in front of the gate (quite literally an island, in the case of a castle surrounded by water defences) separated from the main gatehouse and from the approach road by drawbridges. There's a decent example of a small D-shaped barbican at *Goodrich Castle, Hereford and Worcester*, while the approach across the moat to the much later castle at *Bodiam, Sussex* involves crossing three separate drawbridges.

Later trends were for the towers of the curtain wall to be round, not square (again, because round towers were stronger) and for the walls of smaller castles to be drawn closer together, producing a small, compact type of castle often known as a courtyard castle (a good example of a castle that uses both ideas, though it was heavily altered in later years, is

Tattershall Castle, Lincolnshire – the finest example of castle-building in brick from the mid-1400s.

Skipton Castle in *Yorkshire*). Some courtyard castles were so compact that the inner courtyard became nothing more than a light well, as at *Nunney Castle* in *Somerset* and *Old Wardour Castle* in *Wiltshire* (though both of these are more fortified houses than castles).

By the late 1300s, small cannon were beginning to be used both as defensive and offensive weapons (the West Gate at *Canterbury, Kent*, built in 1380, is said to be the first building in England designed to be defended with guns). Surprisingly, this had little impact on castle design; Bodiam, for example, was built around this time, but its walls were too thin to stand up to cannon-fire. Before long, artillery would make castles obsolete and would produce the forts of the 1500s.

Meanwhile, though, the great trend in the 1400s was for keeps and gatehouses that harked back to the feudalism of several hundred years before, though they were now often built of brick. One of the main spurs for this was the widespread social unrest of the time. Great lords tended to have large retinues of paid soldiers but were not necessarily sure of their loyalty; and so the lord's private accommodation was often set apart in a keep that protected him, his family and his wealth from his own soldiers as much as from his enemies.

Portland Castle, Dorset – typical of the small artillery forts, designed to resist cannon-fire, built by Henry VIII.

A QUICK GUIDE TO ABBEYS

ONE OF THE MOST PLEASING THINGS about visiting abbey ruins – apart from their tendency to be picturesque and set in beautiful countryside – is that they were all built to a similar layout, so you soon start to recognise elements of the design that are familiar from other abbeys. The idea of this short piece is to give you a head start in knowing what to look out for, and to act as a brief glossary of terms relevant to abbey architecture.

Abbeys were usually founded by small parties of monks on land donated by a rich benefactor. The monks were generally under an obligation to settle in 'waste places' (that is, untamed countryside) but they had a knack for choosing spots that in later years would become excellent farmland.

They nearly always settled in sheltered valleys next to rivers or large streams (which they used for their mains drainage – the drains are one of the most interesting aspects of abbey design) and this choice of idyllic location is one of the major factors in the appeal of the ruins to the modern visitor. The monks would first build a wooden church and lodgings, organise their farming and income, then set about building themselves a great abbey church in stone.

THE CHURCH is, of course, the most important building of an abbey and was the first part to be built in stone. It is cross-shaped in plan and is always aligned east-to-west, with the main door usually at the west end and the altar at the east.

THE NAVE is the west end of the church, where the congregation would gather for services. Sometimes this public area of the church would be cut off from the monks' part to the east by a ROOD SCREEN. On either side of the nave there are generally AISLES which, since the nave points west-to-east, are on its north and south sides. Because the abbey cloister is to the south of the nave, the SOUTH AISLE is sometimes missed out of the design.

THE TRANSEPTS are the arms of the church, sticking out to north and south. They often housed chapels.

THE CROSSING is in the middle, where the transepts meet the main body of the church. Its main feature is usually a set of tall arches and cross-vaults.

THE CHOIR (OR QUIRE) is at the east end of the church, right by the crossing. This is where the monks would gather to celebrate services.

THE PRESBYTERY is the extreme east end of the church, where the high altar stood, with important shrines or chapels behind it.

AN APSE is a curved end to a building, usually at the east end of a chapel.

THE CLOISTER is on the south side of the church (a most practical arrangement, since it would be sheltered from colder winds and would get the best of the sun), tucked into the corner of the church formed by the nave and the south transept. This was a private courtyard in which the monks spent a good deal of their daily lives. It would generally have a covered walkway down each side and a grassy yard in the middle.

The cloister was, most importantly, the focal point for all the functional rooms and buildings of the abbey.

Although the image of the cloister is as a secluded garden where the monks strolled in quiet contemplation, it was actually used for many more prosaic activities: it was where the monks would have their heads shaved or hang out their laundry.

THE SACRISTY is usually the first building of the cloister, right next to the south transept. In here were stored the valuable objects and garments used during services.

THE CHAPTER HOUSE is usually right next to the sacristy. This was just about the most important room in the abbey. Every day, the monks would gather here for about an hour to listen to the reading of a chapter of The Rule of St Benedict, which set down the pattern by which monks were supposed to live their lives. This was also a forum for announcements or discussions of matters affecting the community of the abbey.

THE PARLOUR was generally a small, narrow room with benches along each wall, and it usually stood near the chapter house. In silent orders, this was the only room in which monks could talk.

Castle Acre Priory, Norfolk, is a particularly pleasing mixture of older ruins and later, more intact buildings.

Roche Abbey, near Rotherham, Yorkshire – even at a very ruinous abbey like this, you can get an excellent idea of the buildings around the cloister and what they were used for.

A SLYPE is a passageway that leads out of the cloisters. In a ruin it usually looks a little superfluous, but of course there would have been no other way out of the cloister without walking through a room.

THE WARMING HOUSE was the only room apart from the kitchen in which a fire was allowed. It was usually a small room with a huge fireplace (which makes it an easy one to spot in a ruined abbey). Quite often, the warming house was right next to the dormitory and the refectory and was equipped with completely outsized fireplaces so that its warmth spread to the neighbouring buildings.

THE DORMITORY (OR DORTER) where the monks slept was on the first floor on the east side of the cloister, above the chapter house, parlour and so on.

THE NIGHT STAIR led direct from the first-floor dormitory into the south transept of the church, so that the monks had direct access to the church when they were woken to celebrate the night-time services.

THE LATRINE (OR REREDORTER – literally 'behind the dormitory') was always placed at the back of the dormitory and was set over a stream which acted as a main sewer. Clearly monks were very fussy about their sanitary arrangements.

THE REFECTORY (DINING ROOM) was usually on the first floor of a large building on the south side of the cloister. This was an important room. As the monks ate, a brother would read improving texts to them.

THE LAY BROTHERS' DORMITORY often took up the third side of the cloister (the west side), with various rooms such as store-rooms and cellars in an undercroft beneath it. The lay brothers were non-religious members of the community who did most of the hard work (farming and so on).

THE KITCHEN generally stood in a separate building behind the refectory to reduce the risk of fire spreading through the abbey.

THE ABBOT'S HOUSE was quite a large private house befitting his status as a wealthy landowner.

DON'T MISS...

THE ABBOT'S HOUSE at *Muchelney Abbey in Somerset*.

THE REFECTORY AND THE DORMITORY at *Cleeve Abbey in Somerset*.

THE VAULTS BELOW THE REREDORTER at *Netley Abbey in Hampshire*.

GENERALLY... the finest abbey ruins in England: FURNESS ABBEY in *Cumbria*; FOUNTAINS ABBEY and RIEVAULX ABBEY *in Yorkshire*; CASTLE ACRE PRIORY *in Norfolk*.

About this book

The County Chapters

Each chapter covers a single county. The only slight problem is that the borders have changed a good deal in the last 30 years, and have been particularly distorted by the creation of lots of new 'unitary authorities', which has produced such ridiculous inventions as Bath and North East Somerset ('Banes' to its friends).

I've chosen to ignore such recent creations, and instead I have reverted to a kind of 'ideal England' of simple, old-fashioned counties.

Apologies to Rutland, however: England's smallest traditional county, resurrected in the late 1990s, is bundled in with Leicestershire.

Other eccentricities are that Yorkshire is treated as a whole (as are East and West Sussex); Humberside doesn't exist (it's either in Yorkshire or in Lincolnshire); the whole of the north-east between Yorkshire and Northumbria is put under the heading 'County Durham, Tyne and Tees'. Bath, incidentally, is back in Somerset where it belongs.

I make no apologies for any of this: I think the counties as they stand are in the form that is most readily understood by most people.

Regional sections

The chapters are organised into regional sections and placed in an order which I think best reflects the way most of us think about the country. You'll find the south-west at the start of the book and the north-east at the end.

I know this can be a·little tricky at times, but it does work better than the most obvious alternative, which was simply to place all the counties in alphabetical order. The chapters are listed in their regional sections on the main Contents page on page 5, so they shouldn't be too hard to find. Generally, though, I would imagine that the county map on page 9 will prove to be the easiest way of finding a chapter rapidly.

Listings within chapters

The entries in each chapter are organised in alphabetical order, but there may be a couple of places where you will have to turn the page to find a place that, alphabetically, should occur earlier. This mostly occurs with important places that require a whole page to cover them adequately, and I'm afraid it's impossible to avoid when we're trying to fit everything onto the page.

The 'See Also...' sections

At the end of each chapter is a brief round-up of some other places of interest in the county. In some cases, these are places that are shown as castles on maps (especially tourist maps) but cannot actually be visited; in other cases, they might be places that are called 'Castle' or 'Abbey' but are actually stately homes. In either case, knowing what it really is might save you a wasted journey.

Other entries in the 'See Also...' section are historic places that don't quite fit the brief of the book, but which might still be of interest; and there are quite a few less important archaeological sites that could be of particular interest to local people. I'm afraid there isn't space to give very detailed directions or descriptions, so you will generally have to seek these places out for yourself.

OWNERSHIP

Many castles and abbey ruins are in the care of English Heritage or the National Trust, but a substantial minority are privately owned or are publicly owned by another institution, such as a county council.

The main difference this makes is that sites in the care of English Heritage tend to be good value and maintained to a very high standard, whereas a privately owned site might be more expensive or not quite so well presented. National Trust sites have slightly less helpful opening hours and tend to be more expensive.

You can take out membership of English Heritage and the National Trust and get free access to their sites. I would recommend membership of both organisations. English Heritage runs all the most interesting ruins, so you'll get more mileage from membership, but the National Trust looks after huge amounts of countryside on which many of the most important ancient monuments stand, so it's good to be contributing to the upkeep of these places.

PRICES

If we were to give exact admission prices, the book would be out of date before it was even printed; so instead, we have given a guide by using a scale of prices, as follows:

£	Cheap (a pound or less)
££	Good value
£££	Rather expensive
££££	Very expensive

Generally, I would say that a site that costs ££££ is not worth seeing.

OPENING HOURS

Again we couldn't possibly give full details, so we have tried to suggest what you can expect.

'*Usual hours*' means that a site is open roughly during normal shop hours, seven days a week. It also means open all year. In the case of English Heritage, for example, their major sites are open 10 am to 6 pm daily – but in winter they close at 4 pm. (Some, in winter, are closed on Monday and Tuesday.)

'*Slightly limited hours*' might mean a site has a shorter opening day or is open less in winter, but you still have every chance of finding it open if you just turn up.

'*Limited hours*' means you should certainly check before setting off. Telephoning the local Tourist Information office is usually easiest.

DIRECTIONS

A road atlas should be enough to get you in the right area, and after that most sites are clearly signposted. If not, then I have provided directions which, though brief, should be enough to lead you straight there. I've been to all these places and the directions are written from personal experience, so they should work. If you have problems, I would be very grateful to hear from you about them.

Please note...

I have done my level best to ensure that all the details are correct, but I'm afraid we cannot accept any responsibility for errors or for inconvenience caused. Access to private land in particular can change, and it is not to be assumed that rights of way or rights of access exist.

CASTLES
& ANCIENT
MONUMENTS
OF ENGLAND

COUNTY BY COUNTY

Cornwall

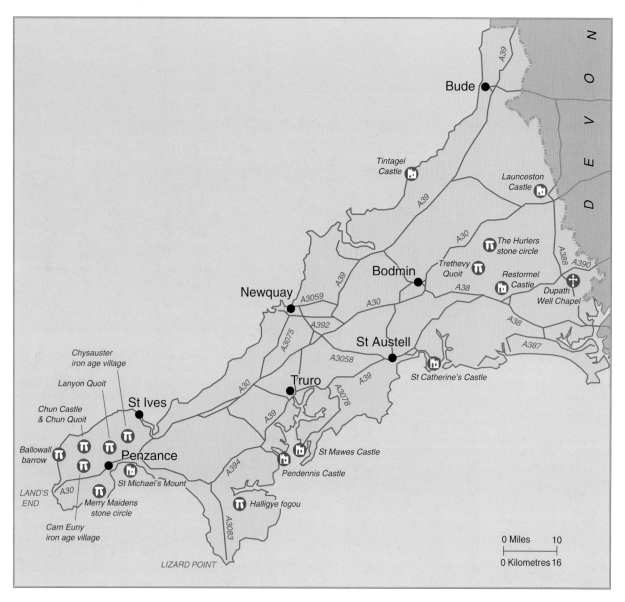

CORNWALL has a wealth of ancient sites which are unusual, well-preserved and set in beautiful landscape. Particularly outstanding are the iron age village at *Chysauster*, where each of the houses is surrounded by a courtyard of outbuildings, and the extraordinary underground passageway known as a 'fogou' at *Halligye*. The county also boasts a couple of small but very pleasing medieval castles: *Restormel Castle*, near Liskeard, is an especially fine example of a circular shell keep, while *Launceston Castle* is a real one-off, its own shell keep having been topped off by a squat, dark, heavy stone tower which now leans at a slightly disconcerting angle. There's also a rare little treasure in the east of the county in the form of *Dupath Well Chapel*, where a spring bubbles up inside a small stone-built shrine in an echo of the pre-Christian worship at watery places.

One of the 'courtyard houses' in the iron age village at Chysauster, where Celtic people lived at the time of the Roman invasion of Britain.

Ballowall Barrow – strange and interesting, in a rocky kind of way, and it's got great coastal views.

BALLOWALL BARROW

English Heritage • Free • Open access at any reasonable time

A very unusual stone variation on the long barrow, this multiple-walled cairn is not easy to puzzle out. In the centre is a T-shaped pit dug 2m (6ft) into the rock, with steps down into it; four small stone cists around this contained bronze age pottery, and the whole thing is ringed by two walls.

Take minor road west out of St Just town centre for Cape Cornwall; from NT car park follow footpath south along cliff to barrow.

CARN EUNY

VILLAGE AND FOGOU

English Heritage • Free • Open access only at reasonable hours

The jumbled remains, uncovered as recently as 1964, of an iron age village which remained in use in Roman times (it was abandoned between 300 and 400 AD). Crops,

The iron age houses of Carn Euny aren't as exciting as Chysauster's (next page), but it has an underground 'fogou'.

livestock and tin trading would have been the means of subsistence of the people who lived here.

The stone houses were built in the period up to about 100 BC to replace previous wooden ones. Some are like the 'courtyard houses' at *Chysauster* (*next page*), but the only house which is easy to make out (House A, by the entrance to the site) is of a smaller oval design found throughout Cornwall. The most interesting thing in the village, though, is the 'fogou' (*see also Halligye, page 34*), an underground passageway covered by enormous capstones.

Signposted on minor road to Brane hamlet, south-west of Sancreed; small car park; short walk to the village.

CHUN CASTLE

On farmland • Free • Open access on footpaths at any reasonable time

This is another unique and surprising Cornish site. Part of its appeal is that it's on the moors well away from the road, so you have to make the effort to get here, but also it's most unusual. It does need a little imagination to make sense of it, though.

Basically it's an iron age hillfort, except that it's small, round and built of stone. In effect, it's a very ancient castle. It has two circular walls, one inside the other, and just one gate, placed so that anyone coming through the gap in the outer wall would have to turn and walk along under the inner curtain wall before reaching the gate, making it easy for defenders to fire on them if need be. It was occupied in the Roman era and after, and you can make out both round huts and later-style square ones inside the enclosure.

A hundred years ago, the ramparts were still 4m (13ft) high, but a lot of stone was carted away to pave the streets of Penzance.

Footpaths up (you'll need a map) from a) the minor road, signposted Chun Castle, which turns off the Madron-to-Morvah road just north of Lanyon Quoit (see next page) or b) from the track beyond Carne Farm, just south of Morvah.

Left: The rubble-like remains of the stone walls of Chun Castle, a very unusual variety of hillfort.

The view from the 'gateway' of one of the best of Chysauster's 'courtyard houses': ahead is the courtyard itself, with the main house right at the back of the compound.

CHYSAUSTER VILLAGE

English Heritage • ££ • Opening limited (usual hours, April to October only)

This iron age village is undoubtedly the most interesting of its kind in England. It's also good fun to explore for yourself, since you can easily pick out the distinctive features of the village's 'courtyard houses'.

Eight houses are arranged in pairs along a street, with their entrances pointing away from the prevailing south-westerly wind, and each house has an area beside it that the experts describe as a terraced garden. Each house is rather like a farmyard: in front of the main, single-room house, a large wall surrounds a courtyard lined with smaller 'rooms', some of them probably stock pens or sheds. You can see open hearths, stones (or 'querns') for grinding corn, and stone channels to bring water into and out of the courtyard.

It's likely that Chysauster was built entirely during Roman times (the bulk of the pottery found here is dated to the second and third centuries AD) and it seems there were once many more houses in the village, so Chysauster could have been a city of the rough, tough native British who traded with the Romans.

Signposted from B3311 (Penzance to St Ives).

DUPATH WELL CHAPEL

English Heritage • Free • Open access only at reasonable hours

A special place. It's a tiny stone chapel built over a spring, showing the continuity of worship at watery places from pagan into Christian times (the Celts were keen on throwing objects of value into springs, rivers and lakes, which is why we have a tradition of throwing money into wells). The building dates from around 1500, but is probably a rebuilding of a much earlier chapel. Water from the spring runs into a stone trough and then out at the back of the building. Charming and evocative.

Signposted down minor road heading east from just south of Callington on the A388; turn right down second minor road; park near farm and walk through farmyard to the site.

The odd-looking Lanyon Quoit was precariously rebuilt in 1824 after one of its stones crumbled away.

THE HURLERS STONE CIRCLES

English Heritage • Free • Open access at any reasonable time

Set in a strange moorland landscape littered with medieval stone crosses, industrial remains and dramatic rocky outcrops as well as many other ancient stone constructions, this set of three stone circles is one of the largest prehistoric sites in England.

All the stones were trimmed and set to be all of the same height; the central circle originally had a 'floor' of quartzite crystals; the northern circle was paved with granite slabs; and a paved pathway two metres wide linked the three circles. It's not hard to imagine what a very significant monument this must have been.

On Bodmin Moor, just off minor road half a mile north-west of Minions; large car park.

The Merry Maidens are said to have been turned to stone for dancing on a Sunday – a common local legend.

LANYON QUOIT

National Trust • Free • Open access at any reasonable time

This pleasantly eccentric set of stones – remnant of a chambered barrow – is also known as the Giant's Table. The lopsided look is because the structure collapsed in 1815 and was rebuilt in 1824 minus one of its four supporting stones, which had broken.

By road running south-west from the B3306 east of Morvah to Madron; park in layby.

THE MERRY MAIDENS

Private land • Free • Open access only at reasonable times

A true geometric circle, its 19 stones all dressed to make their tops level and flat. Nearby is a pair of tall stones known as The Pipers, and a few yards along the road is the wrecked Tregiffian burial chamber, with a big cup-marked stone at the entrance.

In field by B3315 south from Newlyn, not far west of turning to Lamorna; park in layby.

Below: Probably Bodmin Moor's most famous sight, The Hurlers are three stone circles in a row.

Launceston is a most extraordinary-looking castle, with the high Great Tower built inside an earlier shell keep and now leaning at a slightly dizzy angle.

LAUNCESTON CASTLE

English Heritage • ££ • Usual hours

Not at all an average Norman castle. Launceston controlled a bridge across the Tamar which at the time was the main route into Cornwall. The original earthworks of the motte and bailey, with wooden pallisades, may have been built as early as 1067, when the Exeter area rebelled against William the Conqueror and was slapped down with immense force. Not long afterwards a substantial stone shell keep was built, and in the mid-1200s proper stone walls and gatehouses were added to the bailey, while the powerful High Tower was built inside the shell keep.

A fair proportion of the walls and gates survives, but it's the keep that's the star attraction. The walls are massive, powerful and, in the dark stone, just a little grim and forbidding. The steps that lead up the mound to the keep were originally covered to protect people walking up. Once inside the walls of the shell keep, you can see that the High Tower is leaning, like the famous Tower of Pisa. Climbing to the top of the Tower, you not only get a fine view of the surrounding country, but can also see how cramped even the most important rooms would have been – hardly a life of great splendour, even though the Tower was probably built by Richard Duke of Cornwall, who was one of the wealthiest and most influential men in Europe.

A short walk from the main town centre car park in Launceston.

HALLIGYE FOGOU

English Heritage • Free • Open access only at reasonable hours

A dramatic and mysterious place, Halligye (pronounced 'Halley') is the finest example in England of a 'fogou' - an underground passageway similar to the 'souterrains' found in Scotland. It's not known whether fogous were used primarily for storage, for ceremonial purposes or as hiding places in time of trouble. The small fortified homestead under which the fogou ran, dated from 100 BC to 300 AD, has disappeared. You'll need a torch to explore the full length of the passageway.

On privately owned Trelowarren estate, signposted off B3293 SE of Helston; park in estate car park and ask for a walks leaflet from the craft shop, or pick up the path at top end of car park where it crosses the road; a pleasant 15-minute walk across fields to the monument.

PENDENNIS CASTLE

English Heritage • £££ • Usual hours

One of a pair of small artillery forts built between 1539 and 1545 at the order of Henry VIII. The threat of a Spanish invasion was particularly strong at this time, and the Spaniards had large fleets of heavily armed warships which could make mincemeat of existing defences. Henry had the whole south coast surveyed, and built a bunch of these little castles: the best of the rest are *Deal* and *Walmer* in *Kent*.

Together with St Mawes on the opposite side of the channel, Pendennis would defend the entrance to Falmouth harbour. The guns of each one could only reach halfway across, but together the pair could cover the whole width of the channel.

Of the two, St Mawes is more civilised and adult, but this one is more fun and there's an awful lot more to see, because around the original Tudor castle keep there are lots of later fortifications. In the late 1500s a major set of 'star' fortifications was added, with the intention of making the castle impossible to attack from inland. In Victorian times several major artillery batteries were added, and the fort was still in use during the 1914-18 and 1939-45 wars. It all adds up to an awful lot to look at, though some parts can only be visited by guided

Of the two forts built by Henry VIII on either side of Falmouth harbour, Pendennis Castle has the simpler design.

tours, which take place regularly throughout the day.

To make it all more accessible, English Heritage have added lots of modern reconstructions, complete with sound effects and even, inside the keep, the smell of gunsmoke. It's all rather good fun, and even if you only visit the keep, it's worth coming.

Signposted on headland to the east of Falmouth town centre; car park on site.

ST MAWES CASTLE

English Heritage • ££ • Usual hours

This is definitely the cuter of the two, with the advantage of a less cluttered setting (it's not hemmed in by later fortifications, as Pendennis is) which has allowed it to be surrounded by a pleasant garden including some unusual tropical plants that wouldn't grow anywhere else in England.

Richly decorated, with lots of very fancy details to look out for in the Tudor masonry, St Mawes is an altogether more sophisticated design than Pendennis – the basic pattern is like three drums, with a fourth piled on top – and it's a very pleasant place to poke around. It's also in its 'raw' state inside, where Pendennis has been filled with reconstructions. Don't forget to walk down to the lower fort on the shoreline, built at the same time as the main castle.

Incidentally, you should buy the guidebook just for its description of Cornwall in the 1500s, a wild and rugged piece of country, constantly threatened by Spanish and French raids but hitting back with officially sanctioned piracy. The guide covers both of the castles.

Next to A3078 west of the village of St Mawes; car park on site.

The other, St Mawes, is a rather more elaborate shape and has much more ornate detail in the masonry.

You can walk all the way round Restormel's high walls: here, we're looking back to the gatehouse from above the chapel, with the kitchens to the left.

RESTORMEL CASTLE

English Heritage • ££ • Usual hours

In a pretty countryside setting, the circular keep of Restormel is a fine place to visit. It's justly called the finest unaltered example of a Norman shell keep in England and it now sits in splendid isolation, since the walls and buildings of the rectangular bailey have long disappeared.

The keep, which dates from the early 1200s, has several intriguing features, not least the way that the interior buildings just butted up against the outer wall, rather than being built into the wall. You can clearly see this in the kitchen, where a sizeable gap has opened up between the outer wall and the wall of the building inside. This doesn't necessarily mean that the shell was built much earlier: one theory is that while building the outer keep wall, the builders needed to have constant lines of sight to a central point, so they couldn't build inside at the same time.

The deep well is quite dramatic; and three deep pits make an intriguing puzzle. Were they for water storage?

When you consider that the keep originally had top-quality architectural features like fireplaces and windows in the finest local stone (most of which have been robbed) and would have been rendered and limewashed, in its day it must have been a very smart building.

Clearly signposted from main road through Lostwithiel; large car park.

Restormel Castle is unquestionably the finest example of a Norman 'shell keep' in England.

ST MICHAEL'S MOUNT

National Trust • £££ • Usual hours

The buildings on top of the Mount have included a priory, a castle and an artillery fortress, but since 1659 it has been a house and that's basically all it is now (though in fact quite a lot of the space at the top of the hill is taken up by the church). It's a nice place to visit, with a stroll across the causeway followed by a far more energetic steep climb to the summit, but its historical interest for the explorer of castles isn't huge.

The island has been associated with the 'Ictis' said by a pre-Roman text to be the main base for shipping Cornish tin to the continent, but this is not supported by modern archaeologists. The Benedictine priory was founded in 1135, and some of its buildings form the basis of the present house, including the church and a hall known as the Chevy Chase room, which was the priory refectory.

Reached on foot from car parks on the mainland at Marazion (clearly signposted).

St Michael's Mount is basically a stately home in an eccentric location, though it has been a castle and a priory.

TINTAGEL CASTLE

English Heritage • Free • Open access at any reasonable time

Famous for its spurious association with King Arthur, which draws large crowds here in the summer, Tintagel is not terribly interesting as a castle because there is so little left. But it *is* a fairly remarkable place.

It's a headland – almost an island – joined to the mainland by a rocky spur. The first medieval castle was put up on the headland in the 1100s by Reginald, Earl of Cornwall, and in the 1200s another Earl of Cornwall, Richard, built two walled enclosures on the mainland side, plus a wall and gatehouse on the headland, and connected the two with a bridge. Not a lot remains of any of this, and there's no bridge nowadays, so it's a steep walk down and up lots of steps to get from one side to the other.

Reached by a hilly walk from the centre of Tintagel village (several car parks).

There are plenty of neolithic burial chambers around, but not many are as big as Trethevy Quoit.

TRETHEVY QUOIT

English Heritage • Free • Open access only at reasonable hours

This is the burial chamber of a new stone age chambered tomb which would originally have been covered by an earthen mound. There are a few similar monuments around, but this is a particularly large and distinctive example, its huge capstone sitting at a memorably crazy angle and pierced by a small, round hole. The chamber is divided by a cross-stone which has a piece broken off so that a body can be inserted. It's worth a look.

In a field next to houses just west of Darite village (first left just before the village when approaching from the B3254); signposted.

Tintagel was never the home of King Arthur, but it was home to an unusual and remarkable cliff-top castle.

SEE ALSO...

CARN BRAE HILLFORT, *reached on foot from minor roads to the top of the hill from the B3297 south of Redruth or north from Carnkie* – It's not the large iron age hillfort, rare in Cornwall, that's the main interest here, but a neolithic one. The hill rises to three summits and the eastern one, crowned by a natural rocky outcrop, was defended by a massive stone wall 2m (6ft) wide at the base containing boulders up to 3 tons in weight. Inside the wall were a good many wooden buildings, some of them quite substantial. Vast quantities of leaf-shaped flint arrowheads were found, many of them broken and some stuck in the wall, apparently as the result of an attack – remarkable evidence of a warlike community living in a defended site before 2000 BC. The summit is topped by the remains of a castle tower from the 1100s.

CHUN QUOIT (pictured below), *a few yards down the hill from Chun Castle: directions on page 35* – This is the fine-looking chamber of a neolithic chambered tomb, topped by a huge, curved capstone. Its setting, on open moorland with views to the coast, gives the place a special atmosphere. The chamber was once covered by a round mound 11m (35ft) across.

There are several of these small chambered tombs on the West Penwith moors, other well-known ones being ZENNOR QUOIT and MULFRA QUOIT. Both are also reached by footpaths up onto the moors and are not too hard to track down, if you would like to, using the OS map. Zennor Quoit, like *Trethevy Quoit* on Bodmin Moor (*see page 41*) has two of its upright stones projecting forwards on either side of the entrance to form a small porch, like the 'portal dolmens' of Wales.

The whole of this area is covered with patterns of fields that also date back to neolithic times.

KING DONIERT'S STONE, *next to the minor road north-west of St Cleer*, on Bodmin Moor – A broken carved cross thought to commemorate Durngarth, King of Cornwall.

PENHALLAM, *signposted on minor roads near Week St Mary* – Rather interesting ruin of a large fortified medieval manor house. After a short walk on a woodland path, you come across what looks like a maze of low turf banks; this is what's left of the walls of the house, and though none of it stands to any great height, there is enough to give you a good idea of the layout of the place. It's in such a pleasant spot that you're bound to enjoy a visit. (*English Heritage, free, open access during usual hours – car park gate is locked in the evening.*)

ROUGH TOR HILLFORT, HUT CIRCLES & STONE CIRCLE, *car park is at the end of minor road running east from north end of Camelford* – A notable beauty spot and a great place for a walk. The rocky summit of the hill was incorporated into the defences of a hillfort that had stone-built walls. Remains of huts are to be seen inside. Not far away is an elliptical stone 'circle' called Fernacre, made up of 52 small stones, of which 39 still stand. (*National Trust, free, open access at any reasonable time.*)

ST BREOCK DOWNS MONOLITH (pictured right), *on moor to the west of Bodmin* – Large single standing stone in bleak setting which for some reason is in the care of English Heritage.

ST CATHERINE'S CASTLE (pictured on the left), *15-minute walk to headland (some steep slopes) from Fowey centre* – A funny little fortlet built as part of Henry VIII's coastal defences to guard the entrance to Fowey harbour. It has an artillery platform and a squat stone tower. Not terribly exciting, but the walk is very pleasant. (*English Heritage, free, open access at any reasonable time.*)

STRIPPLE STONES HENGE, *Bodmin Moor, near St Breward, by footpath up past Trippet Stones* – Ruined henge with a large circular bank and internal ditch, inside which is a stone circle of 15 stones, with only four still standing. The entrance to the henge faces towards another circle lower down the hill, the Trippet Stones. Interesting, but fairly remote.

TREMATON CASTLE, *near Saltash* – This is said to be a well-preserved shell keep to rival those at Restormel and Launceston (*see above, page 38 and page 40*) but there is no indication of whether it is open to visitors and I'm afraid I was not able to find out. If you live in the area, you might want to check it out for yourself.

AND...

CHAPEL EUNY BURIAL CHAMBER, *Brane* (owned by National Trust, but entry by permission of farm); TRERYN DINAS CLIFF FORT, *near St Levan*

(dramatically sited on a rocky headland, this is a good place for a coastal walk); CASTLE AN DINAS HILLFORT, *near St Columb Major*; CASTLE DORE HILLFORT, *near Golant*; THE RUMPS CLIFF FORT, *north of Padstow* (National Trust land); TREVELGUE HEAD CLIFF FORT, *near Newquay*; WARBSTOW BURY HILLFORT, *by the A39 at Warbstow*.

PLUS... THE SCILLY ISLES

These beautiful islands, warmed by the tropical Atlantic current known as the Gulf Stream, are just a short trip away from Cornwall by plane. There are a number of minor remains of fortifications from the 1500s to the 1800s (listed below), but the islands' main claim to fame is a series of unique bronze age burial chambers.

Known as 'entrance graves', they are of a design that is unique to the islands, consisting of a cairn (a mound made of stones) surrounded by a kerb built of large stones. Within the mound is a large, rectangular chamber.

A number of these monuments are in the care of English Heritage, all of them on St Mary's, and can be visited free of charge at any time. They are: BANT'S CARN CHAMBERED TOMB; INNISIDGEN UPPER AND LOWER CHAMBERED CAIRNS; and PORTH HELLICK DOWN CHAMBERED TOMB.

The other monuments of this kind scattered across the islands have not been investigated thoroughly by archaeologists. Most are now empty and probably have been for many

years. One typical one that was excavated contained pottery urns along with lots of ash and cremated bone, plus beads of glass and fragments of bronze that may have been earrings.

CROMWELL'S CASTLE, *Tresco* – Small round tower built in the 1600s to guard the anchorage between Bryher and Tresco. (*English Heritage, free, open access at any reasonable time.*)

GARRISON WALLS, *St Mary's* – Large walls and earthwork banks which made up the town's defences from the mid-1700s onwards. Comparable with *Berwick-upon-Tweed, Northumbria.* (*English Heritage, free, open access at any reasonable time.*)

HALANGY DOWN ANCIENT VILLAGE, *St Mary's* – Minimal remains of an iron age village of round houses, near *Bant's Carn* burial mound (*see above*).

HARRY'S WALLS, *St Mary's* – Remains of an unfinished fort of the 1500s. (*English Heritage, free, open access at any reasonable time.*)

KING CHARLES CASTLE, *Tresco* – The modest ruin of a coastal defence fort built in the late 1600s, about 20 minutes' walk from New Grimsby. (*English Heritage, free, open access at any reasonable time.*)

THE OLD BLOCKHOUSE, *Old Grimsby harbour, Tresco* – Ruin of a small gun-fort from the 1500s. (*English Heritage, free, open access at any reasonable time.*)

Devon

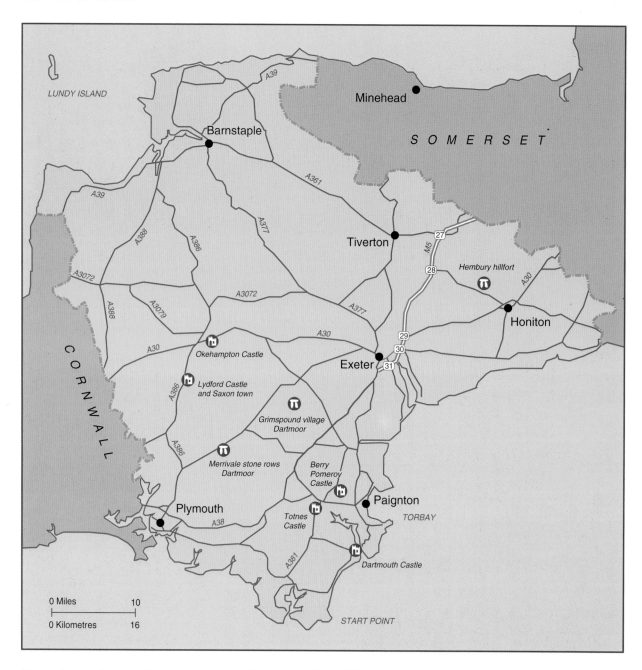

LUNDY ISLAND

Minehead

S O M E R S E T

A39

Barnstaple

A361

A39

A388

A386

A377

Tiverton

M5

27

A3072

28

Hembury hillfort

A3072

A377

29

Honiton

A30

A388

A3079

A30

30

A386

Okehampton Castle

Exeter

31

A386

Lydford Castle
and Saxon town

Grimspound village
Dartmoor

Berry
Pomeroy
Castle

C O R N W A L L

A386

Merrivale stone rows
Dartmoor

Paignton

Plymouth

A38

Totnes
Castle

TORBAY

A361

Dartmouth Castle

0 Miles   10
0 Kilometres   16

START POINT

DEVON is a rural county, but its most outstanding feature is a wilderness: the vast expanse of Dartmoor, littered with the traces of people who lived (and farmed) here 3500 years ago. The region's major monuments, however, are to be found at opposite ends of the county: the hillfort of *Hembury* in the east, and the craggily appealing ruin of *Okehampton Castle* in the west.

Right: The attractive little shell keep at Totnes,
which is an interesting example of an early
Norman castle developed in stone.

44

BERRY POMEROY CASTLE

English Heritage • ££ • Limited hours (April to October only)

This was not so much a castle as a huge fortified house, but it makes an interesting ruin. Its oldest features are the parts you see from the front: the gatehouse, a stretch of wall with a tower at the end, and the L-shaped 'tower house' behind it, which date from about 1480. The gatehouse has recently been restored and has had its roof replaced. On the first floor is a chapel which contains a very old and very rare wall-painting: it's a fresco of the Adoration of the Magi, thought to have been painted in the late 1400s and to be the work of a Flemish artist.

The other interesting surprise at Berry Pomeroy is that, inside the courtyard, you'll find incongruous fragments of stonework from a loggia (a covered garden walkway) in the Renaissance style of the mid-1500s. These fragments are part of a grand house which once occupied the whole of the back wall of the courtyard but which was actually never finished.

Signposted from Berry Pomeroy village, off the A385 between Totnes and Paignton.

Berry Pomeroy is an unusual ruin: in its yard are traces of a splendid Renaissance house that was never finished.

DARTMOUTH CASTLE

English Heritage • ££ • Usual hours

This is an interesting little gun-fort which is directly comparable to the small castles built by Henry VIII (such as *St Mawes Castle* and *Pendennis Castle* in *Cornwall*), though in fact Dartmouth is rather earlier: work started on its construction in 1481. Although it doesn't look like much, when it was built it was one of the most advanced designs in England.

Essentially, the castle is composed of two towers, one round and one square, but joined so as to make one building. On either side of the castle are two gun platforms: open areas protected by a low wall which has openings in it for guns to be fired through (embrasures). Both the ground floor and the basement of the castle are also given over entirely to the guns, with lots of embrasures in the walls, while the

first floor was used as accommodation for the soldiers. Most of the cannon lying about the place, incidentally, were rescued from Dartmouth town where they were in use as bollards.

The most innovative aspect of the design is to be found in the basement, where the gunports were the first in England to be built 'splayed' (widened out) on the inside, so that the gun could be turned slightly and fired at different angles. More entertainingly for the modern visitor, these embrasures also offer attractive views of the harbour mouth.

This building, known as the Old Castle, is not the only one on the headland here. There are fragments of the wall of a much older castle (late 1300s) and there is also a more recent gun battery, known as the Old Battery, which remained in use from the late 1500s right up to the Second World War. (One interesting detail to look out for is the lighting passage next to the magazine: since a lantern could not be used in the same room as the gunpowder, it was stood on the other side of a glass window reached down this narrow passage.)

The castle was part of a network of defences protecting the harbour: on the headland opposite is a fort known as Kingswear Castle and in the town, at Bayard's Cove, there is a simple blockhouse which can be visited.

Signposted on seaward side of Dartmouth.

Left: Dartmouth Castle is actually a fort built in 1481. It's very pretty.

HEMBURY HILLFORT

*By public footpath on farmland • Free •
Open access at any reasonable time*

A good hill for a walk, with fine
views over to Dartmoor. This is the
westernmost of the large iron age
hillforts that are such a major feature
of Dorset, Somerset and Wiltshire:
but the iron age fort was built on top
of a much older neolithic settlement
(very like *Hambledon Hill* in *Dorset*).
It was occupied for less than 200
years, starting about 3300 BC.

Like Hambledon, Hembury seems
to have had both a 'causewayed
camp' and a defensive enclosure of
some kind. This latter enclosure
consisted of a rampart and ditch with
a timber palisade, and at some stage
the palisade seems to have been
burned and the rampart thrown down,
possibly during an attack. Again,
Hambledon shows similar signs of
having been attacked.

Inside the 'causewayed camp' (an
area ringed by a ditch with lots of
gaps in it) were found traces of a hut
and lots of pits, at the bottom of
which were found grains of wheat and
barley, fragments of pottery and lots
of flint tools known as 'scrapers'.
(Human or animal bones don't
survive in the acidic soil here.) Such

finds suggest that it might
and there are traces of
another enclosure nearby
which has barely any
domestic remains and seems
to have been in ritual use.

Abandoned before 3000
BC, the hill was re-occupied
in the iron age, starting
with a small hillfort that
was later enlarged and
strengthened. At some
stage a double bank was
dug across the middle, apparently so
the southern end could be used as a
cattle compound while the north end
was reserved for human occupation.
There weren't any signs of huts, but a
great many slingstones were found,
which suggests that this fort was a
refuge in times of trouble rather than a
permanent settlement.

The Romans also used the site,
which was probably abandoned when
they got here in about 50 BC. It was
very convenient for the Fosse Way.
They rebuilt one of the gates and put
up some large wooden buildings, but
not long afterwards they moved out
and took their buildings with them
(or carefully dismantled them, at
least: the upright posts that supported
the structures were all sawn off at
ground level).

*Beside the A373 north of Honiton; reached
by a short, steep path from the road.*

*The small stone keep at Lydford had the mound piled
up all around it, so that its basement is below the level
of the ground.*

LYDFORD CASTLE

*English Heritage and National Trust • Free •
Open access at any reasonable time*

This plain, squat, heavy Norman keep
isn't terribly big, but it is quite intact
and it's worth a look inside. The keep
was built on top of a particularly
heavy mound (most keeps had to be
built on solid rock). It dates from the
mid-1100s, but its top was altered in
the following century, and at the same
time earth was piled up around it,
burying its basement. Nearby, you can
make out traces of the Saxon defences
of the *burh* of Lydford.

*Easily found in Lydford (signposted from
A386 north of Tavistock).*

*Below: The hillfort at Hembury was built by the Celts,
but the hilltop site was in use in neolithic times.*

Okehampton Castle is a very pleasing pile of rocks: its picturesque qualities outweigh its historical interest.

OKEHAMPTON CASTLE

*English Heritage • ££ • Slightly limited hours
(April to October only)*

This is one of the most attractive castles in England, and it's set in a quiet little valley with a stream running down the side and buzzards patrolling overhead. It's very ruinous, but the tumbledown appearance is part of the appeal of the place and there is more than enough left to give you a very good idea of the layout.

Basically, that layout is as follows. The castle is built on a long, narrow, boat-shaped outcrop of rock which is quite low at one end but climbs to a height of about 30m (100ft) at the other. Here, at the higher end, is a large motte (mound), based on the natural bedrock but with a great pile of shale fragments heaped up against it to make the mound. On top of the mound is a keep; below it is a bailey (courtyard area), with buildings of various kinds ranged round its walls.

Visitors approach the castle from the lower end, up some steps, past one tall fragment of the outer barbican gatehouse and along the course of a long, narrow barbican passageway that led up to the main gatehouse. This passage was intended to constrict attackers as they came to the main gate, making its easier to shoot at them or drop things on them. How high the walls were is not known.

In front of the gate are a couple of walls that probably surrounded a pit crossed by a drawbridge. It was overlooked by a guard-room on the first floor of the gatehouse. Beyond the gatehouse is the bailey – an open courtyard with buildings all round it. The great hall is on your right, and the rooms to your left were lodgings.

Most of these buildings date from the early 1300s, when the castle was completely rebuilt by its then owner, Hugh Courtenay II. Within the great hall, however, there are traces of an earlier hall from the mid-1200s.

Higher up, near the mound, there are a chapel and priest's house on the left, also dating to the rebuilding of the early 1300s. Behind are traces of a later accommodation range. On the right are kitchens of the same later date, probably around 1400.

The keep, which from the entrance looks like nothing more than a single tall finger of stone, is actually a heavy rectangular building that was built in two halves. At the front is the original square stone tower dating from the late 1100s, while behind is an extension added in the early 1300s. The whole thing is satisfyingly heavy and dark, built from slabs of granite, and the drop off the back of the motte is pretty precarious.

Okehampton Castle is mentioned in the Domesday Book in 1086 as being owned by Baldwin de Brionne, Sheriff of Devon; but in 1274 it was described as 'an old motte which is worth nothing, and outside the motte a hall, chamber and kitchen poorly built', which probably explains why it was rebuilt in the early 1300s.

On west side of Okehampton, clearly signposted from the centre of the town.

Grimspound is a village of small bronze age roundhouses surrounded by a wall. Although it has been partially rebuilt, it's still a remarkable survival of some 3500 years ago.

ANCIENT DARTMOOR

ONE OF MANY REMARKABLE THINGS ABOUT DARTMOOR is that its moorland landscape isn't entirely a product of nature, but has formed only as a result of man's intervention. During the bronze age, in the period after about 2000 BC, more land than ever before was being farmed all across Britain, and farming expanded into less favourable areas like the Dartmoor uplands. By about 1200 BC, much of this land had been abandoned again; perhaps because the thin upland soils had been worn out, or because a change in the climate had made it more difficult to grow crops on such exposed land. The fields were left to go to waste and the result is the moorland you see today.

The other result is that Dartmoor is littered with remarkable remains of the bronze age, surviving across wide areas because the land has not been touched since. These include farm settlements and field systems as well as monuments like stone circles and – pretty much a Dartmoor speciality, this one – stone rows.

There are two distinctive types of bronze age settlement known on Dartmoor, and these are labelled 'pounds' and 'enclosed villages'. Pounds were small hamlets with a handful of houses surrounded by a high stone wall which is thought to have been intended to stop farm animals from straying or to protect them from attack by predators or even raids by rustlers. Villages had more houses (usually about 30) and also had lots of low stone walls forming pens or gardens within the perimeter wall of the compound.

There don't seem to have been any fields near the pounds or villages, which are concentrated on the west side of the moor. Instead, fields are mostly found on the eastern side – where the soil and the weather were both better – with small farmsteads scattered among them.

Ancient systems of fields are one of the rarest things to survive in Britain, since good farmland has stayed in use right up to modern times and has been greatly altered as a result, but Dartmoor has provided an ideal place for extensive study. The landscape is divided up by boundaries known as 'reaves', which are mostly dry-stone walls but which might also be banks, ditches or fences. Large reaves define general areas (estates or territories, you might call them) which are divided into fields by lots of smaller reaves. Each field-system appears to have been laid out in one go, in a planned way, rather than developing over the years. Land above a certain height was not enclosed as fields, perhaps because it was left as common land. Interestingly, though, analysis of pollen suggests that the enclosed fields and the open land were used in exactly the same way, as rough grazing for sheep and cattle.

GRIMSPOUND WALLED SETTLEMENT

English Heritage • Free • Open access at any reasonable time

This is a rather fine village of about 20 round stone huts surrounded by a granite wall (the wall has, to some extent, been restored). The village is thought to date to later in the bronze age (after 1000 BC) and to have been a settlement of cattle-farmers. On the west side are areas thought to be cattle pens, while on the north side are smaller huts that might have been used for storage. The entrance to the enclosure has a paved road outside, with a spring nearby.

The round houses have 'porches', stone door jambs, hearths and a stone set in the middle that would have supported a roof-post. Some have raised areas that may have been beds (perhaps 'sleeping platforms' might be more accurate). It's all rather interesting stuff.

On moorland east of a minor road that turns off the B3212 a couple of miles west of Moretonhampstead heading for Challacombe; limited car parking on verge.

MERRIVALE STONE ROWS, STONE CIRCLE & HUT CIRCLES

English Heritage and Dartmoor National Park Authority • Free • Open access at any reasonable time

Any visit to Dartmoor by car is pretty much bound to take you to this area of open moorland, scattered as liberally with ancient monuments as it is with day-trippers.

There are about 60 stone rows on Dartmoor, and three of them are here. Like stone circles, they date from the bronze age and appear to have had a ceremonial use, though exactly what they were for is anyone's guess. The obvious suggestion is as processional ways, like the West Kennet Avenue at *Avebury* in *Wiltshire* (or Carnac in Brittany, France). Near the stone rows are a small stone circle with 11 stones surviving, and a very tall monolith.

Next to the B3357 east of Merrivale village; your choice of car parks.

Enigmatic Dartmoor: one of the double stone rows at Merrivale, with a 'closing stone' at the end.

SEE ALSO...

CORRINGDON BALL CHAMBERED LONG BARROW AND STONE ROWS, *by footpath from South Brent, south Dartmoor* – A neolithic barrow consisting of a large mound with a ruined stone chamber at one end. Nearby are several rows of small stones, some aligned towards bronze age round barrows.

LAKEHEAD HILL STONE CISTS, *near Princetown, footpath through woods from Bellever* – Three large 'cists' (stone chambers) from 'cairns' (stone burial mounds) of the bronze age; one of the cists is surrounded by a 'cairn circle' of six standing stones.

SHOVEL DOWN STONE ROWS, *near Gidleigh on the north-east side of the moor, by footpath up to Shovel Down* – There are lots of stone circles, stone rows, cairns and standing stones in this area.

UPPER PLYM VALLEY, *south Dartmoor* – Six square miles of moor owned by English Heritage and cared for by the National Trust, but the monuments are not as thick on the ground.

TOTNES CASTLE

*English Heritage • ££ • Slightly limited hours
(closed Monday and Tuesday and for an hour
at lunchtime in winter)*

This is a great example of a simple
motte and bailey castle updated by the
addition of a little shell keep. The
motte (castle mound) on which the
keep stands is unusually tall, one of
the biggest in England, and is built of
packed layers of earth, rock and clay.
Initially it was topped by a simple
wooden tower, built in about 1100,
but in the early 1300s the stone shell –
a simple ring of walls – was built on
top of the mound and walls were put
round the bailey below. There was
only ever one basic lean-to building
inside the keep.

*Clearly signposted in Totnes; small council
car park near the castle.*

On top of a very tall mound, Totnes has a great little shell keep built in about 1300 (very late for this kind of keep).

SEE ALSO...

BICKLEIGH CASTLE, *Bickleigh village,
off the A396 south of Tiverton* –
Basically a fortified house from the
mid-1400s, but with bits of an earlier
Norman castle (including a thatched
chapel from the mid-1100s). More
house-like than castle-like to visit.
(*Privately owned, £££, limited hours –
afternoons except Saturday in summer
and certain other days.*)

BUCKLAND ABBEY, *near Plymouth* –
Post-Dissolution house associated with
Sir Francis Drake, incorporating parts
of the church of the Cistercian abbey.
Good monastic barn in the grounds.
(*National Trust, £££, slightly limited
hours – usual hours in summer but
weekends only November to March.*)

CASTLE DROGO, *Drewsteignton, near
Exeter* – Oddly industrial-looking
mock castle built in 1910–1930,
designed by Sir Edwin Lutyens.
(*National Trust, £££, limited hours –
daily except Friday, April to October.*)

COMPTON CASTLE, *Marldon, near
Newton Abbot* – Rather attractive
fortified manor house built from the
1300s to the 1500s. Worth seeing.
(*National Trust, ££, limited hours –
Monday, Wednesday and Thursday
April to October.*)

CROWNHILL FORT, *Plymouth* –
Huge Victorian fort of the 1860s, one
of 'Palmerston's Follies', in a very
original state. Great underground
passageways to explore. (*Landmark
Trust, £££, April to October only.*)

HEMYOCK CASTLE, *Hemyock* – Ruin of
a walls-and-towers style castle; later
buildings on the site are still occupied.
Open to visitors irregularly.

KENT'S CAVERN (PREHISTORIC CAVE
DWELLINGS), *Torquay town centre* –
Open as a tourist show cave with
glibly educational concessions to its
prehistoric past. The amount of stuff
found here (animal bones, tools etc)
makes it an important site.

KIRKHAM HOUSE, *Paignton* – A typical
house of the 1400s. Very interesting.
(*English Heritage, free, open only on
five or six open days each year.*)

MARISCO CASTLE, *Lundy Island* –
Pieces of curtain wall that surrounded
a rectangular tower built in the 1200s.
Not reason enough for making the boat
trip to the island (it's a whole day out),
but there are other reasons to go.

MARTINHOE ROMAN FORTLET, *on north
Devon coast west of Lynton* – Traces
of a small fort garrisoned by a century
of about 80 men. The views are great.

PLYMOUTH ROYAL CITADEL, *Plymouth*
– Large fort from the 1600s, still in
military use so visited by guided tour
only. (*English Heritage, £££, limited
hours – two tours each afternoon, May
to September only.*)

PLYMPTON CASTLE, *near Plymouth* –
Large Norman motte, used as a
viewpoint, with traces of a shell keep.

POWDERHAM CASTLE, *near Kenton,
south of Exeter* – Heavily rebuilt
fortified manor house dating back to
about 1390 in parts but mostly much
more modern, with grand interiors.
(*Privately owned, £££, limited hours –
April to October only.*)

TIVERTON CASTLE, *north side of
Tiverton town centre* – Fragments
remain of a castle of the 1300s with
lots of later house built inside. Dull.
Contains a museum. The oldest bits (a
gatehouse and some wall) can be seen
from the churchyard next door.
(*Privately owned, £££, limited hours –
too complex to specify.*)

AND...

BLACKBURY CAMP HILLFORT & BROAD
DOWN BARROWS, *near Southleigh;*
CHAPMAN BARROWS & LONG STONE,
Parracombe, Exmoor; COUNTISBURY
PROMONTORY FORT, *near Lynmouth.*

Somerset

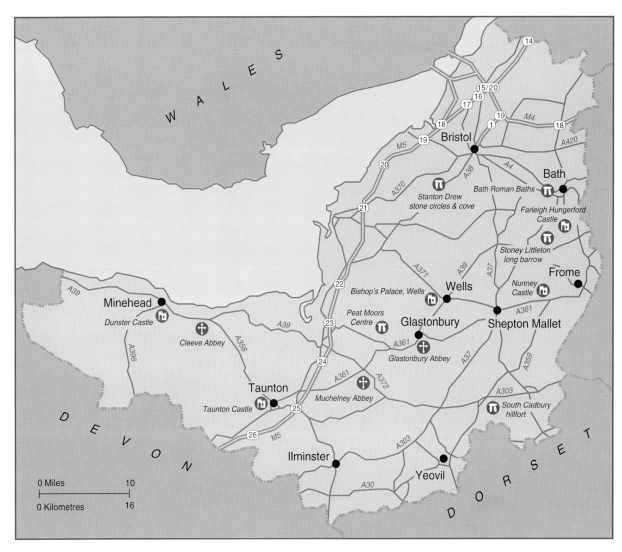

SOMERSET has a very rich history, and it is lucky enough to have notable monuments of all sorts of different types and ages. The oldest is the huge complex of stone circles at *Stanton Drew*, not far from Bristol, which has been shown by recent surveys to have more to it than meets the eye. Particularly enjoyable to visit is *Cleeve Abbey*, where the church has long since disappeared but cloister buildings such as the refectory and the monks' dormitory have survived more or less completely intact, thanks to having been turned into a farm. There aren't any large castles in the county, but there is a very pleasant one at *Farleigh Hungerford*, within easy reach of the Roman town of Bath.

Part of the church at Glastonbury Abbey, with some gorgeous details in the arches.

The main lead-lined Roman hot bath at Bath is only part of a huge temple complex.

BATH ROMAN BATHS

Bath City Council • ££££ • Usual hours

Inevitably this is one of the busiest tourist attractions in the world, with a proportionately huge entrance fee. At peak times it's a struggle to elbow your way through the corridors, lined with museum exhibits, down which you must trek to reach the baths, yet the place still manages to have a faintly mysterious atmosphere.

A few visits to villas will give you the impression that the Romans did little else except take hot baths, but this was far more than a heated swimming pool. Already sacred to the Celts, it became a shrine to the goddess Sulis Minerva, with an extensive temple complex, and among the many dedicatory inscriptions found on stones here is Britain's only reference to a *haruspex*, the priest who read the auguries in the entrails of sacrificial animals.

There's still something magical about the steaming hot water bubbling out of the ground, and the way the extensive suite of Roman baths now lurks in catacomb-like half-darkness under the foundations of the later city. You could spend hours peering at all the many exhibits and reading the unusually excellent guidebook. Altogether, a superb experience.

In centre of city, next to Bath Abbey.

BISHOP'S PALACE, WELLS

Church authorities • £££ • Usual hours

Wells is a lovely little town, with probably the finest cathedral in the country (and the cathedral has a fantastic tearoom, too). The nearby Bishop's Palace is surrounded by a fine wall and moat, with a massive gatehouse to keep the uppity peasantry of the 1300s out, all of which are best seen from the outside (and for free).

Inside the walls are a few greatly updated buildings (including a chapel and the bishop's reception rooms) and some nice gardens containing a few bits of ruined wall. The best bit is the walk outside the walls that takes you to the springs (the wells from which Wells gets its name) where there is a brilliant view of the cathedral reflected in the water.

A very short walk from Wells cathedral.

One of the few genuinely castle-like bits of Dunster is this gatehouse; the rest has been totally updated.

DUNSTER CASTLE

National Trust • £££ • Usual hours

Although it looks fantastic, hanging over the historic village in authentic Gothic horror movie fashion, Dunster is a disappointment to anyone who likes medieval castles since it was rebuilt as a dark and unpleasant house. The Norman motte on which the original castle was built in the 1130s during the slide into anarchy of Stephen's reign survives and is used as a garden. Down in the village there's more to see, including a restored, working watermill, a medieval market cross, a very nice packhorse bridge, and the famous timber-framed Yarn Market.

In Dunster village, east of Minehead.

The outer walls of the Bishop's Palace in Wells look great, but inside there's not much more than gardens.

The gatehouse: 'Shut to no honest person', according to the inscription on the front.

CLEEVE ABBEY REMAINS

English Heritage • ££ • Usual hours

The refectory has its original timber roof; in front of it is a floor of decorated tiles from the late 1200s.

Smashing place. Really fabulous. What makes it very different from most ruined abbeys is that the domestic buildings around the cloister have survived remarkably intact, so it has lots of interesting indoor spaces. As well as being fun to explore, it is also an unusually good place to get an impression of monastic life and to make sense of strange terms like 'reredorter' and 'sacristy'.

Cleeve has recently celebrated its 800th anniversary; it was founded in 1198 and was a Cistercian abbey. Originally the monks would have lived and worshipped in wooden buildings, and it took most of the next 100 years to finish the stone buildings. Its fortunes declined in the 1300s until after 1450, when more money started coming in and some parts of the abbey were rebuilt.

In 1536 the abbey was dissolved, and the huge church was dismantled (all that's left of it is the outline of the foundations on the ground). The other buildings became first a house and then a farmyard, which is why they survived in such a complete state. The main rooms are the refectory, where the monks gathered for meals (it still has its original timber roof), and the dorter, or dormitory (a fine long hall on the first floor), but there are plenty of other bits to see too. There are also a couple of rare treats – a large late 15th century wall painting in a room next to the refectory, and a rather fine clay tile floor, now outdoors, which, thanks to heraldry on the tiles, can be dated to 1272–1300.

Simply enough, don't miss it.

Signposted from A39 west of Williton.

In the monks' dormitory (the 'dorter') on the first floor, there's room for 36 to sleep.

Stairs up to the refectory, where the light pours in through lots of huge windows.

Though there's plenty of Farleigh Hungerford Castle still to be seen, it was once an awful lot bigger.

FARLEIGH HUNGERFORD CASTLE

English Heritage • ££ • Usual hours

Modest but charming, the late medieval castle at Farleigh Hungerford is carefully tended (especially the flowerbeds) by very friendly staff. Although it's not large, it is still the most substantial castle in this part of the world.

Sir Thomas de Hungerford fortified his manor house at Farleigh in the 1370s at a time of widespread invasion scares, but he neglected to get the King's permission and later had to beg for a royal pardon. For the next two centuries the castle and its owners seem to have led a particularly colourful life, with frequent poisoning of husbands by their wives (and *vice versa*). The castle survived the Civil War but was starting to fall apart by about 1700.

What's left today includes an impressively precarious slice of ruined tower and a complete gatehouse, as well as the chapel (once the parish church) and the priest's house (built into the east curtain wall), both of which are pretty much intact and help to make the castle well worth a visit. One particular item of interest is the painting on the wall of the chapel, which was revealed by accident when some of the plaster fell off in 1844. Thought to date from about 1440, it shows Saint George slaying the dragon, though the dragon can barely be made out.

Surprisingly, most of the castle that you see today was actually only the outer court, with relatively low walls and mostly domestic buildings. The main castle was behind, and it's well worth trying to puzzle out some of the maze of foundations.

A couple of miles south west of Bradford-on-Avon; signposted from the A36 a few miles south of Bath.

On the wall of the chapel is a painting of Saint George from the 1440s. Rare early medieval paintings were recently found at a nearby inn, The George at Norton St Philip.

The abbot's kitchen at Glastonbury, which has a huge fireplace in each corner.

GLASTONBURY ABBEY

Church authorities • £££ • Usual hours

It's not the most alluring of ruined abbeys, but Glastonbury does have a couple of particularly good features. One is the unusual funnel-like building which contained the abbott's kitchens; inside there are massive fireplaces and chimneys, with a big vent high up in the centre. The other is the exterior of the Lady Chapel, which was the first building put up after a fire destroyed the original abbey in 1184. The stonework is especially pleasing, with an amazing carved doorway, and underneath, in the crypt, is a well which is thought to have held some special significance.

The ruins of the church are not too exciting, though some of the carving is pretty spectacular. In the middle is the spot where, in 1191, monks claimed to have found the grave of King Arthur – just after the fire, when they needed the money. Hmm…

Right behind Glastonbury high street.

Inside the ruined abbey church at Glastonbury is the site of what is claimed to be King Arthur's grave.

MUCHELNEY ABBEY

English Heritage • ££ • Usual hours

Only foundations remain of the great abbey of Muchelney, built on a large island in the marshes, but one wing of the cloisters, including the former abbott's house, still stands to its full height. It's a great little building, with lots of small, creaky rooms and well-worn stone staircases. It dates mostly from the early 1500s, though it was much altered during its later career as a farmhouse.

In the Abbot's Parlour, which is the principal room on the first floor, there's a big fireplace with a particularly loveable pair of carved stone lions at the top, and some smart wooden panelling. On display in various rooms of the house are appropriately medieval ceramics from the nearby pottery of John Leach.

Also in the village is the Priest's House, a medieval hall house owned by the National Trust and occupied by tenants but open to visitors on summer Sundays and Mondays.

Muchelney village, south west of Somerton.

Muchelney Abbey – all that's left is a building which contained the abbot's lodgings, but it's well worth seeing.

The Abbot's Parlour at Muchelney is highly decorated, with a pair of stone lions over the fireplace.

Left: Nunney castle, its moat still filled with water, is small but very appealing.

PEAT MOORS CENTRE
IRON AGE VILLAGE

Somerset County Council • ££ • Usual hours

An educational project, this 'living museum' features reconstructions of two small iron age roundhouses and a couple of stretches of wooden walkway (one based on the famous new stone age Sweet Track, the other of a later type). There's also a good little one-room museum covering the archaeology of the Somerset peat moors, with a good deal of information about Glastonbury Lake Village. It's really meant for school parties, though.

Clearly signposted on minor road between Westhay and Shapwick.

Woodsmoke hangs under the eaves of an iron age house at the Peat Moors Centre.

Tragically, however, the barrow has been closed for some time after frost and vandals did serious damage to it, and there's no sign of it reopening. To add insult to injury, a site just across the valley was at time of writing being landfilled, which does nothing for the tranquillity of the area.

You have to bear in mind that it was restored in 1858, but the barrow has some really smart stonework, with a fine funnel-shaped forecourt and a huge lintel stone over the entrance. Inside, you used to be able to crawl down a long passageway with seven small chambers, and it was fantastic. One can only hope that it will soon be open again.

Approaching village of Wellow from Bath, turn right along village high street and then turn left (signposted) at edge of village; it's a small single-track road.

NUNNEY CASTLE

English Heritage • Free • Open access any reasonable time

Pretty as a picture, Nunney is a funny little castle of very unusual design. It's classed as a 'courtyard castle' of the French style, with the outer walls giving the main defence and the accommodation buildings set close up against them; but at Nunney, the outer walls have been brought so closely together that the castle is essentially a single keep with a large light well in the middle. It's ringed by a very deep-looking moat.

The only comparable place is *Old Wardour Castle, Wiltshire.* Both were not so much castles as posh houses built by men of a military bent who probably viewed a 'licence to crenellate' as a status symbol in itself. The licence to build Nunney was granted in 1373 to Sir John Delamere, a veteran of the Hundred Years War. Given its modest scale, there's not much to explore here, but it's a very attractive spot.

In Nunney village, just south of Frome off the A361 Shepton Mallet road.

STONEY LITTLETON
LONG BARROW

English Heritage • Free • Open access at reasonable times

One of the finest chambered barrows in England, beautifully set on a hillside in a very pretty valley and reached via a footbridge across a babbling brook and a gentle ten-minute stroll up the hill.

Stoney Littleton barrow is one of the best in the country. Inside is a long passage with seven side-chambers.

Stanton Drew has a lot to offer: this is the smaller north-east circle, with the Great Circle over the rise beyond.

STANTON DREW

STONE CIRCLES & COVE

Privately owned; managed by English Heritage • £ (honesty box, so bring coins) • Every day, 9am to sunset

It's stretching a point to say that Stanton Drew deserves to be mentioned in the same breath as Stonehenge and Avebury, but it's certainly true that this major stone circle is under-appreciated. Perhaps part of the problem is its prosaic setting, on farmland in a small valley, with quite a bit of modern clutter surrounding it. But it has recently received a huge boost to its status following a geophysical survey which came up with remarkable results that put Stanton Drew right at the centre of the current debate on henges.

In fact there are three stone circles here, plus an arrangement of three large standing stones known as The Cove on the other side of the village. The smaller south-west circle is less visually interesting because its stones are smaller and lie flat. The circle that looks best is the other small one, the north-east circle, but the star

attraction, really, is the Great Circle, 113m (370ft) across and the second largest in England after Avebury. This is where the geophysical survey came up with its amazing results.

What was found, using electro-magnetism to probe hidden features of the soil, was a huge, circular henge ditch surrounding the Great Circle, and a series of concentric rings of pits, each pit probably a metre (3ft) across, within the circle of stones. The only comparable finds known to archaeologists are the concentric rings of post-holes from places like Woodhenge (near Stonehenge) and The Sanctuary (near Avebury), so it is

thought that the Stanton Drew pits might contain evidence of posts. This in turn opens up the possibility that within the Great Circle there could have been a huge, round building. Were henges actually great roundhouses, used for feasting, meetings, worship and trade?

The most exciting thing about Stanton Drew is that, because it is as yet unexcavated, it holds out the hope of answers to some of these questions. For archaeologists, this makes it buried treasure in a very real sense.

Signposted in Stanton Drew village, just off the B3130 south of Bristol.

The south-west circle is rather less exciting, with just a few large stones, and those lying flat, not standing.

The three huge stones of The Cove are in the beer garden of the village pub, The Druid.

The huge hillfort of South Cadbury. Was this the real Camelot? Almost certainly not…

SOUTH CADBURY HILLFORT

Private farmland • Free • Open access at reasonable times only

A fantastic hillfort, this, with huge ramparts built about 500 BC and later strengthened with timbers and limestone blocks; but it owes its fame to a theory that it might be the Camelot of Arthurian legend, which unfortunately is incredibly unlikely.

The theory was based on the perfectly reasonable idea that there was a real, historical Arthur around whom the legends grew up, and that he might have been a leader of the native British resistance against Saxon invaders, in the 'dark ages' after the Romans left. South Cadbury was heavily refortified around about 500 AD, and a wooden hall was built. The stronghold of a native king? Well, why not. And with the Camel

There's very little castle to be seen at Taunton, and what little there is, is now home to a museum.

being a local river… could this have been King Arthur's Camelot?

Sadly, it seems not. Even the greatest exponents of the historical Arthur were obliged to conclude that there is no real evidence at all for his existence, and it turns out that many hillforts in southern England were refortified about this time, so there is nothing special about South Cadbury.

All the same, it's worth reading the Penguin paperback by Leslie Alcock which discusses this subject, and it's certainly worth coming to see this excellent hillfort.

Free car park and footpath to the hillfort signposted in South Cadbury village.

TAUNTON CASTLE

Somerset County Council • ££ • Usual hours

This was once a proper castle, with a hall built in the 1100s and a great tower from the mid-1200s, but there's not really an awful lot left of it now except the heavily remodelled hall. Inside is the County Museum, which isn't exactly a bundle of laughs, though it does have a decent archeological section. It's hard to think of an especially good reason to come and have a look round.

In centre of Taunton.

SEE ALSO…

AVELINE'S HOLE CAVE DWELLING, *Burrington Combe, near the 'Rock of Ages'* – This cave contained flint tools and the remains of about 50 humans, dated to around 7000 BC.

CHEDDAR & WOOKEY HOLE CAVE DWELLINGS, *in Cheddar Gorge and not far from Wells town centre* – Both caves are tourist attractions, but both were occupied by humans and have museum exhibits.

CLEVEDON COURT (*National Trust, £££, limited hours*), *just off B3128 west of Clevedon* – This medieval manor house, with a Norman hall, is pretty dull inside, but well worth a cheeky free peek at the exterior.

GLASTONBURY TRIBUNAL (*English Heritage, £, usual hours*), *on Glastonbury high street* – An old merchant's house, now home to an exhibition covering the excavations of Glastonbury Lake Village with lots of finds on display. Pretty good.

GLASTONBURY TOR (*National Trust, free, open access*), *by foot or by bus from Glastonbury town centre* – This famous place is just an unusual hill with a church tower on the top, though the views are superb.

MEARE FISH HOUSE (*English Heritage, free, usual hours*), *signposted on edge of Meare village* – Nice little basic stone dwelling.

STOKE-SUB-HAMDON PRIORY (*National Trust, free, usual hours, but March to October only*), *in North Street, right in the middle of the village* – You can pop in to the derelict Great Hall, but it will only impress keen house-renovators.

AND…

COW CASTLE HILLFORT, *near Simonsbath*; DOLEBURY HILLFORT, *near Churchill*; HAM HILL HILLFORT, *near Stoke-sub-Hamdon*; STOKELEIGH PROMONTORY FORT, *in Leigh Woods, by the Avon Gorge, Clifton, Bristol*; WORLEBURY CAMP, *near Weston-super-Mare.*

Dorset

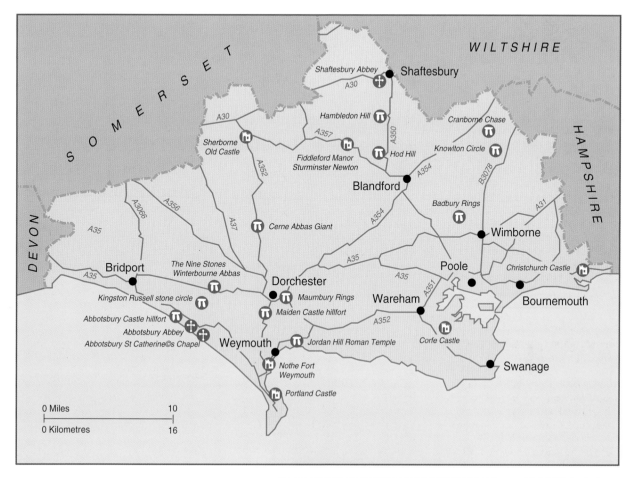

WILTSHIRE

SOMERSET

DEVON

HAMPSHIRE

Shaftesbury Abbey — Shaftesbury
A30

Hambledon Hill
A357
Fiddleford Manor
Sturminster Newton
Hod Hill
A350

Cranborne Chase
Knowlton Circle

Sherborne
Old Castle
A30
A352

A354
Blandford

Badbury Rings
B3078
A31

Cerne Abbas Giant
A3066
A356
A37

A35
Wimborne
Poole
A35
Christchurch Castle

The Nine Stones
Winterbourne Abbas
Bridport
A35
Dorchester
Maumbury Rings
Wareham
A351
Bournemouth

Kingston Russell stone circle
Maiden Castle hillfort
A352

Abbotsbury Castle hillfort
Abbotsbury Abbey
Abbotsbury St Catherine©s Chapel
Weymouth
Jordan Hill Roman Temple
Corfe Castle
Swanage

Nothe Fort
Weymouth

Portland Castle

0 Miles   10
0 Kilometres   16

DORSET is blessed with some of the most
dramatic scenery on the south coast, and many
of its ancient monuments blend perfectly into
the landscape. Indeed, its most notable
monuments are actually *part* of the landscape:
these are the vast iron age hillforts that once
belonged to the Celtic tribe of the Durotriges.
Maiden Castle, *Hod Hill* and *Hambledon Hill*
are particularly fine examples. The county
also has one of the greatest medieval castles,
a favourite of King John, in *Corfe Castle*.
Corfe is also England's most spectacular
example of 'slighting' (the destruction of the
fortifications by blowing them up with
gunpowder, which was ordered by Parliament
after the Civil War). Elsewhere, the open
country to the north of Wimborne Minster is

At Knowlton, a Norman church was built inside the circular bank and ditch of a neolithic henge.

the home of a most unusual monument at *Knowlton Circles*, where a
ruined Norman church stands inside a henge that was just one part of a
vast ceremonial complex in neolithic times.

ABBOTSBURY ABBEY & ST CATHERINE'S CHAPEL

English Heritage • Abbey remains: free, open access at any reasonable time • Chapel: entry is free, but it's not always open.

All that remains of this Benedictine abbey founded in 1044 is one chunk of wall – just about the silliest monument in the care of English Heritage – and a sturdy tithe barn from the 1300s, now a children's 'fun farm' (and pretty hideous too). Coach parties flock to the famous Swannery, another creation of the Abbotsbury monks, making the village a fairly crowded place in the summer; but the scenery round these parts is pretty special, with the unique Chesil Beach – a vast bank of pebbles several miles long – running along the shore to the Isle of Portland.

Between the village and the coast is Dorset's rival to Glastonbury Tor – a little hill with St Catherine's Chapel at the top. The chapel is not especially interesting in itself, but the walk up is rewarded by fine views. Saint Catherine is strongly associated with worship on isolated hilltops – a tradition which very likely contains echoes of pre-Christian worship.

Abbey remains are in Abbotsbury village, west of Weymouth on B3157. The footpath to the top of Chapel Hill is just nearby.

This is all that's left of Abbotsbury Abbey. It's not what the coach parties come for, though.

ABBOTSBURY CASTLE

HILLFORT

Farmland • Free • Open access at any reasonable time

Not all hillforts have grand ramparts, but most offer a pleasant walk with good views, and this is no exception. The hillfort is easily reached, because the road takes you most of the way up the hill, and the views along the coast to Portland, taking in the remarkable Chesil beach, are just spectacular (and I once saw an adder and no less than seven buzzards here).

There's historical interest here too, if you care to look for it: within the ramparts are a barrow and traces of at least nine huts, while a square earthwork on the south west might have been a Roman signal station.

At top of hill, up B3157 west of Abbotsbury.

Abbotsbury Castle is not an exceptional hillfort, but the views are brilliant.

CERNE ABBAS GIANT

National Trust • Free • Open access only at reasonable times

He's rude, he's extraordinary – but is he ancient, or is he a fake? The 55m (170ft) high Giant has always been thought, purely on the style of the image, to date from the second century AD and to represent Hercules 'conflated' with a local god of fertility (Roman gods were often adopted by the natives and mixed up with local gods in this fashion, as Sulis/Minerva at Bath). Recently, however, it has been pointed out that there is no reference to the Giant before the 18th century, which suggests that he may have been created by some local wags around that time.

Belief in the Giant's power has persisted, though. It is still said that women will conceive if they spend midsummer's night on the Giant.

Cerne Abbas village, north of Dorchester, south of Sherborne, right next to A352.

The famously well-endowed Cerne Abbas Giant: is he anything more than an 18th-century joke?

CHRISTCHURCH CASTLE & NORMAN HOUSE

English Heritage • Free • Open access any reasonable time

A comedy castle. All that remains of this tiny keep, built some time after 1160, is two ruined walls about 40ft high with an archway in each. Not worth going out of your way for. The ruins of the Norman Constable's House in the nearby park are pretty enough, but they don't have much of a story to tell. Still, Christchurch is an attractive little town and the priory is well worth seeing, so look in on these two while you're here.

In centre of Christchurch old town, near the priory; park in town centre car parks and wander down the high street.

Christchurch Castle – reminds me of 'Stonehenge' in the film Spinal Tap *(if that means anything to you).*

CRANBORNE CHASE

(OAKLEY DOWN BARROWS, DORSET CURSUS, ACKLING DYKE ROMAN ROAD)

Mostly farmland • Free • Some access by public footpath

This ancient landscape is a great place to get a glimpse of thousands of years of human endeavour. In my personal opinion it's an extraordinary slice of countryside, although to be perfectly fair I would have to admit that none of the individual monuments is especially outstanding. It's more a question of letting your imagination do the walking.

The Roman road of Ackling Dyke (you can still clearly see the *agger*, or main causeway, flanked by drainage ditches) cuts through the Oakley Down barrow group, a Bronze Age cemetery of bowl, disc and bell barrows where bronze daggers and shale and amber beads were among the many objects found during excavation. A footpath travels along the Roman road and is the best way to get a closer look at the barrows.

Across the road, to the south, is a very small surviving stretch of the huge and mysterious Dorset Cursus. This double bank and ditch once ran for 9km (6 miles), but most of it has been ploughed flat.

Its purpose is unknown, though it must surely have been ceremonial. It may have been related to the nearby 'causewayed camp' at *Hambledon Hill (page 62)*, perhaps as part of a great ceremonial landscape. Astronomical alignments have been suggested. Pottery in the ditches dates it to the early new stone age.

You can also see the squared-off end of the Dorset Cursus at Thickthorn Down (beside a minor road off the A354, just north west of Gussage St Michael) where it incorporates two large barrows.

Either side of the B3081, just east of the roundabout on the A354 Salisbury-to-Blandford road, near Sixpenny Handley.

*The ancient landscape of Cranborne Chase: to the right is the bank (*agger*) of the Roman road, with the bronze age Oakley Down barrow group in the middle distance, on the left.*

Once one of the strongest castles in the realm, Corfe is still powerful and dramatic, even in ruins.

CORFE CASTLE

National Trust • £££ • Usual hours

Guarding a gap in the chalk ridge of the beautiful Purbeck hills, Corfe is the finest castle in the south-west of England, in spite of the fact that there's not really an awful lot of it left standing. The castle was very efficiently blown to pieces on the orders of Parliament in 1646, at the end of the Civil War. Although this means there's not much in the way of clambering or exploring on offer, part of the castle's appeal is in the picturesque way the towers are slipping down the hill, while the few remaining pieces of keep have a faintly sinister air which is perhaps an echo of the way it would have dominated the surrounding country.

Corfe is thought to be the place where the Saxon King Edward was murdered in 978 on the orders of his stepmother Elfrida, so that her son Ethelred ('The Unready') could become king. Certainly traces of an important Saxon building, possibly a royal hall, were found under the Norman Old Hall in the West Bailey.

You enter the castle across a bridge (one section would originally have slid or lifted away to close off the castle) over a huge ditch quarried in the early 1200s. Beyond the gatehouse, its towers made of solid stone to first-floor level, is the outer bailey; someone once told me that this is the bit of the castle that the villagers would have been allowed into for fairs and markets, and even if it's not true, it's an evocative image.

The stout gatehouse towers were made of solid stone to first-floor level, with shooting platforms above.

The curtain wall to the right needed only two towers to defend it because the slope outside is so steep. The second of the two towers, higher up the hill, is known as the Plukenet Tower because carved on the outside is the shield of Alan de Plukenet, constable of the castle from 1265 to 1270, rather wittily held up by a pair of hands. It's worth seeking it out. The left-hand curtain wall, defending a shallower slope, has four towers.

Most of this stonework dates from the early 1200s, in the reign of King John.

At the top of the bailey is an astonishing sight, the South-West Gatehouse, split dramatically in half by the Civil War gunpowder. Inside you can see slots for two portcullises and holes into which the drawbars of the gate would have slotted.

Beyond is the West Bailey, getting closer to the inner heart of the castle. This is where the Saxon hall stood, and you should be able to pick out the herring-bone masonry of the original Norman hall, to the left.

Finally you come to the Inner Ward where the typical square Norman keep stood. It was built in the early years of the reign of Henry I, possibly as early as 1105, and later had a forebuilding added to protect the entranceway. Behind it was the Gloriette, a very posh range of buildings thought to have been built for King John and containing a large royal hall as well as the king's private audience chamber.

So there's plenty to see at Corfe, and the scenery around is smashing. Steam trains now run next to the castle on the railway line to Swanage.

Centre of Corfe Castle village, Isle of Purbeck, near Wareham.

If you're in the Sturminster area, you must look in at Fiddleford Manor, with its beautiful interior.

FIDDLEFORD MANOR

English Heritage • Free • Usual hours

Bit of a side-dish, this: it's a lovely little medieval manor house with a superb wooden roof, and it's well worth making a diversion for.

Signposted just off the A357 east of Sturminster Newton; free car park.

JORDAN HILL
ROMAN TEMPLE

English Heritage • Free • Open access at any reasonable time

There are quite a lot of known Roman temples in England and they are, for the most part, really quite dull. Many, including this one, are not in the traditional Roman style (a great big thing with columns on a high podium) but are of a type known as 'Romano-Celtic' which was native to Britain. It

The Romano-Celtic temple at Jordan Hill doesn't look much, but there's a story to it.

involves a tall, square, tower-like shrine called a 'cella' surrounded on all four sides by a lower portico or veranda. Trouble is, all that tends to be left of them is the foundations, so all you see is a square stone path surrounding another square stone path, as here.

Jordan Hill does have an intriguing story to tell, though, because something very odd was found here during excavation. In one corner of the temple was a shaft 4m (13ft) deep with a stone cist at the bottom containing two urns, a sword and a spearhead. The shaft had been filled with layers of ash and charcoal

separated by a roofing slab, and each layer contained the remains of a bird (buzzard, crow, starling or raven). Make of it what you will. Coins dating from the 300s and 400s were also found here, and there were almost 100 burials in the area around the temple.

Signposted turning on to minor road off A353 at Overcombe, just east of Weymouth. Park on road near crown of hill; short footpath to Temple is up small side-road.

KINGSTON RUSSELL
STONE CIRCLE

English Heritage • Free • Open access at any reasonable time

Not a major circle, but a nice spot. It's a small circle of recumbent stones (lying down rather than standing) and is thought to be quite late bronze age. The real beauty of it, though, is that it's nowhere near a road. Because it's isolated on a hilltop in beautiful countryside, and you have to walk to get there, it's superbly atmospheric.

About 20 minutes' walk on footpath across farmland. Follow minor road from Hardy Monument straight across crossroads (the back road to Abbotsbury); park where farm track goes off to right, just before road turns left and drops downhill (please park considerately); walk straight on along footpath where track splits.

Kingston Russell, a small bronze age circle of recumbent stones, is in an ideal setting on open farmland.

THE GREAT HILLFORTS OF DORSET

THE HILLFORT IS Dorset's great contribution to the historical wealth of the nation, and although a fair bit is known about them, there are still many questions left unanswered.

We're pretty certain that hillforts as we know them today were built by the Celts, though hill-top fortifications date back to the stone age (as at *Hembury, Devon*, where a neolithic earthen rampart is thought to have been topped by a wooden palisade).

We know that they weren't much of a barrier to the Romans. After softening up the defences with fire from a *ballista*, a handful of soldiers with shields locked above their heads could stroll up and clean a hillfort out pretty easily. Many of Dorset's hillforts have war cemeteries of Celtic dead dating from the time when Vespasian led the Roman invasion forces along the south coast in 43 AD.

Whether hillforts were normally occupied as towns is not clear, but generally it seems not. In the past they were often equated with the Celtic tribal capitals known as *oppida*, and some may have been, but in pre-Roman times there seems to have been a tendency to build larger tribal capitals on more hospitable sites in the valleys. The theory is that Celtic kings derived their power from the control of trade – not just in status items such as bronze weapons, but also in everday commodities like salt and corn – and that the *oppida* were centres for storage and exchange. The excavations at *Danebury hillfort, Hampshire* have been central to the way this theory has developed.

The main feature of hillforts is the huge earthen ramparts, often with complex gateways intended to ensure that the defenders would have plenty of opportunity to throw spears and stones at anyone attempting to force the gate. Large piles of round stones for use as slingshot are often found. The ramparts were not purely of earth and rubble, however. Often they were 'laced' with timber or fronted with stone walls, and mostly they would have been topped with a timber pallisade. There's a lot more to hillforts than meets the eye.

The most famous hillfort of them all is Maiden Castle, where the ramparts are truly a sight to behold.

BADBURY RINGS

National Trust • Open access • North west of Wimborne Minster, south east of Blandford Forum on B3082.

Not the largest hillfort in Dorset, but one of the best, and very accessible because it's distinctly less uphill than most hillforts. The setting, in rolling open country near the junction of four Roman roads, and next to the avenue of trees that leads to Kingston Lacy house, is splendid, with fine views from the ramparts.

The fort has not been excavated, so its date is uncertain, but it's certainly iron age (Celtic) and was probably built a couple of hundred years before the Romans arrived. Badbury never took off as a town or trade centre the way some large hillforts did, but in

Badbury Rings is a round hillfort topped by trees in which King Arthur is said to live on as a raven.

Roman times there was a market here at the road junction.

Badbury's ramparts are big and well defined (they have recently been restored) and the place really does have an interesting atmosphere, which is probably why so many legends have grown up around it. Badbury was said to be Mount Badon, site of King Arthur's great battle against the Saxons in 518, and a local story tells that Arthur lives on as a raven in the woods in the middle of the fort.

HAMBLEDON HILL HILLFORT
AND CAUSEWAYED CAMP

English Heritage and English Nature • Free • Open access at any time • Footpath up from by the cricket pitch in the village of Shroton

The views over Blackmore Vale from here are beautiful, and the ramparts of the large iron age hillfort are just extraordinary. Huge and steep, they are the most impressive earthen fortifications in the country (with the possible exception of Maiden Castle, but I prefer Hambledon).

But there's something else here, too, and though it doesn't look much, it is very important archaeologically.

Hambledon has been occupied since the stone age, and right in the middle of the hill is one of the mysterious neolithic 'causewayed camps'. Dating from 4000 to 3000 BC, these seem to have been ritual centres in which ceremonies took place that involved cutting ditches and pits, depositing items of value ranging from stone axes and fine pottery to animal and human remains, and filling them in again. A strong possibility seems to be that they were sacred places for excarnation (exposure of the dead), perhaps watched over by the spirits of the ancestors.

Two spurs of the hill (the one you walk up, and the other to the left when you reach the causewayed camp) were protected by neolithic ramparts, thought to have been topped by a wattle breastwork. At some stage it was attacked, and excavations found large amounts of charcoal from the burned breastwork and the skeleton of a young man with a leaf-shaped arrowhead in his chest.

Plenty to think about, then. But the main reason to come here is that it's a good hilltop walk with superb views.

HOD HILL

National Trust • Open access at any time • Steep footpath leaves from small car park on minor road from A350 (north of Stourpaine) to Child Okeford.

This is a fine hillfort, if you don't mind a pretty steep climb to reach the ramparts, but that's not all. What makes this site unique is a Roman camp in the top corner of the fort.

Hod Hill was obviously densely occupied, since in the middle there are traces of lots of huts and storage pits, apparently ranged along streets. In the south-east corner, where you can still make out these huts, there was a large wooden building surrounded by a palisade, which seems to have been the focus for the Roman *ballista* attack, and by its doors great piles of slingstones were found.

The Roman fort, established during Vespasian's invasion campaign, was in the north-west corner, where the ground was higher, giving a commanding view of the country around. Its earth ramparts are very well defined, though of course you can't really make out anything of the

Not only does Hambledon Hill have great, sweeping iron age ramparts, but it's also an important stone age site.

wooden buildings within. It was garrisoned by something like 600 infantry and 250 cavalry for a period of about eight years.

MAIDEN CASTLE

English Heritage • Free • Open access at any time • Access road is signposted south of the town centre in the direction of Weymouth (from the bypass, turn to town centre).

This is, of course, the finest and most famous of them all (though I still prefer Hambledon). The area it covers is vast, the ramparts are truly enormous, the gateways at either end are particularly complicated and in the middle are the traces of a Romano-Celtic temple. On top of this, it was extensively excavated, so an awful lot is known about the different phases of building, between 350 and 70 BC.

The weaker eastern entrance of the fort was attacked by the 2nd Legion under Vespasian, and in a war cemetery just outside the gate the

bodies of 30 Britons were found, each buried with a mug and some food, such as a shoulder of lamb. In the museum in Dorchester you can see the skeleton of one of the defenders, with a Roman *ballista* bolt embedded in the spine.

SEE ALSO...

CHALBURY HILLFORT, *near Weymouth*, best seen from the inland stretch of the coastal footpath; EGGARDON HILL (National Trust), *near Powerstock*, good but only half-accessible; HENGISTBURY HEAD PROMONTORY FORT, *just east of Bournemouth*, probably the most important port for trade with Europe in Celtic times; PILSDON PEN (National Trust), *near Pilsdon*, where an iron age goldsmith's workshop was found; POUNDBURY HILLFORT, *just north of Dorchester*, is cut through by the channel of a Roman aqueduct which brought water to Dorchester.

The claim to fame of Hod Hill is that you can see the earth ramparts of a square Roman fort in one corner.

KNOWLTON CIRCLE

English Heritage • Free • Open access at any reasonable time

This is a unique place: an early and very important henge monument, with the ruins of a Norman church in the middle. And the circle that surrounds the church is not the only monument at Knowlton, either: as at other henge sites, such as Stonehenge and Avebury, it was just one element in a ritual landscape with a whole variety of constructions.

Nearby, topped by a clump of trees, is the vast Great Barrow, which had a ditch around it almost as big as Knowlton Circle itself. Just off to the south, by the road junction, was a much bigger circle, the arc of which can be seen in the curve of trees behind the farm; and there was another henge just to the north. Nothing is known about these monuments from excavation, so it is to be hoped that there are exciting discoveries waiting to be made.

So why was a church built in the middle of the henge in the 1100s? Well, I've heard it said that Christian churches were frequently built on top of pagan places of worship in an effort to blot out the power of the ancient gods in the minds of the simple folk. That may be true, but I can't think of another place where there is evidence of this having happened, so perhaps you should take that one with a pinch of salt.

What is certainly true is that places which were sacred to one set of people were very often taken over as sacred sites by later people, who modified the existing beliefs. Good examples are the *Roman baths at Bath*, where the Romans took over the Celtic goddess Sulis and incorporated her into the worship of their own Minerva, or at *Dupath Well Chapel, Cornwall*, where a Christian chapel stands over a sacred spring which would likely have been a place of worship for the Celts.

Although there's not much to see – the crumbling church walls and the ditch and bank of the henge – it's still a very atmospheric site.

Next to the B3078 near Gussage All Saints; lay-by parking place and entrance a short way down minor road.

Knowlton Circle, where a Norman church was built in the middle of a neolithic henge. It is a splendid spot.

THE NINE STONES, WINTERBOURNE ABBAS

English Heritage • Free • Open access at any reasonable time

Not worth a special trip, but on a sunny day, in the dappled light of the woods and with the breeze rustling the leaves of the trees, these remnants of a 4000-year-old stone circle next to the busy modern main road can be surprisingly atmospheric.

Half-mile west of Winterbourne Abbas, next to A35; park in small lay-by next to barn on north side of road, walk along verge for 50m (55 yds) and cross road (with care!) to the stones, just on the edge on the woods.

Maumbury Rings, originally a henge, was adapted by the Romans to be the amphitheatre for Dorchester.

MAUMBURY RINGS
HENGE & AMPHITHEATRE

English Heritage • Free • Open access at any reasonable time

Starting life as a henge (one element in a massive ritual landscape in the *Maiden Castle* area, associated with a vast enclosure at Mount Pleasant), this monument was turned into an amphitheatre by the Romans and was later used as a gun emplacement in the Civil War. It's not really very exciting, if the truth be told: just two great, curving banks of earth facing each other across the 'arena'.

On southern side of central Dorchester, right next to the brewery.

NOTHE FORT, WEYMOUTH

Owned by local council, operated by Civic Society • ££ • Usual hours

Every south-coast county has its Victorian artillery fort, in an insecure state of preservation after being rescued and used to house a faintly amateurish museum covering the military history of the area. What makes Nothe a bit different, though, is that the building is interesting and the museum exhibits are pretty good.

Nothe is a modern fort, built in the 1870s, and it saw action in the Second World War. It has lots of interesting tunnels, which are dark but not too scary (though a ghost lurks in one, for the kids). The layout of the fort and how it worked are well explained. Best of all, though, is a unique collection of military moustaches. Don't miss it!

In Weymouth, on headland west of harbour; reached on foot or by car from town centre.

Nothe Fort, Weymouth – now home to the nation's finest (if not only) collection of military moustaches.

PORTLAND CASTLE

English Heritage • £££ • Usual hours, but April to October only

This is one of the best-preserved of the gun-forts built by Henry VIII in about 1540 (that is, it's very close to its original condition), but it is not actually one of the most interesting, mainly because there's not really an awful lot to it. Fairly small, and semi-circular in shape, it does look quite pretty on the side that faces the sea, though, and it does have an amusing tale to its name. The story goes that, during the Civil War, a Royalist captain managed to capture the fort by splitting his men into two groups, providing one with Parliamentary colours and getting the other to chase them down the beach. The Parliamentary defenders opened the gates to let in what they thought were comrades in trouble, and effectively surrendered the castle.

Signposted from roundabout at far side of causeway to Isle of Portland.

The semi-circular Portland Castle, captured for the King during the Civil War by a daring act of subterfuge.

SHAFTESBURY ABBEY REMAINS

Dorset County Council • £ • Usual hours

The Saxon King Edward was murdered at *Corfe Castle* in 978, apparently by the will of his step-mother, Elfrida, so that her son Ethelred (later called the Unready) could become king. His body was taken to Shaftesbury Abbey, and here it began to attract miracles.

Almost nothing is left of the abbey, except foundations and a smattering of interesting carved pieces of masonry, but the spot where Edward was buried is still marked and this somehow gives this otherwise uneventful ruin a spark of interest.

Right in the middle of Shaftesbury.

Shaftesbury Abbey is about as ruinous as they come, but it does have an important place in Saxon history.

SHERBORNE OLD CASTLE

English Heritage • ££ • Usual hours

Only the gatehouse and a piece of wall is anywhere near complete, but it's the utterly ruinous bit in the middle of the castle – the remains of a large L-shaped keep – that catches the eye. It's more like sculpture than architecture, but it looks great.

Apart from that, there is really not a lot to be said about the castle. The rectangular circuit of walls, with a tower at each corner and another gate tower, was probably the oldest part, built some time between 1107 and 1135. King John spent some money on the fortifications in the early 1200s, and in the 1590s the castle was the property of Sir Walter Raleigh, whose house – the new castle – is not far away.

On the east side of Sherborne – it is well signposted, but you need to watch out for the turning into a small road leading to the castle at a complicated junction of about six roads. Free car park at the site.

What's left of Sherborne's medieval castle doesn't look much like a large, square Norman keep, but it was.

Hampshire

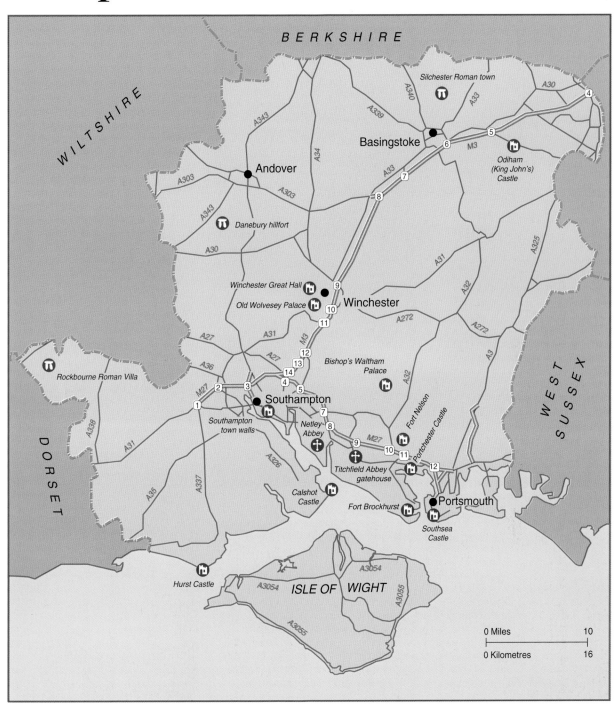

HAMPSHIRE is full of surprises – particularly Roman ones. At *Portchester Castle* there's not only an excellent Norman keep, but also a full circuit of Roman fort walls more than 1700 years old, while at *Silchester* the crumbling walls of a Roman town now surround acres of pasture. And on the outskirts of Southampton you'll find the equally surprising *Netley Abbey,* one of the most beautiful abbey ruins in England.

The keep-like West Tower is the biggest remnant of Bishop's Waltham Palace, but there's lots more to see.

CALSHOT CASTLE

English Heritage • ££ • Usual hours

Like *Hurst Castle (opposite)* and *Southsea Castle (page 76)*, Calshot is one of the small, innovative artillery forts built by Henry VIII to protect the south coast (there are other important ones in *Kent* and *Cornwall*).

The Solent was thought to be particularly at risk from attack by French ships, so a number of these forts were sited here and Calshot, completed in late 1540, was the first to be finished. It is on a smaller pattern than the later castles, with a round, three-storey keep surrounded by a curtain wall and a moat.

In regular use right up to the Second World War, it's a pleasingly neat little building, although it's not an especially exciting place to visit. Go if you haven't seen any of the other forts; the Tudor details are attractive and the views over the busy shipping lanes of the Solent give it a seaside feel.

Here on Calshot Spit, incidentally, was the base for the Schneider Trophy seaplane races of the 1930s in which Supermarine honed the design that eventually became the Spitfire.

Clearly signed from B3053 south of Fawley: drive all the way to the castle if you wish.

BISHOP'S WALTHAM PALACE RUINS

English Heritage • ££ • Usual hours

Two good reasons to come here are the peaceful setting in tree-lined grounds and the attractive crumbling stonework, but this is also a very interesting site historically, giving an insight into an underappreciated aspect of medieval society. It was a massive fortified palace built by the bishops of Winchester, and it reflects their political importance as much as their religious authority. The huge keep-like tower is an expression of feudal lordship equal to any castle, while the one remaining wall of the Great Hall, with its splendid windows, is enough to show that the bishops were very keen to impress guests with their wealth and prestige.

A good deal of this grand design dates from the early 1100s and is down to one man, Henry of Blois. Henry was one of the outstanding characters of his age: after helping to lever his brother, King Stephen, on to the English throne, he started to establish a serious power base by building castles right across his lands (including another fortified palace at *Old Wolvesey, Winchester, page 73*), but when Stephen's fragile reign came to an end in the mid-1150s, Henry had to flee into exile and King Henry II pulled most of his castles down again.

On south side of town of Bishop's Waltham, well signposted on B2177: approaching the town, watch for the sign to the car park.

Calshot Castle, one of Henry VIII's artillery forts, is a very pretty little building, though there's not a lot to it.

Danebury isn't a spectacular hillfort – others have bigger ramparts and better views – but its secrets are known...

DANEBURY HILLFORT

Hampshire County Council • Free
• Open access at any reasonable time

It's not actually the finest hillfort you'll ever see – the ramparts and the views aren't a patch on the great hillforts of Dorset – but Danebury is well worth visiting simply because so much is known about it thanks to detailed excavations in the 1970s by the leading archaeologist and writer Barry Cunliffe. As a result, there is not only a trail of helpful signboards at the site but also an entire museum dedicated to the hillfort – the Museum of the Iron Age, just up the road in Andover.

Built in the 500s or 400s BC, Danebury was home to between 200 and 300 people and might have been an important Celtic town. Within the ramparts (a double bank and ditch) there were two parallel flint-cobbled streets lined with rows of rectangular wooden structures supported by four or six posts (possibly granaries). Evidence of weaving and iron smelting was found, as well as a hoard of 21 sword-shaped currency bars. The ramparts and gateway were strengthened later in the hillfort's career, but by about 100 BC the fort had been abandoned, and when the Romans arrived it was nothing more than a farmstead.

South west of Andover, signposted from A343 Salisbury to Andover road – watch for turn into minor road, heading south, just east of the village of Middle Wallop.

HURST CASTLE

English Heritage • £££ • Usual hours

Hurst was the largest of Henry VIII's forts in the area, built at the end of a long shingle spit which reaches practically to the Isle of Wight, making it easy for the castle's guns to cover the width of the Solent. Its clever positioning was appreciated by the Victorians, who updated it, adding massive gun batteries on either side of the original keep; and its location also makes it quite a nice seaside jaunt for the modern visitor, because the best way to visit is by a short ferry trip (though you can stomp all the way on foot along the spit).

If you go, you'll probably end up making a half-day of it and having a snack in the castle's cafe. The only trouble with this is that there's not actually an awful lot to see at the castle, and by the time you add up ferry fares and entrance fees, it's more expensive to visit than you'd expect.

Hurst castle was finished in 1544, its 12-sided keep and three large, semi-circular bastions giving it positions for 71 guns, though the king could never afford to fit more than 20. In 1803 vaults were added to take larger guns, and in the 1850s the two massive gun batteries were built on either side, making it the fairly dull composite that it is today.

Follow signs from Milford-on-Sea to Keyhaven harbour (car park). Best reached by ferry; walk is 1.5 miles along shingle spit.

Perhaps the best thing about Henry VIII's little gun-forts is the pleasing symmetry of their design, as seen inside the keep at Hurst (above). There are lots of attractive Tudor details, too, like this window and arch inside Calshot Castle (left).

Though there's a keep built by Henry VIII at its centre, Hurst Castle as you see it today is a Victorian gun-fort.

There's lots left of the abbey church – though the north transept, on the left, was carted off to be used as a folly.

NETLEY ABBEY

*English Heritage • Free • Open access
at any reasonable time*

This is one of the most beautiful abbey ruins anywhere in England, hidden in a leafy corner that seems worlds away from the suburbs of Southampton that surround it.

A Cistercian abbey founded in 1239 by monks from Beaulieu, Netley boasted a large, fine church and all the usual monastic buildings grouped around a cloister, but in 1536 it became a victim of Henry VIII's dissolution of the monasteries and was used as a quarry – much of the stone for *Calshot Castle (page 70)* came from here.

The remains were converted into a house, with the abbey church used as a great hall. In about 1700 the house fell out of use and the abbey's career as a picturesque ruin began. In the 1760s, the north transept was carted off to Cranbury Park house near Hursley to be used as a folly.

The greatest part of Netley's appeal is that its treasures are hidden from view and only slowly revealed as you explore. The first view is of the dull, squat shapes left over from the Tudor house, but a doorway takes you through to the cloisters and from there to the remains of the church, where Gothic arches, both broken and intact, soar gracefully. Eventually you will find the block that once housed the monks' sanatorium (hospital) and reredorter (the toilets, basically) where there's an amazing vaulted stone roof, as well as a channel through which a stream once flowed to provide the drainage.

This fantastic vaulted stone roof is underneath what used to be the monks' sanatorium.

In 1544, the owner of the abbey gave Henry VIII a slice of land at Netley on which to build a castle, a companion to *Calshot* and *Hurst*. It's still there, but buried under the late Victorian house now known as Netley Castle. It is just across the road from the abbey, but not open to visitors.

Well signposted from A3025 south of junc. 8 of M27, or from Southampton city centre via toll bridge to Royal Victoria Country Park.

This is the south transept – the one that wasn't stolen. You can see how it would make a good folly, though.

ODIHAM CASTLE (KING JOHN'S CASTLE)

*Hampshire County Council • Free
• Open access at any reasonable time*

The unspectacular remains of a small octagonal keep built in 1207, Odiham castle is still surrounded by traces of earthworks and a moat, though the keep was probably defended just by a wooden palisade, not a stone wall. The castle was used by King John as a staging-post on journeys between Winchester and Windsor and is said to have been one of his favourite places to stay – it's claimed that it was from here that he set off in 1215 to sign *Magna Carta* at Runnymede.

The castle is a pleasant enough goal for a canal-side walk, and it's quite surprising to find it here in the middle of nowhere, but it's pretty run down and is slowly crumbling despite the attentions of the county council.

Just west of North Warnborough, near Odiham, on B3349 south of junction 5 of M3. From the canal bridge by the pub, walk half a mile west along the canal towpath.

King John's little keep at Odiham, which is said to have been one of his favourite places to stay.

The weathered flint walls of Old Wolvesey Palace are really surprisingly interesting – and there's lots of it, too.

OLD WOLVESEY PALACE, WINCHESTER

English Heritage • ££ • Usual hours

Right from its foundation in 662, the see (the bishop's territory) of Winchester shared the power and prestige of the Wessex kings: the bishop owned huge amounts of land, made vast incomes from agriculture and wielded considerable political influence. The first Saxon Bishop of Winchester to build a residence here at Wolvesey was Bishop Aethelwold in the 970s, and when you puzzle out the remains with the help of the guidebook, you'll be forced to agree

with the description of it as 'the first great ceremonial centre of the Anglo-Saxon state'. This was a major-league high-status place.

In 1110 the second Norman bishop, William Gifford, made his own bid to impress his peers by building the West Hall, the largest non-monastic residence of its age. At that time the Anglo-Saxon hall and chapel were probably still used, but when the power-crazed Henry of Blois (see *Bishop's Waltham Palace, page 70*) took over in 1129 he started a programme of building which, by the time of his death in 1171, had created an enormously grand palace with a massive new great hall.

For the next 500 years the palace remained more or less unchanged, but in the 1600s it fell into disuse and in the early 1680s it was demolished to be replaced by a baroque palace that was itself demolished 100 years later.

Some quite substantial parts of the keep, tower and halls from the 1100s remain, as well as much attractive stonework, stout in some places and crumbling in others. It's an enjoyable place to look round: the display boards and guidebook give a good idea of the scale of the buildings, and there are lots of interesting details.

Short, signposted walk from near the cathedral, in Winchester city centre.

PORTCHESTER CASTLE

English Heritage • Grounds: Free • Open access at any reasonable time • Castle: ££ • Usual hours

This is brilliant, this place. Basically it's two little gems on one site. Inside the walls of a square Roman fort – said to be the most complete set of Roman walls in Northern Europe, and still looking pretty much as they did on the day they were completed – stands the only proper Norman castle in the county, with a rather fine keep. The only slight disappointment is that the setting doesn't have quite the atmospheric feel you might hope for, but the harbour views aren't bad.

If you use a little imagination, the Roman walls certainly tell a story. You can make out the joins where the different gangs of builders met up. The D-shaped bastions (not towers) are the original Roman items, and would have had timber floors supporting light catapults. Only the two gateways and the tops of the wall are medieval adaptations or repairs.

The Saxon Shore fort of *Portus Adurni* was the westernmost point of a chain of coastal defences that stretched all the way to Norfolk to protect the south against raiding by Saxons and other Channel-crossing barbarians. It is thought to have been built round about 260 AD, but as early as 300 the troops had left and the timber-built military buildings inside the fort were demolished. A civilian population took over until it was re-garrisoned in 340, and then in 370 it was again abandoned.

In this picture, below, you can see just one part of the amazing circuit of Roman walls at Portchester. Only the gateways are later medieval additions.

The keep of the Norman castle built inside the Roman fort is excellent, with a vertiginous walkway on the roof.

The fort was occupied again in the 400s and 500s, possibly by German mercenaries, and was used on and off throughout the next 300 years. When Portchester was acquired by king Edward the Elder in 904 AD, the fort became a *burh* (as in 'borough'), a Saxon defended settlement.

Visitors have free access to the grounds and Roman walls, but must pay to see the castle. The best bit is the keep, built in the 1120s and doubled in height shortly before 1173. The rooms inside are impressive, as is the view from the slightly scary walkway on the roof. The various kitchens and halls around the keep are of later date and less interesting: at one end is the palace of Richard II. The guidebook is a must.

Signposted from A27 east of Fareham; turn at roundabout for Portchester village; follow road right through village to castle.

Like most Roman villas, Rockbourne has a few small mosaics and a bit of hypocaust. It's not thrilling.

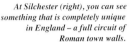
At Silchester (right), you can see something that is completely unique in England – a full circuit of Roman town walls.

still exposed, while the lines of the walls have been picked out in gravel. As with many Roman sites, there's not all that much to see, but the rarity of Roman remains makes any villa (even such a modest one) something of a 'must see' if you're in the area.

Signposted from A354 south of Salisbury (take care: turn is on sharp bend at top of hill) or from B3078 Fordingbridge to Cranborne road; watch for turn to car park one mile south of Rockbourne village.

ROCKBOURNE ROMAN VILLA

Hampshire County Council • ££ • Usual hours

Of the 40 or so Roman villas in Hampshire, this was one of the largest. Like many others, it was built on the site of a Celtic farmstead in about 100 AD and grew in size and splendour before its gradual decline into disuse after 400.

The villa was discovered as recently as 1942 when a farmer, digging out his rabbit-hunting ferret, found oyster shells and tiles. The site was fully excavated, revealing extensive wall foundations, but these were later covered up again. Several mosaic floors and a section of hypocaust are

SILCHESTER ROMAN TOWN

English Heritage • Free • Open access at any reasonable time to exterior of walls

This is a unique and astonishing place, a complete circuit of Roman town walls – crumbling, but none the less the only ones left in Britain – now guarding nothing but fields.

Calleva Atrebatum was built shortly after the Roman invasion of 43 AD as the tribal capital of the Atrebates, the pro-Roman tribe thought to have occupied Sussex and Hampshire (though the walls date mostly from the 200s). The entire town – streets, forum, basilica, temples and baths – is now once again buried under the fields following its excavation (the guidebook, available from other Hampshire County Council sites, has

full details). It apparently flourished right into the 400s and 500s, but was then abandoned completely.

Visitors can walk round the entire circuit of almost 2km (1.5 miles) of walls, and visit the amphitheatre just to the east of the town (though it's reminiscent of a car park). Somewhat disappointingly, the site is difficult to find, badly explained by the few signboards, and hemmed in by farmland jealously defended by 'Keep Out' signs. Such an important relic deserves far better access.

On minor road heading north to Aldershot from the west end of Silchester village; at a bend to the left, turn right down Wall Lane and follow the road to the church.

SOUTHAMPTON TOWN WALLS

Southampton City Council • Walls; free access at any reasonable time • Museums; free entry, usual opening hours

Only recently has Southampton rediscovered its medieval town and castle walls, but it is making up for lost time with a well-signposted wall walk and a number of interesting (and free) museums to visit along the route.

Even compared with famous walled cities like Chester and York, Southampton has a lot to offer . The small God's House Tower archeological museum is excellent, and it would be a great shame to miss the modest but atmospheric Medieval Merchant's House (*English Heritage, ££, usual hours*).

Not many people realise that Southampton still has a fairly complete set of medieval walls and gateways...

In Southampton, follow signs for Old Town.

SOUTHSEA CASTLE

Portsmouth City Council • ££ • Usual hours

One of the forts built by Henry VIII to defend the Solent area, completed in 1544, Southsea castle tied in with the walls and towers defending the docks at Portsmouth. It is known that Henry himself designed one of these castles, and it's thought that Southsea might be the one. Certainly, he stood on its ramparts in 1545 to watch as his fleet sailed out to face the French invaders, and from here he saw the ignominious demise of the *Mary Rose*, the wreck of which was raised in the 1980s.

King Henry VIII stood on the ramparts of Southsea Castle in 1545 and saw the tragic sinking of the **Mary Rose.**

The most accessible of the Tudor forts, Southsea has been remodelled many times over the years but now looks much as it did originally. It's inexpensive to visit, offers an interesting exhibition in the square keep as well as an imaginative audio-visual display, and even has a spooky 'tunnel walk' (actually a brick *caponier* – an underground forward gun position – added in 1814). Good value and good fun.

In Portsmouth, follow signs to Southsea seafront, then to castle; parking on road.

TITCHFIELD ABBEY

GATEHOUSE

English Heritage • Free • Open access at any reasonable time

When the abbey founded here in 1232 was dissolved in 1537, the site was eagerly snapped up by one of the administrators of the abbey's dissolution – a chap called Wriothesley, first Earl of Southampton. He converted the enormous gatehouse into a fine residence, and it's the shell of this house that remains today.

It's not really a terribly spectacular place to visit despite its fine facade, but it does have one special claim to fame. The third Earl of Southampton was a major patron of William Shakespeare, and it is thought possible that the courtyard garden behind the house – set in what was once the abbey cloisters, with a fountain at its centre – may have been the very place in which Shakespeare wrote sonnets, and sometimes held preview performances of his plays, in the late 1500s.

Signposted from A27 Southampton to Fareham road; watch out for left turn into narrow gateway to car park, opposite Fisherman's Rest pub.

The gatehouse of Titchfield Abbey, left, was converted into a house by the Earl of Southampton and may have seen the first performance of several Shakespeare plays.

WINCHESTER GREAT HALL

*Winchester City Council • Free •
Open access during usual hours*

Among all Winchester's many sights
– the cathedral, the museums, the
mill, *Old Wolvesey Palace (page 73)*
and the graceful church at St Cross –
the Great Hall stands out simply
because it is such a lovely building.

Said to be the finest medieval hall
in England, the Great Hall is all that
remains of Winchester castle and
dates from the rebuilding of the castle
by King Henry III in 1222–36. This
also makes it the oldest surviving
building in Winchester.

The famous painted round table
which hangs high on the wall inside
the hall has very little to do with King
Arthur other than that King Edward,
for whom it was probably made in the
1270s, may have been trying to
suggest a rather higher standard of
behaviour to his own barons with this
pointed reference to Arthur's loyal
knights. The table was first painted for
a visit by Henry VIII in 1522.

Sir Walter Raleigh was tried here in
the Hall in 1603, when the court left
London because of the plague. Just
outside the Great Hall, you can also
see a small chunk of Roman wall.

Signposted on foot in Winchester city centre.

*The Great Hall was once part of Winchester castle and
is said to be the finest medieval hall in the country.
Sadly, the famous round table is not King Arthur's.*

SEE ALSO...

BEACON HILL HILLFORT, *near
Kingclere, south of Newbury* – A
sizeable hillfort in a fine position in a
country park; also the site of the grave
of Lord Carnarvon, sponsor of the
Tutankhamun excavations, who lived
at the splendid house at Highclere.

BEAULIEU ABBEY, *Beaulieu estate* –
The modest abbey remains and the
well-designed museum are only worth
the entry fee if you're planning to
visit the Motor Museum and house.

BUTSER ANCIENT FARM (pictured
above), *signposted from A3 south of
Petersfield* – Experimental 'iron age'
farmstead used to test archaeological
theories by putting them into practice;
for example, it has proved that pits
like those found at hillforts are ideal
for storing seed grain. Highlights are a
reconstructed Celtic roundhouse and
ancient varieties of crops and animals.
(*Private trust, ££, usual hours.*)

FLOWERDOWN BARROWS, *in suburbs to
north of Winchester* – Rather dull
group of round barrows in the care of
English Heritage.

MERDON CASTLE, *near Hursley* –
The earthworks of a castle built in
1138 by Henry of Blois, bishop of
Winchester, and pulled down again
in the 1150s. Not open to visitors.

MOTTISFONT ABBEY, *off A3057 just
north of Romsey* – This National Trust
property is better known for its
gardens, but the house still contains
traces of the original abbey.

OLD BASING HOUSE, *near Basingstoke*
– Very interesting remains of a large
fortified house on the site of a
Norman castle. There was a huge
siege here in the English Civil War.

OLD WINCHESTER HILLFORT (pictured
below), *on hill east of Meonstoke* –
Hillfort of single rampart design, in
fabulous position with views to the
Isle of Wight; the wild flowers are
superb in summer.

WINCHESTER WEST GATE (pictured
below), *Winchester city centre* – Most
of Winchester's medieval walls have
vanished, though a good stretch
remains near *Wolvesey Old Palace.*
Just two of five gates survive and this
one is now a small museum with a
friendly curator who will point out
items of interest such as the graffiti
inscribed by prisoners when the tower
was a debtors' gaol. Main attractions
are the building itself, dating from the
12th and 14th centuries; the painted
ceiling; and the trip to the roof. (*City
Council, £, usual hours.*)

AND...

BURY HILL HILLFORT, *just south west
of Andover;* LAMBOROUGH LONG
BARROW, *near Cheriton;* POPHAM
BEACONS ROUND BARROWS, *near
Overton;* QUARLEY HILL HILLFORT,
near Grateley; ST CATHERINE'S HILL
HILLFORT, *just south of Winchester.*

Fort Brockhurst – one link in a chain of astonishingly expensive and pointless forts built in Victorian times to protect the Portsmouth harbour area.

PALMERSTON'S FOLLIES

THE VICTORIANS WERE given to excess in all sorts of ways, not least in their architecture, and one of the most lasting examples of their tendency to completely overdo things is the series of forts that became known as 'Palmerston's Follies'.

In the beginning it seemed like a good idea to bring the south coast's defences into the industrial age by building chains of modern artillery forts next to all the major ports. When Prime Minister Palmerston set things in motion in the 1840s, he was hardly to know that the whole thing would end up as an expensive joke.

The threat that the forts were intended to counteract was from the old enemy, the French. Since the defeat of Napoleon in 1815, the British had complacently assumed that having the best navy in the world was sufficient to protect the nation's shores, but that complacency was shaken by huge advances in the

design of steam-powered, iron-clad warships which were faster, more heavily armed and less reliant on the wind and weather. It was also realised that the French could once again muster a far larger land army than the British could put into the field, which made it vital to protect the coastal ports against attack from inland.

So it was that Palmerston started a programme of expenditure that ran for the next two decades, and in some ways never really stopped. His folly lay not only in the enormous cost of this work, but also in its futility: constant advances in the range and power of rifled guns and in the design of explosive shells made many of the forts obsolete before they were even finished, so the designs constantly had to be adapted and improved and building work had to be started all over again. And by the end of the century, of course, the French had become our allies in any case.

Built low, mostly underground, with shallow angles and great earth banks to deflect shells, the forts were the ultimate development of defensive techniques that had been in use for the previous 300 years. None of them is as appealing as a good stone castle, but they do have a kind of sombre industrial glamour, and they are, after all, the last great fortifications of Britain: the whole idea was made obsolete in the 20th century by the invention of aerial bombing.

FORT BROCKHURST

English Heritage • ££ • Usual hours • Signposted as a left turn at the roundabout on main road to Gosport; car park immediately on left.

The five forts in a line across Gosport peninsula were among the first to be built, in the early 1850s. Some remained in military use until quite recently (and one, bizarrely enough, has just been earmarked for conversion into residential flats), but Fort Brockhurst is owned by

English Heritage and open to the public. Its enormous brick-and-earth ramparts aptly demonstrate the scale on which the engineers were thinking, but the main feature is the moated central 'keep', which the defenders could retreat to if all else was lost. It's rather gloomy inside.

FORT NELSON

Royal Armouries Trust • £££ • Usual hours • On minor road north of A27 between Portchester and Wallington, near Fareham. Watch for signposted turn; car park by fort.

Of the forts that are open to visitors, Fort Nelson is probably the most interesting. Built between 1862 and 1871, it's one of a line of six forts set along Portsdown Hill, high above Portsmouth harbour, facing inland to repulse overland attacks. The fort was recently restored and is now home to the Royal Armouries Museum. This makes it rather more expensive to visit, but the story of these Victorian forts is told most completely here because you can see examples of the kinds of artillery that the forts were designed to withstand. These massive guns are part of a collection of cannon stretching from early medieval times to the present day.

Even for pacifists, Fort Nelson has plenty to offer; especially the gloomy, damp tunnel through the underground magazine to the north caponier. The vast and surprisingly interesting museum includes a corner that's almost an artillery art gallery, with an amazing collection of finely decorated

Red brick, guns and tunnels are the main themes for these Victorian artillery forts.

Right and far right: the gateway and north mortar position of Fort Nelson.

Below: inside the keep at Brockhurst.

ancient cannon. Guns are fired twice a day, there's a clever electronic audio guide and, to top it all, the staff are friendly and helpful. If you only ever visit one Victorian fort, this should probably be the one.

SEE ALSO...

Other forts in the line are still in military use, but FORT WIDLEY (now an equestrian centre) is owned by Hampshire County Council and can be visited by arrangement. To get there, continue along the hillside from Fort Nelson; Widley is shortly after the roundabout on the B2177 Southwick-to-Drayton road.

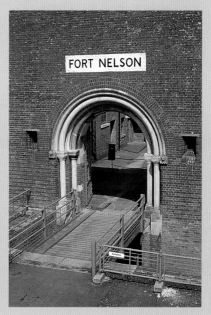

A typical Victorian eccentricity, Spitbank Fort is built on an artificial island right in the middle of the Solent.

Most recent and oddest of the area's Victorian defences are the island forts in the Solent, built of iron-reinforced granite on high points of the sea bed. The nearest is SPITBANK FORT, which is privately owned and can be visited by boat trip from Portsmouth's Historic Harbour (ask at the Harbour's Tourist Information).

If you're keen on military history, you won't want to miss the local museums. The ships at Portsmouth's Historic Harbour are a must (particularly the *Mary Rose* and Nelson's flagship, HMS *Victory*) though it's very busy. Submarine World at Gosport includes a visit to the sub HMS *Alliance*, while the Southampton Hall of Aviation features the Spitfire and the Sandringham flying boat. The D-Day Museum at Southsea has a good reputation; the Royal Marines Museum is nearby, and the Royal Naval Museum is back at the docks.

Fort Widley is part of the same chain of defences as Fort Nelson. It's not normally open, but can be visited.

Isle of Wight

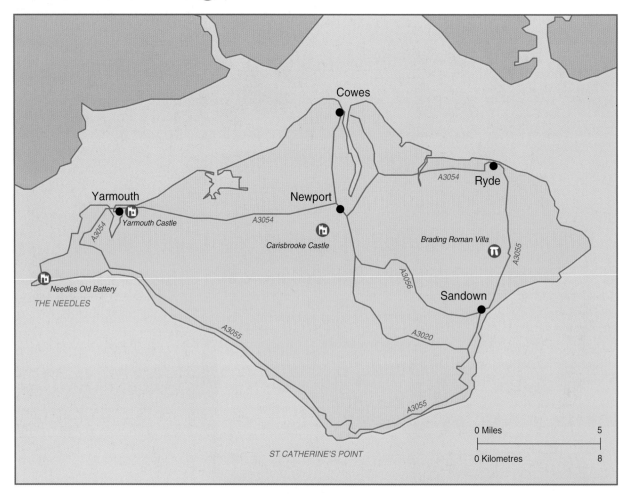

BRADING ROMAN VILLA

Privately owned • £££ • Usual hours

One of the best villas anywhere in England, remarkable not only for its mosaics – which have recently been restored at considerable expense – but also for the wealth of objects of all kinds found here, which are actually on display at the site, rather than having been taken off to some big city museum. Mundane items like loom weights and door catches really help give an idea of what the villa must have been like. In common with all the important villas, it's under a roof and so good for rainy days (see also *Lullingstone* in *Kent* and *Bignor* in *Sussex*). Really, really worth taking the trouble to see.

Signposted south of Morton, off A3055.

As is so often the case with Roman villas, it's the mosaics that are the outstanding feature of Brading villa.

A general view of Carisbrooke, looking from the wall-walk to the small Norman shell keep. Inside the yard are later accommodation buildings, including the great hall.

CARISBROOKE CASTLE

English Heritage • ££ • Usual hours

This is a charming little castle, built right at the heart of the island and certainly the most important and most appealing of the Isle of Wight's heritage sites. It's also the only castle in England occupied by donkeys.

The donkeys are there to show off the workings of a 400-year-old treadmill used to raise water from the well. They perform once an hour, but at various times of day they're to be found wandering around the castle grounds nibbling at the grass borders.

Historically and architecturally, the castle has a bit of everything. There was a Saxon *burh* here, and traces of its wall can be seen in the grass bank on either side of the gatehouse. The tiny shell keep on the motte and the medieval curtain walls date from roughly the 1130s, though with alterations from the 1300s. In the middle is the great hall, which also dates originally from the 1300s, though it has been much altered by later generations (and it's probably the least entertaining bit of the castle).

Finally, the castle was encircled by a set of 'star' fortifications between 1597 and 1600, under the auspices of a trendy Italian fortifications designer: you shouldn't forget to walk around the outside of the castle and take a look at them. Carisbrooke has lots of interesting stories, too, including the details of the imprisonment of King Charles here at the end of the Civil War and the tale of a bowman who single-handedly fought off French raiders in 1377. To get the full story, the guidebook is a must.

Signposted in Carisbrooke, near Newport.

The inside of the gatehouse is fun to explore, with a spiral stair descending in the right-hand drum tower.

The gateway has a very authentic feel, but in fact the wooden doors are fairly modern replacements.

The views excepted, there's not actually an awful lot to see at the Needles Old Battery...

...but one thing that might draw you here is the view of the Needles from this searchlight position.

NEEDLES OLD BATTERY

National Trust • ££ • Usual hours

This small gun-fort was built in 1862 as part of the massive Solent defences, which included lots of big forts in the Portsmouth area (*see Hampshire, pages 78-9*). There's not really an awful lot to see here, but the National Trust has made the best of it with some excellent display boards in a 'Boy's Own' cartoon style, which really do a good job of telling the fort's story in an entertaining way.

Typically for a fort of this era, the whole venture was undermined by an almost comical cock-up: they couldn't actually use the huge guns mounted here, because the chalk simply crumbled underneath them every time they were fired. Eventually a replacement battery was built a little higher up the headland.

The one thing that makes the trek up here worthwhile (it's a blustery twenty-minute walk from the privately owned tourist rip-off car park) is the trip down a winding stair and through a short tunnel to the forward searchlight position, from where the view of the Needles lighthouse is really rather good.

Reached on foot from the Needles car park.

YARMOUTH CASTLE

English Heritage • ££ • Usual hours

Not tremendously interesting gun-fort of late Henry VIII vintage, composed of a whacking great lump of earth (the gun platform) fronted by a wall with some housing behind. All the same, I'd pop in and have a look: there are some interesting rooms in the housing block, and a good exhibition on Henry VIII gun-forts.

Easily found in centre of Yarmouth.

SEE ALSO...

FORT VICTORIA AND FORT ALBERT, *on the coast between Yarmouth and Totland* – A pair of Victorian gun-forts; Albert is inaccessible and Victoria has been converted for modern uses (shops, etc).

GOLDEN HILL FORT (pictured), *signposted from main road between Yarmouth and Totland* – Another Victorian fort, privately owned and operated as a modest museum, but not terribly interesting.

NEWPORT ROMAN VILLA (*Local council, £, usual hours*), *signposted in suburbs of Newport* – This small villa, incongruously set in a quiet street of red-brick Victorian houses, is pretty unremarkable in itself, but it is well presented and explained. Some of the rooms have actually been reconstructed in an attempt to show what the villa would have looked like in Roman times, and there is a small 'Roman garden'.

ST CATHERINE'S ORATORY, *walk up headland from car park signposted on A3055 between Chale and Niton* – This very ancient lighthouse and chapel (it dates from the 1300s) is a very cute stone building shaped like a space rocket. Great views, too. (National Trust; free; open access at any reasonable time.)

AND...

AFTON DOWN BARROWS, *on National Trust land* NE *of Freshwater Bay, off the A3055*; CHILLERTON DOWN HILLFORT, *near Gatcombe, off minor roads* W *of A3020*; FIVE BARROWS ROUND BARROW CEMETERY, *Shalcombe, just* W *of B3399*.

Yarmouth castle is a small artillery fort, with a massive gun-platform at the front and domestic rooms behind.

Wiltshire

RENOWNED throughout the world for the spectacular prehistoric stone circles of *Stonehenge* and *Avebury*, the county has a number of other treasures too…

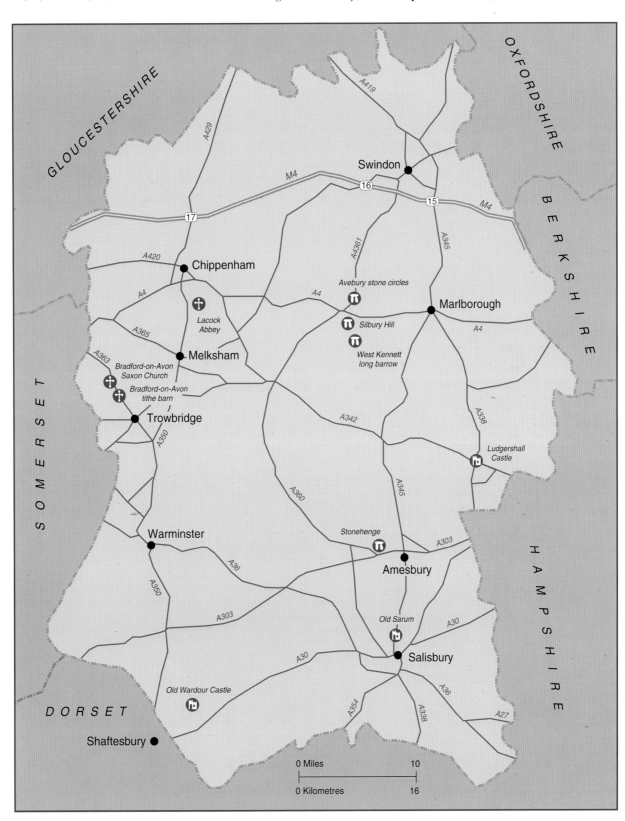

GLOUCESTERSHIRE

OXFORDSHIRE

BERKSHIRE

SOMERSET

HAMPSHIRE

DORSET

A419

A429

M4

Swindon

16

15

M4

A420

A4

Chippenham

A361

A345

A365

Lacock Abbey

Avebury stone circles

Silbury Hill

Marlborough

A4

A363

West Kennett long barrow

Melksham

Bradford-on-Avon Saxon Church

Bradford-on-Avon tithe barn

A342

A338

Trowbridge

A350

Ludgershall Castle

A360

A345

Warminster

Stonehenge

A303

A36

Amesbury

A350

A303

Old Sarum

A30

A354

Old Wardour Castle

Salisbury

A30

A36

A338

A27

Shaftesbury

0 Miles   10

0 Kilometres   16

These monumental megaliths ('big stones', if you prefer) were part of the south-eastern circle, one of two smaller stone circles built inside Avebury's Great Circle.

AVEBURY'S ANCIENT LANDSCAPE

YOU WOULD HAVE to have a heart of flint and a mind of sawdust not to be awestruck by Avebury. The bank and ditch of an immense henge surround an equally immense stone circle, inside which there are several smaller circles. Inside the henge, among the stones, a village later grew up, complete with pub, which surely makes it the only ancient monument inside which you can get a drink. It's just astonishing, it really is – and it retains its power to amaze in spite of

Silbury Hill is a huge man-made mound, built in 'steps' which were then filled in.

the coach parties, though of course to appreciate Avebury at its best you should visit when it's quiet and you can have the place to yourself.

More important, though, Avebury is surrounded by the remnants of a truly remarkable ceremonial landscape with at least three other world-class monuments (the huge mound of Silbury Hill, the Avenue which leads to the henge, and West Kennet long barrow) all of which you simply must go and see when you're here.

The only slight problem is that not a lot is known about any of these monuments, despite quite a lot of excavation in the 1930s; but at least that frees you to appreciate their scale and grace without having to work to understand them.

Current thinking is that henge monuments were originally built in the late stone age and early bronze age (roughly 3000 BC), while the stones were a later addition, dating to around 2000 BC.

AVEBURY
HENGE & STONE CIRCLES

National Trust land • Free • Open access at any reasonable time

The truly enormous bank and ditch, with (most unusually) four entrances, has a massive circle of stones set around its edge. Many stones have been removed over the years, but the south-western quarter of this circle is the most complete part. Within this were two smaller (but still big) stone circles: the one in the south-east has quite a few stones left, and also contained some kind of arrangement of smaller stones, while the other is entirely gone, but surrounded a horseshoe-like setting of three huge stones known as The Cove, two of which are still standing. It's the sheer size of the outer circle and of the stones that makes an impression.

Avebury village; free car park.

AVEBURY: THE AVENUE (WEST KENNET AVENUE)

English Heritage • Free • Open access at any reasonable time

Thought to be a later addition, this avenue ran to the Sanctuary (*see below*). Its stones are set in pairs made up of one taller, thinner stone and one shorter, squatter one, which it is thought might represent male and female. According to a picture-map of the area drawn by William Stukeley in the mid-1700s, there used to be another, similar avenue running west to the Longstones, near Beckhampton.

Alongside minor road running south from Avebury towards West Kennet.

The West Kennet Avenue runs for practically three miles and has 100 pairs of stones.

THE SANCTUARY

English Heritage • free • Open access at any reasonable time

Stukeley witnessed the destruction of a small stone circle here by a farmer in 1745. Excavations have shown that there was previously an arrangement of timber posts, possibly a building. Concrete posts show where post-holes were found, while concrete blocks mark where the stones stood. It's pretty dull, though.

Signposted next to the A4 to the west of West Kennet (parking in lay-by).

SILBURY HILL

English Heritage • free • Open access at any reasonable time

An awesome sight, although it is impossible to known why this huge chalk mound might have been built. There's nothing hidden inside it: Cornish tin miners were brought here in 1776 to dig a shaft right through it from the top, and the Victorians dug a tunnel in from the side, but they didn't find anything. Later digs have proved that the mound is certainly entirely man-made, and was built in 'steps' which were then filled in, all except the top one, which is why the hill has a 'notch' at the top.

By the A4 west of Beckhampton. Car parking in lay-by at viewing point.

WEST KENNET

LONG BARROW

English Heritage • free • Open access at any reasonable time

One of the truly great chambered tombs, with a huge chamber that you can walk right into. It's also one of the biggest tombs in Britain, with a mound over 100m (325ft) long. Probably built around 3000 BC, it remained in use for a thousand years before it was filled to the roof with earth and stones and the entrance was blocked with huge stones. The bones of at least 46 people were found, disarticulated, in the side chambers, along with flints and bits of pottery. More pottery, beads and animal bones were found in the infill. This is a fine monument in a lovely countryside setting, and in spring the wild flowers make it worth the trip on their own.

Brisk ten-minute walk, slightly uphill, on footpath; signposted just across the road from Silbury Hill viewing area.

WINDMILL HILL

English Heritage • free • Open access at any reasonable time

Very interesting to archaeologists, because it's a 'causewayed camp' (*see Introduction*), one of the earliest and most mysterious human monuments. Very dull to the rest of us, though, because there is practically nothing to see.

On foot up track (signposted) from the end of the road through Avebury Trusloe village.

West Kennet chambered long barrow is the biggest (and in many ways the best) monuments of its type in England.

The Saxon church at Bradford-on-Avon is one of the prettiest buildings in England. (On the inside, that is.)

Lacock Abbey was converted to a house in the 1540s and 'Gothicked' in the 1750s.

Within the house, the medieval abbey's cloisters remain pretty much untouched.

BRADFORD-ON-AVON
SAXON CHURCH

Church authorities • Free • Open access at any reasonable time

Such a great little building that it demands attention. For many years nobody even knew it was there, because it was hidden under later rebuilding, but in the 1870s it was revealed and restored. The Saxons weren't very expert at building in stone, but simplicity of style is the great virtue of their architecture. This may well be the oldest standing Saxon building in England.

A short walk from the centre of Bradford-on-Avon, signposted from near the bridge.

BRADFORD-ON-AVON
TITHE BARN

English Heritage • Free • Open access during usual hours

Quite a lot of tithe barns survive all across England. They were used by the abbeys, whose wealth depended on agriculture, to gather and store the crops which were due to them as a tax on local farmers (a 'tithe' being a tenth part, which was the going rate). This one is particularly beautiful.

Again, just a short, signposted walk from the centre of Bradford-on-Avon.

LACOCK ABBEY

National Trust • £££ (house, but it's free to see the historic village) • Usual hours

There's an awful lot going on at Lacock, where the National Trust is helping to preserve an entire village of stone and half-timbered houses, including a tithe barn from the 1300s and an 18th-century lock-up prison. We'll concentrate, though, on the abbey, which was founded in 1232 and converted to a house in the 1540s. In the last century, it was home to the photographic pioneer William Fox Talbot, and there is a photographic museum here in his honour.

The reason Lacock Abbey earns a mention, however, is that quite a decent portion of the abbey cloisters and the rooms that surrounded it (particularly the chapter house and warming room) were left intact when the house conversion took place, and are today in fairly original condition, with exceedingly pretty vaults and arches and plenty of interesting detail. It's only worth going if you want to see the rest of the house too, though.

In Lacock village (free car park signposted) next to the A350 south of Chippenham.

Inside the tithe barn at Bradford-on-Avon, with its superbly graceful roof-beams and single window.

Left: Ludgershall was the hunting lodge of King Henry III. It's not much of a castle, but its craggy weathered flint is attractive.

Bizarre indeed, and not without interest. First things first, though; the castle is pretty dull, mainly because its two main buildings (a keep-like great tower, built around 1100, and a grand accommodation range known as the Royal Palace, constructed roughly 30 years later) survive only to foundation level. Since the castle is the part you have to pay to see, I'd recommend that you look at the rest for free.

Exactly why Salisbury came to be so important to the Normans is not entirely clear – though the hillfort, already strengthened by the Saxons, was practically a ready-made castle – but in 1070 William chose it as the best place to pay off his conquering army, and in 1075 the Norman church authorities made it the centre of the huge diocese which had previously been based at Sherborne in Dorset.

The new cathedral was finished in 1092, but started teetering after a huge storm only five days later and a larger

The foundations of the Norman cathedral at Old Sarum, which fell out of use when the town of Salisbury was built on the river meadows in the 1220s.

one was started instead. In the 1220s, after considerable friction between the church and castle authorities and with the town outgrowing its water supply, a new cathedral and a planned town were built at the place we now know as Salisbury, and the Old Sarum cathedral went out of use.

So there's plenty of historical interest here, all very well explained in the guidebook available from the castle, which makes Old Sarum an interesting adjunct to a visit to the very pleasant town of Salisbury.

Signposted on A345 a couple of miles north of Salisbury; car park.

LUDGERSHALL CASTLE

English Heritage • Free • Open access at any reasonable time

Apart from one big chunk of tower, all that's left of this little domestic castle is a jumble of foundations and some fairly large earthworks. It started life as a timber construction quite early in the Norman period, but the bits you see today date from a much later phase of building, in roughly the 1250s, when the castle was a royal hunting lodge belonging to King Henry III.

More of a fortified residence than anything else, it had a great hall for the king to receive guests and, typically for the time, a kitchen set off to one side to reduce the risk of fire. There were three chapels, all of them apparently in use at the same time.

In the middle of Ludgershall.

OLD SARUM

English Heritage • Grounds: free, open access at any reasonable time; castle, ££, usual hours

Most unusual, in that this is an iron age hillfort with a Norman castle built right in the middle and the traces of a Norman cathedral on the top too.

There's not much left of the Norman castle at Old Sarum: just foundations of the Great Tower and Royal Palace.

The most famous ancient monument in Britain, Stonehenge has regained a lot of its gravity now that you can't actually touch it.

STONEHENGE

English Heritage • £££ • Usual hours (plus later opening in summer months)

OF ALL THE AMAZING things about Stonehenge, perhaps the most remarkable is its capacity to disappoint first-time visitors. Partly it's the car-park clutter, the crowds of visitors from all over the world, the approach to the site through a dismal inner-city subway; but also people say that the stones look smaller than they expected, and far less dramatic, in their prosaic setting between two busy major roads, than they seem in all the atmospheric photographs.

If you've never been to Stonehenge, I'm hoping you might go with lower expectations and be pleasantly surprised. But more important is that English Heritage have recognised the problem of the monument's context and are attempting to do something about it. Their first step has been to rope off the stones themselves, so that

visitors now have to look from a few yards away. Already this has helped a great deal – I could swear that the stones look larger again – and it has solved a real problem of erosion, as well as making it easier to get yourself a decent photo of the stones.

Eventually, it is hoped, the roads will be buried or diverted; a visitor centre and car park will be sited a long way off, with distant views of the monument; and the minority of people who are willing to make the effort will approach on foot, getting a much better idea of the whole ancient landscape which surrounds the henge.

And anyway, Stonehenge is still a truly remarkable place, even if the ambience here is not as magical as you might have hoped. The more you learn about it, the more remarkable it seems, though all the serious guides will point out that we can do little more than speculate about who built it and how it was used. Undoubtedly it

was not a druidic temple, though, since the druids were Celtic priests, and the stones had already been standing for a couple of thousand years by the time the Celts came to Britain. And it certainly did not have a great altar stone on which humans were sacrificed.

What it did have, unquestionably, were astronomical alignments, but this doesn't mean it's the 'ancient computer' that some have suggested. The approach to the stones, along an avenue marked on either side by a bank and ditch, was aligned with the midsummer sunrise (and therefore, looking the opposite way, midwinter sunset). Extra stones outside the main circle, known as the Station Stones, probably mark the midwinter sunrise and midsummer sunset and might have been used to monitor the 18-year cycle of the rising and setting of the moon (personally, I find this quite possible). It has been suggested that other stones in the circle were used to calculate events such as eclipses, but this is not widely accepted.

Incidentally, plenty of other stone circles also show the basic sun and moon alignments.

No other circle, though, was constructed with the same care and technical skill as Stonehenge. The lintel stones were set in place with mortice and tenon joints, a socket-hole in the lintel settling on to a projecting knob on the upright stones. On the trilithons (the arrangements of two massive uprights with a lintel on top, five of which stood in a horseshoe shape inside the circle) the lintels were shaped at an angle, so that they *looked* square from the ground, while the lintels of the circle (and this is something I didn't realise until my last visit) were all shaped to the curve of the circle and linked using tongue-and-groove joints. These methods are clearly derived from woodworking.

You have to bear in mind, though, that the sophisticated stonework represents only the last phase of building at Stonehenge. Through careful excavation, archaeologists have identified three previous phases, all of which were much, much plainer. The first probably dates back to before 3000 BC, when the henge was just a circular ditch around a broken bank, reminiscent of the mysterious 'causewayed camps', with a circle of holes dug around the perimeter (the 'Aubrey holes') which originally contained timber posts.

In the second phase, between 2900 and 2600 BC, lots of post-holes were dug, though what sort of structure these made up is not at all clear. In the third phase, the smallish 'bluestones' were brought here and set up in a double crescent formation (they're stones composed of a blue-grey rock that originates on the Preseli mountains in the south-west corner of Wales, though it has been argued that bits of the same stone might have been found closer to home).

The final triumphant phase of building dates to around 2400 BC, when the avenue that leads up to the stone circle was laid out, and the ring of sarsens and horseshoe of trilithons were built (sarsen is an incredibly hard rock naturally occurring in big boulders on the Marlborough Downs). During this phase the bluestones were reset, though various changes to their arrangement seem to have been made over the next 700 years. By about

The bronze age burial mounds at Normanton Down: nearby is Bush Barrow, where a great treasure was found.

1600 BC, with no more work being carried out, it is assumed that the monument had fallen out of use.

So that's Stonehenge. To make sense of it you should certainly read the guidebook and walk to at least one of the other sites in the area; perhaps the barrows at Normanton Down. For more on the latest debate surrounding henge-type monuments, see *Stanton Drew, Somerset* (*page 57*).

Off the A303 west of Amesbury; buses from Salisbury railway station.

NORMANTON DOWN
BARROW GROUP
National Trust • Free • Open access at any reasonable time

Nowhere else are there so many bronze age burial mounds as around Stonehenge, and you can see the way they were built in cemeteries along the ridges to stand out against the sky.

What makes this group of barrows particularly notable is that one of them is Bush Barrow, where the great Stonehenge treasure (on display in the British Museum, London) was found: it includes bronze weapons, gold

The Winterbourne Stoke group is a good place to see a whole variety of barrows.

ornaments (possibly buckles) and a strange 'ceremonial mace' with a stone head and ivory decoration.

On foot from Stonehenge car park; map provided in guidebook.

WINTERBOURNE STOKE
BARROW GROUP
National Trust • Free • Open access at any reasonable time

This group is a great place to see the whole range of burial mounds, from a stone age long barrow to the rare type known as a pond barrow.

On foot from Stonehenge car park, or from lay-by on A303 immediately east of A360.

WOODHENGE
& DURRINGTON WALLS
English Heritage • Free • Open access at any reasonable time

Woodhenge is an arrangement of post-holes in concentric circles, excavated and marked by concrete posts. It's not much to look at, but it gives you an idea of the scale of what could have been a wooden building (see the guidebook for a drawing).

Just nearby, though you can't really make it out any more, was Durrington Walls, an enormous henge (that is, a circular bank and ditch) which also contained a couple of circular wooden 'buildings'. Again, there are useful reconstruction drawings in the guide.

Signposted off A345 just north of A303.

In landscaped grounds in a secluded valley, Old Wardour Castle is exceptionally pretty.

OLD WARDOUR CASTLE

English Heritage • ££ • Usual hours

In truth it's not really a proper castle, but it's still one of the most enjoyable to visit. It's actually a rather smart fortified house from the last era of castle-building in the late 1300s, taking the form of a tall, hexagonal keep with a courtyard in the middle (actually, it's more of a light well). The only place in England that's at all similar is *Nunney Castle, Somerset*, which dates from the same period.

The man who built Old Wardour, Lord Lovel, obtained a licence from the king to fortify his home in 1393. Lovel had probably, like many other men of his time, made a small personal fortune in the wars against the French, and wished to show off his military credentials in his brand new home. Maybe he picked up a few design ideas on the continent, too, since there is a castle very like it at Concressault in central France.

One whole side was blown away when the keep was slighted in the Civil War, but there are still plenty of rooms and stairways to explore, with great views from the higher levels: kids love charging around the keep and up and down its stairs. Alterations made in the mid-1500s added bigger windows and also some very pleasing architectural details, such as the ornate doorways.

It's a most peaceful and friendly ruin, too, surrounded by lovely landscaped grounds in a secluded hollow in the hills. It's ideal for a picnic on a sunny day. The ruin was used as an ornamental folly in the grounds of the later house (New Wardour Castle, across the lake), with a Gothick pavilion built in front of the castle and a bizarre grotto and stone circle tucked in at the edge of the woods behind it in the 1790s.

The only action Old Wardour ever saw was in the Civil War. In one famous siege of 1643 the wife of the owner, Lady Blanche, and 25 soldiers held the castle against a besieging force of around 1300 men.

Old Wardour was used for the film *Robin Hood, Prince of Thieves*, and a couple of years ago, the gatekeeper was keen to show off the photo album recording how the castle was turned into a film set and would, if you asked nicely, let you hold Kevin Costner's replica sword. If you're a fan of the film, it might be worth asking.

Near Tisbury; signposted off A30 Salisbury to Shaftesbury road – follow signposts down a few small minor roads to reach the castle.

SEE ALSO...

Wiltshire has lots of excellent HILLFORTS, many of them built on the edges of the chalk downs overlooking the valleys below, and they're fine places for a good walk. SCRATCHBURY, *near Warminster (footpath up from B390 opposite the side-road to Norton Bavant)* is a particularly large example, and from its single rampart you can see over to nearby BATTLESBURY, with several rings of ramparts, and also to the odd-looking Cley Hill, which, like Scratchbury, has a barrow on the top. BRATTON CAMP, *near Westbury*, is in a popular country park above the famous Westbury white horse, and there's also a white horse carved on the hillside below OLDBURY CASTLE, *next to the A4 near Calne*. Nearer Swindon is the fairly dramatic BARBURY CASTLE, *on the Marlborough Downs south of Wroughton*. In the Salisbury area there's FIGSBURY RING (National Trust), *signposted from the A30 east of Salisbury*, which has an unusual ditch inside its single rampart, and WINKELBURY, *on the ridge above Berwick St John*, which has some extremely interesting hummocks.

CHISBURY CHAPEL (*English Heritage, free, any reasonable time*), *off the A4 six miles east of Marlborough* – A small thatched chapel from the 1200s.

AND...

There's a heap of barrows to be found: COW DOWN ROUND BARROWS, *on Salisbury Plain, just SW of the junction of A338 and A342*, has 12 bowl barrows and a disc; SNAIL DOWN BARROWS, *on military land SW of Collingbourne Ducis*, had about 30 barrows before the Army drove tanks all over them; GIANT'S CAVE BARROW, *by Badminton Park on the Badminton to Luckington road*, is a ruined chambered long barrow; LUGBURY LONG BARROW, *near Nettleton*, with a huge false portal at the end, had four chambers; TILSHEAD OLD DITCH LONG BARROW, *near Tilshead*, is the longest earthen long barrow in the country.

Sussex

CRAMMED with interesting historic sites, including two outstanding castles: *Pevensey Castle*, with its Roman walls, and the very pretty *Bodiam Castle*.

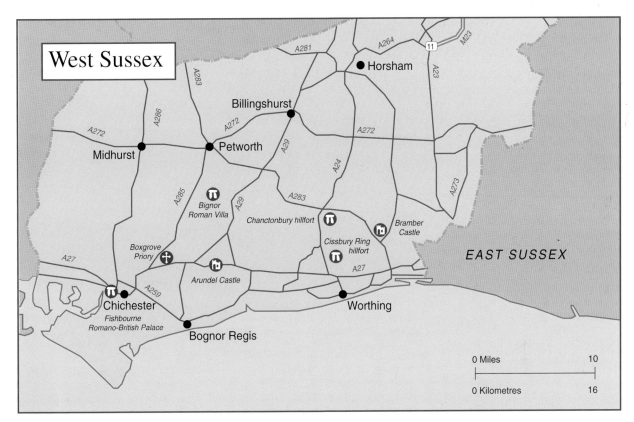

West Sussex

Horsham

Billingshurst

Midhurst

Petworth

Bignor Roman Villa

Chanctonbury hillfort

Bramber Castle

Boxgrove Priory

Cissbury Ring hillfort

Arundel Castle

Chichester

Worthing

Fishbourne Romano-British Palace

Bognor Regis

EAST SUSSEX

A272 · A281 · A264 · A23 · M23 · 11 · A283 · A286 · A272 · A272 · A29 · A24 · A273 · A285 · A29 · A283 · A27 · A259 · A27

0 Miles   10
0 Kilometres   16

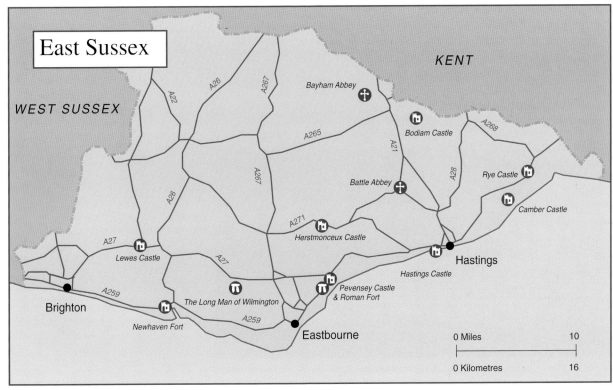

East Sussex

KENT

WEST SUSSEX

Bayham Abbey

Bodiam Castle

Battle Abbey

Rye Castle

Camber Castle

Herstmonceux Castle

Lewes Castle

Hastings

Hastings Castle

Brighton

The Long Man of Wilmington

Pevensey Castle & Roman Fort

Newhaven Fort

Eastbourne

A26 · A267 · A22 · A265 · A21 · A268 · A28 · A267 · A26 · A271 · A27 · A27 · A259 · A259

0 Miles   10
0 Kilometres   16

ARUNDEL CASTLE

*Private trust • ££ (grounds, keep and chapel)
or £££ (also castle interior) • Usual hours*

No castle looks more splendid from a distance than Arundel, its towers rising dramatically above the plain. Trouble is, it's something of a sham. Most of what you see is Victorian mock-medieval rebuilding, topped off in the early 1900s with a couple of immense towers which have an almost industrial look. This part of the building, known as 'the castle', is really just a grand house, with lots of gothicky, baronial rooms, furnished with armour and portrait paintings.

Luckily, though, if you buy a much cheaper 'Grounds and keep' ticket, you get to see all the best early medieval bits of the castle. Arundel is like a smaller version of Windsor: at both castles the original Norman motte dominated not one, but two raised baileys. About 1140, the motte here was topped by a shell keep, now stripped back to something like its

The unusually hard stone from which Bayham Abbey was built means that carved details have survived very well.

The restored Norman shell keep is the oldest and most interesting part of Arundel Castle.

original condition. One nice detail is a 'sally port' that is nothing more than a crane over a trap door, through which some poor soldier was winched down outside the walls so that he could sneak off to spy on the enemy.

The other major feature of this early part of the castle is the barbican gate through which you enter. Built about 1295, it still has its original portcullis and wooden gates, though they swing several feet above the ground because the roadway was later lowered.

Arundel was home to the Fitzalan and Howard families, who in the course of their colourful history had a hand in everything from the deaths of the Princes in the Tower to the many marriages of Henry VIII. I counted eight beheadings, but I may have

missed a few. The fourth Duke of Norfolk lost his head on the orders of Queen Elizabeth I in 1572 for daring to become betrothed to Mary Queen of Scots, which Elizabeth interpreted as an attempt on her throne. Some of Mary's possessions are on display.

In centre of Arundel, off A27 Chichester to Brighton road – free car park in castle.

BAYHAM ABBEY

English Heritage • ££ • Usual hours

The grace and tranquillity of ruined abbeys always appeals, and Bayham is pretty enough not to disappoint, though it doesn't have the scale and splendour of some of the more famous abbeys (*Fountains* and *Rievaulx* in *Yorkshire*, for instance). The remains of a house of 'white canons' (Premonstratensians, who were a kind of Augustinian splinter group) founded not long after 1200, the ruined abbey was 'landscaped' into the grounds of a Georgian house and somehow has the feel of a garden folly rather than a historical ruin. Still, there's some attractive stonework, and the tree growing out of the 'altar' is a splendid sight.

South-east of Royal Tunbridge Wells, clearly signposted from B2169; car park.

Arundel is at its best when seen from a distance, rising above the buildings of the town like a proper castle should.

Nine hundred years ago, Norman knights mounted on war-horses fought their way up this rise to defeat the Saxons who held the ridge at the top.

BATTLE ABBEY
(BATTLE OF HASTINGS SITE)

English Heritage • £££ (includes audio guide) • Usual hours

There's good reason for October 14th 1066 to be the most memorable date in English history, since no other single event had such long-lasting and wide-ranging effects. By wiping out the Saxon fighting lords, a fairly small group of Normans was effectively able to win a kingdom in just a day.

Unless you have a strong interest in military history, a visit to a battlefield is never going to be a hugely thrilling experience – but with an introductory video and an audio tour, English Heritage have done all they can to bring the battle to life. You can skip a lot of the material and still get a decent picture of what happened here 900 years ago.

King Harold's English army had been ready all summer for the expected Norman invasion, but in mid-September marched north to meet another invading army led by the Norwegian King Harold Hardraada. At Stamford Bridge on September 25th the English destroyed the invaders – just a tenth straggled back to Norway – and by October 6th Harold was back in London. Meanwhile, Duke William and his Norman forces landed and established

a base at Hastings, and were raiding royal estates in the area as a deliberate ploy to draw the English to them. Harold moved swiftly to the attack and though he failed to gain the advantage of surprise, he did at least get to choose his ground for the battle.

The English forces were ranged along the top of the ridge where, fighting on foot with swords and axes, they could hold their 'shield wall' against the Norman charges. The Normans, forced to attack uphill, would rely heavily on the power of their cavalry elite, the knights, though the volleys of arrows with which the archers would soften up the English line would also be a key factor.

Harold's forces don't seem to have been depleted by Stamford Bridge (though he does seem to have been short of archers, which may have had a big effect on the outcome) and the sides were pretty much equal at

Just one wing of Battle Abbey still stands. The vaults underneath are very fine.

around 7,000 men each (it amazes me to think that so few were involved).

What won the battle for the Normans was their ability to draw the English down the slopes, sometimes by regrouping after a genuine retreat and sometimes using the classic tactic of pretending to withdraw in disorder and then turning to attack their pursuers. As the day wore on, bold charges by the cavalry were able to break through the English lines and eventually it was one such attack that cut down Harold (who may or may not already have been wounded by an arrow in the eye) and won the day. The Normans were proud to say that some of their most famous fighters were killed that day, but the English had lost nearly all their noblemen.

William ordered the building of Battle Abbey in about 1170 to atone for the blood shed during his conquest of England, and insisted that the altar of the church should be sited on the spot where Harold was said to have fallen. The main remnant is the dorter (dormitory) block, dating from the mid-1200s, which housed the novices' room and the monks' common room, both graced by very attractive vaulted ceilings. Pleasant, but not thrilling: the battlefield is the star attraction here, and that is, after all, just a field.

In Battle village, on A2100 near Hastings; car park free to English Heritage members.

Bodiam is like a toy castle, which is perhaps why it's been voted a children's favourite.

BODIAM CASTLE

National Trust • ££ • Usual hours

It's been compared to a sandcastle – though I think Bodiam is more like a toy fort, with its tall, thin walls and tower at each corner – and at the height of the season the car park is not unlike a beach, with ice creams and deck chairs coming out as soon as the sun shines. The greatest tribute to the castle, though, is that it's still a fine place to visit despite its popularity.

Bodiam owes a good deal of its well-preserved toy castle looks to a careful restoration in the 1920s by its then owner, Lord Curzon. It's a relatively late castle, planned and built as a coherent whole and very little altered afterwards. The royal licence to build it (this licence actually still exists) was granted in 1385 to the colourfully named Sir Edward Dalyngrigge, a rich veteran who had been one of Edward III's generals. In common with many south coast fortifications of the time, it was meant to help defend the area against the uppity French, who had raided Rye and Winchelsea in 1377.

In design, Bodiam was pretty much the ultimate development of the 'courtyard castle', in which the walls and towers were the main defence, with no need for a keep. This left plenty of room in the middle for buildings like cellars, stores, brewhouses and bakeries, which would help increase the castle's revenue in times of peace as well as helping it to survive under siege.

Another big reason for needing a lot of space was that most rich and powerful men of this era would have a large number of mercenaries in their pay, who would need quarters of their own, separate from the lord's staff. At Bodiam there was a large accommodation block for the paid soldiers, with its own kitchen. These mercenaries were not always to be relied upon, however, and so another distinctive feature of the castle's design is that the lord's own quarters could be defended separately.

Beautifully designed though it is, the castle had one small problem. It was built in the days when cannon were just beginning to be used, and before too long, advances in the size and power of the largest guns meant that its walls were just too thin to resist the cannonfire. The castle was, however, very well appointed: it boasted no less than 33 fireplaces and 24 properly drained toilets.

As for Bodiam today: well, access to the tops of the towers and walls is excellent (so long as you don't mind climbing lots of stone stairs), which makes the castle great fun to look around. There are some splendidly large fish in the moat, too, which is now crossed by a straight bridge, but originally had three drawbridges and two gates. One of the original iron-shod oak portcullises can still be seen, and an interesting detail to look out for is the ceiling bosses of the gateways, which are full of 'murder holes' from which defenders could drop nasty surprises.

Just near Bodiam village, signposted from main roads (A21, A268); ample car parking and National Trust tea rooms.

The excellent mosaics at Bignor include this corridor floor, said to be the longest mosaic in England.

BIGNOR ROMAN VILLA

Privately owned • £££ • March to October, usual hours (closed Mondays in March, April, May, October except bank holidays)

Models and plans displayed in the site museum will give you an idea of the vast scale of this Romano-British farm estate, much of which is still being excavated, but it's the striking mosaic floors that are Bignor's star attraction. The villa grew up in the third and fourth centuries on the site of an earlier British farmstead, starting as a four-room house and developing into one of the biggest in Britain. Like many other country estates, it's more likely to have been the home of a British land-owning family who had become 'civilised' by Roman influence, rather than being the property of a Roman 'invader'.

This has to be the only place in England where you can actually set foot on a Roman mosaic floor (well, just on the edge) and the sheer scale of the mosaic flooring in seven different rooms, including a separate bath-house, makes it an exciting experience. On the down side, though, entry is a little bit expensive and, mosaics apart, there's not all that much to see.

Next to minor road south of Bignor village; signposted from A285 south of Petworth and from A29; car park.

BOXGROVE PRIORY

(ABBOT'S HOUSE REMAINS AND PRIORY CHURCH)

English Heritage and church authorities • Free • Open access at reasonable times to remains and to church (contributions to church appreciated); guidebook from church

Once upon a time, Boxgrove Priory had two churches in a row, separated by a screen: one for the monks and one for the people. When Henry VIII dissolved the monasteries in 1536 and the surprisingly small population of ten Benedictine monks was turfed out, the local people grabbed the chance to take over the larger and more splendid monastic church, and so it remains in use to the present day.

The interior of the church is not to be missed: it has some fine, sturdy Norman arches under the tower, which date back to the first building here in about 1120, and you can see a stairway in the north transept (opposite the entrance) through which the monks could nip in to the church directly from their dormitory, to do their sleepy duty in the night offices.

The highlight for me, though, is the fabulous painting on the ceiling of the nave (which is in the Early English style, dating from around 1220, if you're curious). Painted by a Chichester artist called Lambert Barnard not long before the Dissolution, these beautiful flower designs, stylised and yet still natural, are the sort of thing that inspired the Arts and Crafts movement in Victorian times. Just gorgeous.

Other remains of the abbey can still be seen outside the church, and these are cared for by English Heritage. They include the ruins of the separate guest house and a section of arches from the Norman chapter house, but these aren't especially interesting in themselves.

The extraordinary Tudor painted ceiling of the church at Boxgrove is just gorgeous.

In Boxgrove village, just off the A27 near Chichester; look for car park sign.

Left: the most substantial remains at Boxgrove Priory are the walls of the house where the abbot would put up his guests.

SUSSEX (EAST & WEST)

BRAMBER CASTLE

English Heritage • Free • Open access at any reasonable time

One tall chunk of gate-tower wall stands like a great monolith on the edge of the large, levelled castle hill; behind it the original motte, dating from the 1070s, is still very evident, and round the back there's a stretch of curtain wall with the base of another tower. All in all, very little remains of the sizeable castle that once stood here, but it's worth a quick look round if only for the views. The stonework was built in the early 1100s and reworked a couple of centuries later, but not much more is known.

In Bramber, through Upper Beeding village, off A2037 or A283 north east of Worthing.

Above: there's not much left of the castle at Bramber except this piece of gate-tower and the Norman motte.

Below: a real oddity, Camber Castle is a Henry VIII fort that was abandoned when the bay silted up.

The views from Chanctonbury hillfort are amazing, though the walk up to the top is seriously hard work.

CAMBER CASTLE

English Heritage • Exterior: free, open access at any reasonable time; interior: ££, open once a month at summer weekends

A rare ruin of a Henry VIII gun-fort (most of the others were kept in use in some form or another until fairly recent times), the 'castle at Rye' was begun about 1540 but was abandoned even before it went into use, because the bay was silting up so quickly. It's an intriguing curiosity, standing alone on fields flat as football pitches, but none too enlightening unless you visit with one of the occasional guided tours (details from Rye Heritage centre).

Just west of Rye; half-hour walk on footpath from near locks on road to Rye Harbour.

CHANCTONBURY HILLFORT

Area of outstanding natural beauty • Free • Open access at any reasonable time

Topped by 200-year-old beech trees from which the devil is said to spring if you run seven times round it, this great little hillfort built between 400 and 300 BC has bags of atmosphere and is beautifully positioned, with fabulous views over the surrounding country. Well worth the hard slog on foot up the hill to reach it. In the middle there are traces of a small Roman temple (100 to 200 AD) very like the one at *Maiden Castle, Dorset*.

Signposted from A283 east of Washington, north of Worthing; car park; hillfort reached by half-hour walk uphill on track in woods, then turn right along the South Downs Way.

There's not a lot left of Hastings Castle, but equally there isn't a lot else to do at the top of the cliff railway.

Fishbourne Roman palace has one striking mosaic, but otherwise… well, it's not all it's cracked up to be.

CISSBURY RING HILLFORT

National Trust • Free • Open access at any reasonable time

This is a big league hillfort, its sizeable ramparts enclosing a vast area: originally faced with wood, the ramparts have been estimated to contain about 60,000 tons of chalk and would have used as many as 12,000 upright timbers at least four metres (13 ft) in height. Built around 350 BC, Cissbury was abandoned before the Romans came but reoccupied at the time of the Saxon invasions. If you're keen on folk tales, you might be interested to know that the fairies are said to dance here at midnight on Midsummer's Eve.

The hill was in use long before the hillfort was built, though. Outside the south entrance (the end towards the sea), hollows in the ground are the only visible evidence of neolithic flint mines, with shafts sunk 12m (40 ft) under the surface to reach the best seam of flint, and with galleries radiating out into the seam, just as at *Grimes Graves, Norfolk*. Tools of the ancient miners – including antler picks dated to around 2700 BC, scapula shovels and chalk lamps – were found during excavations.

Free public car park clearly signposted from A24 immediately south of Findon (north of Worthing); 15-minute walk up hill.

FISHBOURNE ROMANO-BRITISH PALACE

Sussex Past • £££ • Usual hours

Something of a disappointment, considering that after Hadrian's Wall and Bath's Roman baths, this is probably the most famous Roman site in Britain. Certainly it was a very large villa, but all that is on display are some mosaic floors and a bit of hypocaust, and these are no more exciting than, for instance, the mosaics at *Bignor (page 95)*. In fact, Bignor's are rather better (with the exception of the splendid 'Cupid on a dolphin' mosaic here at Fishbourne). Much of Fishbourne's fame is attached to its dubious claim to be a palace, based on its apparent splendour, but this, unfortunately, is very much in the eye of the archaeologists: very little of it is to be seen today. Museum's good, though.

In Fishbourne, west of Chichester; signposted from A27.

HASTINGS CASTLE

Privately owned • £££ • Usual hours

Here, in October 1066, William the Conqueror built his first castle in England to secure his line of retreat: almost certainly it was a motte with a prefabricated timber tower which he'd brought with him from Normandy. That place in history apart, Hastings castle has little to offer. A few bits of stonework remain from the later development of the cliff-top castle, but they don't tell much of a story.

Near top station of cliff railway, above Hastings old town.

Cissbury is a big hillfort in that it covers a vast area, but the ramparts aren't huge.

The grand facade of Herstmonceux, former home of Britain's top stargazers.

HERSTMONCEUX CASTLE

Privately owned • Grounds and gardens: £££, usual hours • Interior: occasionally open with additional fee

The splendid brick exterior is all that remains of a genuine castle of the early artillery age, built in 1441. Restored as a country house at the beginning of this century and later home to the Royal Observatory (the astronomy museum is just next door), it's now a college for international students. It looks the part from the outside, but there's nothing interesting behind the walls. The college opens the grounds every day and offers tours of the interior about once a week for an extra fee, but unless you *really* want to see the gardens or photograph the castle's facade, I wouldn't bother even with the grounds.

On minor road to south of A271, a few miles north of Eastbourne.

LEWES CASTLE

Sussex Past • ££ (includes museum; discount for English Heritage members) • Usual hours

A decidedly pleasant little castle, the main surviving elements being most of a shell keep and a large barbican gate, both of which you can climb up to look around. The first Norman castle at Lewes was built in about 1070 and was unusual in having two mottes, one at each end of the bailey. Both were later topped by shell keeps, the main one built in the early 1100s.

Lewes saw significant action in 1264, when Simon de Montfort fought and won an important battle nearby against King Henry III. The castle, holding out for the king, was forced to surrender when De Montfort

threatened to execute some of his prisoners, including the king's brother, Richard.

The barbican was built in the early 1300s to protect the fairly weedy Norman main gate, but by then the castle was on its way out: from the early 1400s it slowly declined.

The ticket to the castle also gives you entry to the excellent museum, where there's plenty to see: don't miss the colourful medieval floor tiles or the very rare and unusual Celtic carved stone head, thought to be the representation of a goddess.

Easily found in the middle of Lewes.

THE LONG MAN OF WILMINGTON

National Trust land • Free • Open access at any reasonable time

One of only two human hill-figures in Britain – and the other, the *Cerne Abbas Giant, Dorset,* may well be a fake. You're pretty much free to use your own imagination on who the Long Man is and why he's there, since very little is known beyond the fact that he was restored in the 1870s.

Hill-figures are very difficult to date, as recently demonstrated by the *Uffington White Horse, Berkshire,* where new techniques showed it to be far, far older than the iron age (Celtic)

Who is the Long Man of Wilmington, and how old is he? Well, nobody knows…

date it had been given on stylistic grounds. Similar stylistic comparisons have been made between the Long Man and images of a soldier holding two standards on coins from the 300s, or a warrior with two spears on a Saxon belt buckle from the 600s; or he might be Woden, Thor or Apollo.

My favourite theory, though, crops up in a book called *The Old Straight Track,* full of country lore, where the author suggests the figure might be a 'dodman' or surveyor, lining up two sticks to lay a road in a straight line.

Viewpoint is signposted at the south end of the village of Wilmington, just off the A27.

Lewes Castle has a cute half-ruined shell keep, a superb Barbican gate-tower and an interesting place in history.

Not only a castle, but also a complete circuit of Roman walls – Pevensey is a pretty remarkable place.

PEVENSEY CASTLE
& ROMAN FORT
OF THE SAXON SHORE

English Heritage • Grounds and Roman walls: free, open access at any reasonable time; castle: ££, usual hours

This is an extraordinarily interesting place, in a 'read the guidebook and learn' kind of way, even though the medieval castle is a little bit disappointing. There are four places in Britain where the Normans put a castle inside Roman walls: *Burgh* and Walton *in Suffolk*; *Portchester in Hampshire*; and here. At Burgh no traces remain of the medieval castle, and Walton has been swept away by the sea. Portchester is fantastically impressive, its Norman keep and square circuit of Roman walls both still standing to their full height. Pevensey is less exciting, but it's unusual in several interesting ways.

The Saxon Shore fort of *Anderida* was built later than most of the others (about 340 AD, where the rest were finished by 280) and is the only one that's not the usual regimented Roman square: instead, its walls follow the contours of the small peninsula on which it was built, so it's roughly oval in shape. The main gate was between two large bastions at the west end of the fort (the far end from the castle), with guardhouses tucked in behind the wall. Outside the gate, a ditch, with a wooden bridge across it, cut off the peninsula; to the south of the fort was the sea; and the harbour lay on the north and east, reached by a small, plain gate in the east wall. Unusually, the accommodation inside the walls was just wooden huts, some with tiled hearths, rather than proper stone barracks.

The Romans bailed out of Britain in the early 400s, but the British may have held *Anderida* against the Saxons afterwards; the *Anglo-Saxon Chronicle* records a Saxon victory here in 491, though no archeological evidence for it has been found. The Normans landed at Pevensey in September 1066 and used the Roman fort as their first base. A ditch and pallisaded bank was put in, making the eastern third of the fort into a kind of basic castle.

The first of many sieges here took place in 1088, when Odo, Bishop of Bayeux, the Conqueror's half-brother, held the castle on behalf of Robert, Duke of Normandy, the Conqueror's eldest son, in the war against Robert's brother William Rufus.

As with most castles, a stone keep and walls were built and developed over the next couple of hundred years. Not much of the keep remains, and it's a bit of a mystery, with all sorts of strange, ugly bastions sticking out. Probably it was originally an orthodox square tower. Inside the castle there's not an awful lot to see, apart from the dungeons in the bottom of the gate towers, so if you can rein in your curiosity it's probably just as well to look from the outside. The most impressive part of the castle is the curtain wall, built in the 1250s, with its fat, round towers.

The castle fell into disrepair and decline in Tudor times but, most unusually of all, found a new lease of life in 1940 when it was set up as an observation and command post and the interiors of the towers in the medieval castle were fitted out to house soldiers. Several machine-gun posts, ('pill boxes') were cleverly hidden among the fallen masonry of the Roman walls – and they're still there, if you can find them, English Heritage having decided that the concrete put in by 20th-century soldiers is just as worthy of preservation as the stonework of the Romans and Normans.

Clearly signposted near Westham, off A27 east of Eastbourne; council car park (P&D).

An artillery fort of the Victorian era, Newhaven has been well restored and has excellent museum displays.

NEWHAVEN FORT

Lewes District Council • £££ • Usual hours

This is a Victorian artillery fort, one of 'Palmerston's Follies', built between 1862 and 1871 in an extraordinary position on top of (and under) the white cliffs overlooking the sea and guarding the narrow estuary in which Newhaven docks are set.

A relic of the industrial era in a slightly shabby dockland location, it's hardly a beauty spot, but it does have a certain severe grandeur. The brick buildings within the fort have been spruced up very nicely to house a series of well-presented museum displays, with lots of interactive bits and plenty of sound effects, covering the recent military history of the area (especially the Second World War).

The magazine where gunpowder was stored and the laboratory where it was packed into shells are in fairly original condition, though the gun batteries were much altered for later military use. If you don't mind slogging down and then back up 70 steps, you can drop down a tunnel through the chalk to emerge at the foot of the cliffs in the extraordinary 'caponier', a forward gun position not unlike the 'sally port' of a medieval castle. All in all, it's pretty interesting, though a bit overpriced.

Clearly signposted in centre of Newhaven.

RYE CASTLE

Local council • £ • Usual hours

This funny little keep-like building has been through a number of different uses, most notably as a jail, and is now quite a decent little local museum with a particularly excellent 'diorama'-style display of the local coastline (all that flat farmland where once there was sea). Not particularly outstanding in the castle stakes, but still worth a look if you're in the area.

In the middle of the town of Rye.

This little keep in the middle of Rye is now home to a small local museum.

SEE ALSO...

AMBERLEY CASTLE, *north of Arundel* – This small castle from the late 1300s belonged to the Bishops of Chichester and has a high curtain wall. It is now a smart country hotel. You can visit, provided you arrange it in advance by telephone.

DEVIL'S DYKE HILLFORT, *north of Brighton* – Not the most spectacular hillfort, but great views, and a bus service from Brighton to get there.

EASTBOURNE MARTELLO (THE WISH TOWER), *on Eastbourne seafront* – Can be visited, but only because it houses a puppet museum. Weird. Read about Martellos on *page 106*.

HOLTYE ROMAN ROAD, *off A264 near East Grinstead* – Apparently there's an excavated section of Roman road, surfaced with packed-down iron-smelting waste, to be seen here. I couldn't find it, though.

REDOUBT FORT, *Eastbourne* (pictured) – This round 18th-century artillery fort houses a strange, amateurish military museum.

AND...

BEVIS'S THUMB LONG BARROW, *near North Marden*; DEVIL'S HUMPS bell and bowl barrows, *near Stoughton*; DEVIL'S JUMPS BELL BARROWS, *south of Treyford*; CHICHESTER ROMAN REMAINS, including part of a mosaic in the cathedral (more info in the museum), plus iron age earthworks to the north of the town; FIRLE BEACON barrows, *near West Firle*; MOUNT CABURN HILLFORT, *not far from Lewes*; STANE STREET Roman road (*runs from Bignor to Eartham, north-east of Bognor*).

Kent

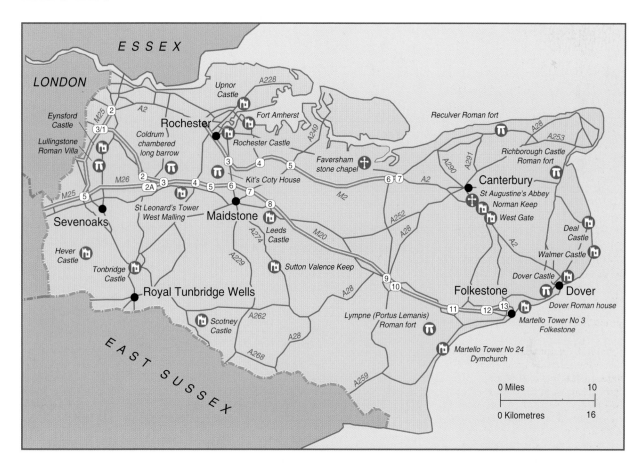

KENT has a greater variety of castles than any other county, but it also has plenty of other interesting historic sites, too. The massive *Dover Castle* remained in use from Saxon times until after the Second World War, but its keep retains a medieval authenticity. Within the castle's grounds you'll also find a Roman lighthouse. *Deal Castle* is the most entertaining of the 'modern' artillery forts built by Henry VIII, with a spectacular design, based on multiple circles, that makes it great fun to explore; while *Rochester Castle* has the largest Norman keep in England – don't miss it (and it's a very easy day trip by train from London, too). Kent isn't short of interesting Roman sites, either. The walls of the fort at *Richborough* are among the most substantial Roman remains in England, while *Lullingstone villa* is certainly the most informative villa in the country; you can even see the footprint of a Roman cat in the clay of a roof-tile.

Upnor Castle is a very charming little artillery fort built in the 1500s to guard the River Medway.

CANTERBURY

THE NATIVE TRIBE of the *Cantii* from whom Kent gets its name called their capital *Durwhern*, but to the Romans this important trading town was *Durovernum Cantiacorum*. The only remaining traces of the Romans' presence are mosaics and a heating system (*hypocaust*) uncovered by wartime bombing and now housed by the Roman Museum (*Butchery Lane*).

ST AUGUSTINE'S ABBEY

English Heritage • ££ • usual hours;
ten minutes' walk from town centre,
down Burgate and across the main road.

Canterbury's place in history was assured in 597 when a turbocharged monk called Augustine arrived on a mission to convert England to the ways of the Roman church. He immediately won the support of Ethelbert, king of Kent, whose Frankish wife, Bertha, was already a Christian. Ethelbert donated an old church 'built long ago by Roman Christians' and here Augustine built the first cathedral in Britain. The present cathedral is on the same spot.

In 598 Augustine was given land outside the city walls on which to make a home for monks sent from St Andrew's in Rome. A church was built here, and later Augustine was buried in a side-chapel called the Porticus of St Gregory. The buildings were improved, pulled down and rebuilt over many years, until in 978 Dunstan gave the monastery the name of St Augustine's Abbey.

Traces of the very first church can still be seen, along with the foundations of lots of later buildings, such as the daring but unfinished 'rotunda' started by Abbot Wulfric II around 1050, or the great Norman church built by Abbot Scolland (1070–87). Sadly, though, there are little more than traces of any of these structures, and the complex pattern of building and rebuilding can only be made sense of with careful use of the guidebook. A visit is an intellectual exercise, not an emotional experience.

Incidentally, at Cliffs End near Ramsgate a cross marks the spot where Augustine is believed to have first set foot in England.

St Augustine was buried in an early church here, and around it the abbey grew up that now bears his name.

The remains of Canterbury's Norman keep are a bit of a disappointment: you can't get inside its walls.

NORMAN KEEP

Local council • Free • Access to exterior only
at any reasonable time; in Castle Street.

Canterbury was more important to the Normans as a strategic centre than a religious one, and here William the Conqueror built his third castle in England (after Hastings and Dover) to secure his line of retreat as he advanced towards London. Like all early castles, Canterbury was probably just a wooden tower with a defensive ditch, but later a classic square stone keep was built.

Canterbury's keep is disappointing today, squeezed into a small public park with no access to the interior, but it has quite a pedigree. It was built by Gundulf, Bishop of Rochester, 'a man very competent and skilful at building in stone', whose previous efforts were the White Tower in London (probably 1079) and the keep at Colchester (1083); Canterbury's keep is in effect a smaller version of Colchester.

WEST GATE

Local council • £ • usual hours; St Peter's St.

Besides having the first cathedral in England, Canterbury can also boast another major first in the form of the West Gate – now a small museum – which was the first building in England designed to be defended by and from guns. The Archbishop of Canterbury was given a licence to build it in 1380, at a time when the towns of the south coast were constantly being raided by the French, who in 1379 had devastated the coastal town of Rye.

The West Gate has a claim to fame: it was the first building in England built to withstand cannon-fire.

Deal Castle is the biggest (and most fun to visit) of the coastal forts built by Henry VIII, with a unique design based on six circles. Its maze-like interior is great fun to explore.

COLDRUM CHAMBERED LONG BARROW

National Trust • Free • Open access at any reasonable time

The most atmospheric prehistoric site in the south-east of England, this partly ruined new stone age tomb is situated in a quiet slice of farmland at the foot of the great chalk ridge of the North Downs. It's an immensely dramatic monument, set on the brink of a slight ridge: the mound is atop the ridge, walled round with massive stones, while the chamber, built from even bigger stones, is set into the 'face' of the ridge, so that you approach it from lower ground.

The mound is oriented east to west, and the remains of 22 people, some of them closely related, were found in the chamber.

Signposted from village of Trottiscliffe; ten minutes' walk from small car park.

On a grey winter's day, the massive ancient stones of Coldrum chambered tomb are sombrely impressive.

DEAL CASTLE

English Heritage • ££ • Usual hours

Of all Henry VIII's coastal defence artillery forts, this early one – built around 1540 – is the largest and probably the most fun to visit.

One of three 'Castles in the Downs' (the others were *Walmer, see below, page 113*, and Sandown, long since swallowed by the sea), Deal has a unique and intriguing design based on six circles. This makes it surprisingly tricky to find your way around, so that the whole thing is rather like a maze; and to add to the fun, there's a circuit of dark, twisty tunnels that runs the full length of the outer walls. This is a place kids have real fun exploring.

Deal Castle is a plainer building with less attractive Tudor detail in the masonry than you'll find in other Henrician forts, so if you want to get a good picture of Henry's coastal castles you would be well advised to visit one of the fancier examples too (perhaps *Walmer, page 113*, or maybe *St Mawes* or *Pendennis* in *Cornwall*). But this is the most likeable of them all, and there is a good, simple exhibition in the basement which shows all the forts built on Henry's orders along the south coast.

On the seafront in Deal, next to the A258; car park on the green by the castle.

Dover's towers and battlements have a squashed look, mainly because the castle was converted to suit artillery warfare in the 1700s. The keep is one of the best in England.

DOVER CASTLE, 'HELLFIRE CORNER' TUNNELS & ROMAN LIGHTHOUSE

English Heritage • £££ • Usual hours

An enormous (and proportionately expensive to visit) English Heritage site with all sorts of claims to fame, not least that the castle was in constant use by the military from Norman times until after the Second World War. The British army finally gave it up in 1956.

It costs a fair bit to get in, but you could easily spend most of the day here, so it's not bad value (and there's one particular thing that I believe is worth the entrance fee in itself).

The four main attractions on the site, in ascending order of interest, are: the Roman lighthouse and Saxon church; the medieval tunnels under the northern wall; the Second World War 'secret tunnels' in the cliff, containing control rooms and a hospital, now known as Hellfire Corner (the guided tour takes an hour); and the Norman keep.

The only trouble with Dover is that all the old stuff has been vastly altered by later generations; so while you want to be impressed by the Roman lighthouse, you're not at all sure how much of it is Roman (actually only the top 6m, or 20ft, was rebuilt, and that as long ago as 1415). Worse, all the medieval towers were truncated in the late 1700s to give the guns a clear field of fire, which is why the castle has such a squat appearance.

All the same, the keep – built by order of Henry II between 1181 and 1188, and the work of a mason known as 'Maurice the Builder' – is very impressive. Typically for a later keep, a forebuilding guards the entrance and the main stairs lead direct to the second floor, which is where you'll find the royal chambers and the real highlight of the castle, the well. It's cleverly lit with a series of lights so that you can see how deep it is – and it really is deep. Worth the entrance fee just for that…

Clearly signposted for cars and for walkers from Dover town centre; car parking on site.

Astonishingly, this Roman lighthouse – one of a pair, either side of the port – survives intact on the Dover headland. Only the top 6m (20ft) are later additions.

Archaeologists have pieced together painted plaster fragments from the walls of Dover's Roman house.

DOVER (DUBRIS)
ROMAN PAINTED HOUSE

Local trust • ££ • Opening hours limited (April to October only, closed Mondays)

Where mosaics are the star attraction at the Roman villas of *Lullingstone* in Kent (*page 110*) and *Bignor* in *Sussex* (*page 95*), it's the wall paintings that grab the attention here, even though the surviving piece of painted plaster is only a couple of feet high.

The painted house was probably a 'mansio' or official hotel (though when you see the colours and themes of the murals, you can't help thinking 'brothel') and it was pulled down to make way for a fort around 270 AD. Basically only a couple of rooms of the house survive, so there's not a huge amount to see; but it would be a shame to miss it if you're in Dover, and the informative if marginally amateurish museum that's been built

Eynsford Castle's appeal is that it's in good walking country, and easily reached from London by train.

around the house gives a good insight into the excellent detective work of local archaeologists.

In New Street, Dover town centre.

EYNSFORD CASTLE

English Heritage • Free • Open access at any reasonable time

The nearest medieval castle to London (though if you're in the north of London, see *Berkhamstead Castle, Hertfordshire*) and although it's not

tremendously exciting, it is, at least, unusual and in a pleasant spot (lots of country walks in the area, and easily reached by train.)

The castle here started life as a wooden building surrounded by a high wall; then in about 1130 a stone hall was built, along with a gate tower and a wooden bridge across the moat, part of which could be lifted up. The irregular circuit of walls was raised in height to 9m (30ft). These walls are still quite impressive, mainly because they look just a bit taller than they have any right to be.

In the middle of Eynsford village, on A225.

FAVERSHAM
STONE CHAPEL

English Heritage • Free • Open access at any reasonable time

The only known, definite example in Britain of a Roman 'temple' that later became a Christian church. You can clearly see the remains of the tiny, square Romano-British mausoleum built in the 300s AD. There's not really much left to look at, but it's one of those atmospheric spots (not unlike *Knowlton Circle, Dorset*) and its unique place in history makes it well worth a look.

In a field by the A2 (London–Canterbury), two miles west of Faversham.

It's small, but it's pretty, and very unusual: Faversham's stone chapel was built around a square Roman temple.

THE BRAVE LITTLE MARTELLO

"Let us be masters of the Straits of Dover for six hours, and we shall be masters of the world" – Napoleon, 1804

NOT SINCE THE NORMANS landed had the south coast of England been under such threat of invasion – and not until Hitler surveyed the white cliffs of Dover through his binoculars in 1944 would it be so threatened again. By 1805, two years after the British had resumed hostilities against the French Republic, Napoleon had gathered an invasion force in northern France and built enough ships and barges to transport 168,000 men to England – an army far greater than the British could muster, even on their own soil.

The British navy was blusteringly confident that it could prevent the French from crossing the Channel. Lord St Vincent declared to the House of Lords: "I do not say that the French will not come; I only say that they will not come by sea." But the Government was not so sure, and started looking for a way to secure its coastal defences at reasonable cost.

Of all the defence works built on this coast over the years – such as the Roman Forts of the Saxon Shore, or Henry VIII's series of quirky little artillery castles – the solution that was finally arrived at in 1805 was both the most modest and the most successful; a chain of 74 small gun towers built along the Kent and Sussex coast between 1805 and 1812 and known as 'Martello Towers'.

The inspiration came from a mildly embarrassing incident during the British invasion of Corsica in 1794. At Mortella Point, a stone watchtower armed with only three small guns had managed to fight off two British warships, inflicting 60 casualties on the British attackers. The British were obliged to build a gun battery 150 yards (140m) away from the tower and pound it for two days before it eventually surrendered.

Drawings and a model of the watchtower had been made at the time, and the idea was now urgently pressed into use – though the design was changed considerably to arrive at the squat, round towers now built out of brick by local builders.

These Martello Towers (how two of the vowels in the name 'Mortella' came to be swopped around is a mystery) had immensely thick walls to protect them against enemy fire, and were armed with a single large gun mounted on the roof. Each individual tower did not need to be heavily armed, because they were placed sufficiently close together to defend each other with crossfire.

A second series of 29 towers (labelled with letters of the alphabet rather than numbers) was built along the coast of Essex and Suffolk but, inevitably, by the time the towers were finished the threat of invasion had faded with the defeat of Napoleon in 1815 at Waterloo. The Martellos never fired a shot in anger.

MARTELLO TOWER NO. 3, FOLKESTONE (LEFT)

Local trust • £ • Usual hours

Of the original 74 Martello Towers built on the south coast, just 25 now remain, nine in their original condition. Some have been converted to private houses, and only two can be visited (not including, that is, the Martello tower at Eastbourne, locally known as the Wish Tower, which is a rather bizarre puppet museum).

Used as a look-out tower in the Second World War, with a shelter added on the roof, Martello No. 3 is now a modest local history museum. Since it's not in its original condition it's not especially evocative of the period and not all that interesting.

On coast to east of Folkestone town centre.

MARTELLO TOWER NO. 24, DYMCHURCH (BELOW)

English Heritage • £ • Opening hours very limited (summer holiday months only)

Number 24 was built in 1808, slotted in among the cottages of Dymchurch so that it could protect the point where one of the main drainage ditches of Romney Marsh cut through the long sea-dyke known as Dymchurch Wall. The tower has been restored to its original state, so this is the better one to visit. There's not a huge amount to see – living quarters on the first floor, gunpowder stored in the basement, big gun on the roof – but for a quick glimpse of an intriguing piece of history, it's worth a visit.

In centre of Dymchurch, just off main road.

The entrance to the magazine at Fort Amherst – inside, raised wooden floors helped to prevent sparks causing explosions in the stored gunpowder.

The first you see of the fort is this chalk cliff: a vast tunnel, cut by French prisoners of war, runs up through it to emerge in the middle of the fort.

Hever Castle, the childhood home of Anne Boleyn, was extensively restored at the beginning of this century by the American millionaire William Waldorf Astor.

FORT AMHERST

Local trust • ££ • Usual hours

This massive fort from the time of the Napoleonic wars, with its brick-built tunnels and earthen ramparts, is a bit like an industrial-era version of an iron-age hillfort. Built on a hillside overlooking Chatham – and under the hill, too, with huge tunnels cut in the chalk – it protected the Royal Navy's biggest docks from an overland attack by an invading power, though its only taste of action was in huge exercises designed to test its defences.

Visits are by guided tour only, with the inevitable periods of boredom as well as moments of enlightenment when things are pointed out that you wouldn't otherwise have noticed. The volunteers who run the place make a huge effort, with costumed re-enactments to convey the details of Victorian military life. It's rather good fun.

Signposted from Chatham town.

The vast stones of Little Kit's Coty House (right) are the exposed chamber from a new stone age chambered tomb.

HEVER CASTLE

Privately owned • £££ • Usual hours

A truly beautiful little moated, fortified house which was the childhood home of Anne Boleyn, Henry VIII's second wife. Behind the stout gatehouse that makes up the whole front end of the building is a lovely timber-framed courtyard – but that's where the beauty ends, because beyond that Hever today is just a tidily restored house with some extremely peculiar furniture. The grounds are crowded with gift shops and coach parties, and the whole thing is something of a heritage theme park experience. It's a pretty place, but ultimately not all that rewarding.

Off B2026 north-east of East Grinstead; clearly signposted from all roads in the area.

KIT'S COTY HOUSE

English Heritage • Free • Open access

Quite a famous monument because of its unusual appearance, Kit's Coty House is actually the stone chamber from a large new stone age tomb. Its name is said to derive from the Celtic for 'chapel in the woods'. The long-vanished mound, 55 metres long, ran from east to west with the chamber at the east end – a similar layout to that of *Coldrum chambered tomb (page 103)*.

It's not terribly easy to find (though of course, an OS map helps): it's just west of the A229, where the road to Burham leaves the road to Aylesford at a sharp corner. The footpath to Kit's Coty runs uphill from by the junction, and the monument is just a few minutes' walk up the hill, in a field to the left of the path.

Just down the hill; a short way along the road, there's another ruined tomb, Lower (or Little) Kit's Coty House. Demolished in the 18th century for building material, this place is also known as Countless Stones, because it's said that its twenty-odd stones can't be counted, and the numbers often found chalked on the stones show that the story is still current.

Directions given above.

Crumbling though they are, the huge walls of Richborough Castle give a real impression of the size and importance of this fort, at the gateway to Roman Britain.

THE ROMANS ON THE SAXON SHORE

WHEN JULIUS CAESAR made his glory-hunting expedition to *Britannia* in 55 BC, it seems that he ignored the people of Kent, marching his troops straight through the county and heading for the other side of the Thames. Yet Caesar's influence on the future of Kent was huge, even though he left Britain later in the year and never came back.

By stomping mercilessly on the rebellious tribe of the Venetii, who controlled the major trade routes from Brittany to south-west England, and by encouraging links between Romanized Gaul and the tribes of south-eastern England, Caesar seems to have changed the entire economic and social map of the region.

When the Romans came to stay, led by the Emperor Claudius in 43 AD, they were welcomed in the south east of England, where trade with the Empire now flowed via the shortest route across the Channel. The port of *Rutupiae* (Richborough), a major supply base for the Claudian invasion, became the Roman gateway to Britain, and this unique role was marked by the construction in about 85 AD of an extremely unusual monument: a massive ceremonial

The landmark towers of the former Saxon minster at Reculver, built inside the walls of a Roman fort and abandoned after the sea cut away the cliff.

archway intended to impress visitors to Britain from the moment they set foot on its shores.

All that can be seen today of the monument is the top of the massive foundation, 40m (125ft) wide and 9m (30ft) deep and solidly built of flints in mortar. It's certainly something to

wonder at. Excavators in the 1920s tunnelled into the middle of it hoping to find a vault, but were disappointed. There's nothing there but solid stone.

It's to the closing days of the Roman empire, however, that the south coast of England owes its most exciting Roman monuments: a series of forts known as the Forts of the Saxon Shore, built to protect the coast against raids and possible attempts at settlement by Germanic barbarians. In many cases, there are substantial Roman walls to be seen at these sites.

RICHBOROUGH CASTLE (RUTUPIAE) ROMAN FORT

English Heritage; ££; usual hours; from Sandwich town centre, follow A257 towards Canterbury and turn down minor road signposted to Richborough; car park at site.

Although Richborough was, as we have seen, a vital port of entry for Romans arriving in Britannia, and a thriving town grew up here, the most prominent remains are the extremely impressive walls – surprisingly high, even if there is not a complete circuit – and encircling ditches of the later

Tumbling down the hillside at Lympne are the remains of a Roman fort sometimes known as Stutfallcastle. Although it is now miles from the sea, in Roman times the fort was probably a major naval base.

Saxon Shore fort, built about 275 AD. The town grew to be extremely large and prosperous (an amazing 56,000 Roman coins were found during excavations) and the guide book is a must to make sense of all the different phases of building which can just about be discerned. There are traces of a late Roman-era Christian church here, too, and Richborough has strong associations with St Augustine's landing in 597. His chapel stood just east of the Roman fort. Although the setting, with ugly nearby industrial plants encroaching on the view, is hardly the prettiest of contexts, this fort is still a fairly exciting site.

LYMPNE (PORTUS LEMANIS) ROMAN FORT

On private farmland; can be viewed from public footpath from near Lympne castle.

Perhaps the most interesting thing about this fort is that it vividly demonstrates the dramatic way in which this part of the Kentish coastline has altered over the years. When the Romans built their fort on this ridge, it was a sea cliff; now the sea is a long way away, across the flat canal-crossed expanse of recovered land. Only a few random pieces of

wall remain, tumbling down the hillside towards the sea, which is probably what gave the place its other name of Stutfallcastle. An altar to Neptune found in the main gateway, which is now in the British Museum, suggests that this was a naval base, possibly the home port of the British fleet in the 200s AD.

RECULVER (REGULBIUM) ROMAN FORT

English Heritage; free entry; open access at any reasonable time; in country park at Reculver, east of Herne Bay.

The twin towers of the church at Reculver, originally a Saxon minster, have long been a landmark for sailors, so much so that when the church was abandoned in the 1700s because it was sliding into the sea, the Admiralty bought the remains. The towers are just as much a landmark today for travellers on the nearby railway line, which in many ways is the best way to see the place, its full romance preserved by distance.

Close up, the towers are not all that romantic, and the remains of the Saxon Shore fort of *Regulbium*, within which the minster was built, is an exception to the general rule that Roman remains are always interesting just because they're Roman. It's basically just a bit of crumbly wall, though there are traces of gateway near the modern shoreline. The fort was built around 210 AD and was abandoned in about 360.

Left: there's half a circuit of fort walls at Reculver, but they're not too exciting.

SEE ALSO...

As well as Richborough, Lympne and Reculver, the other important Roman base on the Kent coast was, of course, Dover (*Dubris*), and you'll get a fair impression of the Roman harbour there from a visit to *Dover Roman Painted House (page 105)* which was probably a hostel at which important visitors would stay when they arrived in Britain. Some remains of the bastion of a fort wall can also be seen.

But there are several Saxon Shore forts in other southern English counties which are even more impressive than the ones in Kent, as follows...

PORTCHESTER, HAMPSHIRE

The best of the lot, with a square circuit of Roman fort walls – said the be the most complete in northern Europe – still standing 5m (27ft) high, fortified with rounded, hollow bastions which would have been equipped with light catapults for defence. Just for a bonus, there's a really good Norman keep built within the walls. (*See page 74.*)

PEVENSEY, SUSSEX

Another good circuit of Roman walls, but this time irregular rather than rectangular, to fit the peninsula on which the fort was built. Again, there's a medieval castle within. (*See page 100.*)

BURGH CASTLE, NORFOLK

The walls are very similar to those at Portchester, though rather more worn and standing on only three sides of the square. Still impressive, mind. (*See page 148.*)

Leeds Castle, built on two islands, looks splendid – but it's not everyone's cup of tea.

LEEDS CASTLE

Privately owned • ££££ • Usual hours (sometimes closed for conferences)

One of the most famous castles in England, though it's actually more of a stately home than a real castle. There are many good reasons for *not* going to Leeds Castle, especially if you prefer a good ruin. Besides giving the same impression of visiting a 'heritage theme park' that you get at *Hever (page 107)*, Leeds is expensive to visit and very crowded. But if for some reason you are obliged to go, it does have one big consolation in the form of the most unusual part of the building, the 'gloriette', kind of a sub-castle attached to the main castle by a narrow bridge but set on its own small island. It looks extremely cute from the outside and has been very sensitively restored on the inside.

Although most of what you see today is 19th-century rebuilding or restoration, the castle is in fact a genuine medieval royal castle with a long history. It was given to King Edward I in about 1278 in part payment of a debt, and he put a lot of work into improving its defences (particularly the water defences) and added a large barbican, now ruined, in front of the main gate that leads to the larger of the castle's two islands.

Clearly signposted from junction 8 of the M20 via the A20.

LULLINGSTONE ROMAN VILLA

English Heritage • ££ • usual hours

Allowing for the fact that the remains of Roman buildings tend to be mere foundations, this is probably the most impressive villa in the country. Discovered as recently as 1939 and roofed over, so that it's now an 'indoor' site – and consequently a very good bet for a rainy day – it not only has enough of the walls left to give you a good impression of what the building might have been like, but also boasts an impressive mosaic floor showing Bellerophon, riding Pegasus, spearing the fire-breathing Chimera.

The excavators also found lots of amazing objects at Lullingstone, including a couple of large busts and the remains of wall paintings on plaster. My favourite finds, though, are some clay roof tiles which bear the footprints of farmyard animals like cats and chickens which wandered across the soft clay while the tiles were laid out to dry.

Completing the picture, several other buildings have been excavated in the area around the villa, including a mausoleum on the hill behind and a large granary near the stream in front. Rather than being a posh country house, the villa seems to have been the farmhouse of a large, prosperous farming estate. A visit will go a long way to giving you a better idea of what this relatively settled and civilised part of the country must have been like in Roman times.

Clearly signposted from A225 near Eynsford.

Lullingstone Roman villa has an amazing mosaic floor (pictured right), but also there is enough of the walls left to give a good idea of what the house was like.

Lullingstone's famous mosaic is best seen from the gallery at first floor level.

Once an important guard point on a major trade route, Sutton Valence has been abandoned since the 1200s.

also responsible for the cathedral at Rochester and the stone curtain walls, but not the keep, of the castle there (*see next page*) and founded a nunnery near West Malling.

Just south of West Malling town centre; follow road through town, and St Leonard's Tower is opposite the country park

SCOTNEY CASTLE

National Trust • £££ • Usual hours

The real draw at Scotney is the gardens. The remains of the castle, with parts of a 17th century house attached, are little more than an ornamental folly next to the lake. All the same, it is a very beautiful spot, and during the summer months you can get a look at the interior of the remaining castle tower. Scotney was first fortified, like many other houses in the area, after the French raids in 1377. Originally the moat surrounded two islands, one of which had a curtain wall with four towers.

Signposted from A21 (take care on difficult turning); car park.

Below: The round tower is all that is left of the castle at Scotney, but it's a very picturesque spot.

ST LEONARD'S TOWER, WEST MALLING

English Heritage • Free • Open access to exterior only, at any reasonable time

It seems a tremendous shame that visitors only get to see the outside of this small Norman keep, because it's a very handsome little building. It was built around 1080 and is thought to be the work of Gundulf, Bishop of Rochester from 1077, who enjoyed a fine reputation as a builder; he was

SUTTON VALENCE KEEP

English Heritage • Free • Open access at any reasonable time to exterior only

This is just a few pieces of wall from a small keep built in the 1100s, and abandoned as early as the 1200s. Sited at the top of the ridge, with extensive views to the south, it was almost certainly built to guard the important trade route from Rye to Maidstone (and very likely to take taxes from everyone who passed, too).

It's a very modest ruin, but it's good to spend a few minutes here looking out over the vale and contemplating the comings and goings of 800 years ago, and you might like to get some lunch in one of the village's pubs.

On east side of Sutton Valence village; turn to east off A274 and follow right-hand (downhill) branch of fork in village road.

Rochester's is the biggest and most impressive Norman keep in the whole of England – it's simply unmissable.

ROCHESTER CASTLE

Rochester City Council and English Heritage • ££ • Usual hours

The largest Norman keep in the country is a splendid sight, dominating the town of Rochester and the Medway estuary, and its interior is impressive too, in a powerful, industrial way. The vast, warehouse-like interior was burnt out and abandoned hundreds of years ago, and looking down into the keep from the roof-walk is a pretty scary experience.

Rochester was hugely important because it guarded the main route from the Channel ports to London, the Roman road of Watling Street, which crossed the Medway here, and it has a very colourful history, having been besieged on at least three occasions. It's only a pity that there's not much to see at the castle apart from the keep. The curtain walls were the work of Gundulf, Bishop of Rochester, who built the White Tower in London and the keeps at Colchester and Canterbury; but these walls were extensively rebuilt between 1367 and 1383 under King Edward III and King Richard II and neglected after the end of the 14th century. The walls are impressive from the outside, but within there is just a public park.

So it's the keep that draws the attention, built shortly after Henry I issued a licence for it in 1127. For all

Inside, the keep is vast and dark, with stairs leading up for a vertiginous view from the top.

its size, there's not that much to explore, so undoubtedly your visit will be more rewarding if you read the history in the guide book before looking round. For example, you'll discover that there's a good reason why one of the towers on the corner of the keep is cylindrical where the others are square. It was rebuilt after a siege in the autumn of 1215, just months after the signing of Magna Carta, when rebellious barons took over and held the royal castle against King John. When the attackers broke through the outer walls and the defenders holed up in the keep, the king's miners dug a tunnel under the tower, until only their wooden pit props were holding it up. On November 25th the king sent out an urgent messenger to bring 'with all speed by day and night forty of the fattest pigs of the sort least good for eating', and the pig fat was used to burn down the props and bring down the tower.

The nearby cathedral (also founded by Gundulf and said to be the second oldest in England) and the old town are well worth a look, too, which makes Rochester a pleasant (and easy) day trip from London.

Easily found in Rochester town centre.

The stout gatehouse of Tonbridge Castle is the main surviving remnant, but the original Norman mound still stands in the trees to the left.

TONBRIDGE CASTLE

Local council • Grounds: open access at any reasonable time; Gatehouse museum: £££, usual hours

Only a gatehouse remains of the castle buildings, along with the mound (motte) of the original Norman castle. There's a decent little museum, but it's something of a 'heritage experience', with an audio tour and lots of waxwork figures, and it's rather too expensive.

Easy to find in Tonbridge town centre.

UPNOR CASTLE

English Heritage • ££ • Usual hours

Although it's really just a modest fort guarding the river Medway and the approach to the great naval dockyards, Upnor is a very pleasant place to visit, in part because of its

The peaceful grounds of Upnor, which in the 1660s fired its guns on Dutch ships raiding up the Medway.

tranquil setting by the river Medway, but also because it's so neat and tidy. The fort was built between 1559 and 1567 on the orders of Queen Elizabeth I and was frequently altered over the years, until in 1668 it was downgraded to be used as a magazine, supplying powder and shot to warships anchored in the river. It had seen action the previous year during a Dutch raid which caused a major rethink of the defences of the Medway estuary.

As you look round the various buildings of the fort – the gatehouse, the main magazine and gun position, and the water bastion that sticks out into the river – there's a pleasant

surprise at every turn, such as the picture of a ship, dating from around 1720, drawn graffiti-style on the walls of the gatehouse, or the beautifully crafted replica powder barrels in the magazine. It's a lovely spot.

In village of Upnor, north of Rochester; from A228, follow signs to village car park.

WALMER CASTLE

English Heritage • ££ • Usual hours

You should probably bite the bullet and take this as a pair with nearby *Deal Castle*, because the two will give you very different impressions of the castles built by Henry VIII. Walmer has been the official residence of the Wardens of the Cinque Ports since 1709, and the upshot of this is that it's more like a stately home than a castle, and very different from the stark simplicity of Deal. Walmer has pleasant gardens, plush carpets, interesting *objets d'art* and bedrooms where Queen Victoria and Wellington stayed, but it's much less fun than Deal, and in comparison it's also rather expensive.

On minor road near shore in Walmer, a couple of miles south of Deal; clearly signposted from A258.

Left: Walmer Castle is a pretty conversion of one of Henry VIII's forts into a grand home. For all its style, it's not as interesting as Deal Castle (page 103).

SEE ALSO...

ADDINGTON PARK CHAMBERED LONG BARROW *and* THE CHESTNUTS CHAMBERED TOMB, *by minor road* W *of Addington,* N *of West Malling* – Two ruined new stone age tombs which are certainly worth a quick look if you're a fan of this kind of thing. The Chestnuts tomb is in a garden: permission needed from the owner.

DOVER WESTERN HEIGHTS and KNIGHTS TEMPLAR CHURCH (pictured, right), *to* W *of Dover town centre* – English Heritage owns parts of the moat of a vast 19th century fort which dominated this hillside, the Western Heights (in a country park, it's best seen from *Dover Castle*). Nearby are the foundations of a round chapel of the mysterious Knights Templar. It's not really very interesting, though.

GRAVESEND FORT and MILTON CHANTRY, *Gravesend town centre* – Right across the Thames from the huge fort at *Tilbury, Essex,* the 18th-century fort at Gravesend helped guard the docks and river. The few magazines and ramparts that are left, in a town park, are more of a local curiosity than an attraction for visitors. The small 14th-century building known as Milton Chantry was once the chapel of a leper hospital; it now houses an English Heritage exhibition. The best reason to stop in at Gravesend is to take the passenger ferry across the river to visit Tilbury Fort.

COOLING CASTLE (pictured above and right) *on minor road through Cooling, north of Rochester* – Amazing. The people who live here have a large ruined medieval castle in their garden; they've looked into restoring it for public visits, but half a million pounds is needed to make it safe. The gatehouse can easily be seen from the road, but please do respect the owners' privacy.

A licence to fortify a house was granted in 1381, at the time of the great French invasion scare, to a local bigwig called John de Cobham; but he decided instead that he would build this castle, completed in 1385. He was anxious, however, to make sure no one (especially the king) thought he was getting ideas above his station, so a copper plaque on the massive gatehouse announces:

Knouwyth that beth and schul be
That I am made in help of the cuntre
In knowing of whyche thyng
Thys is chartre and wytnessyng.

FORT LUTON, *on Magpie Hall Road, to* SE *of Chatham, just off A2* – Bizarre and eccentric use of a smallish Victorian fort as a kind of kids' playground crossed with a local history museum. Amateurish and silly, but if you're an enthusiast of the period it's worth a quick visit for the story of how the army blew up their own fort during exercises.

IGHTHAM MOTE (pictured above), *signposted from Ivy Hatch village, just off A227* E *of Sevenoaks* – This National Trust property (££, *usual hours*) is a smashing little medieval manor house, built around 1340 and surrounded by a moat. Apart from its general picturesque appeal, it's well worth a look for the medieval hall, which is quite similar to – although very much smaller than – the one at *Penshurst Place (next page).*

LYMPNE CASTLE, *signposted in Lympne village, nr Hythe* – Nice but boring, this fortified building from the 1300s comprises a great hall with a tower at each end. Privately owned (*££, opening hours limited to May to September*) and now a conference centre, it's really a country house.

MAISON DIEU (pictured above), *by A2 in Ospringe, near Faversham* – Cute little house from the 1500s, basically a medieval hospital, owned by English Heritage and run by local history society (*££, April to October, weekend and bank holidays only*).

OLDBURY HILLFORT (pictured right), *near Ightham* – In a wooded country park, this is a lovely spot for a walk.

OLD SOAR MANOR, PLAXTOL, *signposted on minor roads near Plaxtol village* – Jointly owned by English Heritage and National Trust (*free entry; usual hours, April to September*), this is just a couple of rooms (chapel and 'solar') from a knight's manor house of the 1200s, but they are very old, very beautiful and very much worth seeing.

PENSHURST PLACE (pictured above), *clearly signposted on minor roads* w *of Tonbridge* – The great hall of this fortified manor house is just amazing, but the rest of it is a dull stately home and admission is pretty expensive (*privately owned, ££££, usual hours*).

SALTWOOD CASTLE, *to* N *of Hythe* – Home of politician Alan Clarke, Saltwood is not open to visitors, although you can see it from the footpath that skirts the walls (please respect the occupants' privacy). It was the palace of the Archbishop of Canterbury and, like the city, was refortified heavily for artillery at the time of the French invasion scares in the 1380s, with a big gatehouse and extensive water defences.

AND...

BIGBURY HILLFORT, Harbledown, nr Canterbury; JULIBERRIE'S GRAVE long barrow, nr Chilham; HORNE'S PLACE CHAPEL, nr Appledore (once part of a house from the 1300s); KNOLE, near Sevenoaks (National Trust; the largest private house in England, built in 1456); ST JOHN'S COMMANDERY, Swingfield (medieval chapel built by Knights Hospitallers, converted to a house in the 1500s); TEMPLE MANOR, Rochester (a manor house from the 1200s built by the Templars).

BUT NOT...

ALLINGTON CASTLE, *Maidstone*, is a modern restoration of a castle from the 1280s which later became a farmhouse and is now a conference centre, not open to visitors; BOXLEY ABBEY, *near Maidstone*, is a private house and not open to visitors; CHIDDINGSTONE CASTLE, *near Hever*, is not a castle at all, but a stately home, and not a very old one at that; CHILHAM CASTLE is a fine house and has a stout tower, built about 1170, in the garden, but is not open to visitors; LULLINGSTONE CASTLE is also a house, though it's worth strolling along from *Lullingstone Roman villa* for a look at the gatehouse.

Surrey

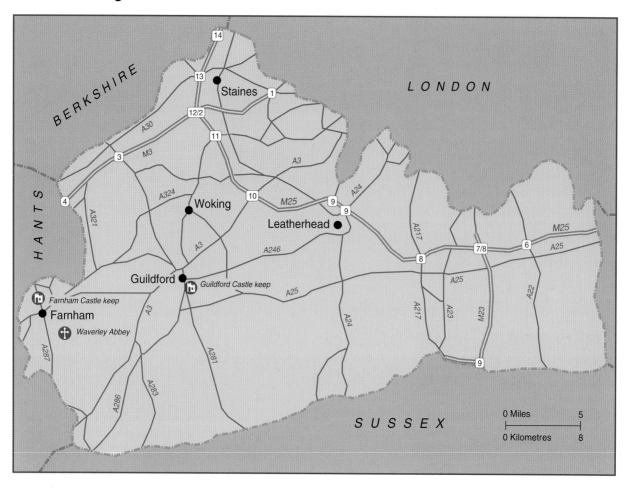

FARNHAM CASTLE KEEP

English Heritage • £££ • Usual hours

Odd place, this. You can tell from old pictures that a few hundred years ago, Farnham was a vast and fine-looking castle, but today the keep – the only part of the much-rebuilt castle that you can now visit – does not have a lot to offer. Certainly it's a formidable structure, the massive 13th-century shell keep walls having been built around, rather than on top of, the original 12th-century mound. But there's not much to see apart from a deep well inside the foundations of the original square tower, which is a candidate for England's most impressive hole in the ground.

The castle's history is rather more interesting than its structure. The original tower was built in the mid-1100s by the colourful Henry of Blois, Bishop of Winchester and brother of King Stephen, more of whose works are described in the chapter that covers *Hampshire*.

Just north of Farnham's rather attractive town centre; parking available at castle, but it's only a short walk up the hill.

GUILDFORD CASTLE KEEP

Owned by Guildford Council, operated by Surrey Archaeology Society • £ • Usual hours

Once you've fought your way through the modern maze of roads that surrounds it, what's left of the old town of Guildford is a pleasant place to stop for a cup of tea. While you're about it, the castle keep is worth a look in at, though there's not an awful lot to see apart from the main fabric

The gatehouse of the keep at Farnham is probably its most attractive feature.

Guildford's keep has survived more or less intact, probably because it was too robust to dismantle.

of the keep which had a later career as the town jail.

Its history is a little obscure, though the original motte may have been one of the earliest Norman castles in England. It was followed by a shell keep and then, in the mid-1100s, by the strong but not especially large stone keep that survives to this day. Its moment of fame came in June 1216 when, like Winchester, Reigate and Farnham, it was captured by Louis, Dauphin of France, whose invasion force had been invited to England by barons rebelling against King John.

Just down the hill from the castle is a surviving medieval gate and the small but interesting (and free) local history museum.

Signposted in town centre, towards the southern end of the old town; parking in nearby streets or car parks.

WAVERLEY ABBEY

REMAINS

English Heritage • Free • Open access at any reasonable time

Quite a romantic ruin, considering the suburban character of the county, Waverley Abbey owes its survival and its current appeal (like *Netley* in *Hampshire* and *Bayham* in *Sussex*) to the fact that it became a ready-made folly in the grounds of a stately home. Waverley was the first Cistercian abbey in Britain, founded in 1128, and in its graceful setting by the River Wey, it's a beautiful ruin. There's just enough left of the 13th-century buildings to give a reasonable impression of the scale and grace of the abbey, and there are a few interesting details to take a peek at.

In grounds of Waverley House; signposted from B3001 a couple of miles south of Farnham; limited car parking; shortish, level walk to abbey ruins.

Waverley abbey is a picturesque ruin, standing in a tranquil riverside setting and easily reached from London.

London

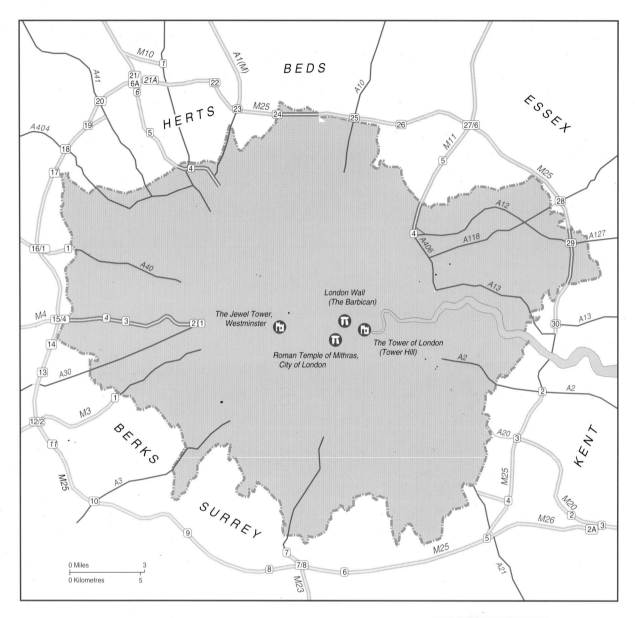

The Jewel Tower,
Westminster

London Wall
(The Barbican)

Roman Temple of Mithras,
City of London

The Tower of London
(Tower Hill)

THE CITY OF LONDON grew up at the lowest point on the Thames that could safely be crossed by a bridge. After the rebellion of the Iceni in 61 AD, during which the town was burned to the ground, *Londinium* became the capital of the province of *Britannia* and the place of residence of its governor, who lived in a splendid palace by the river near what is now Suffolk Lane. At Cripplegate a fort was built, probably to house a ceremonial garrison for the governor; its gate can still be seen. One of the most surprising things about London is that there are still traces of its Roman past here and there, but the most significant monument in the city is the *Tower of London*. Dating right back to the 1070s, the White Tower was the first great stone keep built in England by the Normans, and it's still very impressive.

*Medieval wall,
City of London*

THE JEWEL TOWER, WESTMINSTER

English Heritage • ££ • Usual hours

This is one of the oldest buildings in Westminster, a remnant of the royal palace that preceded the modern Parliament building. It was built in the 1300s by Edward III to house his personal treasure, including his clothes. It now, appropriately enough when you consider where it stands, contains an exhibition on the history and procedures of Parliament. Neither the building nor the exhibition is terribly thrilling, though.

Right next to Westminster Cathedral, opposite the Houses of Parliament.

LONDON WALL

City council • Free • Open access at any reasonable time

Not a lot of people know that there are some quite substantial stretches of the City of London's medieval city wall, nor do they realise that this wall stood on the foundations of a Roman wall, of which quite a bit

This stretch of London's medieval city wall, near Tower Hill tube, is built on Roman foundations.

also still survives. There's a signposted walk along the course of the wall, from Tower Hill tube station to the Museum of London at the Barbican (or, of course, vice versa), with lots of informative signboards along the way. It's a very good way to get in touch with the city's history. You'll learn, for example, that the street called Houndsditch runs on the course of the moat-like, water-filled ditch that ran outside the city wall. This was a foul watercourse used as a rubbish tip and sewer, and it got its name from the number of dead dogs that were usually found in it.

It's interesting to see great slabs of ancient wall and even, in the gardens of the Barbican flats, vast towers. Probably the most dramatic single item is the gate of a Roman fort in the grounds of the Museum of London, which is opened to visitors roughly one weekend a month.

From Tower Hill tube to the Museum of London, Barbican.

Left: The Jewel Tower at Westminster was built to guard Edward III's treasure. And his clothes.

The Temple of Mithras is one of the most unusual sights in London (if not a hugely exciting one).

CITY OF LONDON TEMPLE OF MITHRAS

City council • Free • Open access at any reasonable time

This is a fairly extraordinary thing to find sitting in the streets of London. It's not the most dramatic of monuments to look at, but it is an important relic of London's Roman past. It was originally found under the foundations of a large building some 55m (180ft) from its present site, and was moved wholesale to preserve it. Also found were various statues and cult objects, including a head of the god Mithras and a carving of the bull-slaying which was part of the legend associated with the god. These are on display in the Museum of London.

Mithras was the Zoroastrian god of light, and his worship required a strict adherence to a demanding code of personal morality. There were seven stages of initiation to get through, each of which involved passing physical and psychological tests. Mithraic temples were set underground and designed to look like caves. Most of the ones found in Britain are next to forts, but this one appears to have been built and used by city merchants.

On the south side of Queen Victoria Street, a short walk west from Mansion House tube.

At the heart of the Tower of London is the White Tower, the first Norman keep to be built in England.

THE TOWER OF LONDON

HM The Queen • ££££ • Usual hours

This is one of the greatest medieval castles of England, and it's well worth seeing despite the steep entrance fee and the vast numbers of visitors.

At the heart of the castle is the great Norman keep called the White Tower. (Like most keeps, it would have been whitewashed – there's a castle called White Castle in Wales that got its name for the same reason.) Details like the corner turrets are later and contribute to its Tudor appearance, but this is basically the keep as built in 1079 or shortly after.

The castle has seen many later alterations and additions from the 1100s through to Victorian times, most importantly the conversion to a concentric pattern by Edward I around 1300 – but it retains an authentic medieval feel. The Tower has played such a prominent part in English history that even fripperies like the ravens, the Beefeaters and the Crown Jewels don't detract from its interest.

By the Thames at Tower Bridge; a short walk from Tower Hill Underground station.

SEE ALSO...

ALL HALLOWS BY THE TOWER ROMAN VILLA, *in the crypt of the church, near the Tower of London* – Fragments of wall, some tile floors and a few musty museum exhibits. Not thrilling, but it is appealingly old-fashioned. (*Church authorities, £, usual hours.*)

THE BRITISH MUSEUM, *not far from Tottenham Court Road tube* – Has all the finest archaeological treasures of Britain on permanent display, and it's free to get in. Utterly brilliant.

CAESAR'S CAMP HILLFORT, *Wimbledon Common* – An iron age hillfort, but not in good condition and overrun by a golf course. Not very interesting.

WESTMINSTER ABBEY CHAPTER HOUSE, *near the Houses of Parliament* – A large, round room with the most fascinating medieval clay floor tiles. Highly recommended. (*English Heritage, ££, usual hours.*)

WESTMINSTER HALL, *now part of the Houses of Parliament* – Sadly you can only get to see it on a tour if you're British and you write to your MP. When this vast hall was built by William Rufus in about 1090 it was the largest hall in Europe, though the bad-tempered king is said to have complained that it was not half big enough. A true national treasure.

WINCHESTER PALACE, *Southwark* – The remains of a medieval palace of the Bishops of Winchester consist of nothing more than a couple of bits of wall and a broken rose window. (*English Heritage , free , open access at any reasonable time.*)

Berkshire & Oxfordshire

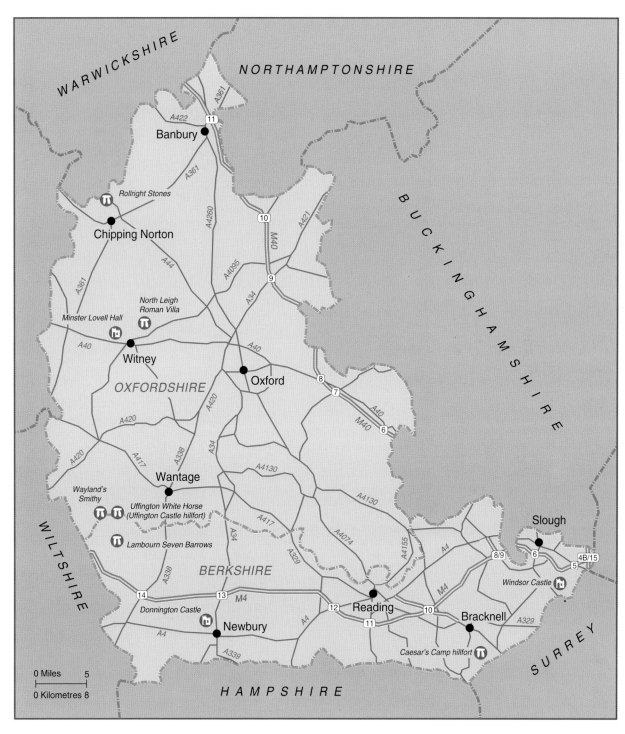

TWO OF THE FINEST prehistoric sites in England have belonged to first one,
then the other of these counties in recent years: they are *Wayland's Smithy*, a
superb neolithic chambered long barrow situated on the ancient track known
as the Ridgeway, and the truly glorious *Uffington White Horse*.

Donnington Castle was a favourite of Elizabeth I. It was already a ruin, but surrounded by earthworks, when one of the greatest sieges of the Civil War took place here.

CAESAR'S CAMP

Royal Estates • Free • Open access at any reasonable time

Trees have recently been cleared from this large hillfort, making its size easier to appreciate. Set in a wooded country park, it's an excellent place to go for a good walk. Not much is known about the fort, though, because the site has never been excavated.

Off A322 south of Bracknell, on B3430, in country park (clearly signposted, car park); it's a fairly long walk to the hillfort.

Caesar's Camp – a big hillfort in good, wild woodland, yet not far from London.

DONNINGTON CASTLE

English Heritage • Free • Open access during usual hours only (no cars after 6.30pm); interior occasionally open.

Strangely, Donnington's greatest moment came during the Civil War, when there was no more of the castle standing than there is today. The sole surviving gatehouse was surrounded by a highly effective set of 'star' earthworks, and the Royalist garrison held out for two years against a series of Parliamentarian sieges, until finally the firepower of a gigantic mortar – the effects of one shot from which can be seen in a massive, brick-patched hole in the walls of the gatehouse – persuaded the defenders to surrender.

In its heyday, this modern, cosy castle (built late 1300s) was one of Queen Elizabeth's favourite houses. The surviving gatehouse makes a very pretty romantic ruin, but there isn't an awful lot to see.

Signposted from centre of Donnington village (just north of Newbury on B4494).

Lambourn is an ideal place to see the various kinds of earthen barrow, including a rare disc barrow.

LAMBOURN
SEVEN BARROWS

English Nature • Free • Open access at any reasonable time

This is a good collection of different kinds of earthen round barrows, set in lovely, sweeping chalk downland. There is a fine 'disc barrow', one of several types usually associated with important female burials.

A few miles north of Lambourn, off B4001, about a mile along minor road to Uffington; small car park near the bend in the road.

From inside the walls, Windsor Castle somehow manages to look rather less huge and grand than it does from outside. On the left here is St George's Chapel.

WINDSOR CASTLE

*Royal palace • ££££ • Usual hours
(sometimes closed for state business)*

Naturally enough, what draws the crowds to Windsor is that it's the home of royalty. Certainly it's a very fine-looking castle (though you have to remember that it owes as much to Victorian rebuilding as it does to medieval military architects), and it dominates the small town of Windsor with an authentic sense of royal authority, but it actually looks its best from outside. I'd recommend that you wander around, get a good look at the outside of the castle – maybe pop down to the river, or spend some time in Windsor Great Park, with its splendid avenue of trees – and save the vast entrance fee (nearly £10) for shopping or a good meal.

If you can't resist the lure of a royal palace, then you pays your money and you gets access to three specific parts of the castle. First there's the opulently furnished state apartments – the reception rooms for important visitors, if you like – where the Wellington Room, a dining room with an enormous table in the middle, is particularly impressive. Here, too, is the Long Gallery, recently restored after the great fire and looking particularly sumptuous.

The other main areas of the castle you can visit are the lower ward, where you can see the changing of the guard every day at 11 o'clock, and St George's Chapel, which isn't really all that exciting, though attached to it is the ornate Albert Memorial Chapel, Victoria's shrine to her dead husband.

In Windsor town centre; you can't miss it.

The Round Tower – originally a Norman shell keep, but greatly rebuilt in Victorian times – is home to the Queen's private apartments, so you're not allowed in.

This is the approach to the castle gate. You can come this far and get a closer look at the walls and towers without paying, which I think is a smart move.

SEE ALSO...

WALBURY CAMP HILLFORT, *on ridge south of Inkpen* – Very large, and in an impressive setting on the highest point on chalk in England, but access to the ramparts is very limited, so it's really not worth a special trip. Close by is COOMBE GIBBETT LONG BARROW (also called Inkpen Beacon) – A big earthen long barrow sited imposingly on the crest of the ridge.

The ruins of Minster Lovell Hall, in a very pretty riverbank setting, are as close as Oxfordshire gets to a castle.

MINSTER LOVELL HALL

English Heritage • Free • Open access at any reasonable time

The attractive ruin of a fortified manor house from the 1400s, in a very pleasant setting on the banks of a small river called the Windrush. The remains are very substantial, with high walls and some interesting doorways, though there aren't any upstairs rooms or indoor spaces.

The area is well known for its old stone villages and pleasant walks and, if you don't fancy taking on anything more strenuous, there's a short, easy walk from the Hall to see the exterior of a medieval dovecote.

Signposted in Minster Lovell village, just off A40 west of Witney; short walk from car parking area through churchyard to hall.

NORTH LEIGH ROMAN VILLA

English Heritage • Free • Open access at any reasonable time

Little remains except foundation-level walls, but it is enough to show that this was a big, wealthy country house. Originally it had four wings around a square courtyard, but only three wings are visible. A modern building in one corner covers the mosaic floor of the dining room, which you can only peer at through the windows: you can make it out well enough to tell that it was a rather classy piece of work: it's in the local style known as 'Cirencester school', like the mosaics at *Chedworth, Gloucestershire.*

Signposted from A4095; ten-minute walk from lay-by on minor road north of the village of East End.

ROLLRIGHT STONES

STONE CIRCLE

& CHAMBERED TOMB

Rollright Trust • £ • Usual hours

This is one of the best-known of England's smaller stone circles, and it's also Britain's most easterly circle. It's not very grand or dramatic, however, and it does seem to puzzle visitors who are expecting it to look like Stonehenge or Avebury.

There are actually three monuments in a small area here: the stone circle, a ruined burial chamber and a single standing stone. The three are linked by a legend that they are a king and his men turned to stone by a witch. The monuments are believed to have been built at more or less the same time, about 2000 BC.

The stone circle, known as the King's Men, is thought to have originally had about 105 stones forming a continuous wall except for one small entrance gap. The stones are said to be uncountable, and there is a tradition that anyone counting them three times and getting the same total each time can have a wish granted. (The guide leaflet states that there are 'seventy-something',

The single standing stone at Rollright known as the King Stone owes its shape to a habit among sightseers in the 19th century of hacking pieces off to take home.

The five stones known as the Whispering Knights are the remains of a stone age burial chamber of a type known as a portal dolmen.

Big, but flattened: North Leigh Roman villa isn't hugely evocative. The building on the right covers a mosaic floor.

though I have it on good authority that there are actually 77).

It's an odd place: far less dramatic than you might expect, as we've said already, and yet it does have an indefinable frisson of ancient mystery to it. Apparently, in the 1700s, young people used still to gather here for dances and feasting on midsummer's eve, which does suggest that echoes of the long-lost ceremonial traditions have lived on.

Just across the road from the stone circle is the King Stone, a single standing stone that may have been a marker for a bronze age cemetery but could equally well have been associated with the circle or have been part of a burial chamber. It owes its unusual shape to a trend among 19th-century visitors for hacking lumps off the side of the stone to take home as souvenirs.

Most people miss out on the third monument in the group, which is just a short walk down the road and along a footpath on the edge of a field. This group of five stones is known as the

Rollright stone circle, also known as the King's Men, originally consisted of closely set stones with just one gap.

Whispering Knights, and it's a ruined stone age burial chamber of the type known as a 'portal dolmen', with two of the uprights forming a 'doorway' partially blocked by another upright. The huge capstone has fallen.

It's certainly an unusual group of monuments, but the circle is really the only outstanding one.

Next to minor road between Little Compton and Great Rollright, just off A3400.

UFFINGTON WHITE HORSE
(UFFINGTON CASTLE HILLFORT)

English Heritage and National Trust • Free • Open access at any reasonable time

The Uffington White Horse is easily the finest and most interesting of all the chalk-cut hill figures in England, and recent investigations have shown that it is far more ancient than anyone could have imagined.

There are lots of white horses around, and most are quite modern (though some are thought to have been re-cut on top of older figures). Uffington was always considered to be very much older: possibly Celtic, because the free-flowing lines of the design are so similar to Celtic art. Recently, though, a new technique very similar to radio-carbon dating was used to establish the date at which the chalk was first exposed, and this showed that the White Horse dates back to around 2000 BC. Excavations also established that the shape has been altered surprisingly little over the years by the regular re-cutting that it receives.

Naturally the best place to see the

Just recently, experts discovered that the Uffington White Horse is an astonishing 4000 years old.

horse is from the valley below, but you can get right up next to it (the area gets a lot of visitors, so you have to walk some distance from the car park). Just above the hill figure is an iron age hillfort: its ramparts aren't large, but they were originally lined with sarsen stones.

Behind the fort runs the ancient track of the Ridgeway, with the stone age tomb of *Wayland's Smithy* (*next page*) just a short walk away. The area drips with ancient history, and the views are fabulous, too.

Signposted from B4057 west of Wantage.

Wayland's Smithy is undoubtedly one of the finest ancient monuments in England, in a very atmospheric setting.

WAYLAND'S SMITHY

English Heritage • Free • Open access at any reasonable time

This is one of the most atmospheric places you could wish to find, its air of cathedral-like sanctity and serenity enhanced by the fact that you can only reach it on foot along the ancient track of the Ridgeway. It stands off to the side of the track in a grove of beech trees: leaves rustle in the breeze, and dappled light plays on the massive sarsen stones which form the facade of the huge monument.

The technical details are secondary to the feel of the place, but it has been excavated with great care and a great deal has been learnt about its development. Like many of the great chambered tombs, it started life as a wooden mortuary structure, with a stone floor, covered over with a long earth mound. Only about 50 years after this first structure was built, around 2800 BC, it was incorporated into the great wedge-shaped earth mound you see today, 55m (180ft) long and surrounded by a kerb of sarsen stones. Behind the facade, a passage leads through an antechamber to a cross-shaped burial chamber in which the remains of eight people (but no thigh bones) were found.

Legend has it that the Norse god Wayland the Smith made shoes for the Uffington horse, and it is said that a traveller on the Ridgeway whose horse has lost a shoe can leave the horse by the tomb, put a coin on a stone and come back later to find the horse shod and the money gone.

A half-hour walk on the Ridgeway from Uffington National Trust car park. (Can be accessed by unmetalled road up the hill from Compton Beauchamp to the Ridgeway.)

SEE ALSO...

BROUGHTON CASTLE (pictured right), *off the B4035 near Banbury* – Started life as a moated, defended manor and grew up into a pleasant house. The moat's still there, the gardens are rather charming and the tour of the house is quite enjoyable, culminating with a walk on the roof. Very nice. (*Privately owned, £££, limited hours – several afternoons a week.*)

DEDDINGTON CASTLE, *on the east side of Deddington* – The remains consist of earthworks only and really aren't all that interesting. (*English Heritage, free, open access.*)

HOAR STONE CHAMBERED BARROW, *off B4022 south of Enstone, down minor road on the left to Fulwell, in trees to right of road a few yards down* – remains of a neolithic barrow made from *very* big stones. Neglected, but quietly impressive.

AND...

ALFRED'S CASTLE HILLFORT, *south-east of Ashbury on footpath from B4000*, said to be where King Alfred's army gathered in 871; CHASTLETON BARROW FORT, *south-east of Chastleton (near Moreton-in-Marsh)*, has a big rampart, which was stone-faced, but no ditch; DYKE HILLS PROMONTORY FORT, *on path from south end of Dorchester-on-Thames*, defended on three sides by rivers; SINODUN HILLFORT, *Little Wittenham, footpath from car park on the road to Brightwell* – in a fine setting with excellent views. ALSO: Wroxton Abbey, near Banbury, is a house (now a school) and not open.

Gloucestershire

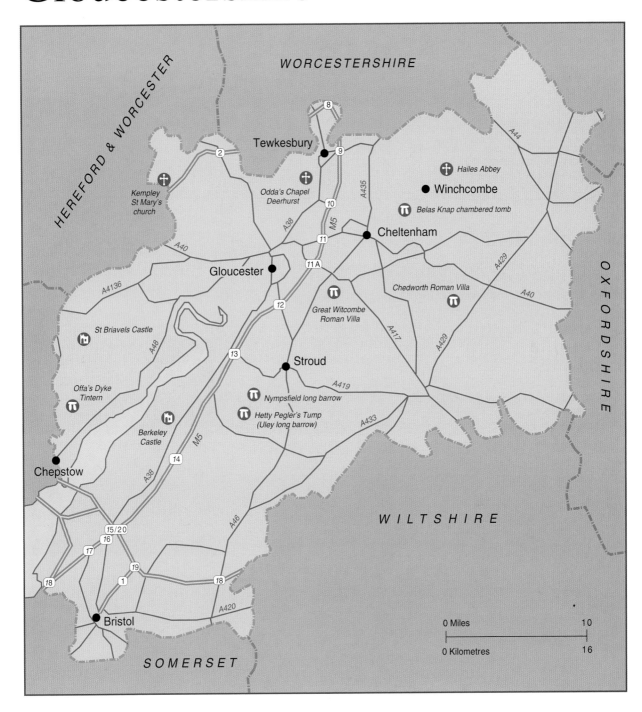

GLOUCESTERSHIRE's intriguing landscape, from the Severn to the Cotswolds, shows significant evidence of occupation from neolithic times and was one of the most populous parts of Britain during the Roman period. Its most pleasing monument, however, is the painted church at *Kempley, St Mary's.*

COTSWOLD-SEVERN CHAMBERED TOMBS

If Gloucestershire has a particular claim to archaeological fame, it is the county's excellent chambered tombs, monuments which are among the oldest buildings in the world. Because the tombs in this area are built from similar materials and share certain architectural details, they are grouped together and are thought to represent a local cultural tradition.

One feature shared by many of the Cotswold-Severn tombs is a 'horned' forecourt built from dry stone walling, which must surely have had some ceremonial purpose, though of course nobody knows what.

The brilliant thing about Hetty Pegler's Tump is the long passage you have to crawl down to reach the chambers.

BELAS KNAP

English Heritage • Free • Open access at any reasonable time; 20-minute walk (uphill, naturally) on the Cotswold Way – the start of the walk is clearly signposted on a minor road off the B4632 south of Winchcombe.

This is an exceptionally large and unusual monument. The long mound is enormous, with a fine dry-stone forecourt at the north end in the middle of which is a false entrance. The genuine burial chambers, almost big enough to stand up in, are on the sides of the mound, two on one side and one on the other with a fourth in the tail end of the mound. The bones of at least 38 people were found in the chambers. It's very imposing, but the next one is more approachable...

You have to see Belas Knap to appreciate it: it's big and brooding and brutally impressive.

HETTY PEGLER'S TUMP (ULEY LONG BARROW)

English Heritage • Free • Open access at any reasonable time; signposted on west side of B4066 just north of Uley.

The beauty of this chambered tomb is that it has a long passage to crawl down, for that authentic sense of ancient mysteries lurking deep within the bowels of the earth. It's not *too* scary, but you will need a torch. Originally there were two pairs of chambers, one each side of the passage, and although two have now been blocked, you can still get in to the other two. As well as bones in the chambers, excavations uncovered two skeletons outside the entrance, along with the jaws of boars.

BEST OF THE REST...

NYMPSFIELD LONG BARROW (*English Heritage; free; open access at any reasonable time*), *in country park beside the B4066* – Just along the ridge from Hetty Pegler's Tump is a country park with splendid views over the Severn valley, and just a few metres away from the car park is this ruined but restored chambered tomb. The mound and the stones that formed the roof of the passage are missing, so it's like a dissected version of a tomb. Worth a quick look.

Nympsfield chambered tomb, just along the ridge from Hetty Pegler's Tump, is ruined.

SEE ALSO...

Several more tombs in the Cotswold-Severn group can be viewed if you're keen, but none of them is especially exciting. Two are in the care of English Heritage (both free; open access at any reasonable time). The trouble with NOTGROVE LONG BARROW (*signposted right next to A436*) is that, after excavation, it was covered over with soil, so it's now just a shapeless grassy mound. WINDMILL TUMP LONG BARROW (*near road from Rodmarton to Cherington*) is the best of the also-rans, but you'll need a decent OS map to find it.

Others include: LEIGHTERTON CHAMBERED LONG BARROW, *near school north west of Leighterton village;* RANDWICK CHAMBERED LONG BARROW, *on National Trust land north west of Randwick church;* WEST TUMP CHAMBERED LONG BARROW, *near Brimpsfield, south of Birdlip.*

There's actually more genuine medieval castle at Berkeley than is at first apparent, but it's the mix of styles from many different ages that gives the interior its appeal.

BERKELEY CASTLE

Privately owned • £££ • Usual hours

Berkeley is really more of a stately home than anything else, still owned and occupied by the same family that has lived here for 850 years, but it has retained some of the feel of a medieval castle and is actually a rather enjoyable place to visit. Quite a lot of sensitive restoration and renovation has been carried out in the 20th century, and the result is a very clean and tidy interior that displays its oldest features to good effect.

The castle gives a pleasing feeling of being a living thing with its roots in the past and the impact of historical events still shows in the fabric of the building, the most marked example being a breach in the shell keep inflicted by Parliamentarian forces in the Civil War, which the owners are still forbidden by law to repair.

It's not immediately easy to make sense of the layout of the castle, but basically the Norman shell keep is on your left as you enter, and the other accommodation buildings are all built against the circuit of walls which surround the small bailey.

The motte is thought to have been put up by William FitzOsbern, one of William the Conqueror's commanders at the Battle of Hastings, who was in charge of the Norman invasion of south Wales. After King Henry II gave his permission for a stone castle in 1117, the mound was supported by stonework and the shell keep was built on top, so that in effect the keep surrounds the mound (a fairly unusual arrangement, but similar to *Farnham Castle* in *Surrey*). The area inside the keep is now a sheltered garden.

The first building you enter on your tour of the castle (guided tours are available if you prefer) is one of the towers of the keep, with a room in which King Edward II is said to have been held prisoner before his murder. This is the most famous event in the castle's history, but the guidebook skirts round the details, perhaps because the main reason his barons didn't like Edward was that he was homosexual, and popular legend has it that he was killed, in what someone considered an appropriate fashion, by being impaled on a red-hot poker.

The rest of the house is rather more fun than the first couple of rooms, with a great variety of detail surviving from different eras. The nice thing about this multi-period mix is that you can skip swiftly past the bits that don't appeal and concentrate on the things that catch your eye, so while everyone else is peering at the portrait of Nell Gwynne on the Grand Stairs (the flight dates from 1637), you can be taking in the fine workmanship of the embroidered silk wallpaper.

Best room of the lot is the Great Hall, which has not changed a great deal since it was built around 1340. The wooden-beamed roof is basically original, though it was greatly altered in 1497, and the wooden screen across the end of the hall dates from the 1500s, with most of its painting being of that era. The stained glass in the windows, however, is modern.

Berkeley isn't a grand, imposing house and was never a particularly big castle, either, but in a quiet way it has quite a lot to offer.

In Berkeley village, signposted from A38 north of junction 14 of the M5.

The huge holes in the mosaic floor of the dining room at Chedworth Roman villa are the result of damage by the roots of trees when the villa lay undiscovered.

The most important excavated rooms at Chedworth are covered over by modern buildings.

There isn't a great deal left of the Roman villa at Great Witcombe, but you can see that it had superb views.

CHEDWORTH ROMAN VILLA

National Trust • £££ • Usual hours

There's something rather musty and uninspiring about this place, and it's hard to see why it has a reputation as one of the finest villas in the country. Its notable features are a fine mosaic floor in the dining room, in the local artistic style known as 'Cirencester school', and an extensive bath range. As well as traditional 'damp heat' baths (like a Turkish bath), Chedworth also had a trendy 'dry heat' sauna-style bath added later.

Posh though these bits are – and they clearly show that this villa was more of a country mansion than a farmstead – it doesn't add up to a very satisfying experience, and you get no real impression of how the villa might have looked in its heyday. If you've seen a mosaic and a *hypocaust* (underfloor heating system) before, Chedworth has nothing new to offer – except possibly the shrine to a water goddess built around the spring that supplied the villa's water. Perhaps the spring explains the odd location of the villa, in a spot where the sun disappears very early in the day.

Off minor road west from Yanworth to Compton Abdale or Withington; signposted from A40 and A429 north of Cirencester.

GREAT WITCOMBE ROMAN VILLA

English Heritage • Free • Open access at any reasonable time (occasional tours give access to mosaics)

Perhaps it's just the setting that makes this villa so much more pleasant than Chedworth, because in all honesty there's rather less to see. Only low stone walls remain, giving you some idea of the floor plan, but it's enough to suggest that this would have been a fine country house in a splendid location with views across the valley (altogether much more like a modern country house than you might expect). There are the remains of a mosaic and a bath-house, but these are only open about five days a year when there is a

The wooded cliffs overlooking the River Wye aren't the best place to see much of Offa's Dyke, but you do get an excellent view of Tintern abbey in Wales.

guided tour (details from poster on site, by phone from English Heritage or in their Visitors' Handbook).

Clearly signposted down turning off minor road between Birdlip and Brockworth, south east of Gloucester off A46 (towards Gloucester from Great Witcombe village).

OFFA'S DYKE, TINTERN

English Heritage • Free • Open access at any reasonable time

Built in the late 780s by Offa, ruler of the Anglo-Saxon kingdom of Mercia (the Midlands equivalent of Wessex) to keep out the Welsh tribes, the dyke was a fortified boundary running from the Severn estuary in the south to the Dee estuary in the north. As well as a bank and ditch, it had a wooden palisade and watch-towers and was guarded by regular patrols.

The reason we mention it here is that this is the only section of Offa's Dyke in the care of English Heritage, but in fact this is not a good place to see the remnants of the dyke (see *Shropshire* for more details). The goal of this pleasant walk is a viewpoint known as the Devil's Pulpit, with a fine view of Tintern Abbey on the far side of the River Wye.

Half-hour walk through woodland and across fields from Forestry car park (signposted) off B4228 north of Chepstow; follow left fork of forest track and turn right when it comes out on a rough road, then shortly turn left at footpath signpost.

The cloister arches are just about all that's left of Hailes Abbey, but it's still an attractive and interesting ruin.

HAILES ABBEY

Owned by National Trust and operated by
English Heritage • ££ • usual hours

There's not much of Hailes Abbey left standing except the arches of the cloisters – but they're very attractive arches, and as you poke around you'll discover enough interesting detail to keep you entertained for a while. The jumble of original stonework and later rebuilding in the arches to the left of the cloister is particularly good fun. This is where the chapter house stood, where the Cistercian monks would gather each day for the reading of a chapter from the Rule of St Benedict, and the importance of the room in the daily lives of the community was reflected in its rich decoration. Roof bosses on display in the site museum show traces of red paint and gilding.

The abbey was one of the last Cistercian houses in England, founded about 120 years after the first at *Waverley, Surrey* as the fulfilment of a vow made by Richard, Earl of Cornwall. Caught in a great storm at sea in October 1242, he promised to found a religious house if he survived. In 1245, his brother, King Henry III, gave him the manor here at Hailes so that he could fulfil his vow.

The abbey hit the big time in 1270, when Richard's son Edmund donated a vial said to contain the blood of Jesus Christ, authenticated by the Patriarch of Jerusalem, who later became Pope Urban IV. A new east end of the abbey church was built in a style known as a 'chevet', with five chapels sticking out – its plan can still easily be seen in the foundations that remain – and here a shrine was placed to house the holy relic. The shrine attracted many thousands of pilgrims over the next two centuries, and their donations helped make the abbey relatively wealthy, but at the time of the dissolution the 'Holy blood' was pronounced to be "honey clarified and coloured with saffron".

Signposted down minor road to Hailes off
B4632 north of Winchcombe.

KEMPLEY
ST MARY'S CHURCH

English Heritage • Free •
Usual hours

This is just brilliant: a small Norman church with fantastic wall paintings, some of them dating back to the early 1100s. What's great about this is not simply that these are rare and interesting images (though of course they are) but that it shows how the Normans would have decorated their buildings. A good example is the typical deeply recessed arch window, the niche of which is covered with a chequered pattern. This kind of paintwork would have been just as common in castles.

The best way to find it is to follow signs from the B4024 east of Much Marcle.

If it doesn't look much like an Anglo-Saxon chapel, that's because Odda's Chapel became part of a house.

ODDA'S CHAPEL, DEERHURST

English Heritage • Free • Open access during usual hours

A small Anglo-Saxon chapel that was later incorporated into a farmhouse. It's pleasingly plain, with a very ancient feel, although it does look a bit like a barn.

In Deerhurst village, near Tewkesbury.

ST BRIAVELS CASTLE

English Heritage • Free • Open access to exterior at any reasonable time and to interior of bailey on summer afternoons

This small castle is now home to a youth hostel, and since it's in the middle of a quiet village in fine walking country, it must be a great place to stay. For non-residents it's not quite so interesting, but it's worth a look if you're passing.

There's a reasonable circuit of walls and moat to be seen, but the main feature is the huge gatehouse, built in the 1290s by Edward I. There was a square great tower, too, but this finally collapsed in 1752. The castle was used in the 1200s as an arsenal for iron crossbow bolts made in the surrounding Forest of Dean.

In the middle of St Briavels village, just off the B4228 between Chepstow and Coleford.

The most interesting feature of St Briavels Castle, now one of the country's most attractive youth hostels, is a huge gatehouse with two cylindrical towers.

SEE ALSO...

ASHLEWORTH TITHE BARN, *by minor road to river from Ashleworth village* – This large barn from the 1400s is a fine building (*pictured below*), but it's still in use by the farm, so you're not really free to poke around. (*National Trust, £ contribution, open access during usual hours in summer.*)

BLAISE CASTLE, *near Bristol* – Not a castle but an 18th-century house now owned by the City Council; there are some enjoyable walks in the grounds.

CIRENCESTER ROMAN AMPHITHEATRE, *a short walk from town centre* – This is a massive set of earthworks, consisting of two large, curved banks either side of an 'arena'. There are plenty of slight traces of Roman buildings throughout the town. (*English Heritage, free, open access at any reasonable time.*)

CRICKLEY HILL HILLFORT, *on National Trust land near Little Witcombe* – One of the oldest defended sites in Britain, dating from 3500 to 2500 BC and starting life as a causewayed camp. Lots of stone age arrowheads were found, and traces of a burned palisade suggest warfare. It was rebuilt as a hillfort around 700 BC.

GLOUCESTER BLACKFRIARS, *Gloucester town centre* – Remains of a small priory church from the 1200s which boasts an original roof of a rare type, but is used as offices and not very easy to get to see (*English Heritage, very limited access*).

GLOUCESTER GREYFRIARS, *Gloucester town centre* – Uninteresting remains of a Franciscan friary church from the late 1400s and early 1500s (*English Heritage, free, open access at any reasonable time*).

HORTON COURT, *off A46 north of Chipping Sodbury* – A gorgeous little manor house (*pictured left*), but only the Norman hall is open to visitors (*National Trust, £, limited hours – only Wednesday and Saturday.*)

KINGSWOOD ABBEY GATEHOUSE, *signposted in Kingswood village* – Cute, but not hugely interesting. (*English Heritage, free, key from shop opposite during shop hours.*)

LYDNEY HILL ROMANO-BRITISH TEMPLE COMPLEX, *near Lydney, Forest of Dean* – An extraordinary place, with a large temple to Nodens, a Celtic god of healing and hunting, plus precinct and guest accommodation, built in the 300s inside a hillfort. Visits only by permission from Lydney Park Estate.

THORNBURY CASTLE, *Thornbury* – The last great fortified manor house of England, built around 1500, but much rebuilt and not open to visitors.

AND...

MINCHINHAMPTON COMMON DEFENCES, *on the Common* – Celtic earthworks on National Trust land; PAINSWICK BEACON HILLFORT, which is not so attractive; ULEY BURY HILLFORT, *on hill above Uley*, which is rather good.

Hereford & Worcester

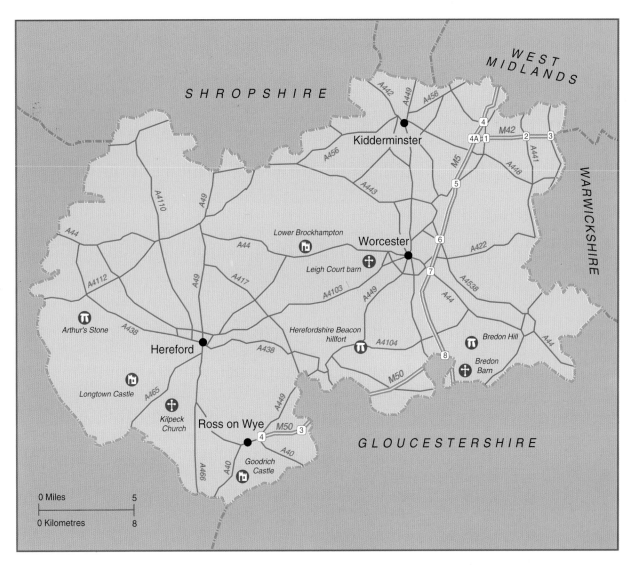

SHROPSHIRE

WEST MIDLANDS

A442
A449
A456

Kidderminster

4
M42
4A 1
2 3

A456

M5
A448
A441

A443

5

WARWICKSHIRE

A4110

A49

A44

Lower Brockhampton

Worcester

6
A422

A44

A4112

A49

A417

Leigh Court barn

7
A4538

Arthur's Stone

A438

A4103

A449

A44

Hereford

A438

Herefordshire Beacon
hillfort

A4104

Bredon Hill

8
Bredon
Barn

Longtown Castle

A465

Kilpeck
Church

Ross on Wye

A449

M50
3

M50

GLOUCESTERSHIRE

4

A40

A466

A40

Goodrich
Castle

0 Miles   5

0 Kilometres   8

HEREFORD AND WORCESTER is a modern composite of two lovely old rural counties. The hills and valleys in the west of the region offer some of the most attractive (and least visited) scenery in England. Wales is but a stone's throw away, with a number of excellent castles lurking on the other side of the border, and on the English side there's a medieval fortress to rival any of them in the shape of the compact and charming *Goodrich Castle*. Equally memorable is the impressive arrangement of stones that makes up the neolithic burial chamber known as *Arthur's Stone*, while the area's most attractive historic building is *Lower Brockhampton*, a small, half-timbered, moated manor house accompanied by an equally picturesque gatehouse, which has stood in a secluded valley for more than 600 years.

Witley Court, a splendid Italianate mansion abandoned in the early 1900s, is now one of England's finest ruined stately homes (and a great spot for a picnic).

133

ARTHUR'S STONE

English Heritage • Free • Open access at any reasonable time

This remarkable monument is the exposed burial chamber of an unusual neolithic tomb. The roof is a vast slab of stone weighing 25 tons, supported by nine smaller uprights. At one end is an entrance passage that ran at right angles up to the end of the chamber, and just the thought of crawling into it in the dark, with that huge weight of stone above, gives a slight hint of what the place might have been about when it was built.

Right next to a minor road on the ridge south of Bredwardine: clearly signposted from B4348 (Ewyas Harold to Hay-on-Wye road) at Dorstone.

Although it's now broken by frost, the huge capstone of Arthur's Stone was a single slab weighing 25 tons.

BREDON BARN

National Trust • Free • Open access at any reasonable time

This isn't classed as a tithe barn, because it didn't belong to an abbey, but it served the same function of storing the season's produce from a large estate farm. Since it belonged to a manor house, it's what's known as a 'manorial' barn.

What makes this one especially interesting is that, over one of the doorways, it has an upstairs room used as an office by the steward whose responsibility it was to account for all the produce. The perks of the

The unique thing about the barn at Bredon is an upstairs room which was the steward's office.

job included a fireplace to keep warm by, and a toilet in the corner. It's a rather lovely building, and it dates from the late 1300s.

Indicated by a hard-to-spot signpost down a tiny lane on the edge of Bredon, near where the road for Tewkesbury leaves the village.

BREDON HILL HILLFORT

English Nature land • Free • Open access at any reasonable time

Bredon Hill is one of the finest pieces of walking country in England, like an island of national park afloat in a sea of ordinary farmland. The hill is important for its wildlife, and the views are special (particularly across to Wales and the Malverns or south towards Gloucester cathedral).

Just as a bonus, there are two hill-forts on the hill. The smaller one, Conderton hillfort, has a single stone rampart and ditch, and dates to about 300 BC, when it may have been just a cattle compound. It became a village of round huts, but was abandoned before the Roman invasion.

Bredon is a promontory fort, with natural defence provided by cliffs on two sides, and with a double rampart cutting it off from the rest of the hill. The outer rampart is built of dry stone and dates to about 300 BC, while the inner one is made of clay and was dug in about 150 BC.

Bredon seems to have been attacked and destroyed at about the time of the birth of Christ, perhaps by raiders from the tribe of the Belgae. The bodies of more than 60 young men were found, hacked to pieces, near the burned remains of the main gate, and it appears that a row of severed heads was displayed on poles by the gate.

Clearly visible from Strensham services on the M5 near the junction with the M50. Reached by tracks up from Great Comberton, Kemerton or Overbury.

Bredon Hill: easily spotted from a service station on the M5, this is a superb place to go for a walk.

It's not difficult to pick out the square Norman keep, built in grey stone, which is the oldest part of the castle.

GOODRICH CASTLE

English Heritage • ££ • Usual hours

This is a super little castle, with a bit of everything: a Norman keep which you can climb to the roof of, via a precarious spiral stair; high walls and towers, with a wall-walk at parapet level; a big gatehouse, with murder-holes and portcullis slots; even a dark dungeon and an interesting toilet.

It's also an ideal castle for people who like to poke around without reading the guidebook, partly because it's easy to make sense of everything (and you'll see it all in one easy loop round, provided you start by turning left inside the gatehouse) and partly because not an awful lot of its history is known in any case. It took its name from the owner of the first castle here, a chap called Godric, at about the time of the Domesday book (1086). Most of its stonework dates from the late 1100s, when it was owned by William de Valence, a son of Isabella of Angouleme, widow of King John. Forced out of his homeland in Poitou by the French conquest of the province in the 1240s, William was a bit of a lad even by the standards of

his time: he was exiled twice (1258 and 1264) when his support for King Henry III got him into trouble with the barons, and he took part in the Crusade of 1270–1273.

One bit of the guidebook you should read, however, is the excellent description of domestic arrangements in the castle, gleaned from its accounts for the year 1296. Details like the 'pipe' of wine (700 bottles) shipped in from Bristol at under £4 the lot, or the fact that a messenger could be sent to London and back in ten days, really bring the castle to life.

The great thing about Goodrich is that as well as the obvious appeal of its larger buildings, there are also lots of interesting details to be picked out. Passing through the gate, for example, note the murder holes above and pop down the small passage at the side to the guard's chamber: very small, but cosy, with a fireplace, windows on three sides to keep watch at and a loo at the other end of the passage. Turn left inside the castle and, after a quick look at the chapel, you can climb the stairs to the upstairs part of the

gatehouse, where there are two large rooms with big fireplaces. In the far one, over the gate passage, you can see not only the slots in which the portcullis ran but also recesses in the wall for its counterweights and a pivot hole for the roller around which the ropes were wound. Perhaps it's just me, but I love this kind of detail.

The square Norman keep is rather older than the rest and built from different stone, grey stuff thought to have been carted here from the Forest of Dean, whereas the rest of the castle is built from the dark red sandstone quarried from the ditch. Incidentally, don't forget to make your way out through the sally port in the basement of the solar and have a look at the angled bases of the towers.

Goodrich is great at any time of year, but the best time to come is in the spring, when vast numbers of housemartins nest here and are constantly flitting in and out through its doors and windows.

Signposted from A40 north of Monmouth and from minor roads near Welsh Bicknor.

HEREFORDSHIRE BEACON

National Trust land • Free • Open access at any reasonable time

A hillfort with spectacular views, since it's built right on top of the Malvern hills. Also known as British Camp, it's one of the most popular spots in the Malverns for dog-walking and kite-flying, and it is reached by a footpath up from a large car park beside the main road, so you can hardly expect it to be quiet – but the ramparts are impressive enough to make it worthwhile. The odd-looking lump at the top is the remnant of a medieval castle mound. Be warned that the walk up is really very steep, particularly at the outset.

Next to the A449 south of Little Malvern.

From Herefordshire Beacon, an iron age fort in the Malvern hills, the views in all directions are absolutely superb.

The little church at Kilpeck boasts a remarkable series of Saxon carvings all round the edge of the roof.

KILPECK CHURCH

Church authorities • Free (donations greatly appreciated) • Open access to exterior at all times and to interior during usual hours

This tiny church is one of England's greatest art treasures, though I, for one, had never heard of it until I stumbled across it by accident while looking for the neighbouring castle.

All round the top of the walls is a series of projecting stone corbels, each one of which is carved as a different figure – some human, some animal – with remarkable wit and skill. The carvings are very beautiful, in a lively, entertaining kind of a way. And they're really old, too – mostly late Saxon, though with some early Norman decoration too. It's an utterly unique place, and I can't praise it highly enough. Go and have a look.

Clearly signposted at Kilpeck village, off the A465 south of Hereford.

LEIGH COURT BARN

English Heritage • Free • Open access during usual hours only

This is probably the most famous barn in Britain – though you might find it hard to believe that a barn *could* be famous. It owes its notoriety partly to an extensive recent restoration and partly to its remarkable timber construction, which is rather special, the whole thing being supported by arches formed from two great slices of tree. The barn was built in the 1300s to serve Pershore Abbey.

It's something of a surprise to see that the exterior of the building looks very ordinary: the low supporting walls are made of brick, and must surely be the result of later rebuilding. Perhaps because of the recent restoration, it looks almost brand new, like a Barratt home. The setting could be more welcoming, too, because the barn is practically in the front garden of someone's house. Don't let this put you off, though.

Signposted by the church near the village of Leigh, beside the minor road to Bransford.

The roof of the medieval barn at Leigh Court is beautiful, with arches formed from two great slices of tree.

Tucked away in a remarkably secluded spot, Lower Brockhampton is one of the prettiest buildings in England.

LOWER BROCKHAMPTON

National Trust • £££ • Limited hours (Wednesday to Sunday afternoons, April to October only)

Its picture postcard looks are the main attraction of Lower Brockhampton, but there's plenty of historical interest here, too. This small moated manor house of the mid-1300s is typical of a kind of defensive dwelling which was once quite common across the country but has largely vanished. Most manors of the kind either developed into larger houses or were abandoned. It's not uncommon, if you're looking at a detailed Ordnance Survey map in search of places of archaeological interest in your area, to come across traces of a moat in a field which show where a house very like this would have stood.

There's not an awful lot to see inside the house because its layout is so simple, the single large hall being by far its most important room.

Signposted from the A44 east of Bromyard.

LONGTOWN CASTLE

English Heritage • Free • Open access at any reasonable time

This is not the most exciting castle ruin you're ever likely to come across, but it's not without interest, and it stands in a fine location in hilly country not far from the famous book town of Hay-on-Wye.

The unusual cylindrical keep, supported by three projecting buttresses, is the castle's most notable feature. It was built in the early 1300s, but the mound on which it stands is rather older, probably dating back to the years just before 1100. One side of the tower is ruined, which means that you can't climb up it at all, but you can see where a flight of stairs led to the higher floors, running up the inside of one of the buttresses.

Besides the keep, there is also a surviving stretch of high stone curtain wall, pierced by a gateway. In front of this, the area that used to be the castle's bailey is clearly defined by the banks that surround it. There are interesting reconstruction drawings on signboards which show clearly how the castle's defences would have dominated the tiny village.

Signposted at the north end of the village of Longtown.

Hidden among trees, the round tower of Longtown Castle is set on a mound that's high enough to offer good views.

MORE TINY CASTLES...

HEREFORDSHIRE IS UNUSUAL in that it is littered with the remains of small border castles. Some of these amount to little more than a couple of chunks of wall, but the remains of others would undoubtedly be restored and open to the public if it weren't for their out-of-the-way location.

Although most are on private land, some of these tiny castle ruins are in fields with access by a permissive footpath, while others are open to the public for a few days each year (perhaps as part of a national initiative such as the Open Gardens scheme or the annual Heritage Weekend every September, or in connection with a local event such as a village fete). Details are too irregular to be published here, and in any case would be of little use to most readers: but if you live in the area or are a regular visitor, it would be worth keeping an eye out for notices.

The following are some places you could investigate for yourself. You never know what you might find...

BRAMPTON BRYAN, *on the A4113 west of Ludlow* – A stone curtain wall with towers and a square gatehouse was added in the mid-1300s to an earlier motte castle. The old castle has pretty much disappeared under later rebuilding. The grounds are occasionally open to the public.

BREDWARDINE, *on the B4352 east of Hay-on-Wye* – There are traces of the walls of a rectangular keep built in the late 1100s.

CLIFFORD (pictured above), *north of Hay-on-Wye* – Has a circuit of walls on a mound, with five round towers. It's in someone's garden.

HUNTINGTON, *on minor road near Hergest, south-west of Kington* – A motte castle with two baileys had a tower added in the late 1100s, and there are supposed to be some traces of it still visible.

KILPECK, *by the church (see page 136)* – A shell keep was built in the early 1200s on an earlier motte. There are some fragments of wall, but it's all very overgrown. There are hopes that it might be cleared and investigated by English Heritage, if an agreement can be reached with the landowner.

SNODHILL, *near Dorstone, off B4348* – An early motte castle, with bailey, on a hilltop; the stone remains include parts of an oddly shaped stone tower from the 1200s, with drum towers either side of the gate. Can be approached by a permissive footpath.

Others include PEMBRIDGE, RICHARDS CASTLE (once a large castle with an unusual octagonal keep) and WILTON, near Bridstow.

SEE ALSO...

CROFT CASTLE, *off the B4362 north of Leominster* – Of a simple design (a quadrangle with a round tower at each corner), it was built in the late 1300s but has been converted into a house. It's an attractive building, but few of its rooms are open, so even as stately home, it's disappointing. (*National Trust, £££, limited hours.*)

CROFT AMBREY HILLFORT, *as above* – Superb large hillfort reached on foot from the car park at Croft Castle, dated to as early as 1000 BC.

HARTLEBURY CASTLE, *near Stourport* – Not a castle, but a house which from 1675 was the residence of the Bishops of Worcester. State Rooms are open at times: the rest is the Worcestershire County Museum, which is fun in an eccentric, old-fashioned way. (*Local council, ££, usual hours.*)

KING ARTHUR'S CAVE, *Whitchurch, near Monmouth* – Small cave in which flint tools of the old and middle stone ages were found, along with bones of mammoths and woolly rhino.

MIDDLE LITTLETON TITHE BARN, *near Evesham* – One of the biggest in England, dating from the 1200s and still used. (*National Trust, £ donation, afternoons in April to October.*)

WIGMORE CASTLE, *on the A4110 north of Leominster* – This site has recently been taken over by English Heritage and was due to open to the public in 1999. There are traces of stone walls from the 1100s on top of an earlier mound. Much rebuilding took place in the mid-1400s, when the castle was owned by Edward IV and Richard III. (*English Heritage, access not confirmed – probably free, open access.*)

WITLEY COURT, *off the A4133 west of Droitwich* – There are actually quite a few shells of ruined stately homes dotted around, but this is probably the most splendid of them. It's a very graceful building, and the grounds make a great place for a picnic. Entry is a little expensive if you're not an English Heritage member, though. (*English Heritage, £££, usual hours.*)

Shropshire

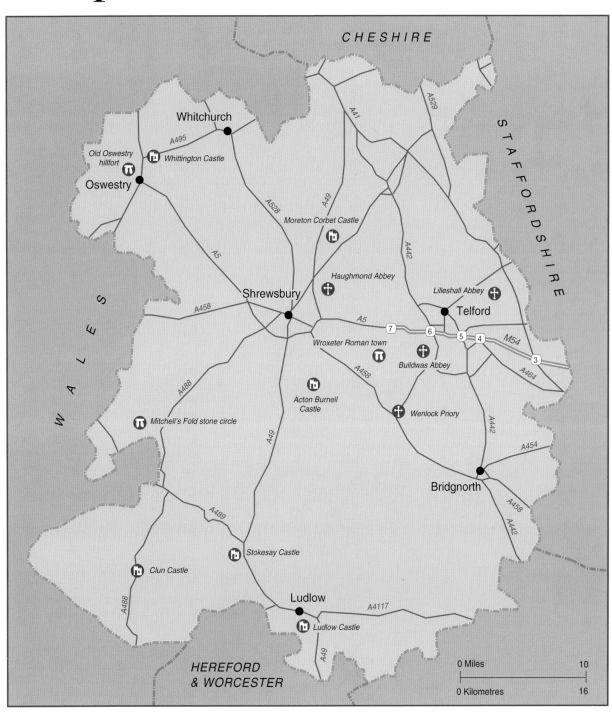

Shropshire has an abundance of smaller medieval remains, including several obscure but very pretty abbey ruins, and it also has some excellent iron age forts on its rolling hills. The county's grandest ruin is *Ludlow Castle*, but its most appealing historic place is undoubtedly the medieval manor house of *Stokesay Castle*, the great hall of which is one of the best in England.

Buildwas Abbey is plain in appearance because it was completed by about 1200 and hardly altered afterwards.

ACTON BURNELL CASTLE

English Heritage • Free • Open access at any reasonable time

The remains of a large fortified manor house built in the 1280s by Robert Burnell, Chancellor of England, this attractive ruin in pink sandstone is pleasingly simple in design. It was basically a big, rectangular keep-like building two storeys high, with a little tower at each corner, and it must have looked extremely grand in its day. One word of advice: don't come on a summer weekend, when the place is crawling with foreign students staying at the nearby school.

Signposted in Acton Burnell village, reached by small country roads south of Shrewsbury.

BUILDWAS ABBEY

English Heritage • ££ • Limited hours (April to October only)

This is an attractively simple and straightforward ruin, tucked away in a quiet little valley not far from Ironbridge (which, thanks to its industrial heritage, has become a busy little tourist town). There are two particularly fine things to see at Buildwas Abbey: one is the ruined church, its plain Norman pillars and arches striding purposefully along each side of the nave; the other is the chapter house, which has a very attractive vaulted roof and a recently exposed floor of interesting old tiles.

Most of the church is still standing. It's unusual in that it was completed by about 1200 and hardly touched thereafter, whereas most abbeys were continually altered and updated during their working lives. This explains its pleasing simplicity.

Although the buildings along two sides of the cloisters have more or less disappeared, the chapter house is flanked by a sacristy and a parlour both of which are still roofed.

Buildwas was founded in 1135 as a daughter-house of the vast and powerful *Furness Abbey* in *Cumbria*. Like Furness, Buildwas belonged to the Savignac Order, which joined up with the Cistercians in 1147. Buildwas did not found any daughter-houses in its turn, but it developed connections with a number of smaller abbeys in Wales and Ireland, including Basingwerk in Clwyd, Strata Marcelli in Powys and Strata Florida in Dyfed. In such a way did the tentacles of power of Furness Abbey extend throughout Britain.

The abbey's history was mostly pretty quiet. Its lands were ravaged in 1406 by followers of the Welsh rebel leader Owain Glyndwr, but apart from that the most notorious episode that took place here was the murder of the abbot in 1342, allegedly by a renegade monk called Thomas Tonge.

Signposted off the A4169 south of Buildwas, between Ironbridge and Much Wenlock.

Acton Burnell was a large fortified house with a small tower at each corner, and must have looked pretty splendid.

CLUN CASTLE

English Heritage • Free • Open access at any reasonable time

Quite an interesting little ruin, dominated by huge earthworks and featuring the remains of a largeish keep built around 1160. For some peculiar reason, the builders decided to set the keep on the side of the mound, which rather undermined its defensive strength. The top of the mound was ringed round with an irregular circuit of walls, one tower of which survives. Not a lot is known about the castle's history.

To one side of the town of Clun; riverside parking place for pleasant walk to the castle is signposted.

The peculiar thing about Clun Castle is that the keep was built on the side of the mound, exposing it to attack.

HAUGHMOND ABBEY

English Heritage • ££ • Usual hours (but April to October only)

There are quite a few small abbey ruins in Shropshire, but this is just about the most enjoyable to explore, with lots of interesting features to see as you poke around. The largest remnants are the abbot's house at the front of the site and the remains of the splendid chapter house, tucked away towards the back.

As is so often the case, the Abbot's house has survived principally because it continued in use as a residence after the abbey was dissolved in 1539, using the cloister as a sheltered garden. When the house burned down in the Civil War, the remains were rebuilt as a farm. Its most unusual feature is the large, ornate bay window at the end of the abbot's private chambers,which is clearly a later alteration but pre-dates the abbey's dissolution.

The abbey church was demolished after the Dissolution, and it is now visible only as an outline on the ground, but the nearby chapter house is in surprisingly good condition. It has three large, richly decorated arches at the front, dating from the late 1100s, with statues of saints among the shafts of the arches added in the mid-1300s. Inside, there is a timber ceiling which may date to around 1500, when the chapter house was rebuilt on a slightly smaller scale.

The abbey's early history is not know, but it flourished after Henry II came to the throne in 1154. Its main patrons, the FitzAlan family, had been staunch supporters of Henry's mother, Matilda, throughout King Stephen's troubled reign.

Signposted on the B5062 east of Shrewsbury.

Below: The abbot's house at Haughmond Abbey is the largest remnant of this very enjoyable ruin.

LILLESHALL ABBEY

*English Heritage • ££ • Limited hours
(April to October, weekends only)*

This is a pretty ruin, with a lovely big arch at the west end of the long church (of which quite a good deal still survives). The best bit is a spiral stair that you can climb to look out over the interior of the church. There are also some attractive pieces of the chapter house and neighbouring rooms. Lilleshall was an Augustinian abbey (like *Haughmond, previous page*). Most of the stonework of the church dates to the late 1100s and early 1200s.

Signposted down minor road between the A518 and the B4379 north of Telford.

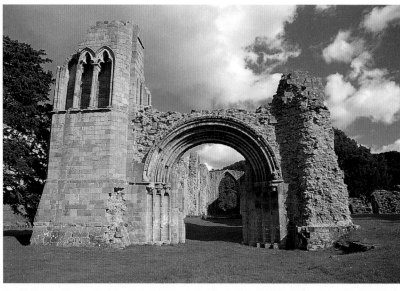

The big arch in the west end of the church is the most attractive feature of Lilleshall Abbey, a small but pretty ruin.

MITCHELL'S FOLD

STONE CIRCLE

English Heritage • Free • Open access at any reasonable time

In a fine setting on heathland with great views across to the Welsh hills, this is a small stone circle of the bronze age. There are now just 16 stones, ten of them still standing, but their spacing shows that there would have been more. A short way away is a single stone known as The Altar.

On lower slopes of Stapeley Hill, reached by footpath from the village of Middleton (in country east of Montgomery); map advised.

The small stone circle of Mitchell's Fold is one of the most remote and peaceful monuments of its kind in England.

Moreton Corbet: in the foreground is the keep of the original castle, with the Elizabethan house behind.

MORETON CORBET CASTLE

English Heritage • Free • Open access at any reasonable time

An unusual little site. In its later days it ended up as more of a country house than a castle, but originally it was defensive in appearance and intention. At the front is the older part: a small, triangular walled enclosure with a fat little rectangular keep from around 1200. Beyond is the ruin of a grand house with elegant details: this is of Elizabethan date, built for Robert Corbet in about 1579.

Signposted on B5063 north of Shawbury; watch carefully for final turning (which is not signposted for castle) down small side-road labelled Moreton Mill.

Looking over the inner bailey of Ludlow Castle from the top of the keep, which was built in the early 1100s.

LUDLOW CASTLE

Privately owned • £££ • Usual hours

One of the biggest ruined castles in England. There's lots to look at, including an excellent keep which, though it doesn't have any floors, you can climb right to the top of for superb views over the castle and the surrounding countryside.

The large outer bailey, now a grassy lawn, was first enclosed in the late 1100s and is thought to have been used to muster troops for the invasion of Ireland in 1171. Most of the buildings in the outer bailey are later additions, though the gatehouse through which you enter the castle is a much-altered version of the original. There isn't much to see, with the exception of a tower over on the far side called Mortimer's Tower, which originally was a small gatehouse protecting a rear entrance to the river: it has been rebuilt over the years, as you can see inside. The only other thing to detain you in the outer bailey is the ice house in the moat, which may have started life as a magazine.

Forward, then, to the inner bailey, which is where all the real action is. The basic layout of the curtain walls is just as it was when the castle was first built in stone, before 1100. There were four open-backed flanking towers, three of them on the west side, plus a large gatehouse which was later rebuilt to become the keep.

The other really old building here is a round Norman chapel dating from the early 1100s, which is a most attractive and unusual design. Similar round churches were often built in imitation of the Church of the Holy Sepulchre at Jerusalem by knights who had seen it when on crusade.

On the far side of the inner bailey is a large accommodation range, the oldest parts of which are a great hall and a solar block to its left, dating from about 1290. Steps lead up from the inner bailey to a modern wooden platform at the level of the original hall floor, which would have had an undercroft underneath. It is thought that the slightly decrepit wooden doors here may be original.

There are interesting stairways and passages to explore in the solar block to the left of the hall and also in the later accommodation to the right of it. The later part of the range includes the Garderobe Tower, built around 1330, which contained a number of guest rooms each with its own toilet – quite a luxury at the time.

The accommodation block in the rear right-hand corner, behind the Garderobe Tower, and the grander one at the front of the inner bailey, by the keep, are both Tudor. The latter, called the Judges' Lodgings, was completed in 1581 and has typically fancy Tudor details in its windows and fireplaces.

Ludlow's history is extensive. It was *de facto* capital of Wales from 1530 to 1641, when the Council of the Marches sat here, and it is said to have been home to the 'Princes in the Tower' (Edward and Richard, sons of King Edward IV) before they were taken to London in 1483.

Right in Ludlow town centre.

Old Oswestry is a fine big hillfort. Its unique feature is a series of vertical cross-banks on either side of the gate.

OLD OSWESTRY HILLFORT

English Heritage • Free • Open access at any reasonable time

Shropshire has plenty of hillforts in more scenic locations, but the great virtue of this one is that it's readily accessible. It's also one of the largest forts in England, with fine ramparts. There's a particularly interesting arrangement on either side of the main gate, where vertical cross-banks divide a wide, open area between the ramparts. Round huts with thick stone walls were built inside the fort, which is thought to have been occupied from about 500 BC until about the time of the Roman conquest.

On outskirts north of Oswestry, off the 'B' road to the A495 and Gobowen: turn down Coppice Drive and right onto Llwyn Road.

WENLOCK PRIORY

English Heritage • ££ • Usual hours

Another of Shropshire's not-so-very-big abbey ruins, set in pretty gardens which make it a pleasant place to visit. By far its outstanding feature is the chapter house, decorated with elaborate arcading, which is both the earliest (late 1100s) and the most attractive surviving building of the abbey.

The remains generally are fragmentary, though the south transept of the church still stands to almost its full height and there's a piece of the south aisle of the nave that is complete enough to have an upstairs room. An interesting early feature is the *lavatorium*, an elaborate fountain at which the monks would have washed before meals.

Wenlock started life as an early Christian monastery, founded before 690 by Mercian royalty. It was refounded as a daughter-house of Cluny, in France, in about 1080. In 1101 the grave of St Milburga was 'discovered' and her remains were put in a shrine in the church. Because of its French connections, the priory was seized by Edward I in 1295 and had a huge annual fine imposed in 1337 following the start of the Hundred Years' War, but in 1395 it achieved English 'denizen' status.

Near the centre of Much Wenlock town.

Right: At the foot of the south transept of Wenlock Priory is the earlier chapter house, prettiest part of a pretty ruin.

Offa's Dyke, near Edenhope Hill: originally it was 8m (25ft) from the bottom of the ditch to the top of the bank.

Offa's DYKE

OFFA WAS KING of the central English kingdom of Mercia from 757, and during his reign Mercia came to dominate the other kingdoms of Anglo-Saxon England in the same way that Wessex would do later.

At the time, the kingdom of Mercia stretched from the Wye in the west to the Fens in the east and from the Mersey, Trent and Don in the north to the Thames in the south. Offa was able to expand his kingdom with victories in battle over the men of West Sussex in 771, Wales in 778, Wessex in 779 and possibly also the Northumbrians, and in 785 he managed to gain control of Kent. Now effectively the ruler of the whole of England south of the Humber, he went on to become a player on the European stage, establishing cordial relations with the Pope in Rome and with Charlemagne in France. The fat pennies which Offa minted were Europe's finest currency of the time.

The decision to build the Dyke was taken some time in the late 780s, no doubt with the idea of ending Welsh raids now that the Mercian borders with its Anglo-Saxon neighbours were no longer so hotly disputed.

Only quite recently have archaeologists realised that the Dyke was not just a boundary marker, but was actually a fortified frontier comparable with Hadrian's Wall. With teams of labour from tribes all over England each working on one stretch, it may have been built in just one summer, and thereafter it seems to have been manned and patrolled on a regular basis.

The top of the bank, 8m (25ft) above the bottom of the ditch, was surmounted by a wooden palisade in some places and by a stone wall in others. It may also have had towers and signal beacons, but there is no trace of large gateways.

One slight mystery about the Dyke concerned its course at the northern end, where it was thought to run to the sea near Prestatyn. More recently, excavations showed that there was no trace of a dyke here, and instead it is now believed that from Treuddyn (near Mold, in Wales) the Dyke followed the same course as another earthwork known as Wat's Dyke, to reach the Dee estuary at Basingwerk, where there was a Mercian fortress and monastery.

There isn't an awful lot to see of Offa's Dyke, unfortunately, but the bits that do survive (as a greatly reduced bank and ditch) almost all offer good walking in open country with fine views.

Some of the best stretches are highlighted in a very handy leaflet produced by Shropshire County Council, complete with maps, which is available free of charge from Tourist Information offices. Alternatively, of course, you could walk the long-distance footpath which runs from Chepstow to Prestatyn: there are several good walking guides which detail its course.

STOKESAY CASTLE

Stokesay Castle is one of the most attractive buildings in England, with an authentic early medieval feel.

English Heritage • ££ • Usual hours

This is just about the prettiest building in England, but it's also a fine example of a fortified manor house of the late 1200s (and bits of it, in fact, are even older). Its remarkable state of preservation is due, at least in part, to the fact that its historical importance was recognised only a century or so after it was abandoned.

Stokesay continued to be occupied long after the Civil War: it was ordered to be slighted in 1647, but only the curtain walls were pulled down. It was still lived in by members of the Baldwyn family, who owned, it right into the early 1700s, although it later came to be used as outbuildings by the neighbouring farm.

In the early 1800s, its value as one of the finest 13th-century buildings anywhere in England was gradually recognised. In 1869 it was bought by the Allcroft family, who fortunately had the good sense to restore it carefully rather than rebuild it in a trendy Gothic style. It was opened to the public as early as 1908.

The early history of the place is fascinating, and it's well worth sitting down with a cup of tea (the castle has a tea shop in the grounds) and reading up on it in the guidebook. Just a taste: the manor of Stokesay was owned by feudal lords who leased it out while they were away crusading, and in 1281 the lease was bought by Lawrence of Ludlow, England's biggest wool merchant, for the price of a sparrowhawk.

There are four main buildings (not including the tremendously pretty gatehouse, which is much more recent, dating to around 1620, and is not open to visitors). The most important is the high-roofed hall, in the middle, which retains its authentic barn-like early medieval feel. Towards the south end of the hall is an octagonal hearth sitting in the middle of the floor, positioned so that it was closer to the important people at the high table. There were no chimneys or fireplaces in the days when the hall was built.

To the left of the hall (looking from the castle courtyard) is the solar block, with the lord's private living room on the first floor. This room is lined with remarkable Jacobean wood panelling, thought to have been put in in the mid-1600s but probably carved 30 to 40 years earlier. When some of the panels were removed for cleaning, earlier decoration was uncovered – Tudor roses in red paint on the whitewash – but this has now been covered up again.

Next building to the left is the keep-like South Tower, the most obviously fortified part of the castle. A licence to crenellate was obtained for it in 1291. It's not clear what its rooms were used for: most likely either as private apartments for the family, or as guest rooms.

Right back at the other end of the hall, reached by a wooden stair, is the North Tower. This was originally a plain defensive tower with tiny arrow-loops for windows, but in the late 1200s it was remodelled as comfortable apartments. The fabulous windows date from the 1600s.

Signposted by the A49 south of Craven Arms.

WHITTINGTON CASTLE

Local council • Free • Open access at any reasonable time

This odd little ruin is sadly neglected, but it's interesting. There are the foundations of a big, square keep, surrounded by a close-set curtain wall with towers. There's also quite a decent twin-towered gatehouse. Most of it dates to about 1220.

In the middle of Whittington.

It seems that the main reason people come to Whittington Castle is to feed the ducks in the moat…

WROXETER ROMAN CITY

English Heritage • ££ • Usual hours

In some ways this is an extraordinary place, though as is often the case with Roman remains, you have to put your imagination to work.

It's the remains of *Viroconium*, the fourth-largest city of Roman Britain. The thing that dominates the remains is one tall but fairly crumbly chunk of wall, which has stood there since about 125 AD. The whole site exposed to view here was a vast, civic bath-house, and this wall was part of a great exercise hall (*basilica*) about 70m (250ft) long and 20m (65ft) wide – think of a medieval cathedral and you'll get an idea of how big it was.

Beyond the remains of the basilica are various other rooms of the baths, with a wide expanse of hypocaust pillars under what would have been the hot and warm rooms. Down in the far corner are a couple of buildings that were not part of the baths, and these are thought to have been a small marketplace (like a little arcade of shops) and a pair of offices.

That, unfortunately, is the limit of the visible remains. The rest of the city lies buried under the fields and has mostly not been excavated, though its general layout is known from the study of aerial photographs. The defensive bank and ditch of the city ran in a circuit almost two miles (3.7km) long.

A finely carved inscription makes it clear that *Viroconium* was lived in by the local tribe of the Cornovii, and that the huge public buildings (like the baths) were erected shortly before 130 AD as part of a campaign by the emperor Hadrian to encourage civic life to flourish in Britain.

Signposted off the B4380 west of Shrewsbury.

The exposed ruins at Wroxeter are the remains of a huge civic bath-house, with an exercise hall 70m (250ft) long.

SEE ALSO…

BURY DITCHES HILLFORT, *near Bishops Castle* – There's a good leaflet produced by Shropshire County Council's Archaeology Unit which describes this and several more of the county's best hillforts. This one is a small but interesting fort set among forestry.

BOSCOBEL HOUSE, *between Telford and Wolverhampton* – Restored timber-framed hunting lodge of the 1600s, with the famous Royal Oak in which King Charles II hid from Cromwell's troops after the Battle of Worcester in 1651. (*English Heritage, £££, usual hours.*)

BRIDGNORTH CASTLE – A single chunk of Norman keep in a town park, notable for the extreme angle at which it leans.

CAER CARADOC HILLFORT, *near Chapel Lawn* – Small but perfectly formed fort with inturned entrances at each end. The views are great.

CAER CARADOC HILLFORT (another one), *on a tall, steep hill near Church Stretton* – Lived in by the Cornovii before Wroxeter was built. In a fine position, but the track up, on the east side of the hill, is steep. Three other spectacular hillforts are CAYNHAM CAMP and TITTERSTONE CLEE *near Ludlow* and THE WREKIN *near Telford* – the last may have been the capital of the Cornovii.

LANGLEY CHAPEL, *not far from Acton Burnell Castle* – Cute but not especially notable medieval chapel with wooden fixtures of the 1600s. (*English Heritage, free, open access at any reasonable time.*)

SHREWSBURY CASTLE, *Shrewsbury town centre* – Not tremendously interesting building based on an earlier castle but dating from the 1800s, housing a military museum.

WHITE LADIES PRIORY, *near Boscobel House (above)* – Ruin of the church from a small priory of the late 1100s. (*English Heritage, free, open access at any time.*)

Staffordshire

HEAD NORTH to discover the most scenic parts of the county, where the attractive ruin of *Croxden Abbey* sits in a quiet valley.

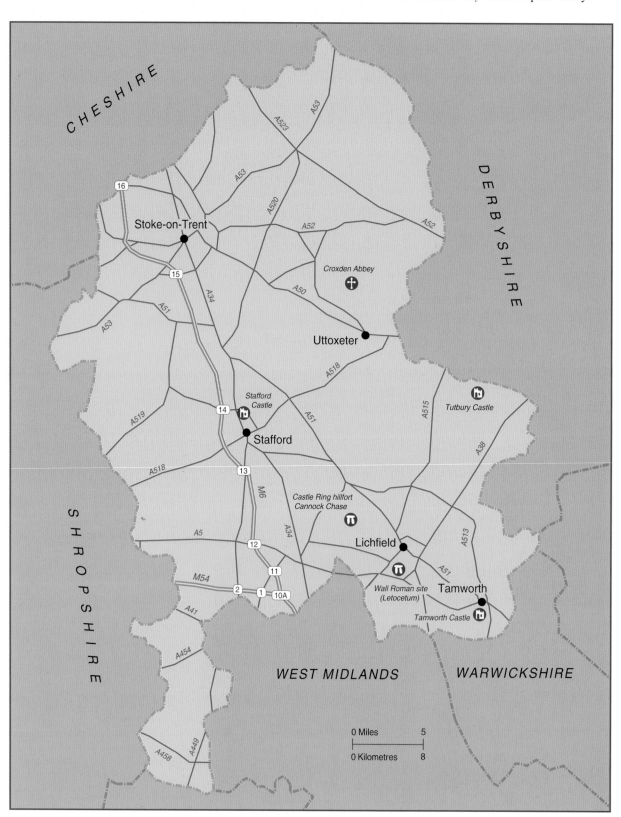

CHESHIRE

DERBYSHIRE

SHROPSHIRE

WEST MIDLANDS

WARWICKSHIRE

A523
A53
A53
16
A520
15
Stoke-on-Trent
A52
A52
Croxden Abbey
A34
A50
A51
A53
Uttoxeter
A519
A518
Stafford Castle
14
A51
Tutbury Castle
A515
Stafford
13
A38
A518
M6
Castle Ring hillfort
Cannock Chase
A5
A34
12
Lichfield
A513
11
M54
2
1
10A
Wall Roman site
(Letocetum)
Tamworth
A51
A41
Tamworth Castle

0 Miles   5
0 Kilometres   8

A454
A458
A449

Croxden Abbey is an excellent mixture of dramatic church remnants and small but interesting details to explore.

CROXDEN ABBEY

Privately owned, but in the care of English Heritage • Free • Open access during usual hours only

Easily the most attractive monument in the county, this ruined Cistercian abbey has lots of interesting corners to explore. Not a great deal is known about its history beyond the fact that it was established in 1176 and, as the signboards at the site explain in a slightly bewildered attempt to find something to say, it made most of its income from its sheep.

Freed from any obligation to understand the history of the place, you're at liberty to wander around and simply appreciate its beauty. Obvious highlights include the arches of the east side of the cloisters, and the towering remnants of the west end and the south transept of the church, as well as a fantastic passageway which still has its roof.

You should also poke around for less obvious details, too, of which there are plenty to be discovered.

Initially it's not at all clear which way the abbey church was aligned, but you soon realise that the village lane cuts right through it. On the other side of the road is what's left of the most important part of the church, the east end, and you can see from the outline of the foundations that it had a 'chevet'-style end, with five sticking-out chapels, similar to the one at *Hailes Abbey, Gloucestershire*. This was quite rare in English churches.

In Croxden, near Hollington, off A522 near Uttoxeter; signposted from minor road between Hollington and Rocester.

CASTLE RING HILLFORT, CANNOCK CHASE

Cannock Chase Council • Free • Open access at any reasonable time

This is not an especially exciting hillfort, but it is a great spot for a woodland walk. It's also very accessible, because you don't have to slog up the hill on foot to reach it: the car park is just a few yards away from the start of a walk that takes you round the full circuit of ramparts.

The hill is the highest point in the forest of Cannock Chase, and there are some excellent views. The ramparts vary according to defensive requirements, with two banks and ditches on the north and west sides but five on the south east, where the adjoining ground is lower.

On the edge of Cannock Wood village; signposted from all the minor roads in the area.

Left: Castle Ring is a decent hillfort with good views, and it's an ideal place for a stroll.

STAFFORD CASTLE

Lord Stafford and Stafford City Council •
Site: Free • Open access any reasonable time
• Visitor centre: £ • Slightly limited hours
(closed Mondays and in winter months)

If ever a castle deserved points for effort, it's this one. The council has spent many years researching the site and restoring the earthworks of what was once a sizeable Norman castle. The visitor centre does a good job of recreating the castle in its medieval heyday, and signboards throughout the site are very informative.

Ultimately, though, earthworks are all that is left of the original castle, which had more or less fallen apart by the 1600s. In the early 1800s it was partially rebuilt and the towers that top the mound today are of this age, which makes it an early example of Gothic revival, but not a real castle.

Clearly signposted on west side of Stafford, near A518 to Telford.

The stone buildings of Stafford Castle are mostly Victorian Gothic, but the Norman earthworks are extensive.

TAMWORTH CASTLE

City Council • £££ • Usual hours

This is a pretty little shell keep, clearly Norman in origin but with quite a few alterations made through the years. The building itself is very likeable, but it houses a museum which is a bit of a mixed bag (the entrance fee is as much as the average cinema ticket, and it delivers rather less in the way of entertainment).

The oldest of the many alterations to the shell, and the highlight of a look round the interior, is a very attractive two-storey great hall with a timber roof dated to the mid-1400s. The castle's setting is pleasant, in a public park next to the river.

Signposted in Tamworth; a good approach is to follow signs from A5 and park by the water meadows for a ten-minute walk across the bridge over the river to the castle.

Tutbury Castle is one of many places in which Mary, Queen of Scots was imprisoned.

TUTBURY CASTLE

Privately owned (Duchy of Lancaster) • ££ •
Limited hours (April to September only)

This is a castle with a turbulent history. It was owned in the early 1300s by the rebellious Thomas of Lancaster (*see Dunstanburgh Castle, Northumberland*), but it was already in decay when Mary, Queen of Scots was imprisoned here. Perhaps unsurprisingly, Mary loathed the place, describing it as sitting on a mountain in a plain, 'exposed to all the malice of the heavens'. Today, it's easy to share her distaste. This isn't the most attractive area.

Tutbury was a large castle, sitting on a huge outcrop of rock overlooking the River Dove. There was an early Norman timber castle here, but this was dismantled by Henry II around 1175 and the site was derelict for about a century. Most of the walls and towers date to the mid-to-late 1300s, but there isn't much of them left.

Signposted in the village of Tutbury.

The well-preserved Norman shell keep of Tamworth Castle is very charming, though it's not so interesting inside.

WALL ROMAN SITE (LETOCETUM)

Owned by the National Trust, managed by English Heritage • ££ • Usual hours

There's not as much to see here as you might hope for. Essentially it's the remains of two substantial buildings: a large bath-house, and what is thought to have been a *mansio*, a hotel for travellers on official business. In themselves, the foundations of these two buildings are not vastly interesting, although they do give you the impression that Wall was a municipal site of some size.

The exact scale of the town, though, is a little unclear, and even a careful read of the guidebook comes up with more questions than answers. Wall started life as a military fort on Watling Street, the Roman road that ran from the main Channel port at Richborough in Kent all the way to Chester. It may have been a base of the XIVth Legion at the time of Boudicca's revolt in 61 AD. Around the fort, some kind of civilian town grew up, and it has been suggested that when the military focus pushed

The Roman site at Wall was a town, and its two main buildings were a bath-house and a mansio *(official hotel).*

further north in the early 100s, the town became an administrative centre.

It is possible that there is a lot more of the Roman town waiting to be uncovered: there are lots of intriguing reports, dating back several hundred years, of stone being taken from Roman buildings in the area and of

objects being found (including what sounds very much like a life-size clay statue of the goddess Minerva). In the meantime, though, this place promises a lot more than it delivers.

Signposted in village of Wall, next to the A5 just south of Lichfield.

SEE ALSO...

CHARTLEY CASTLE (pictured), *next to the A518 near Stowe-by-Chartley* – It's a real surprise to see this fairly substantial ruin right by the main road. It's on private land and not open to visitors (and it's not even easy to park on the verge for a quick look, so you'll have to settle for saluting it as you whizz past). The castle has a motte on which are visible the foundations of a cylindrical great tower (it looks very like the one at *Longtown, Hereford & Worcester*). There were two baileys separated by a ditch, and a curtain wall with half-round towers was built around the inner bailey. The stonework is probably from the 1200s.

THOR'S CAVE, *near Wetton, reached by public footpath* – This rather fantastic, huge, arch-like cave set high on a hill above the River Manifold is a fine goal for a reasonably strenuous walk, but it also has historical interest, since it was occupied both in the old stone age and around the time of the Romans (200 BC to 300 AD).

AND...

Two rather unusual barrows deserve a mention – though, like Thor's Cave, their main appeal is their scenic setting on the edge of the Peak District, near the famously picturesque Dovedale. ILAM TOPS LOW ROUND BARROW (*Ilam Moor, on ridge west of Dovedale*) is a large mound made of alternating layers of earth and stones, covering a

pit which contained the remains of a bull on a bed of charcoal, with human remains above. LONG LOW BARROWS (*at end of road south-east from Wetton*) is a unique arrangement of two limestone mounds joined by a wide bank faced with upright stone slabs. The larger of the two mounds covered a big stone chamber that contained 13 skeletons and three leaf-shaped flint arrowheads.

Warwickshire & the West Midlands

THE OUTSTANDING FEATURE of this part of England is undoubtedly the magnificent *Kenilworth Castle*, a palace fit for Queen Elizabeth I, but there is plenty more besides…

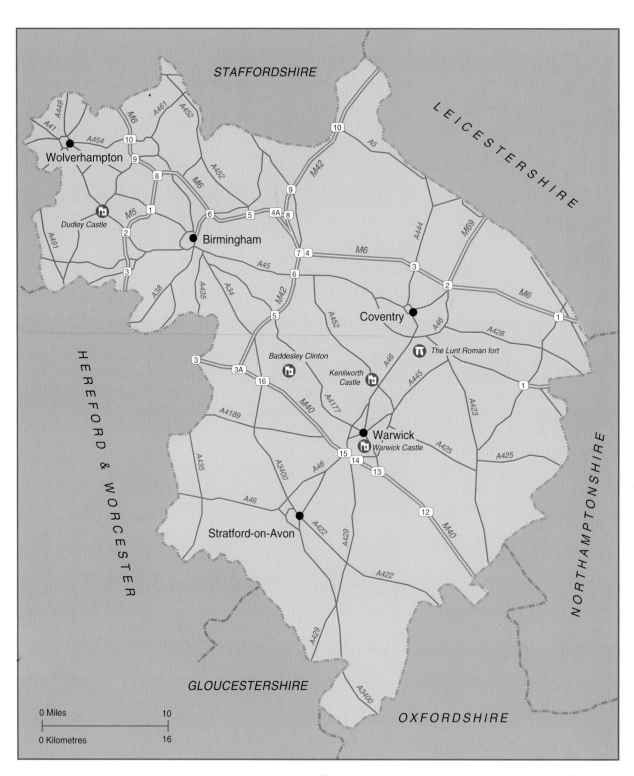

STAFFORDSHIRE

LEICESTERSHIRE

A449
A41
A461
A452
M6
A454
10
9
Wolverhampton
8
A452
M6
9
M42
10
A5
M5
1
6
5
4A 8
Dudley Castle
2
Birmingham
7 4
M6
A444
M69
A491
3
7 4
A45
6
3
A38
A435
A34
M42
6
5
A452
Coventry
A46
M6
1
3
A428
Baddesley Clinton
The Lunt Roman fort
3
3A
16
Kenilworth Castle
A46
A445
1
HEREFORD
A4189
M40
A4177
A423
Warwick
Warwick Castle
A425
A425
A435
A3400
A46
15
14
13
& WORCESTER
A46
12
M40
Stratford-on-Avon
A422
A429
NORTHAMPTONSHIRE
A422
A429
GLOUCESTERSHIRE
A3400
OXFORDSHIRE

| 0 Miles | | 10 |
| 0 Kilometres | | 16 |

BADDESLEY CLINTON

National Trust • £££ • Slightly limited hours (closed two days a week and in winter)

This is a nice little moated manor house, built in the mid-1400s on the site of an earlier house and adapted a good deal in the late 1500s (so it's basically Elizabethan).

The interior of the house was quite substantially refurbished in Victorian times, so it's not as 'original' as you might imagine, though it does have an authentic feel, with wood panelling all over the place. Rather dark and dusty for some tastes, though.

Baddesley Clinton represents a type of defensive house of which few decent examples have survived. Kent is the best place to look for comparable fortified manor houses. *Ightham Mote* (*in the 'See Also...' section on page 114*) is rather older than Baddesley Clinton – and prettier, too. *Penshurst Place* (*page 115*) has no moat, but it's a comparable defensive house with a particularly memorable Great Hall, while *Hever Castle* is certainly the most beautiful house of this kind, despite the 'Gift Shoppe' clutter all around it.

Baddesley Clinton has its own shops, including a tea shop and a secondhand book shop (unique for a historic property, as far as I'm aware). It also has a well-documented history packed with lively characters – well worth reading the guidebook for.

Clearly signposted from A4177 Warwick to Solihull road near village of Chadwick End.

Baddesley Clinton is widely held to be one of the best-preserved medieval moated manor houses in England.

Sheltered by the walls of Dudley Castle is a graceful accommodation range of Elizabethan date.

DUDLEY CASTLE

Dudley and West Midlands Zoological Society • ££££ • Usual hours

The first thing you need to know about Dudley Castle is that it's in the middle of a zoo, which makes it very expensive to visit if you don't want to see the animals. But it's a decent ruin, and watching sealions swimming in the shadows of the medieval walls is something of a unique experience in English castle-visiting.

The remains include half a square keep with a round tower at each corner – it was blown in two when the castle was slighted after the Civil War – and a circuit of walls around a large inner ward, with a grand accommodation range along one side. You can climb a spiral stair to the top of the keep for superb views.

The castle has a long history, built as a motte in 1071 and rebuilt in stone in the 1130s. It was besieged by King Stephen during the civil conflict with Mathilda, and was demolished by Henry II in 1175 because its then owner, Gervaise de Paganel, had supported a rebellion by Henry's son, Prince Henry. The site was derelict until the mid-1200s, when permission to refortify the castle was granted to a descendant of its former owner called Roger de Somery. His son John, a notorious villain, continued the work through to the early 1300s, financing it by robbery and extortion.

The splendid accommodation range dates from the mid-1500s, when the castle was turned into a palace by John Dudley, Duke of Northumberland, who masterminded a plot to put Lady Jane Grey on the throne and was executed by Queen Mary.

Signposted in Dudley town centre; next to the A461, three miles from junction 2 of the M5.

Left: in front of Dudley Castle's keep, you'll find meerkats messing around.

The splendid-looking walls of Kenilworth Castle, with Leicester's Building in the centre and the keep to the right.

KENILWORTH CASTLE

English Heritage • £££ • Usual hours

Kenilworth is one of the country's largest and most splendid castles – though it's not *quite* as interesting to explore as you might hope, because the massive red sandstone buildings that look so fine from a distance are actually rather more ruinous than they at first appear. All the same, there's more than enough to see at Kenilworth to make it worth going out of your way for.

The castle was always an important Royal stronghold, standing right at the heart of England, but it owes much of its size and splendour to its later career as an Elizabethan palace fit for a queen. From 1563, Kenilworth was owned by Robert Dudley, Earl of Leicester, who was a great favourite of Queen Elizabeth – it is said that she almost married him – and he rebuilt it largely for her benefit. Records exist of a 19-day royal visit in July 1575, when the Queen was entertained in the most lavish manner imaginable. One of the castle's most impressive features in its day was the extensive water defences, with a huge lake on which a great naval battle was enacted for the Queen's enjoyment.

Robert Dudley's renovations included two large buildings, one a modern accommodation range known as Leicester's Buildings, which is at the front in most photographs of the castle, the other a new gatehouse on the far side of the castle, known (unsurprisingly) as Leicester's Gatehouse, which has remained in use right into modern times. He also modernised the older buildings of the castle – adding large Tudor windows in the thick walls of the square Norman keep, for example.

The original stone castle, including the keep, was built around 1122, but it was greatly improved by King John in the early 1200s. John added an outer curtain wall with towers and arranged a system of dams and sluices which turned the marshes and streams around the castle into a deep moat and huge lake. The next great phase of building came just before 1400, when John of Gaunt built a grand palace down one side of the original inner ward, overlooking the lake.

It is this part of the castle that is the most interesting to explore. The grandeur of John of Gaunt's Great Hall is still apparent in the roofless ruin, and at each end of it there is a strong tower which you can climb at least part of the way up, with views out across the country and back across the rest of the castle.

The keep is slightly disappointing. Although it looks solid enough from one side, it was broken in half by Civil War slighting, and you can only get up to first floor level. The later modifications, including the large Elizabethan windows, mean that it retains very little of its simple, brutal Norman splendour.

So the buildings within the castle walls are a little disappointing, but the guidebook recommends several walks which will help you appreciate its exterior, including visits to the medieval pleasure-grounds in which Henry V's banqueting hall stood, and the nearby ruins of Kenilworth abbey.

Clearly signposted just to the north of Kenilworth town, off the A452.

THE LUNT ROMAN FORT

*Coventry City Council • ££ • Limited hours
(usual hours during school summer holidays,
weekends only rest of the year)*

This is one of the most fun to visit of
all the Roman sites in England,
though the bits that are most fun
aren't Roman at all – they're recent
reconstructions, in timber, of the walls
and gate of a Roman legionary fort.
The reconstructed gateway has a
serious purpose, too: it was built by
soldiers in a weekend using only tools
like those the Romans would have
used, and the timbers were set in the
original post-holes. Admittedly it
won't hold your interest for long once
you've clambered up the ladders to
the top level, but it does get you
interested in what is, in fact, quite an
important site.

The fort was in use between 60 and
80 AD and was almost certainly
central to the crushing of the rebellion
of the Iceni led by Boudicca. It has
one particularly unusual feature: a
circular arena now interpreted as a
ring in which horses were trained. The
conclusion is that this was a major
supply base of the period.

There's also a reconstruction of
what looks like a barrack block, but in
fact rests on the foundations of the
original granary, and this houses quite
a decent little museum.

In village of Baginton, near Coventry.

*The reconstructed Roman fort gateway at The Lunt is
far more memorable than the usual knee-high remains.*

WARWICK CASTLE

Corporately owned • ££££ • Usual hours

There are several superb things about
Warwick castle: specifically, the huge
gatehouse and barbican, and the two
massive towers known as Caesar's
Tower and Guy's Tower, all of which
were built in the mid-to-late 1300s by
Thomas de Beauchamp, a favourite
commander of Edward III who fought
at Crecy and Poitiers.

Although these are incredibly
impressive examples of late medieval
military architecture, they don't save
the castle from its modern fate as a
very busy tourist trap, owned by the
same people who run Madame
Tussaud's, London's famous
waxwork museum. Its fancy modern
exhibits might appeal to the kids, but I
really couldn't recommend it.

In Warwick town centre.

SEE ALSO...

BRANDON CASTLE, *next to the minor
road to Wolston, near the church* –
There are reasonable traces left of
this small castle which had an
unusual H-shaped keep. It's on
private land and not open, but the
castle has some history which may
be of interest if you're local.

BURROW HILL HILLFORT, *Corley,
near Coventry* – Has just the one
rampart, made of earth and rubble
laced with timber, but it's in quite a
decent location.

HALESOWEN ABBEY, *signposted in
Halesowen off the A456* – There's
not much left of the abbey founded
in the early 1200s by King John, but
it's interesting. Just two slight
hitches: it was built into a farm in
Victorian times and it's not open
very often. (*English Heritage, £,
summer weekends only.*)

KINVER EDGE, *near Stourbridge* –
More a beauty spot than anything
else, with woodland walks on a high
sandstone ridge with great views,
but cut into the face of the cliff are a
number of extraordinary cave-like
'rock houses' which were occupied
from medieval times right up to the
1950s. There's nothing quite like it
to be seen anywhere else in the
country. (*National Trust, free,
access to rock houses basically
Wednesday, Saturday and Sunday
afternoons though other parts are
open usual hours.*)

WAPPENBURY FORT, *in the village of
the same name* – Notable because
the village has developed inside the
ramparts of an iron age fort, though
the vast rampart of gravel and clay
is not terribly well preserved except
on the east and north-west sides.

AND...

CHESTERTON ROMAN FORT, *on both
sides of the Fosse Way near
Chesterton Brook* (impressive
banks and ditches); MEON HILL
HILLFORT, *near Quinton* (double
rampart and ditch on three sides);
OLDBURY HILLFORT, *near Hartshill.*

The interior of Warwick Castle. Though its towers are fantastic, the place is just a bit too much of a theme park.

Bedfordshire, Buckinghamshire, Hertfordshire & Northamptonshire

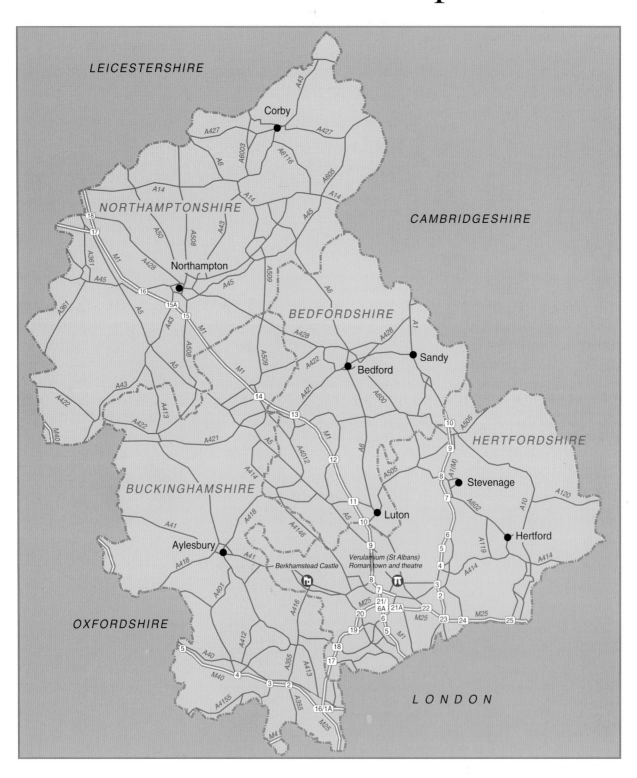

The vast, sweeping earthworks at Berkhamstead make it a great example of a Norman motte and bailey castle.

BERKHAMSTEAD CASTLE

English Heritage • Free • Open access during usual hours

A pleasant, enjoyable ruin dominated by its earthworks, with two circuits of great sweeping grass banks and a double moat (mostly dry, despite the presence of lifebelts) enclosing some pretty high stretches of curtain wall. To one side, there's a mound with some traces of a stone tower. In fact, like *Pickering in Yorkshire*, Berkhamstead is a rather good example of an earthwork motte and bailey castle later enhanced with the addition of stone walls.

Berkhamstead was built by William the Conqueror's half-brother, Robert of Mortain, and was a royal castle for most of its life, but it was generally held by some notable person on behalf of the king. The tower on the mound was a shell keep built around 1160, when the castle was in the care of Thomas Becket. The curtain walls were built in stone at the same time. King John strengthened the walls with round towers and added 'wing walls' which run up the motte.

A square building (the foundations are over by the wall near the curator's house) is thought to have been a three-storey tower built by Richard, Duke of Cornwall, who was given the castle in 1227 by his brother, King Henry III. In about 1300, the castle was given to Edward I's wife.

Signposted in Berkhamstead town centre; by the railway station.

BUCKINGHAMSHIRE SEE ALSO...

GRIM'S DITCH, *near Great Hampden* – This massive linear earthwork runs for 40km (25 miles) across the Chilterns, and it's typical of a kind of dyke that is thought to be a boundary. This one might be iron age, possibly a limit of the territory of the Catuvellauni, but other similar dykes are almost certainly later (eg Bokerley Dyke, Dorset, which is thought to date from the late 300s, or the Saxon-era Wansdyke in Somerset).

IVINGHOE BEACON, *Ashridge* – One of the oldest hillforts in England, occupied before 700 BC. There are traces of round and rectangular huts in the middle. This is fine country, with great views. (*National Trust land, free, open access at any reasonable time.*)

WEST WYCOMBE HILLFORT, *West Wycombe* – Small round fort within the ramparts of which West Wycombe church was built. Nearby is the mausoleum of Sir Francis Dashwood, founder of the Hell Fire Club, which is what makes the place noteworthy.

AND...

BODDINGTON HILLFORT, *near Wendover* (fort with a single rampart made of chalk, flint and turf); BULSTRODE FORT, *Gerrards Cross* (large fort with double ramparts); CHOLESBURY FORT, *surrounding Cholesbury church*; PULPIT HILL HILLFORT, *near Princes Risborough*; THORNBOROUGH BARROWS, *Thornborough*; WHITELEAF BARROWS, *near Monks Risborough*; WYCOMBE CASTLE, *Castle Hill* (remains of a Norman motte and bailey castle).

HERTFORDSHIRE
SEE ALSO...

BISHOP'S STORTFORD CASTLE (ALSO CALLED WAYTEMORE CASTLE), *in park on Bridge Street, at centre of the town* – An interesting local oddity. On a long, oval mound there are the overgrown foundations of a long, rectangular tower. The tower, which had chambers in two of the corners, was built some time in the early 1100s. The castle was updated by King John in the early 1200s. (*Local council, free, open access to view from outside only during usual hours.*)

HERTFORD CASTLE (pictured above), *clearly signposted in town centre* – The thing that is called 'The Castle' today is actually a tall brick-built gatehouse, dating from the late 1400s but greatly restored, together with some later buildings adjoining it. These buildings are now the offices of the local council. Next to them, though, is part of a circuit of walls surrounding an area now used as a town park, with the original castle motte standing to one side. The walls form roughly half of the original circuit, and there is a round tower at one end and a D-shaped tower in the middle. The walls are thought to date from

about 1170, and the motte is believed to have had a small cylindrical tower built on top of it. (*Local council, free, open access to grounds and exterior during daylight hours.*)

WELWYN ROMAN BATHS, *signposted at junction 6 of the A1(M)* – The remains of the bath-house of a Roman villa, preserved in a steel vault right under the motorway. The baths, dating from after 200 AD, are the usual jumble of bits of hypocaust, flue and furnace. Not a thriller, but of definite local interest and remarkable for its situation. (*Local council, £, Saturday and Sunday afternoons only.*)

AND...

ARBURY BANKS IRON AGE FORT, *near Ashwell* (a defended farmstead – excavations found one big round hut in the middle); RAVENSBURGH CASTLE HILLFORT, *near Hexton* (the largest hillfort in eastern England, it may be the *oppidum* that Cassivellaunus defended against Caesar in 54 BC; but permission to visit is need from the landowner); SIX HILLS BARROWS, *near Stevenage* (from the Roman era); THERFIELD HEATH BARROWS, *near Royston* (a neolithic long barrow and later round barrows near the ancient track of the Icknield Way); WHEATHAMPSTEAD DYKE, *Wheathampstead* (iron age earthwork).

BEDFORDSHIRE
SEE ALSO...

BEDFORD CASTLE, *Bedford town centre* – Unfortunately barely anything is left of the castle except a mound and some fragments of stone, but there's a small free local museum next door which has a model of the castle and details of its interesting history.

BUSHMEAD PRIORY REFECTORY, *signposted on minor roads west of Eaton Socon* – The entire refectory building remains intact, complete with its original roof. It's quite pretty. (*English Heritage, free, limited hours – weekends in July and August only.*)

FIVE KNOLLS ROUND BARROWS, *near Dunstable* – Good group of seven round barrows. One of them had about 90 bodies buried near the surface:

about 30 of these had their hands tied and were thought to have been executed in the 400s, while the others had all been hanged in medieval times and later. An interesting example of a grisly gallows site.

HOUGHTON HALL, *near Ampthill* – Ruin of a manor house from the 1600s, parts of which are said to be by Inigo Jones. It's rather attractive, and it's a good place for a stroll in the grounds. (*English Heritage, free, open access at any reasonable time.*)

SHARPENHOE CLAPPER HILLFORT, *near the A6 north of Luton* – This is a small promontory fort cut off by a single large rampart. Although the rampart is probably medieval, under it are traces of a much earlier palisade. This is an excellent piece of country, with good views. (*National Trust land, free, open access at any reasonable time.*)

WAULUD'S BANK, *near Luton* – An interesting large earthwork dating back to the new stone age, the exact function of which is not known but which is thought to have surrounded a settlement. It's a huge chalk bank, 2.5m (8ft) high in places, with a wide ditch outside it, and it curves round to cut off an area inside a bend of the river. Lots of neolithic pottery and flint arrowheads have been found.

AND...

GALLEY HILL BARROWS, *near Streatley* (pair of small barrows which again was the site of a gallows); MAIDEN BOWER FORT, *near Dunstable* (small, circular iron age fort); WREST PARK GARDENS, *off the A6 near Silsoe* (large gardens in grounds of a house, laid out in the late 1700s; *English Heritage, £££, weekends April to October*).

VERULAMIUM (ST ALBANS)
ROMAN WALLS & THEATRE

Roman walls: English Heritage • Free •
Open access at any reasonable time;
Theatre: Local council • ££ • Usual hours

In many ways this is the most impressive archaeological site for miles around, but if you want to get much out of the place, you will have to work at it.

The immediately visible Roman remains are extensive, but not terribly dramatic: they consist of a long stretch of town wall and a pair of Roman rooms with hypocaust and mosaic, now protected by a modern building. These remains are set in a large, grassy park about 10 minutes' walk from the cathedral. They can be seen free of charge at any time.

Much of the rest of the Roman town of *Verulamium* lies buried under the playing fields, and to make sense of it you will need to pay a visit to the excellent museum (*Local council • £££ • Usual hours*). Standing right by the park, the museum explains the Roman town very well indeed, and it also houses some fine mosaics.

The single most impressive remnant is the Roman theatre, which is a short, signposted walk away on the other side of a main road. Its shape is very well preserved, but in itself it doesn't give you much of a feel for what might have taken place here.

Within the grounds of the theatre, there are also the foundations of various shops and houses, one of which had an underground vault thought to have been a shrine.

This is the only Roman theatre in Britain you can visit. Animal shows took place on a raised stage in the centre.

Before it became *Verulamium*, St Albans was the tribal capital (*oppidum*) of the Catuvellauni, and the banks and ditches that protected the Celtic town can still be seen at Prae Wood (directions are probably best obtained from the museum). Like many Celtic towns, it stood near the junction of two rivers, and their modern names – the Ver and the Lea – no doubt have some relation to the Roman name of the town.

Verulamium started as a fort, grew into a small town and in 69 AD was wiped out in the rebellion of the Iceni. Immediately afterwards it was rebuilt on a vast scale, with a splendid forum and basilica (market place and town hall, basically). Eventually it became the biggest and wealthiest town of Roman Britain. There was a sophisticated water supply, and the town boasted a great many fine houses, decorated with top-quality mosaics and Italian marble.

St Albans later achieved lasting glory as the place of execution of the first Christian martyr in Britain, St Alban, who was killed here in about 305 AD. The large and splendid medieval cathedral that is the ultimate monument to his subsequent canonisation has, ironically enough, a good deal of Roman brick in its walls.

Signposted in the centre of St Albans.

NORTHAMPTONSHIRE

The county has two quite important castles which might be of interest, although neither is the kind of major medieval ruin with which this book is chiefly concerned.

FOTHERINGHAY CASTLE, *off the A605 near Peterborough*, is famous mainly because Mary, Queen of Scots was executed here in 1587. Even then it was pretty much a house, with little in the way of fortifications; it was said that you could jump over its walls. (*Privately owned, £££, limited hours.*)

ROCKINGHAM CASTLE, *by the A6003 north of Corby*, is now far more like a grand house but is based on an early Norman motte castle with two baileys. Henry II took control of it in the 1150s and King John put some work into it, but the most impressive feature is a large gatehouse built by Edward I in about 1290. (*Privately owned, £££, limited hours.*)

SEE ALSO...

BARNWELL CASTLE, *Barnwell village* – A stone castle from the late 1200s of a very unusual design: basically a square of walls with odd clusters of towers at all four corners, plus a big gatehouse. There isn't much of it left and it's open infrequently. (*Privately owned, free, very limited hours.*)

BOROUGH HILL HILLFORT, *by the radio mast, near Daventry* – Sizeable iron age fort protected by two banks.

RAINSBOROUGH CAMP, *Newbottle, near Aynho* – Good fort with double rampart: excavations found that one entrance had a timber-lined, cobbled passage leading to two stone-lined guard chambers. This gate was attacked and burned in the 400s BC.

Cambridgeshire

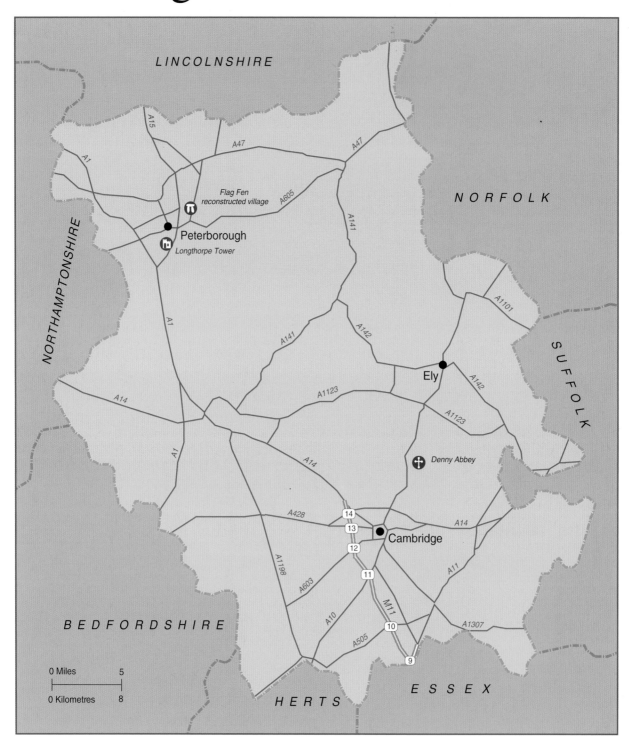

CAMBRIDGESHIRE'S jewels are its university town and the majestic cathedral
at Ely, but the superb medieval wall paintings at *Longthorpe Tower* near
Peterborough are just as memorable in a quiet, modest way.

The farmhouse at Denny Abbey was converted from the abbey church, as the big arch clearly shows.

DENNY ABBEY

English Heritage • ££ • Usual hours

This is an unusual place, and rather good fun. Denny started life as a Benedictine abbey in about 1159, but in 1170 it was given to the Knights Templar, who seem to have used it as a retirement home for old knights. After the Templars were suppressed in 1309, Denny became a community of Franciscan nuns.

The abbey church started by the Benedictines was finished to a smaller plan by the Templars, but the Franciscan nuns converted it into living accommodation. After the Dissolution in the 1530s, it became a farmhouse. It has now been stripped back to reveal layers of stonework going right back to the first church, and this makes it a surprisingly fascinating place to visit.

Signposted off the A10 north of Cambridge.

Right: The interior of Longthorpe Tower is decorated with wall-paintings that are old, rare and very entertaining.

FLAG FEN

Charitable trust • £££ • Usual hours (guided tours Easter to October only)

Major excavations continue to reveal the timber remains, preserved in wet mud, of a bronze age village and a platform which may have had a religious function. There are also reconstructions of buildings and old breeds of animals like sheep, pigs and goats. All in all, though, it's not very interesting.

On the eastern edge of Peterborough, signposted from the A47 and A1139.

LONGTHORPE TOWER

English Heritage • £ • Limited hours (weekends April to October only)

The tower is part of a fortified manor house from about 1300, but the real attraction is that the walls of the first-floor room are covered with paintings from the early 1400s. Said to be just about the finest of their era in northern Europe, the paintings are not only old, they're also drawn in a lively style which is immensely appealing.

Signposted off the A47 west of Peterborough.

The reconstruction of a small bronze age roundhouse at Flag Fen, with a modern Tamworth pig.

SEE ALSO...

ANGLESEY ABBEY, *near Cambridge* – House dating from 1600, built on the site of an Augustinian abbey. The gardens, with arboretum and a mill, are famous. (*National Trust, £££, limited hours.*)

BUCKDEN CASTLE, *near Peterborough* – Former fortified residence of the Bishops of Lincoln, now owned by the Peterborough diocese and not normally open to visitors.

ISLEHAM PRIORY CHURCH, *Isleham village, near Newmarket* – Rare example of a round-ended early Norman church which has survived because it was later used as a barn. Very plain, but well worth a look. (*English Heritage, free, key from nearby house.*)

AND...

DUXFORD CHAPEL, *by Whittlesford railway station*, is not particularly interesting, and nor is RAMSEY ABBEY GATEHOUSE, *Ramsey*. In an area with so little in the way of hills, WANDLEBURY HILLFORT, *near Cambridge*, is quite a good one.

Norfolk

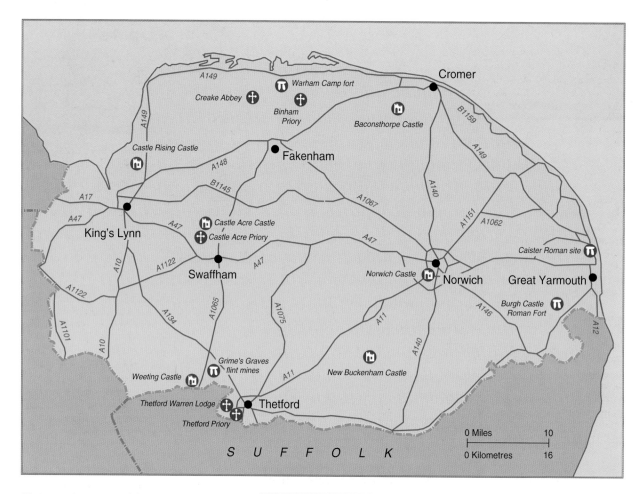

NORFOLK has a surprising number of very fine Norman buildings, and a tour of the county will show you all sorts of examples of beautiful stonework from the Norman period. 'Blind arcading' (arches in relief on a wall, with no actual opening) is a characteristic feature of the classy castle keeps in the area: *Norfolk Castle*, now used as a museum, is the most ornate, but the keep at *Castle Rising* is far more authentic. There are some especially attractive early Norman arches to be found in the church at *Binham Priory*, which is still in use as a parish church. The county's finest historic place, however, is a rich mixture of later architectural styles: at *Castle Acre Priory*, you'll find everything from shapeless crumbling flint to a splendid Tudor window.

Castle Acre Priory is a particularly beautiful ruin, weathered flint being just one of its aspects…

BACONSTHORPE CASTLE

English Heritage • Free • Open access at any reasonable time

This is not strictly speaking a castle at all, but it has a castle-like feel to it because the main part of the ruin is a square of walls surrounded by a moat (or, to be more accurate, bounded on three sides by a moat and on the fourth by a very picturesque lake, which feeds the moat). Baconsthorpe was a large fortified manor house, built in the late 1400s (without royal consent, which it was generally wise to seek) by a man called John Heydon. He was a ruthless and ambitious self-made man who played the dangerous game of supporting whichever side looked likely to win in the Wars of the Roses (1455–85).

The largest buildings are two gatehouses. One is a sizeable three-storey affair guarding the bridge across the moat; the other, placed some distance in front of the main 'castle', was built later and in a more decorative Tudor style.

The circuit of walls and towers inside the moat survives to a reasonable height, but there aren't any stairs or rooms to explore. It's a pretty ruin, though, its waterside setting adding greatly to its appeal.

Down a clearly signposted farm track from the village of Baconsthorpe.

As well as this picturesque moated ruin, Baconsthorpe Castle also has a very attractive Tudor gatehouse.

BINHAM PRIORY

English Heritage and church authorities • Free • Open access at any reasonable time to ruins (usual hours for church)

This is a priory of two halves: part one is a large set of crumbling flint ruins, cared for by English Heritage, while part two is the nave of the Norman priory church, which still stands pretty much intact (though minus the aisles along each side) and which is used as the parish church. The church is a rather charming mixture of graceful, simple Norman arches and desperately clunky later repairs, such as the bricked-up window above the door. It would be a great shame to pass this way without having a look inside. The ruined part of the priory, on the other hand, is a good deal less interesting, but you can make out where some of the principal rooms stood, such as the Chapter House and the Warming Room.

The Priory was founded as an offshoot of St Albans Abbey in 1104, and is remarkable for the number of unsavoury and disreputable priors who were in charge of the place. (The guidebook available from the church contains a good brief history.) In one episode in 1212, after the prior had been removed by the Abbot of St Albans, a local nobleman called Robert Fitzwalter actually laid siege to the Priory in an attempt to get his man reinstated. This greatly irked King John, who is said to have exclaimed 'By God's feet, either I or Fitzwalter must be King of England!' before sending armed men to chase off the besiegers. The prior from 1317, William de Somerton, was so obsessed with alchemy that he sold most of the Priory's valuables to buy materials for his experiments. Of such stuff was medieval England made…

In the village of Binham.

Left: The nave of the Norman priory at Binham is still in use as the parish church, and the interior is lovely.

BURGH CASTLE ROMAN FORT OF THE SAXON SHORE

The walls of the Roman fort of Burgh Castle are more than 1600 years old and still stand up to 5m (16ft) high.

English Heritage • Free • Open access at any reasonable time

A very classy Roman ruin which demands comparison with the similar fort at *Portchester, Hampshire*. Burgh doesn't have a Norman castle, however, and nor does it have a complete circuit of Roman walls – one side has disappeared entirely. But all the same, at first sight, as you approach on foot over the fields, it's a very impressive monument. For the full length of one of the long sides of the fort, the wall stands to more or less its original height, punctuated with a number of solid round bastions. These bastions would have been armed with light catapults or spear-throwing *balistas*.

There's one angle from which the slight decay of Burgh is actually preferable to the perfection of Portchester, and that's when you make your way round the side to see that one of the solid bastions has actually broken off and rolled, more or less in one piece, several yards down the hill. The fact that it didn't just disintegrate is something of a tribute to the work of the Roman builders. The collapse of the bastion clearly shows that these structures were built outside the wall, not bonded with it (though they were joined at the top, as you can see from the weathered join between the wall and the corner bastion a short distance away). You can also see the square socket on the top of the bastion which the catapult was mounted in.

The fort of *Gariannonum* was built in about 275 AD to control the Waveney river and, like all the Saxon Shore forts, to prevent Saxon raiders from making inland incursions. There was also a quay alongside the fort, traces of which have been uncovered.

The fort was destroyed in the mid-300s and in 630, St Fursa built a monastery within its walls. Fairly early in Norman times, a motte castle was constructed in one corner, but there isn't any sign of it now because the mound was levelled in 1839 to help restore the site to something more like its Roman appearance.

An easy five-minute walk, on level track and across a grassy field, from church at Burgh Castle; signposted down minor roads off the A143 west of Great Yarmouth.

This may have been a boarding house in the Roman town at Caister.

CAISTER ROMAN SITE

English Heritage • Free • Open access at any reasonable time

The remains here are minimal, and in the rather unattractive surroundings of a modern housing estate. There's a stretch of town wall and the footings of a row of buildings, but none of the walls survives above foundation height. There's also a piece of paved street. It's all a little dull, but it's a lot more interesting on paper, because this was a small port which grew wealthy from trading expeditions across the North Sea to the Rhine.

Signposted off the A149 at Caister-on-Sea.

Pleasing in its external appearance, the keep at Castle Rising also has a very interesting interior.

CASTLE RISING CASTLE

English Heritage • ££ • Slightly limited hours (closed Monday and Tuesday in winter)

One of the nicest keeps in England, dating from about 1140. Part of its appeal lies in its attractively detailed exterior, featuring typical Norman decorative themes but without the flamboyance of the keep at *Norwich* (*opposite*). Equally satisfying is its cube-like shape, quite different from the usual tall, rectangular military tower. (It's not as tall as it is wide: just over 15m (50ft) high, but nearly 21m (70ft) across on the narrower side, though it would have been slightly taller with parapets and the tops to the towers at each corner.) There's also something friendly about its setting, in a bowl formed by the massive earthwork bank of the inner bailey that surrounds it.

Perhaps most pleasing of all, though, is the interior, which is very easy to make sense of and which gives the impression that it hasn't been altered a great deal over the years, so that you get a good feel for the way its Norman builders intended it to function. The forebuilding that protects the entrance stair, on the other hand, has been altered a great deal, with windows and fireplaces from its later career as a small house. It seems that when the keep itself deteriorated and fell out of use, this forebuilding continued to be lived in.

When you come to the top of the stair and emerge inside the keep, you're at first-floor level, standing at one end of the original great hall. There's a passage inside the thickness of the wall that takes you right to the far end of the hall, where there's the most unusual arrangement of an upstairs kitchen, complete with brick hearth and chimney.

A spiral stair in the corner next to the forebuilding leads down to the basement and up to the roof (but unfortunately visitors aren't allowed out at the top). There's a similar stair in the diagonally opposite corner of the keep.

The interior of the keep is split in two unequal halves by a dividing wall, and another passage in the thickness of the wall leads from the great hall through to the smaller half and emerges in the chapel. This stood at the head of another first-floor room which would have been the great chamber – the lord's private apartments. Below both the great hall and the great chamber, the high-roofed basements would have been used only for storage.

Apart from the keep, there's a gatehouse, built at roughly the same time as the keep, and the remains of a chapel. There's also the ruin of an early Norman church with a rounded end, which pre-dates the keep and was partially buried when the earthwork bank was built, by which time it was presumably no longer in use.

The castle played its only notable part in history when King Edward III sent his mother Isabella to live in isolation here after a plot against him involving her lover, Roger Mortimer.

Clearly signposted from the A149 King's Lynn bypass to the north of the town.

CASTLE ACRE CASTLE

The great sweeping banks of the earthwork ramparts at Castle Acre are the most impressive feature of the castle.

English Heritage • Free • Open access at any reasonable time

Huge earthworks totally dominate the remains of this early Norman castle, with a vast, sweeping bank encircling a wide bailey, and a high mound overlooking it at one end. There is, however, some stonework too. On top of the mound is all that's left of an intriguing keep-like structure, surrounded by a later curtain wall that looks almost like a shell keep, while between the mound and the bailey is a very crumbly gateway.

The building on top of the mound was converted into a keep in about 1140, when the fragile reign of King Stephen meant that a lot of unlicensed castles were springing up. Originally, though, it was a large defended manor house which is thought to have been one of the earliest stone structures in any English castle. It consisted of two rectangular blocks side by side, with the main rooms on the first floor and two wells in the basement, and it was one of the first buildings in England to have proper fireplaces. It was built between 1070 and 1080 by William de Warenne, one of William the Conqueror's best men, who later became the king's Chief Justiciar.

The other interesting aspect of Castle Acre, now a quiet village, is that it was a carefully planned town surrounded by its own walls. One of the gateways, the Bailey Gate, still stands in the village, as do the earthworks on which the town wall stood (they are between the village and St James's church).

On the edge of Castle Acre village: reached by clearly signposted footpaths.

CREAKE ABBEY

English Heritage • Free • Open access at any reasonable time

There's not much of this Augustinian abbey left – just the ruins of a few parts of the abbey church from around the crossing. It's quite pretty, though.

Signposted down a track from the B1355 to the north of North Creake.

There's quite a number of smaller religious ruins in Norfolk, of which Creake Abbey is about the most substantial.

Three of the finest features of the priory: the west end of the church, the Prior's house and the Tudor gatehouse.

CASTLE ACRE PRIORY

English Heritage • £££ • Usual hours

This is one of the most pleasant and enjoyable historic sites in England. Castle Acre Priory was founded in the 1080s by William de Warenne, owner of Castle Acre's castle, as an offshoot of a priory that he had previously established at Lewes in Sussex. Both Lewes and Castle Acre were Cluniac priories, owing allegiance to the great mother house at Cluny in France.

The Cluniacs were not so obsessed with austerity as, say, the Cistercians who built *Fountains Abbey* in *Yorkshire*, so their churches tended to be fairly ornate. One of the highlights here is the soaring west end of the priory church, dating from the early 1100s, with much of its decorative detail still looking as fresh as a daisy.

It's far from being the only highlight, however, because the marvellous thing about this extensive ruin is its variety. There's a lot of attractive crumbly flint round the back, where you can make out all the buildings of the priory cloister.

The big oriel window of the Prior's bedchamber was added in the early 1500s to bring the room up to date.

Especially noteworthy is the Chapter House, which stood two storeys high so that direct access from the monks' dormitory to the church wasn't possible: instead, there's a flight of stairs on the other side of the parlour.

The careful planning of domestic arrangements at monastic sites is always fascinating, and particularly so in this case. The stream at the bottom of the site, for example, was exploited by three different buildings: the mill, which used it for power, and the kitchens and latrines, which used it for drainage.

Perhaps most entertaining of all, though, is the range of rooms next to the west end of the church which formed the Prior's house. This is an attractive blend of early stonework with later alterations, and it offers a rare opportunity to explore some upstairs rooms and interiors. There aren't too many monastic buildings in England with roofs and floors, but the Prior's chapel and bedchamber both have their original roofs from the 1300s and ceilings from the 1400s. Much of it was decorated with a motif of white and red roses to celebrate the joining of the houses of Lancaster and York by the marriage of Henry VII and Elizabeth of York in 1485.

Signposted in centre of Castle Acre village.

GRIME'S GRAVES
NEOLITHIC FLINT MINES

*English Heritage • ££ • Slightly limited hours
(closed Monday and Tuesday in winter)*

An utterly unique experience, this is your chance to put on a hard-hat and climb down a ladder into a neolithic flint mine some 4000 years old. At the bottom of the kiln-shaped mineshaft, a touch over 9m (30ft) below the surface, you can peer into galleries that radiate in all directions, down which the stone age miners crawled in pursuit of the main seam of flint.

Be aware, though, that the mine is not as glamorous as some photos make it appear: it's kept pretty dark to discourage plant growth, and the galleries are really tiny. Once upon a time, visitors were allowed to crawl down them; but not now.

The area all around the single excavated mineshaft is covered with round hollows in the ground which are the tops of hundreds more mines.

Clearly signposted from both the A134 and A1065 in the north of Breckland Forest.

Hollows in the ground are the only visible trace of hundreds of neolithic mineshafts at Grime's Graves.

NEW BUCKENHAM CASTLE

*Privately owned • £ • Usual hours
(but closed on Sundays)*

An odd but engaging place to visit, with a 'secret garden' kind of feel. You have to ask for the key at the garage and let yourself in through the gate (which means you're guaranteed to get the place to yourself). Behind the gate there's a bridge across the moat, which incorporates stonework from a gatehouse of the late 1200s. Beyond that there's a circular earthwork rampart, which you can walk right round, and this encloses a

The keep at New Buckenham Castle was probably the first round tower built in England – and the largest.

flat, grassy inner bailey with the ruin of a large round tower tucked away on the far side.

This is thought to have been the oldest round keep in the country, built around 1140, and it was probably also the largest. It now stands about 6m (20ft) high, but originally may have had as many as four floors. Inside, it is divided in two by a cross-wall.

On west side of New Buckenham village, beside the B1113. Key from the garage just across the road.

NORWICH CASTLE

Local council (houses the county museum) • £££ • Usual hours

This large keep, beautifully decorated with the 'blind arcading' that the Normans were so fond of, was built around 1130. It was greatly restored in the 1830s by Anthony Salvin, but it is said to be very authentic.

It's a pleasant surprise to find that the restoration hasn't really been continued inside the keep. Instead, the whole of the interior has been treated as a single large space which makes a very splendid museum gallery, with a huge arch across the middle (very like the one at *Hedingham Castle, Essex*) replacing what was presumably a dividing wall. The interior walls are all blackened, as if by fire.

There's a number of rooms and passages in the thickness of the wall that you can look into, but if you pay a small fee (£) you can take one of the hourly guided tours around otherwise inaccessible bits of the keep. The museum, incidentally, is very good.

Easily found in the middle of Norwich: use city centre car parks.

Because the keep at Norwich was restored in the 1830s, it now looks very much as it did when built. Pretty, is it not?

THETFORD PRIORY

English Heritage • Free • Open access at any reasonable time

This is a less than romantic ruin in a town park. The remains are extensive in the sense that they cover a lot of ground, but there's little more than foundation-level walls. A few tall but very crumbly pieces survive at the crossing of the church, and one building, the prior's house, still stands to its full height thanks to the fact that it was occupied after the priory was shut down. There's also a gatehouse of the late 1300s which is in much better condition, but this is on private land adjacent to the priory ruin and though it is supposed to be accessible, you shouldn't bank on it.

Thetford was an important religious centre from Saxon times, and was the home of the East Anglian bishopric before it moved to Norwich in 1094. The priory was founded in 1104 as an offshoot of Lewes Priory in Sussex, which in turn was related to the great monastery of Cluny in France. Thetford Priory's heyday came in the 1200s, when a large Lady Chapel was built amid tales of visions by local people. Holy relics, including a fragment of Christ's purple robe, were 'discovered' inside a statue of the Virgin Mary, which brought pilgrims flocking to the place, usually in search of cures. A boy who was run down by a hay wagon and killed is said to have

Thetford Priory was one of England's foremost places of pilgrimage in the 1200s, but there's not much left now.

been brought back to life after his parents prayed to the Virgin Mary.

The town of Thetford was such an important religious centre that it once had as many as 22 churches, and the ruin of one – the Priory of the Holy Sepulchre – is also in the care of English Heritage and can be visited. It's just a short walk away. Elsewhere in the town are the remains of a Dominican friary and a Benedictine nunnery, but these are not normally open to visitors.

Signposted on the western side of Thetford.

THETFORD WARREN LODGE

English Heritage • Free • Open access at any reasonable time

Located some way outside Thetford on the edge of the forest, this is an interesting little early medieval house which is supposed to have been the dwelling-place of a kind of gamekeeper working for the Priory.

Signposted on the B1107 a couple of miles west of Thetford.

WEETING CASTLE REMAINS

English Heritage • Free • Open access at any reasonable time

The ruin of a fortified manor house surrounded by a moat, some of it built as early as the 1100s.

Signposted in Weeting village, by the church.

Weeting Castle was a fortified manor house with a two-storey hall and a three-storey tower, but there's not a lot left.

Thetford Warren Lodge is a rare and interesting example of a two-storey Norman house.

WARHAM CAMP

IRON AGE FORT

Private farmland • Free • Open access at any reasonable time

This is the only notable monument of the iron age in the region, which in itself makes it worth a look. It's a rather good circular fort with two banks and ditches, probably built by the Iceni round about the time of the birth of Christ. There's an explanatory signboard on the site.

The original entrance was probably on the lower side of the fort, where the channelling of the small river has destroyed the ramparts.

Heading south on the minor road from Warham to Wighton, the fort is down a wide, gated track on the right where the road begins to level out at the top of the hill. Please park carefully.

Warham Camp is an iron age fort built around 2000 years ago (probably by the Celtic tribe of the Iceni).

SEE ALSO...

BURNHAM NORTON FRIARY REMAINS (pictured right), *in Burnham Norton village, near the school* – One wall of a church and a very pretty gatehouse are all that's left, with a local council signboard to explain the site.

BRANCASTER ROMAN FORT, *Brancaster* – The earth ramparts of the fort of *Brancodunum* are visible, but the real reason to come here is for a pleasant walk on National Trust land beside the north Norfolk coast.

CAISTER CASTLE, *near Caister-on-Sea* – The brick-built tower here is the most prominent building of what is classed (with *Tattershall Castle, Lincolnshire* and *Herstmonceux Castle, Sussex*) as one of the best examples of a brick castle from the 1400s. Unfortunately it isn't open to visitors, although there is some sort of car museum in the grounds which is open in the summer months.

CAISTOR ST EDMUND ROMAN TOWN, *near Norwich* – There's a large Roman town buried under fields here, which is pretty exciting as a concept even if there isn't very much to see. Best place to start is with the interesting display in Norwich museum, but also there are explanatory signboards on the site. The town of *Venta Icenorum* was set up in about 70 AD, not long after the uprising of the Iceni, and its original timber buildings were rebuilt in stone in about 150 AD. They include a forum, basilica, baths and temples.

CLAXTON CASTLE, *near Norwich* – There are the remains here (a wall with six towers) of a small castle built in about 1333, but they are in the grounds of a private house and not open to the public.

COW TOWER, *Norwich* – Norwich had extensive town walls, and this round brick tower used to be part of the defences. It now stands on its own in a park by the river. (*English Heritage, free, open access.*)

NORTH ELMHAM CHAPEL (OR CATHEDRAL), *North Elmham village* – One of the most eccentric historic sites in the country, this started life as a wooden Saxon cathedral and went on to become a Norman chapel which was later converted into a fortified house by a local bishop. Bizarre. It's not much to look at, though. (*English Heritage, free, open access.*)

OXBURGH HALL, *south-west of Swaffham* – Large and very fine moated manor house built in 1482. It's a really good example of a later

fortified house, and has extensive gardens as well as such frippery as embroidery by Mary Queen of Scots. (*National Trust, £££, limited hours – afternoons only, closed Thursday and Friday, April to October only.*)

PEDDARS WAY ROMAN ROAD – miles of it is now a long-distance footpath, but there isn't an awful lot of evidence of the original Roman roadway or drainage ditches.

AND...

ARMINGHALL HENGE, *Bixley, near Norwich;* HOLKHAM FORT, *north-west of Holkham;* LITTLE CRESSINGHAM ROUND BARROWS, south of the B1108.

Suffolk

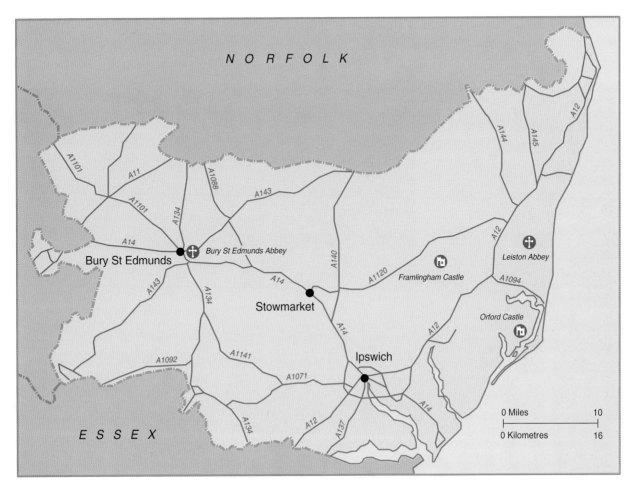

SUFFOLK was once just a part of Norfolk, and it shares much of the rural character of its neighbour. Its country villages are particularly pretty, and it has some very scenic coastline. It is also home to two of the most interesting castles in England: *Orford Castle*, with its attractive cylindrical keep, and *Framlingham Castle*, which is an early example of a castle that had no keep, its principal defence being a circuit of tall walls with many towers, each of which could be cut off and defended separately. Both castles are well worth seeing, though Orford is the more pleasing to explore.

Right: The walls at Framlingham Castle, built about 1190, still stand to something like 13m (45ft) in height.

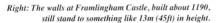

171

BURY ST EDMUNDS ABBEY

English Heritage and local council • Free • Usual hours

Bury St Edmunds Abbey was, of course, the abbey in which St Edmund was buried, which was enough to make it one of the most important in the country. For the most part its once-splendid buildings have crumbled completely away, but even in a scattered and fragmentary condition it's an interesting place. There's a lot to see, and you could spend a couple of hours taking it in.

King Edmund was killed in battle by the Danes in 870, shot through with arrows and then decapitated, but his body immediately began to attract miracles: a magical wolf crying "Here!" led his followers to the loose head. In 903, the sainted king's remains were brought to Bury, where there was already an important monastery founded by Sigebert, King of the East Angles, in about 633. After the Normans arrived, and especially after William the Conqueror confirmed the Abbey's independence in 1081, the serious building work started. Eventually it became one of the wealthiest Benedictine abbeys in England, with Saint Edmund's remains housed in a magnificent shrine behind the high altar in the east end of the church.

The organic shapes of the flint remains can only hint at the scale and grandeur of Bury St Edmunds Abbey.

There's a vast, rambling assortment of crumbling flint-and-mortar remains scattered throughout the town park, which is enough to give you a good idea of the scale of the place. It's well explained by a trail of signboards.

There are also quite a few intact pieces – in particular the huge, richly ornamented Norman tower which doubled up as a gateway and bell-tower for the neighbouring church – and these show very clearly what a prestigious place this was. There's even a bridge that once carried the town wall, its arches capable of being defended with portcullises.

And, to show that Bury St Edmunds can offer something that you won't see anywhere else, there's an extraordinary set of houses which seem to have grown organically, like fungus on a rotting oak, out of the broken stones of the west end of the church. All together, it makes for a very intriguing ensemble.

Clearly signposted as 'Historic Bury St Edmunds' on the east side of the town.

SEE ALSO...

BUNGAY CASTLE (pictured right), *in the middle of Bungay* – Remains of another castle of the Bigod family, Earls of Norfolk. It has a gatehouse composed of two hollow round towers, and the base of a large, square keep, under which there is a short tunnel said to be a mine dug during a siege. Indifferently cared for, it's not much to look at. (*Local council; free access during shop hours: key from nearby shops as advertised on signboard.*)

EYE CASTLE, *Eye* – A Norman motte with some remains of stonework and a Victorian folly on top. It's in a park and can be visited free at most times.

LANDGUARD FORT, *in Felixstowe* – A small artillery fort built in the mid-1700s to guard the harbour mouth, and

adapted over the years. (*English Heritage, ££, Sunday and bank holiday Mondays in summer only.*)

LINDSEY ST JAMES CHAPEL, *signposted near Lindsey village* – a tranquil little thatched Norman building from the 1200s, in a very quiet bit of country, but hemmed in so that it's hard to appreciate the exterior. (*English Heritage, free, access to interior during usual hours.*)

ST OLAVE'S PRIORY REMAINS, *next to the A143 at Fritton* – Not much is left except a vaulted undercroft said to be one of the earliest built from brick. (*English Heritage, free, usual hours.*)

WEST STOW ANGLO-SAXON VILLAGE, *clearly signposted off the B1106 and A134 between Bury St Edmunds and Thetford* – One of England's major reconstructed sites, like *Butser Hill* in *Hampshire* and *Flag Fen* in *Cambridgeshire,* but where those are pre-Roman sites, this is Anglo-Saxon. There are reconstructions of typical buildings derived from excavated timber remains both here and on other sites across northern Europe, including a great hall of the kind in which the Saxon lord would have feasted his men at arms. (*Charitable trust, £££, usual hours in April to October.*)

FRAMLINGHAM CASTLE

English Heritage • £££ • Usual hours

This is an interesting and unusual example of a type of castle that's distinctly different from the average, and it has survived in extraordinarily good condition. It was built in 1190 by Roger Bigod, Earl of Norfolk, to replace his father's castle, which Henry II had destroyed in 1175.

What was unusual about the castle was that it didn't have a keep, relying instead solely on the strength of the curtain walls, which were designed so that they could be defended in a very flexible way. Sections of the wall that were under pressure during an attack could easily be supported by extra men. At the same time, the design gave a large enclosed area which allowed plenty of room for mustering troops or corralling animals, as well as for the necessary buildings. The walls are remarkably tall and strong (13m or 45ft high and 2.5m or 8ft thick), with 12 square, hollow towers projecting from the walls to give excellent fields of covering fire.

The only drawback of the castle's layout from the point of view of the modern visitor is that it doesn't leave

There's a complete circuit of tall walls at Framlingham, which is an unusual variety of keepless castle.

you with a lot to explore. Basically all you can do is climb up to the wall-walk around the top, then follow it round until you get right back to where you started from. The most entertaining bits are the gaps at each of the towers, which the modern walkway crosses on solid footbridges: originally, these gaps were spanned by precarious plank gangways, which could easily be thrown down to thwart attackers who had managed to scale one section of the wall.

The Tudor brick chimneys, added in the late 1400s or early 1500s, are quite amusing: most of them don't actually have a fireplace underneath. They were purely decorative, intended to make the place look more like a comfortable, classy modern house.

The most notable building inside the walls was a Great Hall, but this has disappeared under the poorhouse built in the 1700s which now houses the visitor centre. Outside the walls you can see the Prison Tower, which covered a stair to a small postern doorway high up in the wall.

Clearly signposted in Framlingham.

The flint decoration on the east end of the church at Leiston is quite unlike anything you'll see elsewhere.

LEISTON ABBEY

English Heritage • Free • Open access at any reasonable time

There's not terribly much left of this Premonstratensian abbey, and it feels uncomfortably like it's in the garden of the post-Dissolution house (now privately owned by a musical charity); but there are a couple of beautiful details in the unusual stonework of the church (arcading infilled with glassy black knapped flint). There's also a restored Lady Chapel, but it's not always open.

Signposted by the B1122 north of Leiston.

ORFORD CASTLE

English Heritage • ££ • Usual hours (but closed Monday and Tuesday in winter)

This excellent keep is one of the most enjoyable to visit in the whole of England. It's basically cylindrical in shape, but with three large buttress-like projections, which are big enough to have rooms inside, plus a kind of forebuilding two storeys high. This design gives the keep a satisfying simple-but-complex appearance. Once there was also a circuit of stone walls and towers (seen still standing and strong in an engraving from 1600) but these are long gone.

It was built between 1165 and 1173 by, naturally enough, that great keep-builder King Henry II. Compared with the great cylindrical tower at *Conisbrough Castle, Yorkshire*, which belonged to Henry's brother, Orford's keep is quite grand inside, managing to pull off the trick of round rooms and thick walls without feeling too cramped. The wide spiral stair that runs all the way up one of the projecting lobes, giving access to all the floors from the basement to the roof, is particularly grand and elegant. Like most spiral stairs in castles, it runs clockwise so that a defender coming down the stairs would more easily be able to wield his sword right-handed against an attacker coming up.

The keep has all the features typical of a building of its period and size. The basement, where the well is, was used for storage and could only be reached from inside. The entrance is up external steps to the first floor, emerging in the Lower Hall (probably the public rooms). Above this is the Upper Hall, which would have been private chambers.

In the thickness of the walls there's an intriguing variety of passages and rooms, with some interesting and unusual details. There's a small kitchen right beside the Lower Hall, with a fine shallow stone sink, and halfway up the stairs to the next floor is a chapel. Several of the passages are for toilets, and on the outside walls of the keep you can see the chutes from which these discharged. In one passage there's a sink-like stone construction which is said to be a Norman urinal.

Orford is one of the country's two great cylindrical keeps (the other is at Conisbrough in Yorkshire).

Eventually the stair brings you out on the roof, from where the views out over the coast are excellent. Up here there is also a small bakehouse in one of the turret-like tops of the three projecting lobes of the keep. The oven makes use of clay tiles, some of which are decorated: these would have been used here because they were 'seconds', and are thought to be among the earliest decorated tiles anywhere in England.

The castle was built here partly because Henry was encouraging the development of a new port and town, but also as a decisive move in his continuing war of nerves with Hugh Bigod, Earl of Norfolk, (*see also Framlingham Castle, previous page*). Henry had pretty much won the argument by the time he returned the castles at Framlingham and *Bungay (previous page)* to the Bigods in exchange for a large fine in 1165, but the king didn't have a powerful royal castle between London and Norwich. He kept hold of the Bigod castle at Walton, on the coast near Felixstowe, until Orford was finished, at which point Walton was destroyed.

Orford had an uneventful history after that, apart from its capture in 1217 by the French during the unruly period after the death of King John.

Easily found in the village of Orford.

Essex

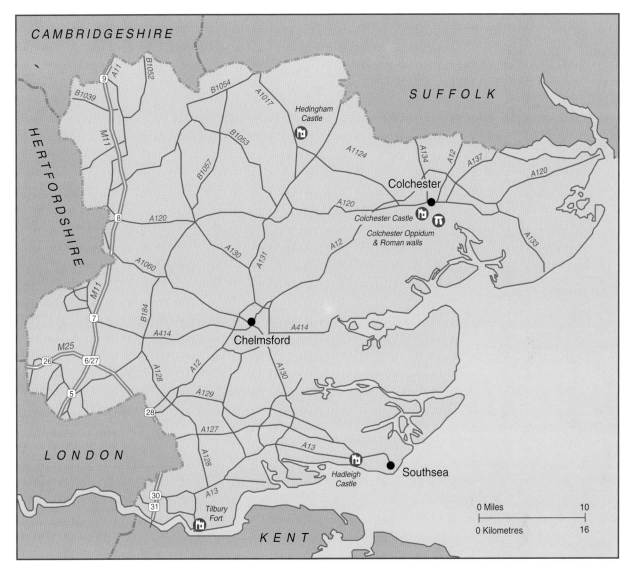

ESSEX is never going to be much of a holiday destination, but it is fortunate enough to have several of the most unusual and important historic sites in the country, within easy striking distance of London. Colchester is the oldest recorded town in Britain, and its Roman origins live on in the foundations of *Colchester Castle*, where one of the earliest and most unusual Norman keeps is built on top of a temple dedicated to the deified emperor Claudius. There's another excellent Norman keep at *Hedingham Castle*, while *Tilbury Fort* is a fine example of how military fortifications developed in the post-castle era.

The extraordinary lifting bridges over the moat at Tilbury Fort, seen from behind the ramparts.

175

COLCHESTER CASTLE

Local council (contains a museum) • £££ •
Usual hours (except Sundays, when it's open
summer afternoons only)

This is an astonishing building. It was
either the first or the second great
Norman keep in England (depending
on who you listen to), built in a hurry
some time between 1075 and 1085
following major raids by the Danes.
So pressing was the need for it that at
first floor level you can see traces of
battlements put on so that the keep
could be defended when it was only
partly built.

It's such a big building that it's
hard to believe it was a keep, but just
imagine what it would have looked
like when it was four storeys tall
rather than the present two: the top
two floors were demolished after the
castle was sold for scrap in 1683.

Even more remarkably, the keep is
set firmly on the foundations of an
enormous Roman temple. This temple
was dedicated to the deified Emperor
Claudius, who led the Roman
invasion of Britain in 43 AD and made
a triumphal entry into captured
Colchester at the head of his troops.
Where most temples would have been

The extraordinary keep of Colchester Castle is one of the oldest in England, built on top of a Roman temple.

built on a solid stone base, this one
was founded on vaults filled with
sand. These vaults form the
foundation of the Norman keep, and
have now been excavated.

The keep now houses a museum,
which is very good but doesn't give
you much of a feel for what the
Norman interior might have been like.
Both the Roman vaults and various
parts of the keep that are not usually
open to visitors can be visited on a
guided tour (*every day, hourly, £*).

In the middle of Colchester, off the High St.

HADLEIGH CASTLE

English Heritage • Free • Open access at any
reasonable time

This modest ruin is in an interesting
setting overlooking the Thames
estuary. Its main feature is a large
ruined round tower, but there are also
pieces of curtain wall and remains of
a gatehouse with a barbican in front.
Most of this stonework dates from
just before 1370, when the castle was
rebuilt by Edward III.

Signposted from the middle of Hadleigh.

Right: Hadleigh Castle is a pretty little ruin, and it
features in a number of paintings by Constable.

HEDINGHAM CASTLE

Privately owned • £££ • Limited opening
(Usual hours, but Easter to October only)

This impressive Norman keep stands alone on the top of a hill, the rest of the castle that surrounded it having long vanished to be replaced by a posh house. It's in remarkably original condition, except that in the early 1700s two huge holes were smashed in the east side and fitted with barn doors, so that the basement could be used to park carriages in.

There are two things about the exterior of the keep that give it a very authentic early Norman look. First, the windows are tiny, minimising the chances for attackers to gain entry or weaken the structure (and the higher ones, which are more than just slits, are typical simple Norman arches). Second, a touch of grandeur is added by the occasional fine detail in the stonework, such as the zig-zag chevron moulding of the doorway.

The keep was built in about 1140 by Aubrey de Vere, son of one of William I's most important knights, whose father had been rewarded with extensive estates in south-east England. Its architect was William de Corbeuil, Archbishop of Canterbury, who had previously designed the vast keep at *Rochester, Kent,* of which Hedingham is said to be a three-quarters-size copy.

The entrance is, as is usual, by stairs to the first floor, and at some time a forebuilding was built to cover the stairs, but it has since been ruined. Inside, the first floor is now used as a shop and cafe, which probably makes the keep the oldest fortified building in England in which you can have a cup of tea.

A single spiral stair in one corner, its stone treads replaced with brick in the 1500s, leads down to the basement and up to the higher floors. The basement was used for storage and is thought to have had a well on one side, and a cesspit into which the toilets drained on the other. There's actually still a faint smell of drains in one corner, but there could be another reason for this.

It's upstairs, on the second floor, that the real surprise of Hedingham is waiting. Rather than being divided in two by a supporting wall, like the

The keep at Hedingham was built as a three-quarters-size version of the keep at Rochester in Kent.

keep at Rochester, this room has a huge arch right across the middle. It's pretty remarkable. The room, known as the Banqueting Hall, is two storeys high, with a gallery halfway up running round all four sides of the room. In the thickness of the wall are various alcoves, chambers and passages leading to toilets, and the arches that give access to these side-chambers are really splendidly decorated, further enhancing the impression that this was a room designed to impress.

Further up is another floor said to have been divided by hangings and used as sleeping accommodation. (It's a little hard to picture the Earl and his wife bedding down in an alcove in the corner, as described by an explanatory

signboard, but it does make you consider the makeshift nature of the accommodation offered by keeps, which explains why they were often only used in times of crisis.) The stair continues to the roof, but unfortunately visitors can't follow.

The castle was besieged and taken in 1216 by King John, but re-taken the following year by the forces of Louis, Prince of France, of whom Hedingham's owner was a supporter. It's said that there was a secret tunnel from the basement of the keep to the fishponds, and that, during one of these sieges, the defenders threw fresh fish at the besiegers to show how well they were eating.

Signposted on the A604 at Castle Hedingham.

TILBURY FORT

English Heritage • £££ • Usual hours

This is the finest example in England of the post-medieval equivalent of the castle, built in the late 1600s and influenced by the latest ideas from Europe on how to build ramparts to withstand artillery fire and how to shape them so that every inch could be defended with covering gunfire.

Unfortunately, to appreciate its design you have to see it from the air. At ground level it doesn't look much, with the exception of the fascinating lifting bridges over the moat. Even these, though, you can't get close to. Access generally is very poor, with only a much later magazine block and one underground magazine on view.

Clearly signposted, near Tilbury docks.

The paved pentagonal parade ground of Tilbury Fort, with (on the left) the red-brick powder magazines of 1716 and (on the right) the Officers' Barracks, dating largely from about 1772, which is lived in as houses.

SEE ALSO...

BARTLOW HILLS BARROWS, *on footpath near Ashdon* – Rare group of round barrows from the Roman era.

BRADWELL ROMAN FORT OF THE SAXON SHORE, *on footpath to Bradwell Point* – Mostly ruined fort of *Orthona*, with one round bastion and some wall next to a small chapel from the 600s.

COALHOUSE FORT, *near East Tilbury* – A decent example of a Victorian brick-built fort, but open only irregularly. (*Private trust, ££, eight days a year.*)

COGGESHALL GRANGE BARN, *Coggeshall near Colchester* – Dating from the 1200s, this is said to be the oldest timber-framed barn in Europe. (*National Trust, ££, open Tuesday, Thursday and Sunday afternoons April to mid-October.*)

COLCHESTER OPPIDUM (Lexden and Bluebottle Grove earthworks) – Dykes protecting *Camulodunum*, the tribal capital of the Trinovantes captured by the Catuvellauni in about 10 BC. (*English Heritage, free, open access.*)

HARWICH REDOUBT, *Main Road, Harwich* – Small circular fort of the Napoleonic era. (*Private trust, £, open Sundays only except in May and August when it's open all the time.*)

LAYER MARNEY TOWER, *signposted off the B1022 south of Colchester* – Very ostentatious (and very tall) brick-built gatehouse of a Tudor house, built between 1515 and 1525. (*Privately owned, £££, afternoons except Saturday, April to September.*)

MERSEA MOUNT BARROW, *near West Mersea* – Unusual barrow of the Roman era with a brick vault at its centre. In the early 1900s a passage was installed to the vault and a key is supposed to be available from a nearby house, but the place has a derelict air.

PLESHEY CASTLE, *Pleshey village* – Substantial earthworks of a motte castle with a vast bailey are all there is to see, though some stonework has been excavated. (*Privately owned, visits by arrangement only.*)

PRIOR'S HALL BARN, *Widdington* – Interesting medieval barn of the local 'aisled' design. (*English Heritage, free, weekends April to October.*)

SAFFRON WALDEN CASTLE, *by the museum* – A whacking great lump of stonework is all that remains of a large keep from the 1200s. (*Local council, free, open access to exterior only.*)

ST BOTOLPH'S PRIORY, *Colchester* – Ruin of the church of the oldest Augustinian priory in England, with an attractive arcaded west end, but it's in a grubby town park frequented by the kind of people society has abandoned.

ST JOHN'S ABBEY GATEHOUSE, *Colchester, not far from the station* – Quite a pretty little building of the 1400s which is all that remains of the Benedictine abbey. (*English Heritage, free, open access.*)

STANSTED MOUNTFITCHET CASTLE – A reconstruction of a Norman motte and bailey castle, with animals and such like. (*Privately owned, £££, mid-March to mid-November daily.*)

WALTHAM ABBEY, *Lee Valley Park* – The Abbey was the burial site of King Harold after the battle of Hastings and was the last in England to be dissolved in 1540. The west end of the Norman church has remained in use as the parish church, though it was restored in Victorian times. It has some amazing early Norman pillars. Quite a place, really. There is also a gatehouse from the late 1300s in the next-door country park. (*Church authorities, English Heritage and Lee Valley Park, free, open access in usual hours.*)

AND...

There are two hillforts within spitting distance of London in *Epping Forest* – AMBRESBURY BANKS and LOUGHTON.

Leicestershire

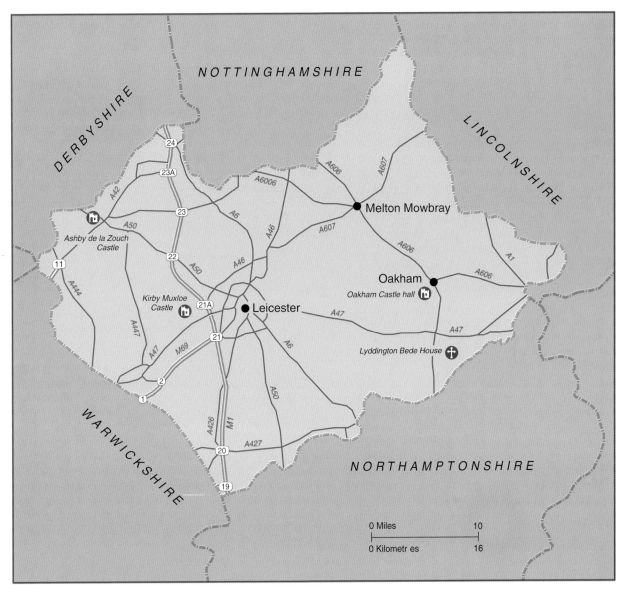

LEICESTERSHIRE'S most important castle, in the county town of Leicester, has long since vanished, but the county has two particularly good examples of later medieval castles. Both were built in the 1470s by the same man – William, Lord Hastings, who was Lord Chamberlain to King Edward IV. *Ashby de la Zouch Castle* is notable for the dark, mysterious underground passage that runs from its keep to its kitchens, while *Kirby Muxloe* is an attractive little moated castle built in brick.

At Kirby Muxloe, a man was employed to sit up all night and watch the level of the moat, so that it didn't flood the castle.

ASHBY DE LA ZOUCH CASTLE

English Heritage • ££ • Usual hours
(but closed Monday and Tuesday in winter)

The 'Wow' factor here is supplied by a dark, twisty tunnel that runs from the basement of the keep to the cellar of the kitchen about 15m (40ft) away. This tunnel is delightfully spooky, with a rather uneven floor, and it really is pitch black inside, so you need to bring a torch (though I believe they will lend you one at the entrance if you ask nicely).

Half the keep – or Hastings Tower, to give it its proper name – was blown completely away in 1649 when the

Lyddington Bede House started life as one wing of a grand residence of the Bishops of Lincoln.

There are tales of underground passages at many castles, but Ashby de la Zouch actually has one you can explore.

castle was slighted, but in one corner is a spiral stair that you can climb right to the top, from where the views are rather fine. The Tower is named after its builder, William, Lord Hastings, who was Lord Chamberlain to King Edward IV, and though it looks like a typical Norman keep, it is actually much more recent: the licence to build it was granted in April 1474. This makes it rather newer than, for example, the brick-built keep at *Tattershall Castle, Lincolnshire*.

The climb to the top of the keep and the dive down the dark tunnel are about all the castle offers in the way of things to explore, but the layout of the remaining buildings – kitchen, buttery, hall, solar and chapel, in that order – is interesting. The oldest parts are the hall and the buttery (which was originally the solar – the lord's private chamber). These date back to about 1150, when an earlier Norman manor house was rebuilt in stone.

Signposted in Ashby de la Zouch; some car parking is available right by the castle.

KIRBY MUXLOE CASTLE

English Heritage • ££ • Limited hours (April to October, weekends only)

Very much a partner for *Ashby de la Zouch Castle, above*, since it was built in 1480 by the same chap, the first Lord Hastings. Kirby Muxloe is built from brick, a far more typical material of the age, and surrounded by a moat. Surviving records reveal that a man was paid to sit up all night watching the level of the moat to make sure that it didn't rise too high.

The castle was a classic layout: a square of walls with a tower at each corner, plus a tower halfway along three of the sides and a large gatehouse halfway along the fourth. Only one corner-tower and the gatehouse are still standing, which means there isn't terribly much to look at, and perhaps that explains why the opening hours are so short. Shame, though, because it's rather a pretty spot.

Signposted off the B5380 west of Leicester.

Oakham Hall is the great hall of a Norman fortified manor house built as early as 1180, although it does look rather like a Victorian public library.

LYDDINGTON BEDE HOUSE

English Heritage • ££ • Usual hours

An interesting old building (with the slight reservation that, for what it is, it's a little expensive, unless you're a member of English Heritage). It started life in the 1300s as one wing of a country residence of the Bishops of Lincoln. In 1600 it was converted into almshouses, and thereafter it provided homes for pensioners for over 300 years.

The downstairs is split into a series of tiny rooms with their own fireplaces, but upstairs the large rooms, with ornate decoration, give some idea of the grandeur of the place in its earlier days. The highlight is the attic room, where you can see the underside of the stone roof-tiles pinned to the wooden beams.

In Lyddington village, signposted off the A6003 between Corby and Uppingham.

OAKHAM GREAT HALL

Local authority • Free • Slightly limited hours (afternoons only on Sunday)

This funny little building looks like a late Victorian school hall or library, but in fact it's the hall of a fortified manor house that was built in about 1180 and is still in remarkably good condition. It is used as a courtroom, and its walls are lined with the ceremonial horseshoes presented to the town by royalty whenever they visit, as a symbolic version of an ancient tax. Well worth a brief look.

In the town of Oakham, in Rutland.

Kirby Muxloe, just on the outskirts of Leicester, is a rather attractive brick-built castle from the late 1400s.

SEE ALSO...

BELVOIR CASTLE, *Vale of Belvoir* – Possibly the most rebuilt castle in England, it's now a Gothic house of the early 1800s by James Wyatt. The site has been fortified ever since a motte castle was built here before 1089; a later castle was destroyed by King John, and another was blown up by Parliament after the Civil War. All the old stuff has long since vanished (*Privately owned, £££, limited hours.*)

BURROUGH HILL HILLFORT, *near Melton Mowbray* – Big fort which may have been the pre-Roman capital of the local tribe, the Coritani.

LEICESTER JEWRY ROMAN WALL, *Leicester city centre* – The Roman town of Ratae was the tribal capital of the Coritani. There's a bit of Roman wall 9m (30ft) high, probably part of a large civic bath-house, with a decent little archeological museum. (*English Heritage, ££, usual hours.*)

Nottinghamshire & Derbyshire

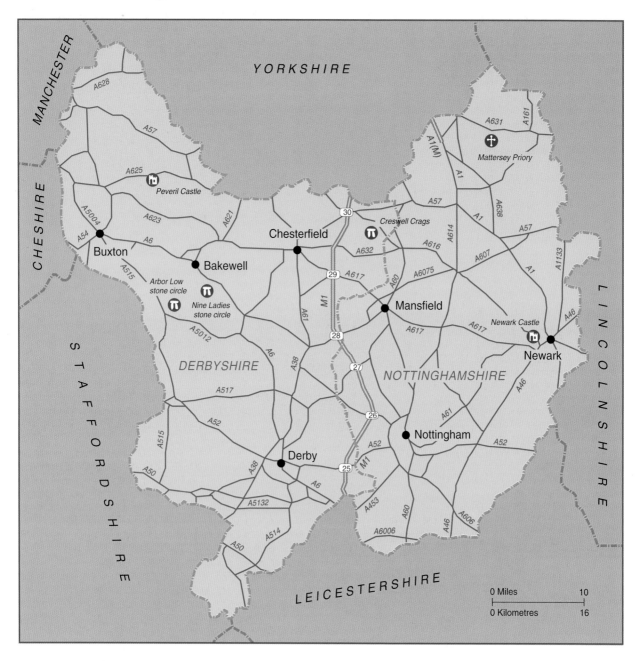

DERBYSHIRE'S hills offer the most dramatic scenery of the two counties, although the fertile farmland of Nottinghamshire has its own gentle charm. It's in the splendid setting of the Peak District National Park that the most exciting monuments of the region are to be found – the dramatic stone circle at *Arbor Low*, and the small but surprisingly forbidding *Peveril Castle*.

MATTERSEY PRIORY

English Heritage • Free • Open access at any reasonable time

This funny little place stands in fields near a farmhouse at the end of a long, bumpy, pothole-riddled track. (It's a better idea to walk than to drive; it takes about 15 minutes.) According to an informative signboard on the site, Mattersey was typical of hundreds of smaller religious foundations which were once scattered all over England. And it really is small – almost comically so, the undercroft arches that are the main surviving piece of the building looking like a half-size model of a proper abbey.

Signposted down a rough track from the village of Mattersey on the B6045.

Mattersey Priory is a tiny little ruin, the few bits of remaining arch looking like a model of a 'proper' abbey ruin.

NEWARK CASTLE

Local council • Free • Open access to exterior only during usual hours

From the far bank of the River Trent, this is a cracking-looking castle, but from the other side you realise that it's something of a facade: the tall walls that face the river are just about all that's left. There is, however, rather a good display on the history of the castle in a modern visitor centre in the park next to the ruin (it's free to get in) and there are also occasional guided tours which show you into bits of the ruin that aren't normally open.

Newark was owned throughout its life by the Bishops of Lincoln, who built the first castle here in about 1130, and the oldest part is the large gatehouse, from roughly that date. Most of the rest of the castle is from the early 1300s. It was a quadrangle of tall walls, with towers at the corners and halfway along each wall. Newark's greatest claim to fame is that King John died here in 1216.

In the middle of Newark, by the river.

Newark Castle, on the banks of the River Trent, is where the troubled life of King John drew to a close.

SEE ALSO...

NOTTINGHAM CASTLE, *in the middle of Nottingham city centre* – Trades to some extent on associations with Robin Hood, but in the first place he was a fictional character, and in the second there is barely anything left of the medieval castle. The only surviving building is a greatly restored gatehouse of the 1300s. Nottingham was actually a very large castle, but it was completely destroyed after the Civil War on the orders of Oliver Cromwell. The grounds are now a public park, and in the middle there is an ugly, squat, early Victorian house which is now the City Museum. (*Local council, ££, usual hours.*)

RUFFORD ABBEY, *off the A614 in Sherwood Forest* – Ruin of a house dating from the 1600s which was built from the remains of a Cistercian abbey founded in the 1100s. The grounds are now a country park, and it's more a place for a good walk than anything else. (*English Heritage and local council, free, usual hours.*)

OXTON CAMP HILLFORT, *on Robin Hood Hill, near Oxton* – Small triangular fort with two entrances: near one is a mound that contained Roman coins and a Saxon burial.

ARBOR LOW HENGE

English Heritage • £ (landowner's access charge, honesty box) • Usual hours

A good, big monument with great views across interesting countryside. The henge, of the new stone age, has a ditch dug 2m (6ft) deep into solid limestone, while the arrangement of 50 stones dates to the bronze age. Originally, the stones probably stood upright. A 'cove' of stones in the middle faced the extreme midsummer setting point of the moon.

Signposted down minor road off the A515.

The 'recumbent' stones of Arbor Low were probably meant to stand upright, but weren't bedded in properly.

Robin Hood's Cave, at Creswell Crags, is where the earliest example of British art was found.

CRESWELL CRAGS

Local council • Free • Usual hours

Just about the only place in Britain where you can get an insight into the people of the old stone age and middle stone age. It's a small gorge with low cliffs on either side, and the cliffs contain caves that were lived in by Neanderthals some 43,000 years ago, by early *Homo Sapiens* about 30,000 years ago, and by middle stone age people 12,000 years ago. To this last date belong the first examples of British art – scratchy drawings, on pieces of bone, of a horse and a man. They were found in one of the caves here, and you can actually see them in the site museum.

Museum apart, there isn't too much to see. Setting out on foot, you follow a path around the pond in the middle of the gorge, peering into the caves through iron gratings. Luckily, however, there are guided tours three times a day of the inside of Robin Hood's Cave, where the horse's head drawing was found.

Signposted off the A616 south of Creswell.

NINE LADIES STONE CIRCLE

English Heritage • Free • Open access at any reasonable time

This tiny but appealing stone circle is part of a bronze age burial ground. There are about 70 small cairns in the area, and excavations of some of them uncovered about 80 cremations with grave goods including flint and bronze daggers, axes and beads of faience (natural glass). The moor is a lovely place for a walk, with excellent views.

On Stanton Moor, east of the minor road from Stanton in Peak to Birchover; 15-minute walk on footpath from this road.

Nine Ladies stone circle, on Stanton Moor: there were at least three more like it in the area just 200 years ago.

PEVERIL CASTLE

English Heritage • ££ • Usual hours

It's hard to think of another English castle in such a dramatic setting as Peveril, or one reached by such a steep walk. Perched high on a crag above the busy tourist town of Castleton, Peveril overlooks the largest of the town's famous caves (now called Peak Cavern, though its earlier name, mentioned in an engraving of 1727 reproduced in the guidebook but a little too fruity to repeat here, is far more colourful).

It's not a very big castle, but its use of the rocky terrain to enhance its defences gives it an interesting touch of the grim and forbidding. Two small gorges give natural protection to two sides of the triangular castle compound, with the steep hill up which you approach the castle doing almost as good a job on the third side. The wall on this side may be the oldest part of the castle, dating back to before 1100.

In 1155, when Henry II came to the throne, the owner of the 'Castle of

Peveril Castle is perched high on a crag above the town of Castleton, with the dramatic peak of Mam Tor behind.

Peak' was a chap called William Peverel, who foolishly resisted the new king's authority and was stripped of his lands. Peveril thus became one of the smallest and most obscure royal castles. The little keep was built by Henry II in 1176, though it's hardly the kind of thing you associate with England's great keep-building king.

The only other significant building was a large hall of the early 1200s built just inside the long outer wall,

but another interesting aspect of the castle's layout is that a bridge near the keep led to an outer bailey on the other side of the gorge. The main reason for this arrangement was that the outer bailey could be reached by a much less steep track up from the town, which made it possible to bring up carts carrying supplies.

Reached by a steep 15-minute walk, uphill all the way, from the town of Castleton.

SEE ALSO...

BOLSOVER CASTLE, *in Bolsover* – A romantic Jacobean house built in imitation of a medieval castle on the site of one. Quite pretty. *(English Heritage, £££, usual hours.)*

MAM TOR HILLFORT, *near Castleton* – Large hillfort in a splendid location dating back to before 1100 BC. Traces of huts were found inside, built of two circles of posts.

AND...

CASTLE NAZE PROMONTORY FORT, *near Chapel-en-le-Frith*; HOB HURST'S HOUSE BURIAL MOUND, *on farmland near Chatsworth* (an unusual square barrow with a ditch and bank); FIVE WELLS CHAMBERED BARROW, *near Taddington* (interesting cairn with two back-to-back chambers); MINNINGLOW CHAMBERED TOMB, *north of Ballidon* (big mound with four burial chambers, two still topped by capstones).

Lincolnshire

LINCOLN'S CATHEDRAL is worth travelling a very long way to see, and the superb brick keep of *Tattershall Castle* is almost as fine.

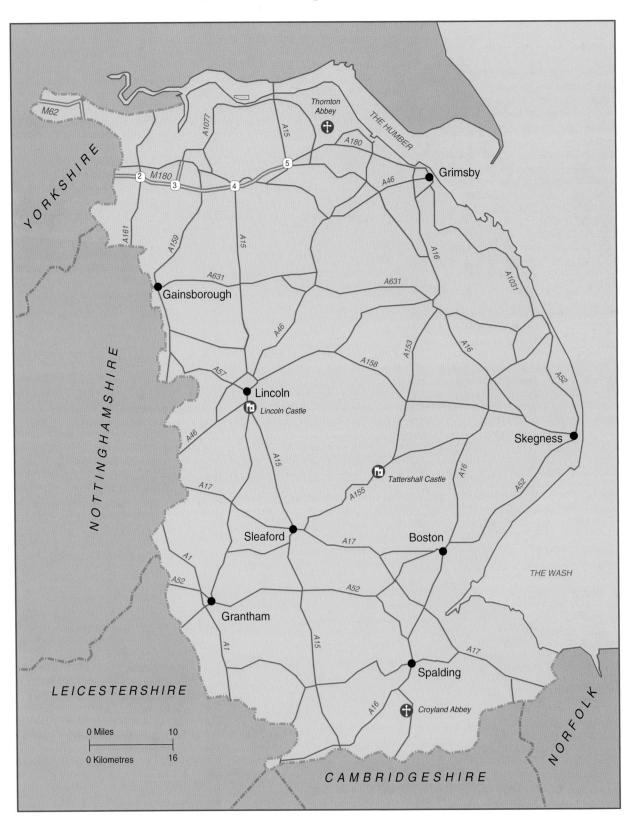

YORKSHIRE

THE HUMBER

M62

A1077

A15

Thornton Abbey

A180

M180

A46

Grimsby

A161

A159

A15

A631

A631

A16

A1031

Gainsborough

A46

A158

A153

A16

A52

NOTTINGHAMSHIRE

A57

Lincoln

Lincoln Castle

A15

Skegness

A46

A155

Tattershall Castle

A16

A52

A17

Sleaford

A17

Boston

A1

A16

A52

THE WASH

A52

A52

Grantham

A1

A15

Spalding

A17

LEICESTERSHIRE

A16

Croyland Abbey

NORFOLK

0 Miles 10
0 Kilometres 16

CAMBRIDGESHIRE

CROYLAND ABBEY

Church authorities • Free • Open access at any reasonable time

This is an extraordinary thing to come across in the flat fenland of south Lincolnshire. It's the ruin of a large Benedictine abbey, part of which (the north aisle of the church and the later ornamental tower) has been converted into the parish church, while the vast, ornate west end of the abbey church just stands there, right alongside the church tower.

The fabric of the west end dates from the 1200s, but the remarkable statues that decorate it are from the 1400s. It's well worth bringing a pair of binoculars or something so that you can look more closely at the statues, and the guidebook available from the church will tell you who they are.

The abbey is supposed to date right back to 699 AD, when it was founded by St Guthlac, and is said to be the burial place of Hereward the Wake (the Saxon who led an anti-Norman resistance movement) and his mother, Lady Godiva. Magdalene College at the University of Cambridge owes its existence to an abbot of Croyland.

Not far away, in the middle of the town, is a vastly unusual three-way bridge built in the late 1300s to replace a similar wooden bridge.

In the small town of Crowland.

The ruins of the chapter house at Thornton Abbey can't compete with the vast gatehouse, seen in the distance.

LINCOLN CASTLE

County council • £££ • Usual hours

Next to Lincoln's glorious cathedral, the castle is a distant second best (perhaps even third best, since the Bishops' Palace is rather good). There's a decent circuit of high walls, with a good wall-walk along one stretch, and there are fine views from the Observatory Tower by the gate.

This tower stands on top of one of Lincoln's two mottes: on the other is a Norman shell enclosure called the Lucy Tower. None of the towers is especially interesting, however.

Within the walls, there are also some more recent buildings. There's an early Victorian court building, designed by the man who created the British Museum, Sir Robert Smirke, and there are prison buildings of Georgian and Victorian date, one of which houses an exhibition displaying one of the few surviving copies of *Magna Carta*. More interesting to look at than you might think, it's the highlight of a visit to the castle.

In the old part of Lincoln, by the cathedral.

THORNTON ABBEY

English Heritage • Free • Open access at any reasonable time

The ruins of the Augustinian priory are pretty minimal, though with a few interesting details, but the main attraction is the astonishing brick gatehouse dating from the late 1400s. The interior is open occasionally for guided tours.

Signposted on minor roads west of Barton-on-Humber.

The remarkable ruined west end of Croyland Abbey. And how did that arch get to be that shape?

The Observatory Tower at Lincoln Castle was built to keep an eye on prisoners in the castle grounds below.

TATTERSHALL CASTLE

National Trust • ££ • Usual hours

This is a fine keep by any standards, but it's also the best example in the country of a later brick-built castle. And it's good fun to look round, too.

The keep was built by Ralph, Lord Cromwell, not long after he was made Lord Treasurer to Henry VI in 1433. He was not the most modest of men: his motto was 'Have I not the right?' and the interior of the building is covered with decorations intended to proclaim the prestige of its owner.

There are five floors in all, starting with a basement used for storage, followed by a parlour on the ground floor where everyday business was carried out. The upper storeys are reached by a spiral stair with a beautifully carved handrail: the hall is on the first floor, an audience chamber occupies the second and the third was a private chamber. All the rooms are large, with ornate fireplaces. Above this is the roof, with great battlements: the drop from the machicolations is pretty scary, and the views from the upper-level wall-walk are superb.

The castle was seized by the Crown in 1471 and remained in royal hands to the time of Henry VIII, after which it was owned and lived in by the Earls of Leicester. They abandoned it in the 1690s. In 1910, the keep's fireplaces were ripped out and sold, and it might have been demolished, but Lord Curzon bought and restored it (as he also did with *Bodiam Castle, Sussex*).

Clearly signposted in Tattershall village.

The superb keep of Tattershall Castle is the finest example in England of a later brick-built castle building.

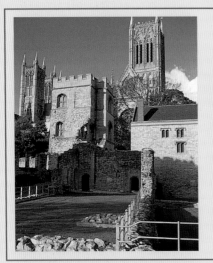

SEE ALSO...

BOLINGBROKE CASTLE, *in the village of Old Bolingbroke* – Knee-high ruins of a castle with five towers and a twin-towered gatehouse, the birthplace of King Henry IV. Quite interesting. (*English Heritage, free, open access at any reasonable time*.)

GAINSBOROUGH OLD HALL, *signposted in Gainsborough* – Very entertaining medieval house from about 1460, consisting of two accommodation wings on either side of a central hall block. The hall is excellent; the kitchens, in their own separate extension, are superb; and at one end of the hall block is a small tower that you can climb right to the top of. A great combination. (*English Heritage and local council, ££, usual hours*.)

LINCOLN BISHOP'S PALACE (pictured left), *by the cathedral in Lincoln* – There are only little bits left of various buildings that stood on this site, but it's a most enjoyable mixture. There's a particularly good undercroft under the East Hall, dating to the 1100s. Most visitors to the cathedral don't even realise the Palace is here, and it's ridiculously cheap to get in. Go. (*English Heritage, £, usual hours*.)

Cheshire

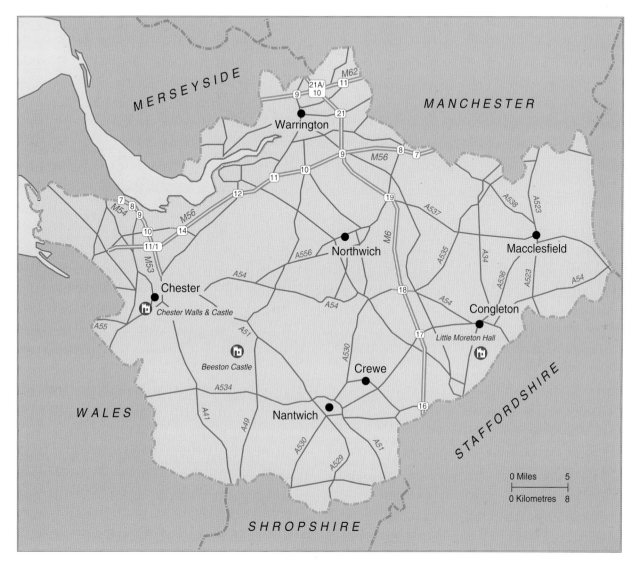

CHESHIRE has been a border county since Roman times, when the fort of *Deva* at Chester was right on the front line, and yet it has surprisingly little to show for it in the way of fortifications. Apart from the medieval town walls of Chester itself, long stretches of which incorporate the Roman fort wall, the county's most notable monument is the dilapidated castle at *Beeston*, its ruinous state compensated for by its splendid hilltop position. Don't miss, though, the gorgeous timber-framed medieval manor of *Little Moreton Hall*, one of the most pleasing old buildings in England.

On a rocky outcrop in the highest corner of a high hill, the inner bailey of Beeston Castle is cut off by a wide ditch now spanned by a soaring bridge.

The square block on the right is the back of the twin-towered gatehouse defending Beeston's inner bailey.

BEESTON CASTLE

English Heritage • ££ • Usual hours

The star of the show at Beeston is the hill on which the castle was built, rather than the scattered remains of walls and towers. It's a massive outcrop of red sandstone that rises out of the Cheshire plain, and it was, not surprisingly, used as an iron age hillfort centuries before the medieval castle-builders got to work. The views are breathtaking, especially when you've earned them with a long, steep walk to the top.

The castle was started in 1225 by Ranulf, Earl of Chester, but it was still unfinished when his successor, John, died without an heir in 1237, at which point the earldom and its possessions were taken by the King, Henry III. Although both Henry and his son, Edward I, used the castle to gather troops and supplies for campaigns against North Wales, Beeston was not needed as a royal residence, so the castle never really had any domestic accommodation apart from some timber buildings in the outer bailey.

Since it was built in a time when keeps had gone out of fashion, the castle's main defences were its two circuits of walls: one around the inner bailey, on the rocky summit of the hill, protected by a rock-cut ditch; the other sweeping around the lower slopes of the hill to form the outer bailey. Both circuits of wall had plenty of projecting towers, so that the wall could be defended by crossfire, and each had a large gatehouse with twin D-shaped towers.

Quarrying for stone on the hillside in the last 300 years has destroyed much of the outer bailey's walls, and the only building that really gives much of an impression of the medieval castle is the gatehouse of the inner bailey, with the modern footbridge soaring rather dramatically across the ditch to meet it. Within the inner bailey is a rather marvellous well, cut some 125m (400 ft) deep into the rock, and if some naughty person is tempted to drop a small stone into it, you'd be foolish not to listen out for the splash.

With its lack of any substantial walls and buildings, then, Beeston is not so much a castle as a viewpoint with added historical interest; but it's a pleasant spot to visit.

Signposted near village of Beeston, on minor roads off the A49 south of Tarporley.

CHESTER ROMAN REMAINS, MEDIEVAL TOWN WALLS & CASTLE (AGRICOLA TOWER)

Walls and Roman remains: City Council • Free • Open access at any time; Castle, Agricola Tower: English Heritage • Free • Open access during usual hours only

Chester is quite proud of its scattered Roman remains, but in fact there isn't anything of any great interest. The legionary fortress of *Deva*, home to the 20th Legion from 88 AD, was intended to keep an eye on the Celts of northern Wales, where resistance to Roman rule was at its strongest. The wooden fort was rebuilt in stone after 100 AD, and there are traces of it in the basements of several shops in the centre of town, as well as surviving stretches of Roman wall under the later medieval walls at the northern end of the city, with bread ovens to be seen on Abbey Green.

A sizeable civilian town grew up next to the fort, its entertainment needs satisfied by an amphitheatre with a crowd capacity of 8,000, one part of which can be seen just outside the modern Newgate. Right by the

Newgate are the foundations of one of the corner towers of the Roman fort, and in a garden next to the wall there are the columns of a Roman temple.

Roman Chester was also a sea-port, but the silting-up of the River Dee was a factor in the abandonment of the fort in the 380s. Traces of Roman quay can be seen near the racecourse.

The best thing about present-day Chester, though, is its circuit of medieval walls (though the gateways and towers have regularly been rebuilt right up to modern times). No visit to the city is complete without a walk all the way round: it takes a couple of hours, and there are signboards and leaflets to help you make sense of it.

There was once a large and very important castle at Chester, but there's barely a trace of it left now. William the Conqueror built a motte-and-bailey castle here in 1070, just outside the remains of the Roman fort, but the first building in stone took place in the 1100s and one square tower of this date survives. Known as the Agricola Tower, it houses a chapel with slight traces of medieval wall paintings. Unfortunately, though, it's unbelievably dull. Nearby are bits of wall which show evidence of the adaptation of the castle as an artillery fort in the 1600s and 1700s, but there is nothing of any substance to be seen.

All in Chester city centre: Agricola tower is reached on foot through the car park at the law courts.

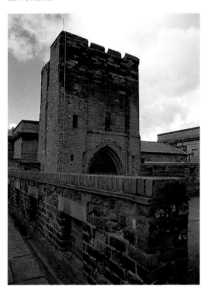

The Agricola Tower is just about the only surviving piece of the huge medieval castle at Chester.

Little Moreton Hall is one of the prettiest buildings in England, and it's not lacking in historical interest, either.

LITTLE MORETON HALL

National Trust • £££ • Slightly limited hours (closed for much of winter, open weekend afternoons in November and December, open daily except Monday and Tuesday mornings from mid-March to end October)

This is one of the most beautiful historic buildings you'll ever set eyes on, and it's probably the finest timber-framed manor house in the country. Its beauty is not just in its design and construction (some of the wood-carving is glorious) but also in the way the building has settled in over the years, the timber twisting and bending into eccentric shapes. Nowhere is this more apparent than in the glorious, airy Long Gallery at the top of the house.

Little Moreton Hall dates from the mid-1400s, which makes it about a century younger than the fortified manor house of *Stokesay Castle, Shropshire* or the pretty moated house of *Lower Brockhampton* in *Hereford & Worcester*. The comparison is well worth making, because both the older houses have a typical medieval layout with the hall as the main room, used for sleeping and eating as well as receiving guests. Little Moreton is, by contrast, a modern house.

The Hall is one of the Trust's busiest sites, and they put on plenty of extra entertainment (free guided tours, a discovery trail for the kids, actors in Elizabethan dress and so on).

Signposted off the A34 south of Congleton.

SEE ALSO...

CASTLE DITCH FORT, *Eddisbury Hill, near Delamere* – Sizeable fort with double rampart and ditch, built before 100 BC and destroyed by the Romans.

MAIDEN CASTLE HILLFORT, *near Bickerton* – A small promontory fort, protected on one side by cliffs which were dug out to make them steeper. Dates back to about 400 BC.

NORTON PRIORY, *near Runcorn* – Minimal excavated remains and a good vaulted undercroft, plus a decent museum. The extensive gardens are probably more of a draw, though. (*Privately owned by charitable trust, ££, usual hours.*)

SANDBACH SAXON STONE CROSSES, *Market Square, Sandbach* – Fine big stone pillars intricately carved with Saxon designs, dating to the 800s.

Lancashire

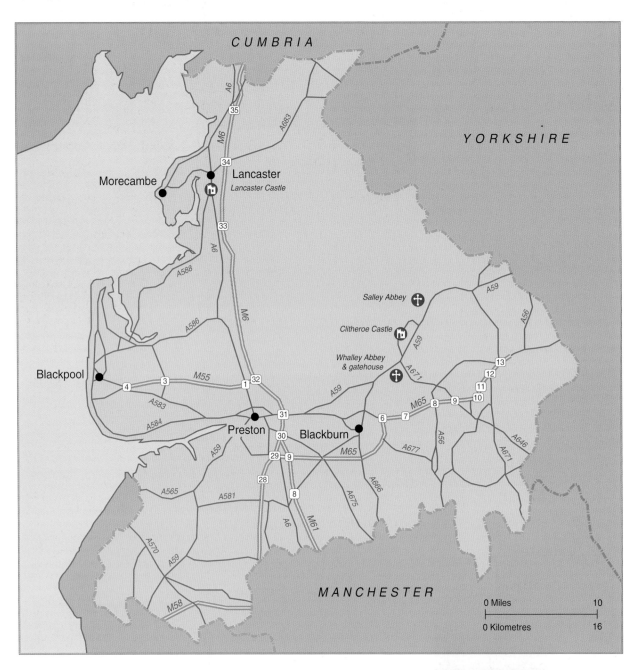

Map of Lancashire showing towns including Morecambe, Lancaster, Blackpool, Preston, Blackburn, and sites such as Lancaster Castle, Salley Abbey, Clitheroe Castle, Whalley Abbey & gatehouse. Bordered by Cumbria, Yorkshire, and Manchester. Scale: 0–10 Miles / 0–16 Kilometres.

LANCASHIRE has, for most of its career, been a quiet, pastoral county far removed from the trouble and strife to the north and south. Its only large castle is at the county town of Lancaster, which saw its heyday after 1399 when it became the property of Henry IV, Duke of Lancaster – but since it currently serves as both law-courts and prison, it isn't really much of a visitor attraction. The county's most pleasant historic site is *Salley Abbey*, an extremely attractive ruin in a quiet slice of country not far from Lancashire's most scenic parts: the Pennine hills, Ribblesdale and the Forest of Bowland.

CLITHEROE CASTLE

Local council • Free • Open access during daylight hours

This small castle is not much to write home about – just the remains of a plain little keep perched on top of a hill and surrounded by a public park – but it looks rather good from a distance, and it's certainly worth a quick visit if you're in the area, if only for the views from the top.

The keep was probably built in the mid-1100s, though not a great deal is known about its history. It is said to be one of the smallest 'great towers' in England and it did not even have a fireplace or a toilet.

At the centre of the town of Clitheroe.

The tiny keep at Clitheroe, set high above the town, actually looks rather grand from a distance.

The great gatehouse of Lancaster Castle, built by Henry IV after 1400, is the main gate to the prison.

LANCASTER CASTLE

HM The Queen and Lancaster City Council • £££ • Usual hours

The modern Lancaster castle is actually a prison (a role performed by most castles at one time or another, so it's an appropriate enough function for the castle in modern times). Its most impressive feature is the great gateway, probably built by Henry IV in about 1400, which you can appreciate free of charge from the outside. Most of the rest of the medieval castle was destroyed after the Civil War and rebuilt as a prison and law courts some 200 years ago. You can visit parts of the building on a guided tour, but it concentrates on the court rooms, which are in the Gothic revival style, and the legal history of the last 200 years. If you're not interested in these subjects, the tour is expensive and a little dull.

With luck, things should get better. Eventually the old-fashioned prison is bound to close, and visitors will gain access to parts of the old castle like the remains of a large Norman keep.

Clearly signposted in Lancaster town centre; a very short walk from nearby car parks.

SALLEY ABBEY

English Heritage • Free • Open access at any reasonable time

There's not really an awful lot left of this Cistercian abbey founded in 1147, but it's a very pretty ruin, in a lovely, peaceful setting on the edge of a small village in a wide river valley. It's a good spot for a picnic.

One thing to look out for when you poke round the ruin is the flight of night stairs, which would have run from the church to the dormitories so that the monks could tiptoe down to prayers in the middle of the night.

You can also have a bit of fun (or perhaps give the kids something to keep them occupied) by hunting around for a few smaller details, too, because there are several carved stones in incongruous places which have probably been recycled. Look out for a stone with a sword in it and an interesting Celtic cross.

In Sawley, signposted from A59 – abbey is through village on right.

It's very pretty, is Salley Abbey, with its well-kept lawns and its pleasant, quiet location.

193

The former main gate of Whalley Abbey, this is the only ancient monument you can drive through.

WHALLEY ABBEY

GATEHOUSE

English Heritage • Free • Open access at any reasonable time

The gatehouse of the aforementioned abbey and its earliest building, dating from the early 1300s. It's an impressively large gateway, with attractive vaults and arches, and it has the unusual distinction of being the only building in the care of English Heritage which you can drive right through on a public highway. Originally there was a chapel on the first floor which could be used by guests staying at the abbey.

Right next to Whalley Abbey, as above.

WHALLEY ABBEY

Church authorities • ££ • Usual hours

The post-Dissolution house at Whalley Abbey is now a conference centre, with the abbey ruins in its grounds.

The Cistercian abbey at Whalley wasn't actually founded here, but rather was moved wholesale in 1296 from Stanlaw on Cheshire's Wirral peninsula, where the monks had been suffering an appalling run of bad luck. By the 1270s, 100 years after it was established, Stanlaw Abbey was being flooded to a depth of almost 2m (6ft) by high tides every spring, so the monks applied to the Pope for permission to go to a new home in Lancashire. The arrangements took years, and in the meantime their church tower was wrecked by a gale and the abbey was destroyed by a huge fire. Even after the move, the Whalley monks squabbled with their brethren at Salley, just along the valley, over supplies of corn, and were sued for a huge amount of money by the Bishop of Lichfield over rights to appoint a vicar to the local church. After just 20 years here, they were sufficiently fed up with the bleakness of the country and the lack of trees for timber and fuel to consider a move to Toxteth in Liverpool, but in the end they stayed put.

In the course of the next 150 years the monks eventually managed to build their abbey, starting with the church and finishing with the extensive abbott's lodgings. After the Dissolution, the abbott's house and the infirmary were dismantled and a large house was built on the site (it's now a conference centre for the Diocese of Blackburn). The church was pulled down not long afterwards, but its foundations were uncovered again by excavations in the 1930s.

Today, some parts of the cloister buildings are still standing, but mostly what you see is the outlines of the foundations. It's less like a historical ruin and more like an attractive formal garden. At times it's more informative than nearby *Salley Abbey* (*previous page*), but it's certainly not half as pretty.

Well signposted, provided you turn off A59 for Whalley first; car parking.

SEE ALSO...

RIBCHESTER ROMAN FORT, *off the B6425 north of Blackburn* – There's a good little museum here which contains some astonishing objects, but the Roman fort is mostly buried under a massive medieval church. A short walk away are the minimal remains of a bath-house. (*Private trust, ££, usual hours.*)

WARTON OLD RECTORY, *north of Carnforth* – Remains of a stone-built medieval house. Worth seeing. (*English Heritage and local trust, free, usual hours.*)

AND...

BLEASDALE CIRCLE, *near Bleasdale Church* (barrow with a timber circle on the top, dating from 1800 BC); CASTERCLIFF CAMP HILLFORT, *near Nelson*; PIKESTONES CHAMBERED LONG BARROW, *on Anglezarke Moor.*

Cumbria

THE LAKE DISTRICT is absolutely littered with top-class historic sites, especially *Furness Abbey*, *Brougham Castle* and *Hardknott Roman fort*.

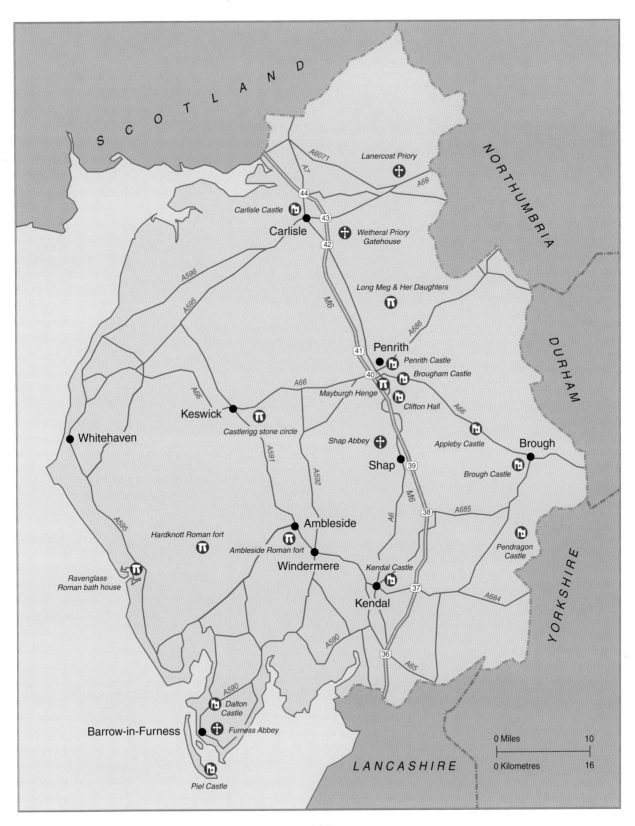

SCOTLAND

NORTHUMBRIA

DURHAM

YORKSHIRE

LANCASHIRE

Lanercost Priory

Carlisle Castle

Carlisle

Wetheral Priory Gatehouse

Long Meg & Her Daughters

Penrith
Penrith Castle
Brougham Castle

Mayburgh Henge
Clifton Hall

Appleby Castle

Brough

Keswick

Castlerigg stone circle

Whitehaven

Shap Abbey

Shap

Brough Castle

Hardknott Roman fort

Ambleside

Ambleside Roman fort

Windermere

Pendragon Castle

Ravenglass Roman bath house

Kendal Castle

Kendal

Dalton Castle

Barrow-in-Furness

Furness Abbey

Piel Castle

A6071
A7
A69
A596
A595
A6
A686
M6
A66
A591
A592
A66
A685
A684
A65
A590
A590

44
43
42
41
40
39
38
37
36

0 Miles ———— 10
0 Kilometres ———— 16

It's a very nice spot, this, beside the lake at Ambleside, and there's a Roman fort to add a dash of interest.

AMBLESIDE ROMAN FORT

National Trust and English Heritage • Free • Open access at any reasonable time

With Hadrian's Wall not far away and the fabulous *Hardknott Roman fort* (*page 203*) just up the road, this modest site seems hardly worth mentioning, but it's in a pleasant lakeside location on the edge of the Lake District's best shopping town, and that's reason enough to visit.

The fort was called *Galava*, and guarded the road from the Pennine passes at Brougham to the Cumbrian coast at Ravenglass. The foundations of several buildings are visible, including a corner tower and several accommodation blocks.

Reached by a short walk through the public park from the car park at Waterhead.

APPLEBY CASTLE

Privately owned • £££ • Usual hours

This is a mildly eccentric but pleasant little place, where an effort has been made to provide entertainment for visitors without turning the grounds into a theme park. There are extensive, well cared-for gardens with diversions such as aviaries, deer and farm animals for the children.

At the centre of the grounds is a courtyard enclosed by a wall – this was the bailey of the medieval castle – and at one end stands the house, which dates largely from the late 1600s, while at the other end is the small but impressive keep, also known as Caesar's Tower. It was built about 1170 (though it was restored in the late 1600s) and the nice thing about it is its authentic feel. There's a long, steep and very narrow spiral stair to the roof and on a clear day the views are just great.

Just on the edge of the town of Appleby.

BROUGH CASTLE

English Heritage • Free • Open access at any reasonable time

Brough is absolutely smashing for a small castle with free access, though you do have to watch out for the rampaging hordes of free-range

The keep of Appleby Castle is rather excellent, with an authentic feel to it and superb views from the top.

chickens from the neighbouring farm. The castle was built in the corner of a Roman fort in about 1090, and was one of the first in England to be constructed in stone. Some of the walls are of this early date and show the herringbone pattern typical of Norman masonry.

There are two main buildings: a broken square keep of four storeys, which dates from the late 1100s, and an accommodation block that incorporates a large round tower in one corner known as Clifford's Tower. Between them is a large courtyard paved with stone in a very similar fashion to *Brougham Castle* (*opposite*) just down the road.

The castle was extensively renovated by Anne Clifford in the mid-1600s, but not long afterwards much of its stone was taken away and used to repair Appleby Castle.

It's quite a romantic ruin, the only slight disappointment being that the flight of stairs which leads to the top level of the tower is currently closed up, and there is no indication as to whether it might be opened up again at some stage. The views from the top must be pretty exceptional.

Signposted from the A685 Kirkby Stephen road just south of its junction with the A66,

Left: Brough Castle is rather good, with a large keep and a big round tower at either end of a paved yard.

BROUGHAM CASTLE

English Heritage • ££ • Usual hours

You have to go a long way (and you'd have to cross the Pennines, too) to find a better castle than Brougham. It's a most enjoyable castle to visit, sited very pleasantly on the banks of the River Eamont. It boasts an impressive gatehouse and a large keep which you can climb right to the top of, thanks to a spiral stair in one corner. Once you've reached the top, you can walk round three sides of the keep to find, tucked in the corner, a surprisingly ornamented little chapel.

Like nearby *Brough* (*opposite*), the castle was built on the site of a Roman fort, which probably explains the similarity of their names, especially when you consider that another Roman fort not far away at Bainbridge in North Yorkshire is known as Brough-by-Bainbridge. The name 'Brough' is probably the same word as the Saxon *burh* (or borough), meaning a defended town. It's easy to see why the route across the Pennines now followed by the A66 was so

Undoubtedly the region's best ruined castle, Brougham has a large keep which you can climb right to the top.

important to the Romans, and the fort at Brougham, the Roman *Brocavum*, guarded the junction of this trans-Pennine route to York with the main east coast highway to Scotland.

The outline of the Roman fort can clearly be seen in the field next to the castle, but it's on private land and cannot be visited. In fact, the fort is not in original Roman condition in any case, because it was used as a ready-made bailey for the castle and its ditches were modified.

Brougham, Brough and Appleby castles all share a history, in that they were all owned by a Norman lord called Robert de Vipont. He built the keep at Brougham, as well as a large accommodation block to the east of it, some time before 1228. Before this date, both Brough and Appleby are known to have seen action in various disputes with the Scots (both were captured in William the Lion's invasion of 1173-4, for example) but Brougham is not mentioned, so it is assumed that it was not yet built. Later, all three castles passed to

Robert, Lord Clifford, who between 1290 and 1314 made sweeping changes to Brougham Castle, adding an extra storey to the keep to contain a comfortable private apartment for himself and his family (including the small chapel mentioned above) and developing the gatehouse right next to the keep so that it almost became the kind of great gatehouse tower that was then considered the ideal form of defence for a castle.

The most endearing character associated with the three castles, though, was Lady Anne, the last of the Cliffords, an eccentric old lady who was so disgusted by Parliamentary victory in the Civil War in 1645 that she retired from London life and retreated north to restore the castles to their former Royalist glory. Oliver Cromwell is said to have dismissed her with the comment: 'Let her build what she will, she shall have no hindrance from me'.

At Brougham, just off the A66 a couple of miles east of Penrith. Well signposted.

The tower of Clifton Hall was part of a defended manor house, heavily adapted over the centuries.

CLIFTON HALL

English Heritage • Free • Open access at any reasonable time

This little tower from a manor house from the 1400s was much altered over the years. A stair climbs to second floor level. Look in if you're passing.

In village of Clifton, on A6 south of Penrith.

DALTON CASTLE

National Trust • £ • Limited hours (Saturday afternoons)

This funny little keep is very like the type of defensive dwelling known as a 'pele tower', except that it was never lived in. Rather, it was a public building, built in the early 1300s as a law court and gaol for *Furness Abbey* (*see page 202*), and its existence is proof of the extraordinary secular power of the abbey, which owned the land and the people for miles around.

The Castle remained in use as both court and gaol into modern times, and has been extensively altered over the years. It's not especially interesting to visit, though if the guide is willing, you can climb down a ladder into the windowless dungeon.

In the middle of Dalton-in-Furness.

Dalton Castle has always been used as a law court and a gaol, and still has the air of a public building.

CASTLERIGG STONE CIRCLE (THE CARLES)

English Heritage and National Trust • Free • Open access at any reasonable time

This is unquestionably the most pleasing of all England's smaller stone circles. Not only is the setting distinctly beautiful, but also the monument was skilfully sited by its neolithic builders so that it seems to be the focal point for the hills around. If that sounds a bit daft, you'll just have to go and see for yourself.

The stone circle at Castlerigg is a national treasure, though more for its setting than for the monument itself.

This is thought to be one of the earliest stone circles in Britain. It is located near a pass to Borrowdale and within easy reach of several good sources of stone for axes. Top-quality axes of Lake District stone are found all over the country, and seem to have been traded as prestige goods.

The 'circle' is actually pear-shaped, with an entrance on the northern side, facing the River Greta, marked by a pair of particularly large stones. The most unusual feature –

unique, in fact – is a setting of 10 stones in a rectangular shape at one side of the circle. Your guess is as good as anyone's when it comes to what the function of this feature might have been. Excavations in the 1880s revealed nothing but charcoal.

Castlerigg is a great place to have to yourself, but it does get very busy in summer. It looks best in snow.

Signposted on minor roads off the A66 to the east of Keswick.

CARLISLE CASTLE

English Heritage • £££ • Usual hours

Like Dover Castle in Kent, Carlisle has the blunted look of a Norman keep adapted later for use with artillery.

Carlisle is rather like Dover Castle, at the opposite end of the country, in that it has a rather squashed look as a result of its medieval battlements being adapted for the artillery age. It has also – again, like Dover – remained in military use right into modern times, and in fact still has Army accommodation grouped around the parade ground that stands behind the gatehouse. One's first impression on visiting the castle is that it might be a little too tidy and functional to be of much interest, but in fact the substantially intact keep makes it well worth a visit.

You won't be surprised to learn that the fat, square keep is the oldest part of the castle. It was started by Henry I in the 1120s, but was completed by King David I of Scotland, who took control of the north of England during King Stephen's precarious reign (1135–54). The keep is divided in two by a wall running down the middle, with substantial rooms on the three

upper floors reached by a spiral stair in one corner. Several rooms contain displays covering the history of the castle, and you can climb up a steep ladder to the roof. In a small side-chamber on the second floor are some extraordinary carvings, which are thought to have been made by prisoners in the 1480s.

The only other substantial old building of the castle is the outer gatehouse through which you enter. Although it's based on a tower built in about 1168, most of what you see today dates from the complete remodelling of the building in 1378–83 on the orders of Richard II. The gatehouse acted as both prison and exchequer (a bit like a bank), but it was also home to the Warden of the castle, with the result that the main rooms are very similar to the rooms of a manor house of the same period. On the first floor is a large hall, with a kitchen and service area at one end and a private chamber (solar) at the other separated by interesting screens.

Both the castle and the town of Carlisle feature heavily in the history of conflict between Scotland and England, from the expedition of William II in 1092 to crush the marauding bands who were raiding into Cumbria, right up to the Jacobite rebellion of 1745, when Bonnie Prince Charlie briefly held the town as a rearward base for a march that took him as far south as Derby, before he was eventually forced to flee back to Scotland in total disarray.

The adaptation for artillery took place mostly in the 1540s at the behest of Henry VIII, and was largely the work of an engineer from Moravia called Stefan von Haschenperg, who seems to have been regarded by the locals as a bit of a cowboy: 'A man that will pretend more knowledge than he hath indeed'. The alterations to the keep's battlements and the 'half-moon' battery in front of the inner gatehouse were both his work.

In Carlisle town centre; use city car parks.

FURNESS ABBEY

English Heritage • £££ • Usual hours

The beautiful and extensive ruins of Furness Abbey are sheltered from the winter weather in a very quiet valley.

This is one of the finest abbey ruins in England and, luckily for the modern visitor, it's not half as well-known as it was in the 1800s. At this time, with the Romantic movement was in full swing, abbey ruins were in vogue and William Wordsworth's book *Guide to the Lakes* helped to make Furness into an unmissable attraction for any tourist visiting the region. Visitor numbers swelled in the 1840s and 1850s, when a new railway, described by Wordsworth as a 'pestilential nuisance', passed alongside the abbey and a huge hotel was constructed right next-door to the ruin.

By the early 1900s the abbey was providing a Grand Day Out for hundreds of trippers at a time. Fortunately it's a good deal quieter now, and you can explore the ruin in the tranquility which it deserves.

When Henry VIII passed the law to dissolve the monasteries in 1536, Furness was the second wealthiest abbey in Britain (the richest was *Fountains Abbey* in *Yorkshire*). Although its history is not known in detail because the abbey's records have not survived, enough is known of its resources and its influence to show that there was an astonishing concentration of wealth and power in the hands of the abbot who ran the place. The abbey had daughter houses in Ireland, Scotland and the Isle of Man. It owned most of the fishing rights and farmland for miles around (as well as lots of land in the Lancashire hills) and operated iron mines, quarries, forges and mills.

In the early 1300s, the abbot was granted the legal rights – unique for a religious leader – to act as sheriff and to appoint a coroner, which gave him the power of life and death over the people of the region. He established a court at Dalton-in-Furness in a building which is now known as *Dalton Castle (see page 198)*. Following a Scottish raid led by Robert Bruce in 1322, when the then abbot, John Cockerham, paid a ransom rather than let his lands be ransacked, the abbey was even granted royal permission to build its own castle at *Piel (see page 203)*.

It all builds up to a picture of a place which was not so much a religious retreat as a massive baronial estate, so it's little surprise to find that the abbey kept up with architectural trends like the fad in the late 1400s for tall towers. The tower built at the west end of the church probably stood to a height of 50 metres (160 feet), very like the surviving tower at Fountains Abbey.

The most attractive parts of the abbey ruin are the five remarkable arches on the east side of the cloister, and the chapter house behind; the undercroft of the neighbouring dormitory; and the chapel of the infirmary, at the far end of the site. In the abbey museum there are lots of interesting carved stones, including two extraordinary figures of knights with their helmets on.

Clearly signposted from Barrow-in-Furness town centre (off A590 or A5087).

HARDKNOTT ROMAN FORT

The extraordinary setting of Hardknott Roman fort makes it one of England's most memorable historic sites.

English Heritage • Free • Open access at any reasonable time

This has to be the most splendidly positioned historic site in the whole of England, set in wild country at the top of Eskdale, where the Roman road from Ravenglass climbed up to cross the Hardknott and Wrynose passes to reach Little Langdale and Ambleside. The Latin name of *Mediobogdum* doesn't actually mean 'the middle of nowhere', but it certainly ought to.

The complete circuit of Roman fort walls still stands to shoulder height, with the foundations of a square tower at each corner. In the middle you can see the foundations of granaries, the headquarters building and the commandant's house, while the small group of buildings just outside the gate which you pass as you approach the fort was a bath-house.

The fort was built not long before 100 AD and was in use for little more than 100 years. It must have been a particularly unpleasant posting in winter, especially when you consider that any wood, for building or for fires, had to be brought up from the valley below.

You should be aware that the narrow, twisty and steep road across from Little Langdale is one of the most… errm… *exciting* to drive in Britain. In winter, or if you're at all unsure of your car, you should approach from the other direction.

By the minor road across Hardknott Pass from Boot in Eskdale to Cockley Beck, just below the summit on the Eskdale side.

Kendal Castle has the remains of a fairly large keep, but it's not a tremendously exciting ruin.

KENDAL CASTLE

Local council • Free • Open access at any reasonable time

Not the most thrilling of ruined castles, and inevitably something of a playground for the bored youth of the town of Kendal, which does nothing to enhance its appeal.

Still, the castle is nicely poised at the top of the hill and there is an almost complete curtain wall with one of its round towers in a very healthy state. The main remnant is the bottom of a great tower and neighbouring hall with some vaulting surviving in the basement. The stonework is thought to date from the mid-1100s and the early 1200s, with the great tower probably being the earliest part.

If you're staying in the town and want to explore a little further, the views are fairly rewarding.

Reached by a walk of about 20 minutes from Kendal town centre; the last bit, up the hill on which the castle stands, is quite steep.

Lanercost Priory was built of stone taken from nearby Hadrian's Wall.

LANERCOST PRIORY

English Heritage • ££ • Usual hours

This priory for Augustinian canons was founded in 1169 and built using materials from Hadrian's Wall. The church survives pretty much intact, and its nave and north aisle are used as the present parish church. It has windows by William Morris and Edward Burne-Jones, and a statue of Mary Magdalene high on the wall above the door is said to have been donated by King Edward I.

The ruins aren't very extensive, but there are several interesting bits. The remainder of the church is fairly splendid, with several large knights' tombs from the early 1500s. There is also a decent vaulted undercroft, above which the refectory stood, and in one corner are the remains of a defensive house or pele tower which dates from the mid-1500s.

Easily found in Lanercost village.

'Long Meg' is a tall, pointy outlying stone next to one of the largest stone circles in England ('her daughters').

LONG MEG & HER DAUGHTERS

On farmland next to public road • Free • Open access at any reasonable time

This is one of the largest stone circles in Britain, composed originally of 70 stones of which 59 now remain, 27 of them still standing upright. Long Meg is a tall outlying stone with faint spiral carvings on the side facing the circle. The stones would probably also have been surrounded by a henge bank, with an entrance on the south-west side, near Long Meg.

This is an impressive monument, but I find that there's something a little offputting about the atmosphere of the place – though maybe that's just the 'offerings' left by the cows…

Follow minor road north from Little Salkeld towards Glassonby; watch carefully for the signpost which marks a left turn on to the tiny road that leads to the monument.

MAYBURGH HENGE & KING ARTHUR'S ROUND TABLE

English Heritage • Free • Open access at any reasonable time

Mayburgh Henge doesn't seem much to get excited about, but when you consider the huge communal effort that went into its construction, and the tantalising glimpse it gives into the ritual lives of the people who built it 4000 years ago, it begins to seem like a very important monument.

The huge, circular, amphitheatre-like bank of the henge is built entirely out of football-sized boulders brought from the bed of the nearby river, and it is estimated that the bank contains five million of these stones. There is just one entrance, on the eastern side, and a standing stone in the middle is the sole survivor of a group of four, while another four stones stood near the entranceway.

Henges like Mayburgh are the predecessors of stone circles, and this is one of the best examples in the country.

Pendragon Castle is located slap bang in the middle of nowhere, though the Settle-Carlisle railway runs past it.

Penrith Castle was a large, square thing consisting of four walls around a courtyard. Not terribly pretty.

A short walk away is another unusual henge monument known as King Arthur's Round Table. Not as dramatic as Mayburgh, it's a circular area defined by a large ditch, with two entrances on opposite sides formed by banks across the ditch. Nobody knows what its purpose was, though excavation did reveal that a cremation had taken place in the centre.

The two monuments are thought to be roughly contemporary and to date to between 2500 and 1700 BC.

Signposted just off the A6 near its junction with the B5320 south of Penrith.

PENDRAGON CASTLE

On private farmland • Free • Open access at any reasonable time

In a beautiful countryside setting, this is a small ruin which is well worth having a quick poke around. It was a square tower of a fair old size, said to have been built by Henry II and later owned, as were so many of the castles in the area, by the Cliffords. Legend connects the place with Uther Pendragon, father of King Arthur.

By the B6259 a little way north of Outhgill.

PENRITH CASTLE

English Heritage and local council • Free • Open access during usual hours

Prosaically located on the edge of the town near the railway station, this is a ruin of reasonable size but with no great appeal. It's a later castle, more of a fortified house, built with royal permission in 1397 to a square plan around a courtyard (very like *Castle Bolton, Yorkshire* but without the corner towers). Although the walls are high enough on one side to give an idea of what it must have looked like, there are no entertaining details to explore on the inside.

On west side of Penrith town centre.

PIEL CASTLE

English Heritage • Free • Open access at any reasonable time (but reached by privately run ferry: £££, hours according to demand)

An eccentric oddity, visited by a trip on a small ferryboat which makes for a memorable experience even though the castle isn't all that thrilling. There's quite a lot of the keep left, and it's unusual because it was split in three by internal walls, but you can really only look at it from the outside. There are also substantial walls and towers around the inner bailey.

The castle is another expression of the power and prestige of *Furness Abbey (page 202)*. It was built with royal assent after 1327 to protect the Abbey's harbour here from raids by the Scots. There was, however, already a castle here in the reign of King Stephen in the early 1100s.

On Piel Island, near Barrow-in-Furness: reached by ferry from Roa Island, off A5087.

Wild, windswept and often wet: Piel Castle was built by Furness Abbey to control the harbour that it overlooks.

RAVENGLASS FORT
ROMAN BATH HOUSE

English Heritage • Free • Open access at any reasonable time

By the standards of Roman remains, the walls of this bath house are really remarkably high, so that it actually looks like a building, rather than mere foundations. And it's tucked away in a fairly quiet location, so that you get a pleasant sense of discovering it for yourself. You can easily make out Roman plaster of two different colours on the walls, and there are also traces of colour in the niches. The reason that the walls have survived so well is that they were incorporated into a medieval building.

The bath house stood just outside the ramparts of the fort of *Glannoventa*, which guarded the Roman port here on the Cumbrian coast. The fort's earthworks can be visited on the other side of the railway: there's a path on the left as you return from the bath house.

Reached on foot (an easy, level walk of about 15 minutes) along path signposted from the minor road into Ravenglass, just after it leaves the main road (A595); limited parking in layby by the road.

The remains of the bath house outside the Roman fort at Ravenglass – you won't often see such tall Roman walls.

SHAP ABBEY

English Heritage • Free • Open access at any reasonable time

A largely uninspiring little ruin, but memorable for its remote setting in a tiny, hidden valley which is now occupied mostly by a farm. It was a Premonstratensian abbey founded in the late 1100s. The only building of any substance is the very tall tower at the west end of the church, but most of the rest of the abbey's buildings can be made out from the low walls that survive. The layout is fairly interesting because everything had to be squeezed in next to the stream, with appropriate alterations to the traditional abbey plan.

Reached by a minor road signposted at the north end of the village of Shap, on the A66.

The thing that makes Wetheral Priory gatehouse different from many other priory and abbey gatehouses is that you can take a look upstairs.

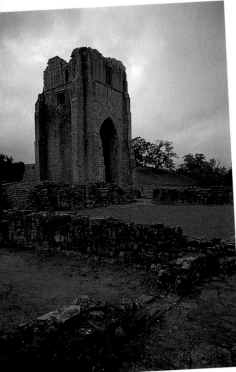

WETHERAL PRIORY
GATEHOUSE

English Heritage • Free • Open access at any reasonable time (interior, usual hours)

This is a very pleasing little building, and although it's one of those modest places where ten minutes is more than enough time to see it all, it would be a shame not to take a quick look if you're in the Carlisle area. The gatehouse of a Benedictine priory, it has survived because it was used as a vicar's residence after the Dissolution.

There are stairs up to a large room over the gateway, and a spiral stair leads to second-floor level.

The gatehouse is also one of the few historically important buildings that you can drive a car through, since the small car park is round the back.

Clearly signposted off the B6263 just south of Wetheral, near Carlisle.

Left: Shap Abbey's most impressive building is the tall tower at the west end of the church.

SEE ALSO...

BEWCASTLE CASTLE, *in remote location north of Hadrian's Wall* – This modest ruin is on privately owned farmland but can be visited, and the farm even sells a guide leaflet. The castle was established as far back as 1092 in the corner of a Roman fort. One wall of the shell-like enclosure stands to nearly its full height. Not too interesting, but in a magnificent bit of wild country.

BOW BRIDGE, *near Furness Abbey* – Basic packhorse bridge on the medieval road to Furness Abbey (*English Heritage, free, open access at any reasonable time*).

CARROCK FELL HILLFORT, *Mungrisdale, footpath from near Mosedale village* – There are about ten or so hillforts in the Lake District, but this is the biggest and the best. It has a single rampart of dry-stone walling, with fine stone facing still visible in places.

CARTMEL PRIORY GATEHOUSE, *Cartmel village* (*National Trust, opening irregular*) – Later used as a school, this is not a terrifically interesting building, though the enormous, famous Priory church nearby is pretty remarkable.

COCKERMOUTH CASTLE, *Cockermouth* - A big castle dating to before 1220 and owned in the late 1300s by the Percy family, Earls of Northumberland, it was slighted in the Civil War and rebuilt as a house. It is privately owned and not open to the public.

EGREMONT CASTLE, *by the minor road to Middletown on edge of Egremont* – Quite a decent little ruin, though only some bits of wall and a gatehouse are anything like intact. The oldest parts date from 1130–1140. It's on public land and easily accessible.

GREY CROFT STONE CIRCLE, *Seascale* – A circle of 12 large boulders, ten of them re-erected following excavations in the 1940s. Right in the shadow of Windscale/Sellafield nuclear plant.

HUTTON-IN-THE-FOREST, *near Penrith* – Stately home developed around a large and rather cute (but very much altered) keep-like pele tower. It's mostly an affair of gracious interiors and pleasant gardens. (*Privately owned, £££, limited hours – three afternoons a week, May to September.*)

KIRKOSWALD CASTLE, *near footpath to Glassonby off minor road heading east from the village* – Small remnant of what was once a very fine fortified house licensed by King John, destroyed by Edward Bruce after Bannockburn and rebuilt in grand style by Thomas, Lord Dacre. On private land and not open to visitors.

MUNCASTER CASTLE (pictured), *near Ravenglass* – One wing of this large stately home is made up of a defensive pele tower from the 1300s (said to stand on the foundations of a Roman signal tower), but it's still basically a house. However, in the grounds is a fantastic owl sanctuary, helping to conserve endangered owls from around the world, which in my book (and this *is* my book) makes the place well worth visiting. (*Privately owned, £££, limited hours – summer months only.*)

NAWORTH CASTLE, *near Lanercost* – Splendid-looking house developed from a large pele tower, but not normally open to the public.

PIKE OF STICKLE AXE FACTORY, *Great Langdale* – Not much to look at, but if you're walking in the area or visiting the pub at Dungeon Ghyll, look up at the rocky scree by the Pike of Stickle and consider that this was one of Britain's biggest sources of stone axes.

SHAP STONE CIRCLES, *all around Shap* – There are a number of stone circles in the area, none of them now in very good condition, and there are some large standing stones which are left over from avenues that connected the circles. Mostly of local interest.

SIZERGH CASTLE, *near Kendal* – Typical example of a stately home of the region that has developed from a defensive 'pele tower' of the 1300s. The pele is quite a large one, and you can easily see how a hall block was added to one side and then, later, two wings were built on to turn it all into a house. (*National Trust, £££, limited hours – April to October only, closed Friday & Saturday.*)

WORKINGTON HALL, *Workington* – Ruin of a fortified manor house which, again, was built up around a pele tower of the 1300s. It's a plain ruin, but worth a look. In a nearby building is a decent local museum. (*Local council, £, slightly limited hours – every day except Monday, Easter to October.*)

AND...

BRATS HILL STONE CIRCLE, *footpath up from Boot, Eskdale*; BURWENS SETTLEMENT & EWE CLOSE WALLED SETTLEMENT, *near Crosby Ravensworth* (iron age villages); CASTLE CRAG HILLFORT, *footpath from end of Thirlmere*; HOLME BANK WALLED SETTLEMENT, *Urswick*; MOOR DIVOCK STONE CIRCLES, *Askham*; RAISET PIKE LONG BARROW, *Crosby Garrett*.

The Roman Wall is at its most exciting as it crosses the rugged country of the Pennines: this stretch is east from Cawfields, heading for the highest point at Winshields Crag.

HADRIAN'S WALL

ONE OF THE MOST EXTRAORDINARY monuments of the Roman Empire anywhere in Europe, Hadrian's Wall is a spectacular memorial to the scale of ambition of the men in charge of the Roman army, and to the sheer hard work of the soldiers who actually had to build it.

Its appeal for the modern visitor is not quite what you might expect, though. Photographs of the wall striding majestically across craggy border country tend to suggest that this is Britain's equivalent of the Great Wall of China, and you picture yourself walking along its top, treading where the soldiers of 1900 years ago also trod. In reality only a few short sections of the Wall stand anything more than knee-high, and for much of its course it has vanished altogether. Of course, there are places where you can walk alongside the Wall for a couple of miles and thoroughly enjoy the drama of its contribution to the spectacular scenery; but for the most part it's inside the museums and among the jumbled walls of the forts that you will start to appreciate what a remarkable place this is – because its true value is as a time-capsule within which thousands of tiny details have survived to tell us the story of the daily lives of the soldiers of the Wall.

THEY SAY THAT THE BEST way to see Hadrian's Wall is on foot, and they're probably right. But on the other hand, all the most exciting parts of the Wall can easily be seen in one day by car, provided you pick and choose a little. Such an itinerary might include a good walk along one of the more scenic parts of the Wall, as well as visits to a couple of the best forts. You'll get a good impression of the whole variety of buildings which helped to make it such a formidable frontier – towers, milecastles, Wall forts and rearward support forts – and you'll have plenty left to explore on later visits if you want to see more.

Although the Wall ran from Bowness-on-Solway in the west to Wallsend on the banks of the Tyne in the east, all the most substantial stretches and all the most interesting monuments are concentrated in roughly the middle third of the Wall's course. This section runs from Banks (just north-east of *Lanercost Priory, Cumbria*) in the west to just the other side of Chesters fort, near Chollerford, in the east. The Ordnance Survey Outdoor Leisure map 43 concentrates on this section of country, though to be honest the average car-borne visitor doesn't really need the detail it provides.

The first thing you should equip yourself with is the excellent leaflet 'A Visitor's Guide to Hadrian's Wall', which is available free of charge from Tourist Information centres. This leaflet includes a road-map that is perfectly adequate for the job, and it shows all the most important sites on the Wall and provides complete information on opening times and charges. It also covers museums, such as the excellent Museum of Antiquities in Newcastle.

Basically, though, all you have to do is drive along the B6318, much of which follows the course of the Roman military road along the Wall, and all the important sites are very clearly signposted.

THE STORY OF THE WALL BEGINS in about 78 AD, when Julius Agricola arrived in Britain to take over as governor. He was a fine military commander with an acute sense of how to do a job properly, and his mission was to beat down the rebel tribes of northern England and then push the conquest north into Scotland. This he did, easily defeating a huge Caledonian army of 30,000 men at the battle of *Mons Graupius*, somewhere near Inverness, late in 84 AD.

Agricola was recalled to Rome not long afterwards, and the Romans failed ever to consolidate their conquest of the Scottish lowlands, but Agricola's systematic approach left an important legacy. He had proceeded by building two main roads, one in the west via Carlisle and the other in the east from York to Corbridge. These roads were linked by other roads crossing the Pennines where possible, one of the most important being Stanegate, which linked the forts at Carlisle and Corbridge.

In Trajan's reign, between 98 and 117 AD, this was effectively the northern frontier and was reinforced with more forts of varying sizes. By the time Hadrian became emperor the region was again a war zone, probably with the Brigantes of northern England acting in concert with their Scottish lowland neighbours. When Hadrian visited Britain in person in 122 AD, he gave the order to construct

Milecastle 42 at Cawfields: a small fort like this, with a gate through the wall, was built after every mile of Wall.

a massive fortified frontier that would establish permanently the northern end of the Roman Empire.

Hadrian's policy was consolidation behind existing frontiers, and he also ordered defensive works along the borders in Germany and elsewhere in Europe, but the sheer scale of the British wall suggests that it had something of a symbolic value. Britain had always been the Wild North to the Romans, which is what gave Julius Caesar's expeditions here in 55 BC such great propaganda value and made the island such an attractive prize for Claudius at the time of the invasion in 43 AD. The monumental wall of stone that Hadrian ordered was a statement of ownership, an assertion of the pride of the Empire.

The original idea was to use the seven forts of Stanegate and to build a wall ten Roman feet (3m) thick, but these plans changed before too long. The work was done in stretches of about five miles, starting from the banks of the Tyne at Newcastle, and was divided between two teams: one laid the foundations and built the milecastles and turrets, while the other followed along building the Wall itself. Unfortunately, by the time the foundation-layers had reached the River Irthing (near Gilsland), the Wall-builders had only got as far as the Tyne crossing (near Chollerford), and so the decision was taken to build the Wall two feet narrower. For much of the central part of the Wall, you

can clearly see the broader footings sticking out two feet behind the Wall.

At the same time, probably because of great hostility among the border tribes, it was decided that new forts – and many more of them – needed to be built actually on the wall, with gates opening northward so that troops could readily be sent out to meet attackers. Also, the Wall was extended at the eastern end to meet the Tyne estuary at Wallsend.

The extra work that this would involve was probably the reason for a further economy, which was that the stone wall would not yet be continued west of the Irthing. Instead, the wall and milecastles were built from turf and timber. The 'turf wall' was 6m (20ft) wide at the base and about 4m (13 ft) high, with a timber palisade on the top. Not very much later, the stone wall was extended to the west of the fort at Birdoswald, and eventually it completed its course all the way to the Solway Firth at Bowness.

The finishing touch, after the forts were in place, was the Vallum, a wide ditch flanked by banks 2m (6ft) high, which ran alongside the Wall but a few tens of metres behind it, creating a dead strip of no man's land. This not only helped to protect the rear of the Wall, but also acted to control traffic approaching from the south.

The Vallum could only be crossed at gaps in the banks immediately behind the forts, where the ditch was crossed by a narrow causeway protected by its own gate. The only one of these crossings that is still in evidence is at Benwell, a suburb of Newcastle, and though it's not a lot to look at, you can see the bases of the stone arch of the gateway.

The frontier was largely complete by 120 AD, but after Hadrian's death in 138 AD the succeeding emperor, Antoninus Pius, decided to make another attempt to conquer lowland Scotland. He pushed northward and built a new turf wall from the Forth to the Clyde, now known as the Antonine Wall. It was finished by about 143 AD and the old border was opened up: the milecastle gates were taken down and the ditch and banks of the Vallum were deliberately slighted.

Perhaps predictably, the result was a great deal of trouble with the tribes. For a while the Antonine Wall was abandoned, but by about 158 AD many more troops had been brought in and both walls were restored and manned simultaneously. Within 20 years, a major raid by Caledonian tribes broke through the northern wall. The Romans mounted a punitive expedition to restore order, but decided to withdraw once more to Hadrian's Wall. Thereafter, this remained the northern border of the Roman Empire until after 410 AD, when Rome was sacked by the Goths and the Emperor finally decided to leave Britain to its own devices.

THE BEST STRETCHES OF WALL

BANKS EAST TURRET TO BIRDOSWALD FORT

Alongside the minor road from Lanercost to Birdoswald Fort

This is the best 'drive-by' section, and a good place to start, with the first notable stretches of Wall popping up beside the road and featuring the remains of two turrets (romantically named 51B and 51A).

WALLTOWN CRAGS

Clearly signposted from B6318 east of Greenhead; free parking

A short but very picturesque section of Wall running up and down the rugged slopes of the Crags, plus the remains of a lookout turret (45A) which was built before the Wall and later incorporated into it, as you can clearly see from the masonry.

CAWFIELDS

Clearly signed from B6318 east of Greenhead, north of Haltwhistle; free parking

A fine stretch of 'consolidated' Wall (rebuilt so that it won't fall apart any more) that starts with Milecastle 42.

A good place for a walk eastwards along the Wall, perhaps as far as Turret 41A (it takes about half an hour). You get a particularly good view of the banks and ditches of the Vallum from this area. Also, there are the traces of quite a number of earthwork forts in the fields all around. Just to the west is the fort of *Aesica* (Great Chesters), but there isn't much of it to be seen.

WINSHIELDS

Reached on foot west of the car park at Steel Rigg (clearly signposted off B6318 halfway between Cawfields and Housesteads, opposite turn to Vindolanda)

Probably the most picturesque section of the Wall, and another great place for a good walk. Notable features include the highest point of the Wall at Winshields Crag (from where, on a clear day, you can see the Solway Firth in the west) and Milecastle 40.

SEWINGSHIELDS

On foot east from Housesteads fort

Another good walking section of about two miles in length, with excellent views, and featuring the recently excavated Milecastle 35.

Below: The Vallum, composed of a ditch with a bank on either side, is seen to good effect near Cawfields.

MILECASTLES AND TURRETS

The 80 Roman miles of Hadrian's Wall featured, as a crucial part of the plan, a fortlet every mile – known now as a milecastle – with a gate-tower to allow traffic to cross the wall. Each milecastle had barracks and a kitchen for a small garrison. Between the milecastles there were two turrets, at intervals of a third of a Roman mile. The turrets had steps up to the wall-walk, and could be used both as look-out towers and as signal stations.

BANKS EAST TURRET (52A)

English Heritage • Free • Open access at any reasonable time

This turret marks your first real sight of the Wall at the western end, and it's noteworthy because it was originally built as a free-standing turret on the 'turf wall', before the stone-built one had extended this far. Indeed, when the stone wall was first pushed on west of the River Irthing, this was where it ended. Between here and Birdoswald, there are two more decent turrets right by the road.

Alongside the minor road from Lanercost to Birdoswald Fort.

Poltross Burn is the best-preserved milecastle: the Wall is on the left of the picture, with the barracks to the right.

POLTROSS BURN MILECASTLE

English Heritage • Free • Open access at any reasonable time

This is the best-preserved of all the milecastles, in a pleasant, sheltered spot, reached by a footpath from the station at Gilsland which crosses the stream on a footbridge. You can see the typical pattern of the milecastle, with the gate in the wall and barrack blocks behind it, and there are three or four steps from the bottom of the flight which led up to the wall-walk.

Clearly signposted at Gilsland station: a five-minute walk to the milecastle.

BRUNTON TURRET (26B)

English Heritage • Free • Open access at any reasonable time

This is where the Wall *really* starts at the eastern end, and it is the most substantial turret ruin. In the lintel of the doorway, you can see the hole for the pivot that the door swung on.

By the A6079 south of the B6318 near Chollerford; signposted; parking in layby.

The turret at Banks East was built as part of the 'turf wall', before the stone wall was extended this far.

Brunton is the best example of a turret, and it's not very far from the fort at Chesters.

BIRDOSWALD FORT (CAMBOGLANNA)

English Heritage and Cumbria County Council • £££ • Usual hours

This is the least interesting of the large forts, though it does have an extensive modern visitor centre. The excavated area in the centre has a minimal jumble of remains which are not easy to make any sense of, so the best thing to do here is wander around the circuit of low walls with gates and towers. Behind the fort, there's a dramatic drop to the valley of the River Irthing, and there is an excellent view from the field next to the fort.

The course of the stone wall was diverted from the original 'turf wall' to incorporate the Birdoswald fort, which means that a stretch of turf wall remains visible in this area.

Leading east from the fort is a good stretch of the Wall, and at its end – a walk of about ten minutes – are the remains of Harrow's Scar Milecastle, which again is worth seeing for the way the country falls away to the river valley. Beyond here, the Wall dropped down to cross the river on Willowford Bridge, the remains of which can also be visited (the landowner makes a small charge).

Right next to minor road from Lanercost to Gilsland (signposted from B6318 west of Gilsland); free car park.

The walls and gates of the fort at Birdoswald are well preserved, although there's quite not so much to see inside.

VINDOLANDA FORT AND MUSEUM

Privately owned (charitable trust) • £££ • Slightly limited hours (closed in winter, from mid-November to mid-February)

One very good reason to come here is to visit the site museum, which has a remarkable collection of items found during excavations. It's particularly strong on ordinary, everyday things such as a huge quantity of leather shoes, or the legs and seats of chairs. There is also a collection of Roman writing (displayed as reproductions) which features more remarkable insights into everyday Roman life, including an invitation to a birthday party and a letter about a soldier's socks and underpants. One of the most interesting items is a pair of carved stone slabs which formed part of a counter in the strongroom of the fort, worn down by soldiers leaning on the top as they waited to receive their pay or take out their savings.

The remains at *Vindolanda* aren't as tidy and well-presented as some of the other forts, but that's because excavations and restoration are still in progress. Inside the walls of the fort, which in its visible form dates from about 300 AD, you can see the headquarters building (*principia*), where one slab from the soldiers' pay counter still stands in its original position, and the commander's house. Outside the west gate of the fort is a jumble of remains which represents civilian buildings that grew up on either side of the main road, plus the remains of another commander's house from an earlier fort on the site.

There is more to keep you occupied besides the remains and the museum. In one corner of the site is a reconstruction of the Wall in both its stone-built and its turf-and-timber phases, complete with a stone-wall turret and a milecastle gate of the 'turf wall'. Elsewhere there are gardens with a reconstructed Roman temple, and not far away is the only non-ruined Roman milestone in Britain still standing in its original position by the former Roman road.

Signposted from B6318 between Cawfields and Housesteads; free car parking.

Inside the fort at Vindolanda, where you can see the counter on which soldiers leaned as they drew their pay.

To the left are the granaries and ahead is the commander's house, but it's the dramatic setting you'll remember.

HOUSESTEADS FORT
(VERCOVICIUM)

English Heritage and National Trust • £££ • Usual hours

This is the finest and most famous Roman fort in Britain, and inevitably it's very popular at any time of year. It owes much of its drama to its location, on high ground in fairly wild country, but there is also plenty to see inside the walls.

There are good, readily understood remains of such prominent features as the gateways, granaries and barracks, but most of the main buildings were substantially altered and updated over the years, so they do tend to be something of a jumble of work from different periods.

The most famous building, and by far the easiest to decipher, is the latrine block, next to the angle tower in the south-west corner of the fort (it's to the right as you enter by the visitors' gate in the south wall). Toilet seats of wood or stone covered a sewer which could be flushed out with rainwater from the nearby collecting tank. The stone flags which make up the tank have been worn down at the top, probably by soldiers washing

their clothes (rather than sharpening swords, the guidebook feels obliged to point out). A channel in the floor had running water for rinsing out the sponges which were used instead of toilet paper.

Besides the remarkable fort, Housesteads is also a good base for a one-stop visit to the Wall, since excellent walking is to be had for a couple of miles in either direction. Just a short walk west is Milecastle 37 which has a gate archway that stands almost to head height.

Clearly signposted next to B6318; pay and display car park. It's a steepish 15-minute uphill walk to the fort.

BROCOLITIA
TEMPLE OF MITHRAS

English Heritage and Northumbria National Park • Free • Open access at any reasonable time

Even though it's one of the smallest sites on the Wall, this is definitely a 'must see'. It's the restored remains of a temple dedicated to Mithras, the soldier's god, which stood just outside the ramparts of an infantry fort. The on-site signboard explains it very well. Just nearby, there was also a shrine to the water nymph goddess Coventina, and here an amazing collection of offerings was found, including altars, sculptures and more than 13,000 coins.

Clearly signposted by B6318 west of Chesters, east of Housesteads; free car park.

CHESTERS FORT (CILURNUM)

English Heritage • £££ • Usual hours

Chesters is quite different from the other famous fort at *Housesteads* (*previous page*), and there are two main reasons for this. First, it's in quiet, pastoral lowland country rather than on the rugged uplands. Second, the remains of the fort are displayed in a very different way. Most of it has been left under the fields, with just the most important pieces sticking up through the grass, fenced off to keep the sheep out. This makes it look rather fragmentary, but in fact it's quite a good way of pointing out the significant buildings that you are likely to find in any Roman fort.

Forts were built to pretty much the same pattern throughout the Empire, with the typical 'playing card' layout of walls – a rectangle with rounded corners – and a gate on each side. The forts on Hadrian's Wall came in two sizes, a smaller one for 500 infantry and a larger to house 1000 infantry or 500 cavalry. Generally, the infantry forts were placed 'behind' the Wall, so that just the north gate led out into hostile territory, but the cavalry forts were positioned 'astride' the line of the Wall so that the east and west side-gates were also forward of the Wall. This made it easier for large numbers of mounted men to be deployed fairly quickly.

The most solid building at Chesters is this bath house, but it's the whole ensemble that makes it an interesting site.

All the forts have a similar internal layout, with blocks of barracks (and stables, in cavalry forts) on either side and a central strip comprising granaries, the headquarters building and the commander's house.

Granaries apart, most of these features can be seen at Chesters. You enter next to the North Gate, and to your left are the barracks. Ahead is the headquarters block, where you can get a very good impression of the paved courtyard at the centre of the building. At the back of this block is the strongroom vault, which still had a nail-studded oak door when it was excavated. To the left of the headquarters building is the commander's house, with its heated rooms and private baths reflecting the high status of its occupant.

The most famous building at Chesters – famous mainly because its masonry stands to quite a height – is the bath block outside the walls of the fort. It's certainly worth seeing, with niches in the changing room that could have housed statues, or might just have been where you put your clothes when you stripped off.

Just over the river from near the bath-house are the remains of the Roman bridge, which must have been an extremely impressive construction: there are good drawings in the guidebook, which also has instructions on how to reach it by footpath from Chollerford.

Finally, it would be a mistake to miss out on the small but crammed site museum, which houses lots of pieces of stone (statues, altars and inscriptions) from all along the Wall, as well as a selection of other finds. It's a little dry and dusty by modern standards, but there's no substitute for actual, original Roman stuff.

Clearly signposted from B6318 just west of Chollerford; free car parking.

Left: In front is the strongroom of the headquarters, with the commander's house beyond.

One of the Corbridge granaries, its raised floor allowing air to circulate. It's in good nick for a Roman building.

CORBRIDGE ROMAN SITE (CORSTOPITUM)

English Heritage • £££ • Usual hours

Corbridge started life as a supply base at the time of Agricola's advance into Scotland in 79 AD, but by about 200 it had grown into a town. This makes it an interesting site, though some of the remains can be a little confusing.

The excavated site that you see today is only a small part of the town, which extends under the fields as far as the outskirts of modern Corbridge. The site is split in two by the town's main road, which is part of the Stanegate, the frontier road that crossed England from coast to coast.

On one side of the road are the most substantial buildings, including a pair of granaries, the raised floors of which are in amazingly good condition. The grain stored inside had to be kept dry and well ventilated, and one of the window-like ventilation slots still has a stone mullion in place, which is a real rarity in Roman England. Next to the road, there's a loading platform which was sheltered by a portico with large, round, stone columns.

Beside the granaries is an aqueduct, down which fresh water flowed into the town. At the end of it is the place where a large lead tank stood, in which the water, having run under cover for a long distance, would be aerated before flowing through a fountain into a big stone trough.

Further on is a large building consisting of a set of rooms grouped around a courtyard. It's not known what this building was, or even if it was ever finished. It looks rather like a forum, but may have been a market.

The jumble of low stone walls on the other half of the site is rather entertainingly crinkled, because it has subsided into the infilled ditches of an earlier fort. It's all a bit of a mess, but you can make out a side street in the middle and a number of narrow alleyways leading between the various other buildings, which include a couple of houses, some workshops and a number of temples. Over in the corner is a headquarters building – the home of the administrative departments of the Roman army – with an underground strongroom very like the one at Chesters Fort.

Piecing together the history of the town isn't easy, but it seems to have grow up around the remains of the fourth fort on the site, dating to the time of the Antonine Wall in the early 140s. This fort was the first to have stone buildings, and the foundations of the commander's house and part of a headquarters building can be seen within the later courtyard building already described.

The fort was decommissioned when Hadrian's Wall was remanned about 163 AD, and that's when Corbridge started to become a town. Round about 180, when Scottish tribes broke through the Antonine Wall, there is evidence of burning at Corbridge, but thereafter its growth continued at least into the 300s and possibly beyond.

Signposted by the B6318 west of Chollerford.

Yorkshire

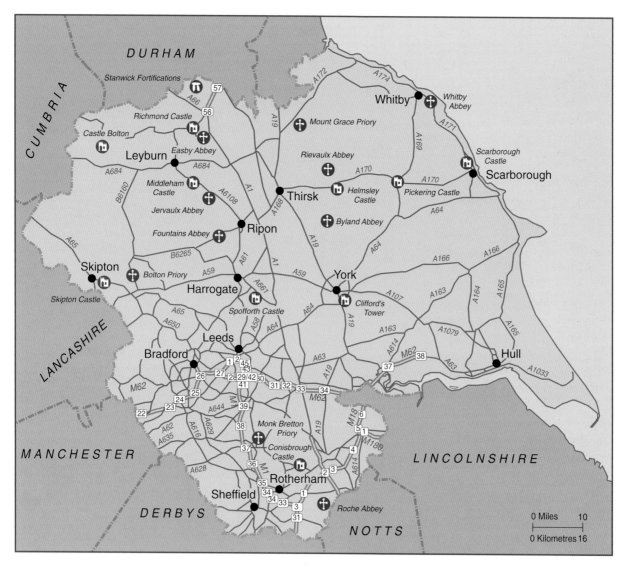

DURHAM

CUMBRIA

Stanwick Fortifications

57

A66

56

Richmond Castle

Castle Bolton

Leyburn

Easby Abbey

A684

A684

Middleham Castle

A6108

Jervaulx Abbey

A65

B6160

A1

A168

Fountains Abbey

B6265

Ripon

A61

A1

Skipton

Bolton Priory

A59

Skipton Castle

Harrogate

A661

Spofforth Castle

LANCASHIRE

A65

A650

A58

A64

Leeds

Bradford

M62

Mount Grace Priory

A172

A19

Rievaulx Abbey

A170

Helmsley Castle

Byland Abbey

A19

A64

Whitby

Whitby Abbey

A174

A171

A169

A170

Pickering Castle

Scarborough Castle

Scarborough

A64

A166

A166

York

Clifford's Tower

A107

A163

A164

A165

A163

A19

A1079

A165

Hull

A1033

A63

M62

38

37

M62

A19

A644

39

22

23

24

25

26

27

28 29/42

41

30

31 32

33

34

Monk Bretton Priory

A62

A635

A616

A629

38

37

A628

36

M1

35

34

34 33

31

3

Sheffield

1

Roche Abbey

Conisbrough Castle

Rotherham

2

3

1

6

6 1

M180

M18

A614

4

LINCOLNSHIRE

DERBYS

NOTTS

MANCHESTER

0 Miles   10

0 Kilometres 16

YORKSHIRE was traditionally divided into three parts known as 'ridings' (from the old word 'thridding', meaning a third), but it has such a strong identity as a region in its own right that we've taken it all as one whole. The result is the largest of our county chapters, and one that has an unfair share of the most spectacular and important castles in England. The best keeps are those at *Conisbrough* and *Richmond*, while there are other good reasons to remember *Helmsley*, *Middleham*, *Pickering* and *Scarborough*. The grand ruined abbeys of *Fountains* and *Rievaulx* speak for themselves, but there are other good abbey remains at *Byland*, *Roche* and *Whitby*. Finally, the county's biggest surprise is the extraordinary set of Celtic earthworks at Stanwick. It won't interest everybody, but it gives a fascinating insight into the British resistance to Roman rule.

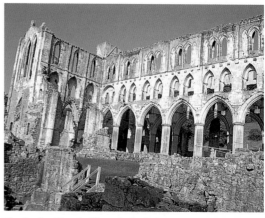

The church at Rievaulx Abbey – England's finest religious monument.

Bolton Priory is in a lovely setting by the River Wharfe. The nave is still in use as the parish church.

Barden Tower is a plain defensive house restored in the 1600s by the eccentric Lady Anne Clifford.

BOLTON PRIORY & BARDEN TOWER

Privately owned • Free (but parking fee charged at Bolton Abbey) • Open access during usual hours only

These two modest ruins stand in the beautiful valley of the River Wharfe, on an estate owned by the Duke and Duchess of Devonshire (of Chatsworth fame). The estate is open to visitors under a simple arrangement by which you pay a one-off all-day fee for car parking and can then wander as you wish.

The Priory (why the estate is called 'Bolton Abbey' is anyone's guess) dates from the late 1100s. Its nave is used as the parish church and the rest of the old priory church stands as ruins, but there's very little left of other buildings.

Barden Tower is a short drive (or a good walk) away, with its own small car park. It's the ruin of a rectangular fortified tower house said to date back to the 1200s, but its big claim to fame is that it was restored by the eccentric Lady Anne Clifford (*see also Skipton Castle, page 227, and Brougham Castle, Cumbria*). It can only be viewed from the outside.

Bolton Abbey estate, by the B6160, off the A59 between Skipton and Blubberhouses.

BYLAND ABBEY

English Heritage • ££ • Usual hours

Nowhere near as spectacular as nearby *Rievaulx* (*page 221*), but what it lacks in grandeur it makes up for in quality. There's a good deal to see behind the much-photographed broken rose window at the west end of the church. Quite a lot of the east wall of the abbey church has survived, and it's enough to show that the church was enormous. When it was built, it was the largest Cistercian church in England. Its masonry was of the highest quality, and what makes it so enjoyable to look round is that, even though only small pieces remain, there are plenty of beautifully constructed details to look out for – even something as simple as the stairs up from the cloister to the church.

The cloister was particularly large, and the guidebook points out that this was where the monks would spend a lot of their time when not at prayer. It was the venue for activities like shaving their heads for the tonsure, trimming their beards and hanging out the laundry, so it was perhaps not the secluded garden you often imagine.

One thing to look out for on the far side of the cloister is the warming room, a very small room with a very large fireplace. This was one of the few places where a fire was allowed, and the monks could sit here and get the chill out of their bones in the winter months.

Opposite the abbey ruins is a very pleasant country pub, so you might wish to time your visit appropriately.

Not far south-west of the village of Wass; clearly signposted from A170 Thirsk to Helmsley and A19 Thirsk to York roads.

Below: The church of Byland Abbey was once the largest in the country, and its details are superb.

CASTLE BOLTON

Privately owned • £££ • Usual hours

This is something of a rarity in that it's a (mostly) ruined castle in private ownership, and though an institution such as English Heritage might be able to lavish more cash on it, the castle is well presented, rewarding to visit and not too expensive. Although it's a relatively modern building (the licence to build it was granted in 1378 by Edward III), it nevertheless feels like a 'proper' castle, especially when you're down in the dark depths of the cobbled courtyard, with four storeys of stone towering above you.

The plan of the castle is a simple square, with accommodation along each side and a tower at each corner. It was attacked by Parliamentary forces in the Civil War but was not actually slighted, and instead owes its present incomplete state to the collapse of the north-east tower in 1761, taking some of the wall with it. The other side of the castle, however, is more or less intact, with many of its original roofs and floors. This part of the castle is home to high-status living chambers and bedrooms, with well-preserved 'garderobe' toilets at the end of small, dead-end passageways.

Mary Queen of Scots was held here, in these very rooms, from July 1568 to early in 1569, and seems to have

Castle Bolton dates from the days when castles were getting more house-like, but its interior looks far more brutal.

spent most of her time knitting and getting her hair done (a new style every day, apparently).

One interesting feature of the castle's design is the way the main gate leads straight into the courtyard, where the five doorways that lead out – all protected by a stout door and a portcullis – have been made to look pretty much identical, giving attackers no clue as to which way to go next.

In Castle Bolton village, clearly signposted on minor roads off the A684 near Aysgarth.

CLIFFORD'S TOWER, YORK

English Heritage • ££ • Usual hours

Clifford's Tower is one of the most extraordinary castle buildings in the country, and very cute with it. It's basically all that survives of York castle, and it owes its idiosyncratic look partly to the unusual height of the mound on which it is built, and partly to its unique 'quatrefoil' plan (like four circles linked together), which was based on French designs. Although it looks a little like a shell keep, it was in fact a great tower with floors: inside, you can see some of the projecting stones (corbels) which supported wooden joists.

The tower was built in the late 1200s on the orders of Henry III, to replace a previous stone tower which blew down in a gale in 1228. (In turn, that tower replaced a wooden building which was burned down during anti-Jewish riots in 1190.) Clifford's Tower is the work of a chap called Henry of Reims, said to have been the king's finest architect, who also worked on Westminster Abbey. The tower stood over a bailey guarded by a stone curtain wall with towers and two gateways, but most of this has now disappeared.

In fact, from the time of William the Conqueror, York had two castles (as did London). Both were destroyed by the Vikings in 1069 and rebuilt.

The cute-looking Clifford's Tower was once part of a major castle at York, most of which has disappeared.

In Tower Street, York city centre.

The keep at Conisbrough is one of the most interesting in the country, with a very authentic feel to the interior.

CONISBROUGH CASTLE

English Heritage • ££ • Usual hours

What a fantastic keep. It's 27m (90ft) high, cylindrical, with six massive buttresses. This design is unique in Britain, though a similar keep is known in France. With smooth walls of finely dressed stone broken by scarcely any windows, it looks immensely strong. It dates from the great era of keep-building, the reign of Henry II, and in fact it was built round about 1180 by Henry's half-brother Hamelin Plantagenet.

There's some debate about whether round towers were considered stronger than square ones, but the keep at Conisbrough proves one thing: whatever the defensive virtues, a round tower on even this scale could never provide accommodation to match that of a large square keep. Although the rooms within have grand fireplaces, they are far from luxurious in size. The floors have recently been restored, contributing greatly to the impression you get of the building, with just a touch of modern theatricals added (sound effects, would you believe) to help it all along. There's an interesting little chapel on the third floor, and the views from the roof are superb.

The curtain walls were added later, but not much later – in the early 1200s. The keep probably owes its survival to the fact that a length of the walls had already collapsed before the Civil War, so the castle wasn't really defensible and consequently escaped slighting by Parliament.

Clearly signposted in Conisbrough village, on the A630 south-west of Doncaster.

Left: The refectory building at Easby Abbey is the prettiest part of this small but attractive ruin.

EASBY ABBEY

English Heritage • Free • Open access at any reasonable time

Tucked away in a quiet spot by the River Swale without the benefit of a decent modern signpost to help you find it, this ruin is surprisingly busy, perhaps because people come here after seeing the castle at Richmond.

There are several pretty buildings, most of them near the entrance: the refectory, straight ahead, with its tall gothic windows, and the guest block on the left, which also incorporates the latrines ('reredorter'). Beyond are the cloisters, where the abbey church is a mere outline on the ground.

The abbey was founded in 1155 by Premonstratensians. One of their customs was a belief in the healing power of bleeding, and every canon was bled six times a year, which made the infirmary (beyond the church) a fairly important building.

A mile west of Richmond, off the 'B' road to Brompton on Swale. Can be reached on foot from Richmond: see the castle guidebook.

Helmsley's defences included two great towers, one later incorporated into the Tudor house (right of picture).

HELMSLEY CASTLE

English Heritage • £££ • Usual hours

Helmsley is a fine castle, even though the building that so dominates the area – the tall, keep-like East Tower – is so utterly ruined that you can't even climb a stair to use it as a viewpoint. In fact, it's not the stone buildings of the castle but its earthworks that give it a unique character. The first thing that grabs your attention when you visit is the hugely impressive set of banks and ditches which define the rectangular castle ground. From the modern entrance, you are obliged to walk around the outside until you reach one of the gateways which stand at either end of the castle.

The earthworks are the remains of the first Helmsley Castle, built in the 1120s by a wealthy landowner called Walter Espec (his other great claim to fame is that he granted the land on which Rievaulx Abbey was founded in 1131). It seems that Walter put his castle here not because the site had any particular strategic importance, but because Helmsley was at the centre of his Yorkshire estates. At the time, the castle buildings would all have been built from wood, and the earth banks would have been topped with timber breastworks.

Before you cross one of the bridges to enter the castle, it's worth walking all the way around the bank and taking a look across the rock-cut ditch at the only stone building which survives more or less intact. The reason this part of the castle is so well preserved is, perhaps unsurprisingly, that it is by far the most recent: this was a Tudor mansion, built in the 1560s on the site of the original hall and domestic buildings of the castle. Inside, it has some reasonably interesting details, including plaster ceilings and wood panelling.

The gateways at either end of the castle are not immediately easy to puzzle out, but both are worth studying. Each one had a barbican – like a small 'island' of defence outside the gate – added in the late 1200s to early 1300s.

The other interesting aspect of the castle's design is that the East Tower, though it looks like a keep, was just one of a pair of great towers. The other – the West Tower – has been incorporated into the end of the Tudor accommodation block. Both towers date to the first phase of building in stone at the castle, in the late 1100s, and at this time most castles still had a single keep as a last refuge in times of trouble. The idea of a castle's main defence coming from strengthened towers on the curtain wall was a later innovation, which suggests that whoever came up with the design for Helmsley was ahead of his time.

One final surprise is that the East Tower wasn't, as you might expect, square: the missing side was rounded. Most of the stone from it still lies in the ditch below, where it landed when the Parliamentarians blew the tower up during the Civil War.

Easily found in the small town of Helmsley; car parking in town square.

MIDDLEHAM CASTLE

English Heritage • ££ • Usual hours

A fine castle, different from many ruins (and rather like an old-fashioned toy castle) in that, rather than sprawling all over a hill, it stands square, forceful and compact on level ground on the edge of a small market town. It's a simple design, with the great keep in the middle – dating from the 1100s – surrounded in about 1300 by a square of curtain walls with corner towers, giving a layout that's very reminiscent of the 'concentric' castles built in the late 1200s by Edward III in Wales. It's also a surprisingly complete ruin, the collapse of one wall allowing you to look into the middle almost as if it were a cutaway illustration.

The only drawback is that the inside of the castle, with high walls looming above narrow interior spaces, is rather cramped, dark and dank. But you can't have everything.

The keep is impressive, and a stair in one corner climbs right to the top so that you can get a crow's eye view of the interior. The ground floor housed kitchens and cellars; one half of the first floor was taken up by a large hall, while the other half was occupied by great chamber, with a smaller private chamber adjoining. It is thought that a third storey was added in the 1400s.

JERVAULX ABBEY

Privately owned • ££
(honesty box, so bring coins)
• Usual hours

Another Yorkshire rarity, this: the privately owned ruin of a Cistercian abbey in the grounds of a large house. It's rather overgrown and neglected, but in fact this makes it a charming place to visit, because you feel as if you're discovering it for yourself. The ruin is currently undergoing a slow but steady programme of restoration, so it remains to be seen whether this unique atmosphere will survive the process of tidying up.

The abbey's name derives from 'Yorevale' (valley of the River Ure). It was founded in 1156 after the first abbot, John de Kinstan, saw a vision of the Virgin Mary while lost in thick woodland with 12 of his monks. The church is more or less completely destroyed, but some of the walls of the dormitories and similar cloister buildings still stand to first floor level.

Signposted next to A6108 a few miles south-east of Middleham.

From the castle, you can see an early Norman motte-and-bailey castle on a nearby hill, which in 1086 was owned by a chap by the name of Ribald. The castle was moved to its present site in the mid-1100s, when the great keep was built, surrounded by just a wooden palisade. In 1270 the castle passed to the Nevill family, and not much later the stone curtain wall was built. However, Middleham is most closely associated with Richard, Duke of Gloucester, later King Richard III, who is said to have been very fond of the place.

Easily found in the small town of Middleham.

Below: Middleham is exactly what you expect a castle to look like, with a square of walls around a keep.

FOUNTAINS ABBEY

The ruins of Fountains Abbey, hidden away in a secluded valley, are dominated by the tall Perpendicular Tower.

National Trust • £££ • Usual hours

The two great Yorkshire abbeys make a fascinating contrast, as different in their appeal to the modern visitor as they are in their style of architecture. Fountains has a secluded feel to it: tucked away in a quiet valley that for several hundred years has been part of the private grounds of a large house, it is protected by careful shepherding of its vast numbers of visitors.

Just about the first part of the ruin you come across is the west end of the abbey church. Dating from the early 1100s, it's built in a plain style, with fat, round columns and simple arches. Next door is another of the abbey's most memorable features: a remarkable stretch of vaulting, nearly 100m (300ft) long, which forms the undercroft of the lay brothers' dormitory. At the far end the stream runs under it, with the toilets ('reredorter') built over the stream.

Together, these two elements characterise the aesthetic appeal of Fountains. It's all about simplicity, scale and repetition, with a distinct austere beauty but none of the soaring grace of Rievaulx.

The fact that the lay brothers' dormitory could sleep 200 is some evidence of the wealth of Fountains in later days, but it certainly wasn't so well off in its early days. It was founded in 1132 by a small group of Benedictine monks from St Mary's in York, but they simply didn't have the resources to make a go of it. In the following year they applied to the Cistercians at Clairvaux in France – themselves established only 35 years before, with a similar intention of returning to the simple rule of St Benedict – for help.

In 1135 Fountains became a Cistercian abbey, and it never really looked back. By the time of the Dissolution in 1539, it was the richest abbey in England. One obvious indication of its later wealth (and also of the immodest tendencies of the then Abbot, Marmaduke Huby) was the building in the early 1500s of the huge tower known as the Perpendicular Tower, attached to the north transept of the church. An earlier example of conspicuous spending is the Chapel of the Nine Altars at the east end of the church, which dates from the early 1200s: it's a very unusual arrangement.

There are lots of interesting details to see elsewhere around the place. The cloister still has a very enclosed feel to it, with some good bits of building just off it, including three big arches that give access to the chapter house. Nearby is the warming house, with a huge fireplace for such a small room (stand inside and take a look up the chimney to get the full effect): it was clearly intended to heat the monks' dormitory and refectory on either side, too.

Fountains Abbey is part of the Studley Royal estate, with extensive water gardens to wander round: and there's also Fountains Hall, built between 1598 and 1604, to see. You could easily spend a whole day.

Clearly signposted on the B6265 near Ripon.

A view of Rievaulx from behind the refectory (left), with the beautiful arches of the presbytery just glimpsed.

RIEVAULX ABBEY

English Heritage • £££ • Usual hours

Rievaulx has a rather more friendly and accessible atmosphere than Fountains, perhaps because it's built on the gentle slope of a wide valley. It's less secluded, but more cheerful. The real highlight is the east end (or 'presbytery') of the abbey church, which is the single most beautiful religious ruin in England, but one of the great things about Rievaulx is the way that this part of the abbey is hidden at first and slowly revealed as you make your way up past the other buildings of the site.

It's not as easy to get a clear idea of the full plan of the abbey as it is at a more ruinous place (like *Roche Abbey, page 225*) but on the other hand there are some remarkable and substantial buildings. Foremost among them is the huge refectory built in the late 1100s, but there's plenty more besides, including the less well-preserved but equally interesting chapter house with a rounded end. One nice detail is that small sections of arcading have been reconstructed from fallen stonework in both the main cloister and the infirmary cloister, to show how the arcades that ran round all four sides of the courtyards would have looked.

The abbey here was founded in 1132 – the same year as Fountains – by no less a figure than Bernard, Abbott of the Cistercian house of Clairvaux in France, with the militant intention of spreading the Cistercian way to northern England and Scotland. Rievaulx was to be the launchpad for a mission. With considerable resources sunk into it, the new abbey was able to found daughter-houses in Bedfordshire and in Scotland as early as 1136.

Rievaulx's glory days arrived when a man called Aelred became Abbot in 1147 (his predecessor resigned to become Abbot of Fountains). Aelred was the foremost religious writer of his day and soon became the most respected figure in the English church, his fame spreading across Europe so that Rievaulx was at the centre of international affairs. Not long after his death in 1167 Aelred was canonised and in the early 1200s the saint's remains were placed in a magnificent shrine of gold and silver in the east end of the abbey church at Rievaulx.

It was at this time that the east end of the church was rebuilt to house the saint's shrine. With its magnificent tall, pointed arches, it is said to be the finest example of the architectural style known as 'Early English'. Don't forget to pop round the back and have a look at the flying buttresses which once supported the high vaults of the church, now ruined to thin, arching strips of supporting stones.

The abbey, like many others, had run up large debts by the late 1200s, and it was sacked by the Scots in 1322 when King Edward II and his army were beaten in battle at Byland and fled to York.

Clearly signposted on the B1257 just west of the small town of Helmsley.

MOUNT GRACE PRIORY

*English Heritage and National Trust • £££ •
Usual hours*

This is a really fascinating place, quite
unlike anything you'll see anywhere
else in the country. It has nothing of
the grace and beauty of Yorkshire's
grand abbey ruins, but that's not the
point. This was an altogether different
kind of religious establishment.

Mount Grace was founded as late as
1398 by the Carthusians, who sought
to recapture the purity of the early
church by living as hermits, each to
his own cell. Rather than doing it in
the wild, though, they gathered
together within the security of the
community. Basically what you see
today is the ruins of a series of these
cells grouped around a very large
open cloister, with the remains of
their fairly modest church on one side.

It wouldn't mean a lot if it weren't
for the fact that one of the cells has
been rebuilt to show how it would
have been. It's less like a cell and
more like a lovely little house, with its
own courtyard garden, complete with
outside toilet. Today's housing
planners, one feels, could learn a lot.

MONK BRETTON PRIORY

*English Heritage • Free •
Open access during usual
hours only*

An interesting if not
terribly attractive set of
remains, the blackened
old stone contrasting
greatly with the modern
housing all around.
There's little left of the
church, and part of the cloister range stands to a reasonable height only
because it was converted into a house after the Dissolution (notice a large,
baronial fireplace halfway up one wall). Possibly the most rewarding detail
is the drainage stream, lined with dressed stone as it passes beneath where
the toilet block would have stood and covered with huge slabs of stone
further on. This is a place that clearly has a few stories to tell, but a lack of
signboards means that you probably won't get to hear them.

Signposted on the east side of Barnsley, by the main road to Pontefract.

It seems very comfortable, yet the
toughness of the Carthusian regime of
constant prayer is hinted at by the
prison where runaways were held
while being convinced of the error of
their ways.

While you're visiting, don't neglect
to pop round the back and see the
well-houses over the springs that
supplied the Priory with water.

Signposted off the A19 near Osmotherley.

The Great Cloister of the fascinating Mount Grace Priory, with (centre of the picture) a reconstructed cell in which a monk lived his hermit-like existence.

PICKERING CASTLE

Pickering is an early motte castle rebuilt in stone. From the gate (centre), the wall climbs up the mound beyond.

English Heritage • ££ • Usual hours (but it closes at lunchtime)

Pickering is a lovely little castle, even though it doesn't have any especially exciting buildings – the shell keep which was once the heart of the castle is completely ruined. Most of the surrounding walls and towers still stand to their full height, though, and the castle is an interestingly coherent example of the way an early Norman motte and bailey was developed by rebuilding in stone. The icing on the cake is seeing the steam trains of the North Yorkshire Moors Railway run past its walls.

There must have been something about this spot that made it of great strategic importance (perhaps it was the roads that crossed here) but in 1069 William the Conqueror chose it as the right place to build a wood-and-earth castle to help him control the territory as he crushed major uprisings in the north of England (and at this stage he still had to watch out for the Danes, besides).

Probably the most interesting aspect of the castle today is that its design still reflects that first castle. The earliest phase of building in stone, under Henry II in 1180-87, was the curtain wall that climbs up either side of the motte and circles the inner bailey, including the gatehouse now known as the Coleman Tower at the foot of the motte. Not long after, the shell keep on top of the motte was added, probably between 1218 and 1236 under King Henry III. Unfortunately, there's not really an awful lot of it left.

Only later, between 1323 and 1326, did the outer bailey get its curtain wall, though it had previously been enclosed by a bank and palisade. Part of this work was a tower behind the keep, now called Rosamund's Tower, which was set into the moat so that a postern gate or sally port could give access to the outside of the walls. It's one of the most interesting bits of the castle today, along with the motte itself and the height of the curtain walls as they cross the moat.

The castle's important buildings were in the inner bailey near the chapel, which is now the only roofed building (its pointy lancet windows are original, but it was heavily restored in Victorian times). These included a hall dating from the early 1100s (actually the castle's first stone building) and a later hall built in 1314, both of which feature large, arched recesses in the wall with a stone seat inside, which may have been where the lord or his steward sat in judgment on local legal disputes when the court was in session.

Pickering was owned by Thomas, Earl of Lancaster, who had the king's favourite, Piers Gaveston, executed at Scarborough in 1312 and rebelled against King Edward II in 1321 (*see Dunstanburgh Castle, Northumbria*). Its main role, however, seems to have been recreational rather than military: it stood on the edge of a large royal forest, and kings often brought their retinues to the castle for the hunting.

Easily found in the middle of Pickering.

223

RICHMOND CASTLE

English Heritage • ££ • Usual hours

The magnificent keep at Richmond totally dominates the castle's remains, but it's certainly not the whole story. Richmond was actually one of the first castles in England to be built in stone, established in the 1080s by Alan the Red, one of William the Conqueror's best soldiers and most trusted advisers. He had been granted lots of land in Swaledale and he chose this site, on high cliffs above the river, as the ideal place for a brand new castle and town.

Although the walls were all strengthened by later rebuilding, the layout of the place remains faithful to Earl Alan's original castle. The most important building at the time was the great hall in the far left-hand corner of the inner bailey, known as Scolland's Hall after Earl Alan's steward. It's well worth taking a closer look at this, even though it's quite severely ruined. It is the oldest building of the castle, and you'll find it easy to make sense of the layout of what was a typical (though unusually large and grand) hall block of the time. The hall itself was on the first floor of the main part of the building, with the lord's private apartment (or solar) across the end: this room was small but comfortable, with windows overlooking the river and a decent-sized fireplace.

Incidentally, the fact that the walls along the cliff edge have largely disappeared reflects the pattern of the first castle: since the cliffs were defence enough in themselves, this side was probably protected by just a wooden palisade.

Equally incidentally, next door to Scolland's Hall is a tower known as the Gold Hole Tower. The guidebook coyly suggests that its name has something to do with a modern legend of buried treasure, but it's my belief that the name has more to do with the fact that this was a latrine tower.

The unusually tall keep was started in the mid-1100s by Conan 'The Little', Earl of Brittany, but inevitably it has connections with England's greatest keep-builder, King Henry II, who controlled the castle, when Conan died in 1171, as guardian of Conan's daughter Constance. At about the same time, all the walls

Richmond's tall keep was built in the mid-1100s by Conan, but the earlier parts of the castle are all Alan's work.

were strengthened and a barbican was placed in front of the main gate, next to the keep.

The keep itself was built on top of the original gate, with the large archway through which traffic originally entered the castle now blocked. Access to the ground floor of the keep was only possible through a spiral stair from the floor above, and in this basement – used for storage – there's a well which was cunningly incorporated into a pillar that supports the upstairs floor.

There is a single large room on the first and second floors, with small chambers in the thickness of the wall on each floor, and above this you can get out on the roof, from where the views really are superb.

The rather ugly modern thing to one side of the keep, by the way, is a block of detention cells dating from Victorian times. The castle was still in military use then, and remained so right into the Second World War.

Easily found in the middle of Richmond.

ROCHE ABBEY

Roche is a lovely spot, but there might be a lot more of the abbey left if it weren't for Capability Brown.

English Heritage • ££ • Slightly limited hours (closed November to March)

This is an interesting ruin in an extraordinarily beautiful spot, for which only hesitant thanks are due to Lancelot 'Capability' Brown, the famed landscape gardener.

He was brought in in 1774 to design the grounds for a new house belonging to Lord Scarborough, within which the abbey ruins lay. Since such picturesque ruins were just coming into fashion, it was decided to make the abbey a feature of the grounds – Brown's first attempt at the 'Gothick' style – but this involved destroying anything that didn't fit the designer's idea of picturesque. Some walls were pulled down so that their stone could be used to enhance other parts of the ruin, and large parts of the buildings of the cloister were simply flattened because they got in the way. Most of the area was then buried under stepped formal grass terraces.

As early as the 1870s, some attempt was made to dig under this artificial landscape to see what remained of the abbey underneath, and in the 1920s the area was systematically cleared and the remains consolidated. The upshot of all this is a rather fine mixture of landscaped surroundings with lots of mature trees, a very picturesque piece of abbey ruin, and an extensive layout of foundation walls from which it is easy to get a good idea of the plan of the abbey. One of the most pleasing features is the large, well-channelled stream which is crossed in several places by the buildings of the cloister.

Roche was a Cistercian abbey founded in 1147 by monks from Newminster in Northumberland, which in turn was a daughter-house of Fountains Abbey. As at all new foundations, the first work would have been to build accommodation and a simple church in timber, and a surviving charter from one of Roche's patrons gave the monks permission to get wood from the forest of Maltby under the supervision of the forester – unless he was unco-operative, in which case they could take it anyway.

There's also a vivid surviving account from the time of the abbey's dissolution in 1538 that tells how the local people immediately descended on the place and plundered everything of value that they could carry, including tiles and paving stones from the floors and lead from the roofs.

If you'd like to take a longer look at this pleasant piece of countryside, there's a circular walk of about 15 miles (though it can be done in shorter pieces) organised by the local council and the Countryside Commission, which takes in several nearby historic sites as well a few pubs. Leaflets are available free from the ticket office.

Signposted off the A634 south of Maltby, near Rotherham.

The keep at Scarborough, like most of England's finest keeps, was the work of King Henry II in the mid-1100s.

SANDAL CASTLE

Local council • Free • Open access during usual hours

A far more interesting site than you might at first think. Although there isn't much of it left, this was a castle of a unique and fascinating design. It lay buried for many years before being revealed by a ten-year excavation begun in 1963.

Basically, the layout was as follows. There was a large keep, made up of a number of rounded towers, on top of the early Norman mound. A covered walkway led down the side of the mound to a double-towered gate, the bottom of which can clearly be seen. A bridge crossed a ditch to a small, strong, half-moon-shaped barbican, which in turn was separated

by the ditch from the inner bailey area which fitted in a semicircle around the barbican. The whole lot was surrounded by a large ditch and bank, with just one gateway (right beside the causeway by which you now reach the inner bailey). You really need to see a plan or an aerial photo to appreciate the beauty of this layout.

Signposted off the A61 south of Wakefield, opposite the turn for the B6132 to Royston.

SCARBOROUGH CASTLE

English Heritage • £££ • Usual hours

Scarborough isn't quite in the top rank of English castles, but it has the advantages of a splendid seaside clifftop location with great views out to sea and along the coast, and it possesses an impressive-looking ruined Norman keep. There are also a few pieces of various accommodation blocks to poke around, and the remains of a Roman signal station on the edge of the cliff.

The layout of the castle is simple enough. The headland needed no defences on the seaward side because

The barbican at Sandal guarded the approach to the keep, with a twin-towered gate as the next line of defence.

of the cliffs, but there's an enormous curtain wall facing the town, with closely spaced towers. Tucked in behind the curtain wall is a raised inner bailey protected by its own wall (mostly ruined), and this is where the keep stands. Below the keep is the gatehouse, in front of which is a strangely-shaped bailey, the sinuous course of its walls and towers following the contours of the hill.

The castle was basically built by Henry II between 1158 and 1168, and the keep dates mostly from then, though it was founded on an existing tower of the 1130s. King John spent a lot of money on the castle (as he did with so many castles) between 1201 and 1216, most of his expenditure going to improve the curtain wall. Henry III also splashed out on improvements, adding the barbican gateway in the 1240s.

Scarborough's most notorious event took place in 1312, when the castle was besieged by rebellious barons after the blood of Piers Gaveston, lover of Edward II, who was governor of the castle at the time. The garrison was starved out and Gaveston surrendered on the promise of safe conduct to London for a fair trial, but the promise was broken and he was summarily beheaded in the castle.

On headland at north end of Scarborough's South Bay; can be reached by footpath from the town, but is not well signposted for cars – it's up Castle Street from the town centre. Free parking on the road, near the church.

Skipton Castle is mostly composed of fat, round towers closely grouped together around a small courtyard.

SKIPTON CASTLE
Privately owned • £££ • Usual hours

Extremely good fun, if a little expensive (it costs as much as a cinema ticket), this is a pleasing little castle. Its layout is basically a half-moon of closely spaced round towers, with short stretches of wall between some of them. The flat side, quite surprisingly, looks out over a steep cliff which drops away to the river gorge below.

The towers date variously to the late 1100s, the 1200s and the early 1300s, but the place was destroyed in the Civil War and then rebuilt to its original pattern by the eccentric Lady Anne Clifford, a firm adherent of the medieval ways of her ancestors, who was born here in 1590 (*see also Brougham Castle, Cumbria*). She was not permitted to return the castle to its former strength, however, and in some of the towers you can see where Lady Anne's thinner walls were put on the base of the very thick originals.

In the middle is a courtyard – gloomy, but appealing in a Gothicky way, and featuring a marvellous twisted tree – surrounded by the Tudor-style frontages of the restored accommodation. Lots of stairs lead in and out of a warren of rooms in the various towers, which makes the interior very enjoyable to explore.

Easily found, right in the middle of Skipton.

SPOFFORTH CASTLE
English Heritage • Free • Open access at any reasonable time

The remains of a fortified house that belonged to the Percy family. Its most interesting feature is the way the undercroft to the large hall is built up against a rock outcrop, so that it's almost as if the place has grown out of the rock. This is the oldest part of the building, dating to the late 1200s. The hall itself was rebuilt later.

Signposted in Spofforth village, off the A661 south of Harrogate.

The remarkable undercroft beneath the great hall at Spofforth uses the rock outcrop as one of its walls.

The remarkable earthworks of the Celtic town at Stanwick run for six miles across the Yorkshire fields.

STANWICK IRON AGE FORTIFICATIONS

One section in the care of English Heritage •
Free • Open access at any reasonable time

This is an extraordinarily large set of earthworks, running in a circuit of some 10km (6 miles) around what was once a town belonging to the Celtic tribe of the Brigantes.

One small section of the earthworks was partially restored after excavation in the 1960s and is in the care of English Heritage. Here the ditch in front of the earth rampart has been revealed and a tiny piece of the stone wall which topped the rampart has been reconstructed. A nearby signboard has a map of the defences, which is a great help if you want to explore further.

The story of Stanwick is a remarkable one, and it starts in 51 AD with Queen Cartimandua, ruler of the tribe of the Brigantes, whose territory covered much of northern England on both sides of the Pennines. She was a wholehearted supporter of peace with the Romans, to the extent that when the British resistance leader Caratacus was defeated in battle and fled to her for protection, she handed him over.

Anti-Roman feeling was growing within the tribe, however, and was stirred up by the rebellion of the Iceni in 61 AD. By 69 AD, Cartimandua's husband Venutius had had enough. At the head of the tribe's anti-Roman factions, he wrested control from his ex-wife (the Romans had to rescue her) and kicked off a general rebellion of the Brigantes.

The earthen rampart was fronted by a ditch and topped by a stone wall, as seen in this restored section.

Although the fortifications at Stanwick started as a small hillfort-like enclosure in about 47 AD and were expanded with the creation of a much larger compound not long after, the full circuit of ramparts was thrown up in about 72 AD as the Brigantes prepared to make their final stand. Much of the 250 hectares of land which it enclosed would have been pasture for the tribe's precious cattle.

Unfortunately, it was a futile effort. The ramparts were so extensive that they could never have been defended properly, and work was not complete when the Ninth Legion attacked the fort and wiped out its defenders in what is presumed to have been the battle that finally ended the Brigantian uprising. Sir Mortimer Wheeler, who excavated the site, described it thus: 'Stanwick is at the same time a very notable memorial to a heroic episode of the British resistance and a monument to its futility'.

By minor road from Forcett to Stanwick.

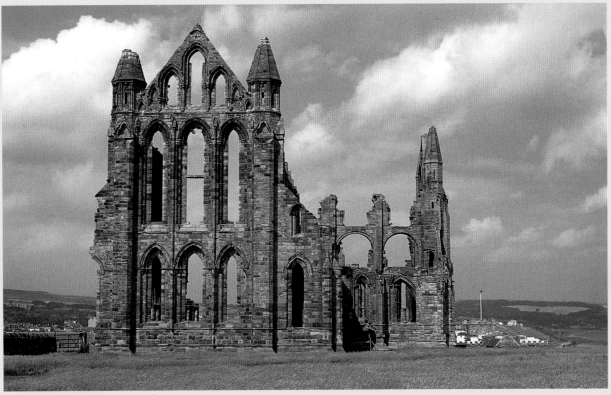

WHITBY ABBEY

English Heritage • £££ • Usual hours

Whitby might not be as splendid as the great Yorkshire abbeys at *Rievaulx* and *Fountains,* and there's a good deal less of it left, but it's still a very pretty ruin.

Unfortunately none of the domestic buildings of the abbey – the refectory where the monks ate, the dormitories where they slept, or the cloisters around which these rooms were set – has survived. In fact only two 'wings' of the church stand to anything like their original height, the east end and the north transept. But this is more than enough to give you a good idea of the church's size and grandeur, and by happy accident it makes a very pleasing composition. As recently as late last century the tower over the crossing was intact too, but it came down in storms.

The Benedictine community at Whitby was founded in the 1070s on the site of a much older religious settlement, a monastery established by Abbess Hilda in 657. Famous for the exemplary lives led by its monks and nuns, Whitby was home to many of the early English saints, including the

It's a very pretty ruin, and Whitby has an important place in the history of the early English church, too.

poet Caedmon, whose verse is the earliest literature in the English language. Hilda's abbey was chosen for the honour of hosting the great synod (meeting) of 664, at which King Oswy of Northumbria had agreed to hear arguments from the great men of the Celtic and Roman churches and decide which rule would be followed in England. For political reasons, it was pretty much a foregone conclusion that he would opt for the Roman ways – as indeed he did.

Excavations have uncovered traces of small buildings from the first Whitby abbey, dating to the 900s. Because lots of artefacts associated with weaving were found, it's thought that they were nuns' cells.

The abbey church that you see today was started in the 1220s and developed over a period of about 200 years. There was already an earlier Norman church on the site, and instead of just knocking it down and starting again, the monks rebuilt it piece by piece. As a result, each part is in a different architectural style.

Also, if you look carefully, you can see that the church is slightly bent, with the western half at a slight angle to the eastern half.

The first stage of rebuilding was the east end, in 'Early English' style with long, pointed windows. The rest could only be undertaken when money was available. In the 1250s, work on the transepts and crossing drove the abbey into debt. By the mid-1300s, when plague was just one factor in a recession that hit the whole of Europe, work on the final stage slowed so much that it was not finished until the mid-1400s. The west end, not much of which survives, has details in the style known as Perpendicular, characterised by large windows and straight tracery.

The abbey was dissolved by Henry VIII in 1539 and its stone used to build a nearby house; the church may have been left alone because it was an important landmark for passing ships.

On headland east of Whitby; reached by car (council car park) or on foot up steep path.

SEE ALSO...

ALDBOROUGH ROMAN TOWN, *Aldborough village, just south of Boroughbridge* – All that remains of this Roman town are some very short stretches of wall, standing to foundation height only, and two small mosaics covered by modern huts. There's a small museum, too. It's hard to see why they bother to keep it open to the public, though perhaps we ought to be grateful that they do. (*English Heritage, ££, usual hours.*)

ALMONDBURY HILLFORT, *Castle Hill, Huddersfield* – Large and interesting hillfort which started life as a small bronze age settlement. In the early iron age (about 700 BC) it developed into a fort with a timber-laced rampart faced with large stones. Later it was expanded greatly, with banks enclosing a series of 'annexes' as well as lots of pasture. It seems to have been burned and abandoned in about 500 BC.

BURTON AGNES MANOR HOUSE, *on the A614 west of Bridlington* – Not to be confused with the nearby stately home, Burton Agnes Hall, this is basically a Norman house, though with additions from the 1500s and 1600s. It's rather good. (*English Heritage, free, open access during usual hours.*)

THE DEVIL'S ARROWS (pictured above), *in field to west of Boroughbridge, beside minor road to Roecliffe, before you reach the A1* – Three most unusual standing stones: very tall and thin, and with weathered tops that look as if they have been carved. One is right by the road, but two others are in a field which you can't get in to because of the crops. The stones are related to an extensive neolithic/ bronze age ceremonial complex between the rivers Swale and Ure involving henges at Thornborough and Hutton Moor.

DUGGLEBY HOWE ROUND BARROW, *just south-east of Duggleby village, by the B1253* – One of the largest barrows in Britain, made from an astonishing 5000 tons of chalk. It contained 50 cremations of the late neolithic/early bronze age (around 2500 to 2000 BC) plus bone pins and arrowheads.

KNARESBOROUGH CASTLE, *in park just off the town centre* – The main remnant is a large keep-like tower built by Edward II in about 1310. Its basements can be visited on a guided tour organised by the nearby town museum, but it's too expensive and inconvenient an arrangement for such a modest monument. (*Local council, ££, limited hours – tours five times a day, May to September only.*)

LOOSE HOWE ROUND BARROW, *on moors north of the road from Rosedale Head to Rosedale Abbey* – Interesting primarily for what was found in it. Excavations found an oak tree-trunk coffin with a body inside laid out on a bed of rushes and straw. A piece of shoe survived, as did an offering of hazel branches and hazelnuts. There was a bronze knife at the hip of the body, and next to the coffin was a dugout canoe 3m (10ft) long. All this is dated at about 1700 BC.

MARMION TOWER, *West Tanfield* – The substantial gatehouse of a manor house which has vanished. Its most notable feature is a fancy oriel window, but you can climb up to a room on the first floor and also follow a stair to second-floor level, though the stair just ends. Nice little building. (*English Heritage, free, open access at any reasonable time.*)

PIERCEBRIDGE ROMAN FORT & BRIDGE, *Piercebridge village* – Strictly speaking, the fort is in Durham, but we won't quibble. The county council has done a good job of displaying the remains of a large stone fort from the early 300s AD; the remains include a stretch of wall, part of a gateway and some buildings just inside the wall, though all of it survives only as foundation-level walls. Out on the edge of town (directions can be gleaned from a signboard at the fort) is a jumble of stonework in a field which is all that is left of the stone piers of a bridge across the River Tees. The river has taken a different course, leaving the bridge high and dry. There isn't really much to look at, but it does make you realise that Roman military engineers were capable of building large and very solid structures. (*County council and English Heritage, free, open access at civilised hours.*)

RIPLEY CASTLE, *Ripley village* – Not so much a castle as a house, though it was originally defended and has retained some castle-like features. The tower dates back to the 1400s and has an unusual roof. (*Privately owned, £££, limited hours – in summer it is not open on Friday or Saturday except in the high season in July and August, and in winter it is open at lunchtime five days a week.*)

RUDSTON MONOLITH, *in the village churchyard by the B1253 to Bridlington* – This is the tallest standing stone in Britain, an impressive 7.8m (25ft) high and weighing 26 tons. Made of gritstone, it was dragged here from Cayton Bay, 12 miles away. It is thought to have been put up around 2000 BC.

ST MARY'S ABBEY, YORK – Some beautiful arches and a good deal of the ground plan of this important early abbey remain in the grounds of the Yorkshire Museum. Inside the museum itself, you can find out more; there is also a guidebook on sale. Well worth seeing. (*City council, free, open access during museum opening hours.*)

SKIPSEA CASTLE, *west of the village* – Earthworks only survive, but it's an interesting motte and bailey castle in which the motte was separated from the bailey by its own moat and also by a marsh, which was crossed by a wooden causeway. The lake that surrounds most of the castle is known to have contained eels, which were a major food source in medieval times. (*English Heritage, free, open access at any reasonable time.*)

THORNBOROUGH HENGE, *in field next to the minor road from West Tanfield to Thornborough* – This is actually one of the most impressive henge monuments anywhere in England: the only other notable one is *Mayburgh Henge* in *Cumbria*. (A henge is a great circular bank surrounding an arena-like area.) There are actually three henges in a row here, all thought to date to the early bronze age (not long after 2000 BC) rather than the neolithic. The northernmost henge, which stands among trees, is said to be the best preserved, but the easiest one to get to is the middle one, standing in a field. This middle henge was built on top of an earlier 'cursus' monument (a long, narrow earthwork like a processional way). When it was built, the bank of the henge was covered with white gypsum from the bed of the nearby river.

WHARRAM PERCY DESERTED MEDIEVAL VILLAGE, *off the B1248 north of Wetwang* – Although there are many examples, right across the country, of villages that were abandoned in medieval times, this is probably the most interesting of the lot, with quite a lot of the church still standing. It's worth going simply to get the story of these deserted villages – you may well find that it helps you make sense of a similar site in your local area – but do get hold of the guidebook first, from any other English Heritage site in the region. (*English Heritage, free, open access at any reasonable time.*)

WHEELDALE ROMAN ROAD, *on the moor south of Goathland* – One of the best-preserved stretches of Roman road anywhere in England (and the only one in the care of English Heritage, as far as I am aware). It is about a mile long and still has its hardcore road surface as well as its drainage ditches to either side. A very

good place for a walk. (*English Heritage and North Yorkshire Moors National Park Authority, free, open access at any time.*)

WHORLTON CASTLE, *on minor road to Whorlton from Swainby village* – Rather an entertaining find, tucked away in a fairly out-of-the-way location near the very pretty village of Swainby. There's a substantial gatehouse of the 1300s but not a lot else (just some vaults from a building that stood in a corner of a small walled enclosure). It's quite intriguing, though. A little further down the lane, there's an interesting half-ruined church, too. (*On private land; open access at any reasonable time.*)

WILLY HOWE ROUND BARROW, *between Wold Newton and Burton Fleming* –

Very large barrow notable mainly for its size, but comparable with *Duggleby Howe barrow* (*above*).

YORK ROMAN REMAINS, *throughout the city* – York (*Eboracum*) was one of the most important forts of Roman Britain, along with Chester and Caerleon, and grew into a large town which remained England's second city right into late medieval times. York also has the unique distinction of being the only place in Britain where a Roman emperor died (Septimus Severus in 211 AD). There are plenty of finds in the city's two main museums, and there are traces of walls and towers in various places around the town, dating mainly from the rebuilding of the fort in the 300s. The most notable is the Multiangular Tower, which was one of the corner towers of the fort.

AND…

ACKLAM WOLD BARROWS, *east of Acklam by the road to Birdsall.*

BROUGH-BY-BAINBRIDGE ROMAN FORT, *near village of Bainbridge in Wensleydale.*

CARL WARK HILLFORT, *on Hathersage Moor, near Sheffield.*

CASTLE DYKES HENGE, *on hill above Aysgarth, in Wensleydale.*

CASTLETON RIGG SETTLEMENT, *by the road from Castleton to Westerdale.*

CAWTHORN ROMAN CAMPS, *north of the road from Copton to Newton-on-Rawcliffe (a unique set of four Roman camps visible as low earthworks).*

DANBY RIGG, *near Danby, track up from North End Farm (lots of stone cairns, standing stones and earthworks in an impressive setting).*

DANE'S DYKES, *near Flamborough (vast earthwork of the iron age that cuts off the whole peninsula of Flamborough Head).*

GILLING CASTLE, *East Gilling (started life as some sort of tower house but is now not open to visitors).*

GOLDSBOROUGH ROMAN SIGNAL STATION, *near Whitby.*

GRASSINGTON SETTLEMENT, *on the moors north of the village.*

HANGING GRIMSTON BARROWS – *Thixendale, by Stone Sleights, on both sides of road south-east of Leavening.*

HIGH BRIDE STONES STONE CIRCLES, *North York moors near Grosmont.*

HUTTON MOOR HENGES, *in angle of A61 and A1 near Hutton Conyers.*

ILKLEY MOOR ROCK CARVINGS & ILKLEY ROMAN FORT, *Ilkley Moor.*

INGLEBOROUGH HILLFORT, *north-east of Ingleton; from B6255 near Storrs Cave, track via Crina Bottom.*

MALTON ROMAN FORT, *Malton town (some ramparts on public land).*

NEWBURGH PRIORY, *near Coxwold* is a post-Dissolution house that has links with Oliver Cromwell. It is open to visitors in the summer.

SCAMBRIDGE LONG BARROW AND DYKES, *east of Allerston, reached by track north from the A170 (big long barrow of the neolithic era, plus lots of iron age earthworks).*

STAPLE HOWE IRON AGE FARMSTEAD, *east of Scampston, south of the A64.*

STEETON HALL GATEWAY, *near Castleford (small but well-preserved gatehouse of the 1300s, in the care of English Heritage: free, access to exterior only during usual hours).*

County Durham, Tyne & Tees

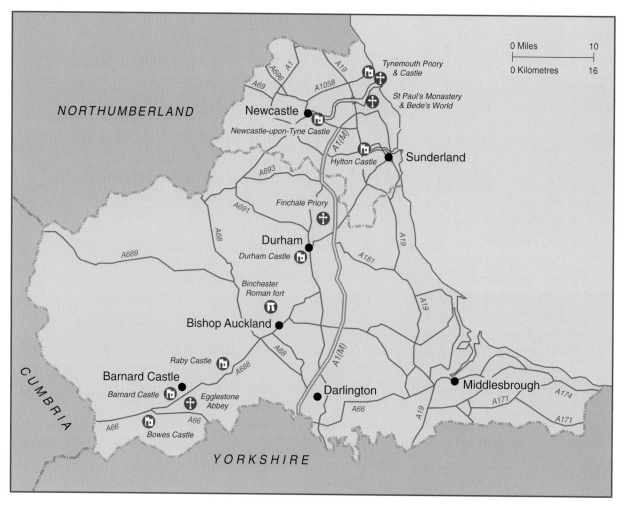

COUNTY DURHAM AND THE METROPOLITAN COUNTIES that are its neighbours have what is probably the most diverse landscape in the country, with large industrial towns just a few minutes' drive away from some of England's finest coasts and hills. The area is full of pleasant surprises, probably the biggest being the splendid Norman keep at the heart of the region's largest city, *Newcastle-upon-Tyne*. Also within spitting distance of the city is a remarkable complex on the headland at *Tynemouth*, where you'll find the ruins of both a castle and a priory. Most appealing for tourists, though, are the river valleys of the Pennines, where the redoubtable *Barnard Castle* sits on a high cliff guarding the approach to Teesdale.

Finchale Priory – one of the region's nicest little ruins.

BARNARD CASTLE

English Heritage • ££ • Usual hours

This is one of the great castles of the north of England, even though the remains aren't quite substantial enough to put it in the top rank. It actually looks its grandest from outside, particularly from down by the river, where you can see the full height of the curtain walls atop the riverside cliffs.

Inside the walls, the most important single feature is the thick-walled Round Tower, which, along with the Great Hall next to it, formed the lord's residence at the heart of the castle. You can get into the vaulted basement of the Round Tower and up to the first floor. There's also a spiral stair which takes you to second-floor level and ends abruptly, which makes a good vantage point. It's enough to tell you that this was never the most elegant or comfortable of keeps.

Apart from that, the remains are a bit of a jumble. Various pieces of curtain wall stride majestically around the inner bailey and span the huge

One of the oldest buildings of Barnard Castle, the massive Round Tower (on the right) is still very nearly intact.

ditch, and you can appreciate the size of the outer bailey which dominated the town. The views over the river are rather beautiful.

The first castle here was built by a Norman lord from Picardy, Guy de Baliol, who was given a large estate in the area by William II as a reward for services during the rebellion of the Earl of Northumbria in 1093. Guy chose the site, but it was his nephew and heir, Bernard de Baliol, who started to build a stone castle here in the 1130s. He also founded the town, following the example of Alan, Count of Brittany, who created a new town and castle at Richmond in Yorkshire some 60 years before. To this day, castle and town bear Bernard's name.

The building programme continued right into the 1180s, but it cost the family more than they could afford. By the time Hugh de Baliol inherited in 1205, he was heavily in debt to the Bishop of Durham, who pressured him into siding with Durham in a dispute with King John. For a while

John took away all Hugh's lands, but by 1213 he was back in favour.

Hugh was succeeded in 1228 by his son, John de Baliol, who became one of the most powerful men in Britain when he married a Scottish heiress (called, spectacularly, Devorguilla of Galloway) and inherited her land and titles in Scotland. After his death in 1269, his wife founded in his memory the college at Oxford that still bears his name (though with an added 'l').

Thanks to the Scottish titles that John married into, his third son, also called John, managed to get voted King of Scotland in 1290 at a council convened by the English king, Edward I. When John got too big for his boots and renounced his homage to Edward in 1296, trouble followed and John ended up as a prisoner in the Tower, though he was later allowed to retire to the family estates in Picardy.

In the middle of the town of Barnard Castle; you can park by the riverside and walk up, or park in the town centre.

The highlight of Binchester is the very well-preserved bath house, now protected by a modern building.

BINCHESTER ROMAN FORT

Durham County Council • ££ • Limited hours (Easter and May to September only)

Only a small section in the centre of this military fort has been excavated and left exposed to view, principally because it includes the well-preserved floor of a bath house heated by an underfloor hypocaust. This is now covered by a modern building and has been partially reconstructed to show in some detail how the room would have looked.

Known to the Romans as *Vincovia*, Binchester was a rearward cavalry fort supporting the front line at Hadrian's Wall. First used between 79 and 122 AD, the site was later reoccupied and the fort was rebuilt in stone in the mid-300s.

Signposted from Bishop Auckland, on minor road north to Newfield and Byers Green.

The keep at Bowes Castle was built by Henry II and is unusual in that it wasn't ever defended by a curtain wall.

BOWES CASTLE

English Heritage • Free • Open access at any reasonable time

The remains of a large keep built by Henry II – *the* great keep-builder – between 1170 and 1187 in the corner of a Roman fort. It looks pretty fine, and you can climb a short flight of spiral stair to first-floor level to look over the interior, but this doesn't add up to a tremendously exciting visit. You can make out where the forebuilding stood, and the door on the first floor which its stairs led to. The keep is thought to be unusual for its time, in that it was never surrounded by other buildings.

In the middle of Bowes village (signposted).

DURHAM CASTLE

University of Durham • £££ • Limited hours (Hourly guided tours: every day in summer months; Monday, Wednesday, Saturday and Sunday afternoons in winter months)

The city – or citadel, even – of Durham is a remarkable place, with the cathedral and castle of the Prince Bishops built on a huge rock outcrop in a loop of the River Wear. As the home of the infamous Prince Bishops, the historical weight of the place is immense, but Durham is also a living city and this is reflected in the fact that the castle has been taken over by the University and has been heavily rebuilt over the years, with the result that it's a shadow of its former self.

The pattern of the castle is pretty much as it has always been, with a keep on top of a mound overlooking a bailey with accommodation around the walls, and there are some very attractive Norman details here and there, but basically it's now more an over-elaborate Victorian creation.

In Durham city centre, near the cathedral.

Durham Castle was heavily restored in the mid-1800s to become a University college, so it's not much fun.

The arches of the church at Egglestone Abbey look pretty fine – and the toilets are rather interesting, too.

The gatehouse-keep of Hylton Castle is an elegant-looking building. It's a pity you can't get inside it.

EGGLESTONE ABBEY

English Heritage • Free • Open access at any reasonable time

This is a small but very pretty ruin in lovely country. The main remnants are most of the west and east ends of the abbey church, with some fine arches, and a well-preserved reredorter (the toilets) at the end of the dormitory range. Don't miss the view of the ruin from high on the other side of the river on the minor road to Barnard Castle.

Near Barnard Castle: signposted from B6277 or minor road from town to Greta Bridge.

FINCHALE PRIORY

English Heritage • ££ • Limited opening (afternoons April to September only, but see main entry)

It was clearly never on a grand scale, but with more of its buildings surviving than most abbey remains this is an interesting ruin, and very good fun to explore. There are lots of excellent details to admire in the church, from the fine tracery in the windows of the choir to the sweet little pinnacle at one end. There's even a spiral stair in a fat, hollow pillar at the corner of the north transept which you can ascend to look

down on the interior of the church (though be careful, because it leads out into thin air). Other notable elements include a fine vaulted cellar beneath the refectory and substantial parts of the prior's lodgings.

The Priory began as a hermitage set up in 1110 by St Godric. The peaceful river valley is now home to a camping site, which charges a small fee for parking but allows free access to the Priory in the winter months, when it's not formally open.

Clearly signposted from either the A167 or the A690 north of Durham.

HYLTON CASTLE

English Heritage and local council • Free • Open access to exterior only in usual hours

This is a very splendid-looking gatehouse-keep that dates from around 1400, and there are some fine carved details high on its walls, but unfortunately you can't do anything but admire its partially restored exterior. Its suburban location means it isn't much of a tourist attraction, but it is set in a well-tended park. Nothing is known about the layout of the castle of which it was a part.

In suburb of Hylton Castle, signposted off A1231 north-west of Sunderland.

There's lots to see at Finchale Priory, which is a fascinating jumble of interesting odds and ends.

NEWCASTLE KEEP

*Newcastle City Council • ££ • Slightly
limited hours (not Sunday or Monday)*

Newcastle-upon-Tyne is lucky
enough to be one of only two major
English cities to still have a castle
(the other, of course, is London) and
although there's not a lot left except
the keep, it is an excellent keep.
Quite apart from anything else, the
view from the roof – with the
famous Tyne Bridge on one side,
and the city on the other – is an ideal
way of getting your bearings if you
are new to the city.

The keep, like all the best keeps,
was ordered by Henry II and is the
work of Maurice the Builder. It was
started in 1168 and took about ten
years to complete. The layout is
pretty much as it was originally,
though with some slight alterations
at various times. The entrance is
through a forebuilding, and the stairs
originally led straight up to the door
of the huge, tall Great Chamber on
the third storey. Off the side of this
enormous room is a chamber inside
the thickness of the wall which
contains the impressively deep well.
Inside the forebuilding, below the
stairs, there's an interesting chapel.

This is certainly one of the finest
keeps in England, and if you fancy
combining castle-visiting with a bit
of city shopping, you're laughing.

*Near the Tyne in Newcastle city centre; car
parks in Quayside are pretty close.*

The work of Henry II, the keep at Newcastle is one of the best in the country – and it's in the city centre, too.

The majestic-looking Raby Castle, with deer in its deer park, has bags of style but lacks medieval authenticity.

RABY CASTLE

*Privately owned • £££ • Limited hours (open
two days a week in spring, every day except
Saturday in summer)*

Raby is more a house than a castle,
and seems always to have been so:
experts say it is poorly defended,
though its walls and towers look the
part. It was built after 1378 by the
great Neville family and developed
over several hundred years into a
palatial residence. As a castle-like
stately home, it's not bad to visit. The
interiors are mostly 1700s and 1800s,
but the medieval kitchen is superb.

A mile north of Staindrop on the A688.

TYNEMOUTH PRIORY & CASTLE

English Heritage • £££ • Usual hours

There's something of a fragmentary feel to the remains of the priory and castle at Tynemouth, as even the guidebook admits, but it's still a rewarding place to visit. The setting has a very seasidey feel, with the ruins located on a rocky headland which has very obvious defensive strength as well as the sense of isolation which seems to have been a prime requisite for monastic sites.

The headland was refortified by Henry VIII after the Priory was dissolved and remained in use as a military establishment right into the 1960s, with the result that most of the original fortifications were destroyed and rebuilt over the years. When the whole thing passed into the care of the nation, many later buildings were torn down to reveal the oldest stonework, and while this certainly makes for a more attractive scene today, it also contributes to that fragmentary feel.

The remains of the Priory are the more obvious attraction, particularly since the east end of the church stands to a considerable height. It was probably left intact at the time of the Dissolution to act as a landmark for ships in the daytime, but it also acted as a lighthouse – carrying on a much older tradition of the monks – with a coal brazier burning in one of the

The remains of Tynemouth Priory are very attractive, and the coastal setting makes it rather special.

towers atop the end wall of the church, until in 1659 the stairs leading to the tower collapsed and a purpose-built lighthouse was erected.

The church is the only real survival of the Priory, but it has some very attractive details. Right at the east end is a tiny chapel, which may have been a private chantry of the Percy family or may have been a Lady Chapel. Although you do have to bear in mind that it was restored in the mid-1800s, it has a very attractive interior with elaborate vaulting (almost too elaborate, in fact). The carved bosses

of the vaults are described in some detail in the guidebook.

The headland was home to an early Christian monastery where St Oswin, King of Deira, was buried in 651. This monastery was destroyed by the Danes in 875, but refounded by the Normans (as a Benedictine daughter-house of St Albans Abbey) in 1085 thanks to the generosity of Robert de Mowbray, Earl of Northumberland. Robert also built a castle here, and in 1095 he held out for two months under siege during a rebellion against King William II. After his capture and a long imprisonment, Robert was allowed to live out a peaceful retirement as a monk at St Albans.

The later medieval castle had a circuit of walls around the entire headland (an unusually long circuit, too, at nearly 1km or 1100 yards) but most of this has disappeared. The only surviving building is the great gatehouse-keep built in the 1390s by Prior John of Wethamstede. It contains typical keep accommodation such as a great hall, with a great chamber above. Although the castle defences were the Priory's responsibility, Tynemouth Castle was also of great strategic importance in the wars with Scotland, and kings often stayed here, so the Crown contributed money to build it.

Clearly signposted on the seafront at Tynemouth, off the A1058.

The only bit of the castle left is the great gatehouse-keep, with a long, narrow barbican defending the entrance.

St Paul's Monastery & Bede's World, Jarrow

English Heritage, church authorities and charitable trust • Monastery ruins: free, open access at any reasonable time • Church: free, hours as Bede's World • Bede's World: ££, slightly limited hours (not Mondays except bank holidays, not Sunday mornings)

Some stonework remains from the early Christian monastery in which the famous monastic historian Bede lived around 700 AD, but it is of no great interest, even though one part of this ancient building survives as the chancel of the parish church.

In an attempt to reflect the importance of this venerable site – and, equally importantly, in an effort to revive an area left derelict by the heavy industry that once sustained it – the ambitious interpretation centre of Bede's World has been established, with a reconstructed Saxon farm of Bede's era. It's not yet entirely

This is where the Venerable Bede lived and wrote 1300 years ago. It's surprising that anything at all remains.

successful, partly because the landscaping will take a good deal of time to mature, but the animals are great and the staff are very friendly.

There are some decent reconstructed buildings, with lots more planned.

Clearly signposted near the Tyne Tunnel.

SEE ALSO...

ARBEIA (SOUTH SHIELDS ROMAN FORT), *clearly signposted in South Shields* – Rather excellent remains of a major Roman supply base, still under excavation and maintained as a museum by the local council, with very good reconstruction of a stone-built Roman gateway and lots of educational events. It's open usual hours (except Sundays in winter) and it's free to get in.

AUCKLAND CASTLE, *Bishop Auckland* – Residence of the Bishops of Durham with some splendid rooms open to the public, but it's all rather modern because it was destroyed in the 1650s and rebuilt after the Restoration. There are some trendy, with-it museum displays. A shelter for deer in the Park is open free to English Heritage members, but otherwise it's *£££, usual hours.*

BRANCEPETH CASTLE, *Brancepeth, near Durham* – Once an important castle of the Neville family, it was massacred by a Victorian restoration, then re-restored by Salvin. Barely anything original remains. It is owned by a firm and used for conferences.

ESCOMB SAXON CHURCH, *signposted at Escomb, near Bishop Auckland* – Extremely interesting, slightly brutal-looking ancient church which is very well explained by lots of information sheets inside the church. Stacks of intriguing detail, with lots of re-used Roman masonry. Access is free during usual hours with key from a nearby house, as directed on a sign. (*Pictured above.*)

GISBOROUGH PRIORY (*English Heritage & local council, £, usual hours except Mondays in winter*), *signposted on eastern edge of Guisborough* – Modest remains of an Augustinian priory, including a gatehouse and the east end of a church from the early 1300s.

LUMLEY CASTLE, *near Chester-le-Street* – This marvellous-looking quadrangular fortified house, which can be seen from the A167, was built in the 1390s by a supporter of Richard II called Lord Lumley, who was deposed in 1399. It is now a hotel.

WITTON CASTLE, *near Bishop Auckland* – an ugly Victorian Gothic imitation in the grounds of a caravan park, used as a pub. Can be visited on payment of a small fee. Not worth it.

AND...

BOWES ROMAN FORT, *on west side of Bowes*, surrounding the church and the castle; GRETA BRIDGE ROMAN FORT, *off the A66 near turning to Brignall*, its earthworks visible next to the Morritt Arms Hotel; REY CROSS ROMAN FORT, *way out in the country west of Bowes, cut through by the A66*, the earthworks of a marching camp that held a whole legion under canvas.

Northumbria

HOME to some of England's finest castles, with the fantastic keep of *Warkworth* and the scenic splendour of *Dunstanburgh* to the fore.

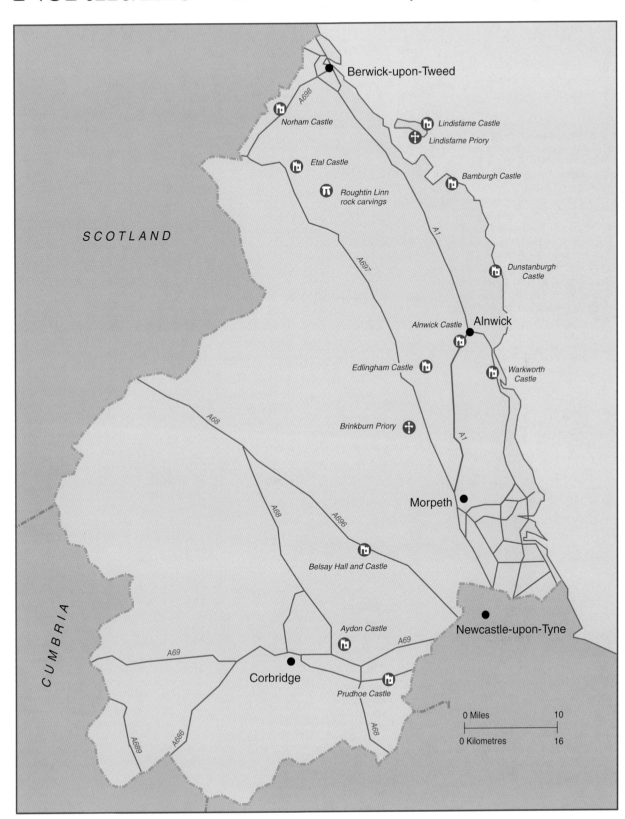

Berwick-upon-Tweed

Norham Castle

Lindisfarne Castle

Lindisfarne Priory

Etal Castle

Bamburgh Castle

Roughtin Linn
rock carvings

SCOTLAND

Dunstanburgh
Castle

Alnwick Castle

Alnwick

Edlingham Castle

Warkworth
Castle

Brinkburn Priory

Morpeth

Belsay Hall and Castle

CUMBRIA

Newcastle-upon-Tyne

Aydon Castle

Corbridge

Prudhoe Castle

0 Miles 10

0 Kilometres 16

Alnwick is a great-looking castle: you get an excellent view from the public footpath on the other side of the river.

ALNWICK CASTLE

Privately owned • £££ • Limited hours
(Easter to September, not mornings)

This is probably the finest example in England of a castle which developed into a stately home, and its Victorian description as 'the Windsor of the north' hits the nail on the head. Like Windsor, its interiors are ornate and lavishly decorated and the fabric of the building has been much altered, though the walls and towers are basically old. Much of the stonework dates from the decades after the early 1300s, when the castle was bought by the Percy family.

Alnwick was rebuilt by Robert Adam in the late 1700s and restored by Anthony Salvin in the early 1800s to give it back its medieval feel.

In the town of Alnwick.

AYDON CASTLE

English Heritage • ££ • Usual hours

Right at the other end of the scale from Alnwick Castle, this is a plain little fortified manor house which is very pleasing in its simplicity.

It's surrounded by a roughly pentagon-shaped circuit of curtain walls, some parts of which date from as late as 1350, but the main buildings were put up – with several changes of plan along the way – between 1296 and 1305. First was the chamber block, with the solar (the lord's private apartment) on the first floor. Next came the larger hall block, at right-angles to the chambers, with a hall and kitchen on the first floor. Later a separate kitchen range was built at right-angles to the hall block, and two stretches of wall were added to form an inner courtyard.

The whole thing survived to be used as a farmhouse in the 1700s and 1800s, but alterations from this period have been stripped away to leave the castle in a condition that seems remarkably complete and authentic. It's a very interesting example of the home of a minor nobleman.

Signposted off the B6321 north of Corbridge.

Aydon Castle is a superbly authentic example of the kind of fortified house that belonged to a lower-league lord.

BAMBURGH CASTLE

Privately owned • £££ • Usual hours

This is just about the finest-looking castle in England, set high on a massive rock overlooking the sea and visible for miles along the coast. Unfortunately it's disappointing to visit, having been 'restored' rather radically in Victorian times with the result that hardly anything original remains. Content yourself with admiring it from afar and take a walk on the superb sandy beach.

It is, however, a place with a long and interesting history. The rock was probably used as a natural stronghold by the Celts and the Romans, but it was certainly occupied in Saxon times and achieved widespread fame as the resting place of the head and right hand of St Oswald. In Norman times Bamburgh became the property of Robert, Earl of Northumberland, who in 1095 foolishly picked a quarrel with King William II which is extensively detailed in the *Anglo-Saxon Chronicle*. The castle was besieged, but held out, and so the King built a siege-castle said by the *Chronicle* to have been called 'Malveisin', which translates as 'Evil Neighbour'. Its garrison

Built on a huge rock, Bamburgh is one of the most splendid-looking castles in England. The beach is great, too.

captured Earl Robert as he tried to sneak off to Tynemouth, and his wife surrendered Bamburgh when they threatened to put out his eyes.

Bamburgh remained a royal castle for much of its life, but its history is not well documented. The keep, which is not unlike the one at Dover in Kent, was probably completed by Henry II. Further work was carried out by King John and by Henry III. In the Wars of the Roses, Bamburgh was held by the Lancastrians and in 1464 it was captured by Richard Neville, Earl of Warwick – the infamous 'Kingmaker' – who pounded it to pieces with artillery before it surrendered.

Easily spotted on the coast at Bamburgh.

BELSAY CASTLE

English Heritage • £££ • Usual hours

This place is tremendously good fun, with a very entertaining little keep tucked away in the grounds of a later house, reached by a half-hour stroll through gardens that have been sculpted artistically out of an old stone-quarry.

The new house, Belsay Hall, dates from the early 1800s and is frankly bizarre. If it were on a larger scale it might be quite graceful, but instead its classical borrowings – particularly the large hall of pillars at the centre of the house – are rather silly.

The earlier Belsay Castle is a ruin of two halves: a tower that dates largely from the early 1400s, and a house that was built on the side in 1614, when the unification of England and Scotland had made the border regions more peaceful.

Although the tower isn't huge, it's just as much fun to explore as many larger keeps. A spiral stair leads to main rooms on three floors – a kitchen on the ground floor, with a hall and a private chamber above – and eventually out on to the roof, where you can pop into one of the turrets and see the long drop to the ground through the holes in the machicolated battlements. There are smaller side-rooms on four levels, one of which is thought to have been a chapel.

Signposted from the A696 at the village of Belsay.

BRINKBURN PRIORY

English Heritage • ££ • Usual hours

This is a rare chance to get the full effect of a monastic church in something like its original condition, though you have to bear in mind that it was restored in Victorian times (in a 'very sensitive and restrained manner', says the guidebook). And very beautiful it is too, with the interior space mostly uncluttered by the paraphernalia of a working church so that you can really appreciate its grace and spirituality.

The architectural style of the church is called Transitional, because it's a mixture of an earlier and a later style. The door on the north side of the church, by the entrance to the site, is a good place to see both styles at work: the rounded arch of the door, with its sharply cut decoration, is typical of the earlier Norman style, while the arcades above (filled-in arches) have pointed tops and floral curves typical of the later style called Early English. The fact that the church took 30 to 40 years to build (late 1100s to early 1200s) explains why it might have fallen between two styles, but inside the church you can see that the lower arches are all pointed, belonging to the later style, while the higher windows are all rounded, following the earlier style. Odd.

The priory was founded by Augustinian canons some time around 1130 and was dissolved in 1536, but the church remained in use until the 1600s, when the roof fell in. As with most priories, a house was built after the Dissolution and this has just recently been placed in the care of English Heritage. Featuring some very attractive early Victorian details, it's currently looking rather stripped and bare while they consider what to do with it, but actually the blank canvas of its interior is almost as appealing as the church itself. It'll be interesting to see what comes of it.

Off the B6344, signposted from the A697 north of Morpeth.

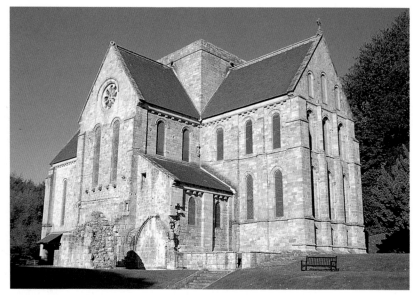

The beautiful priory church at Brinkburn dates from around 1200 and was sensitively restored in Victorian times.

EDLINGHAM CASTLE

English Heritage • Free • Open access at any reasonable time

This isn't a very large ruin, and there is nothing in the way of rooms or upper storeys to explore, but it's rather attractive in a rough and ready kind of way, and set in a lovely slice of country.

It started life in about 1250 as a long hall-house (that is, a house in which the main room was a large hall, though in this case there were quite a few other rooms besides). In about 1340 the keep was added, joined to the hall block by a short forebuilding. In common with many of the tower-houses of the region, it's what's known as a 'solar tower' and contained well-appointed private rooms for use by the lord. At roughly the same time that the keep was built, a gatehouse was added at the front of a roughly triangular courtyard enclosed by curtain walls.

The keep still stands to a decent height, and you can make out many of the fine details of the principal room on the first floor. The turrets are quite entertaining, too.

The nearby Norman church is well worth taking a look inside, with some remarkable pillars and arches, and here you can buy guide leaflets that describe the castle in detail.

Off the B6341 south-west of Alnwick.

Edlingham Castle is a rough and ready ruin in wild and woolly border country. The keep was built around 1340.

The great gatehouse at Dunstanburgh: six storeys tall when it was built in 1325, but falling apart by the early 1500s.

DUNSTANBURGH CASTLE

English Heritage and National Trust • ££ •
Usual hours

The great beauty of Dunstanburgh is its superb setting on a remote headland, with the sea crashing against the cliffs below and the fields rolling away on the landward side like grassy green waves. You have to approach the castle on foot from about a mile and a half away, and this gentle, scenic walk makes a visit to the castle all the more enjoyable.

The odd thing about Dunstanburgh Castle is that it has always been this remote, built on what you might call a greenfield site in the early 1300s by Thomas, Earl of Lancaster. Thomas was one of the most powerful men in the realm and led the English barons in a series of disputes with King Edward II in the early 1300s.

Edward came to the throne in 1307, but from the start many of the lords were unhappy about the influence on him of his lover, Piers Gaveston. Eventually the barons managed to have Gaveston tried by a kangaroo court at Scarborough and executed, with Thomas of Lancaster acting as their ringleader. For a year and a half

the nation was on the point of civil war, until in October 1313 the king finally pardoned the barons. By then, building work at Dunstanburgh was already well under way, and the castle was completed by about 1325.

It would not be surprising, then, if Thomas intended Dunstanburgh to be a stronghold from which he could lead a rebellion. One of the things you notice about the castle is that its walls enclose a vast area, perhaps so a large body of troops could be mustered here if need be (though it also proved useful in sheltering the local villagers, with their animals and possessions, when the Scots raided the area).

The main feature of the castle is the massive gatehouse, four storeys tall and originally topped with two towers another two storeys high. You can still get up to second-floor level on one side, and the views are brilliant.

Around 1380 a new gateway and gatehouse were built to the left of the original, so that the great gatehouse could be used purely as a keep, with an inner ward behind it protected from the rest of the castle.

The other main remnants are a stretch of curtain wall to the right of

the gatehouse, with a couple of towers and a few interesting features, and a tower called the Lilburn Tower which stands on its own looking especially picturesque with the sea beyond. That doesn't really add up to an awful lot of castle, but the location makes all the difference.

Reached by footpath north from Craster or south from Embleton golf course.

The Lilburn Tower, looking out to sea from the ruined curtain wall, is the most photogenic part of the castle.

ETAL CASTLE

English Heritage • ££ • Usual hours

The principal buildings here are a small keep and a gatehouse, which stood at opposite corners of a roughly square walled enclosure. One side of the curtain wall survives, along with parts of a corner-tower: it is thought that a similar tower would have stood in the fourth corner.

The keep started life as a three-storey tower-house in the late 1200s, and was extended by one storey in 1341 when a licence was granted to fortify the building. You can clearly see the join. The hall was on the first

The keep at Etal started life as a three-storey tower, and you can see where an extra floor was added.

floor, with a solar above (complete with a small chapel in the thickness of the wall) and another chamber on the top floor. All three of the upper floors had 'garderobe'-style toilets, with a cess pit in the basement below. In front of the keep was a forebuilding protected by a portcullis.

The gatehouse was almost as big as the keep, with rooms on just two floors but with towers on either side of the gate reaching up another storey. The first floor was reached by external steps, and the ornate windows suggest it may have been used as a chapel.

In all honesty, it's not the most fascinating place. 'Added value' is offered in the form of an unusual exhibition, with commentary on audio tape only, which describes the nearby battle of Flodden (1513), when the Earl of Surrey hastily gathered together a mob of untrained local amateurs and thoroughly trounced a far larger army of Scots.

LINDISFARNE CASTLE

National Trust • ££ • Usual hours

Originally an artillery fort built by Henry VIII, the castle was disused by the early 1800s, and in the 1880s was bought by the editor of *Country Life* magazine, Edward Hudson, who employed the architect Sir Edwin Lutyens to transform it into a cosy country house. The resulting creation

Lindisfarne Castle is an eccentric country house converted in the late 1800s from an artillery fort.

is deliciously eccentric on the outside and very comfortable on the inside, and you would be very happy to get an invitation to stay for a few days. Not much of a castle, then, but a very lovely stately-cottage-cum-folly.

Reached only on foot (ten minutes' walk from Lindisfarne village).

LINDISFARNE PRIORY

English Heritage • ££ • Usual hours

The heart and soul of Holy Island, and if you come at a quiet time it is very beautiful, though it doesn't stand up to the hordes of visitors at peak periods. In truth there's not terribly much to see, the most memorable feature of the ruin being one slender surviving arch over the crossing of the church, known as the Rainbow Arch. Other buildings besides the church are too erratic to make much sense.

When there aren't many people around, though, the island does still retain its ancient air of sanctity. The original monastery here was founded in 635 by Aidan, a monk from Iona who was summoned by King Oswald of Northumbria to become the kingdom's first bishop. Its most famous resident was Cuthbert, one of the earliest English saints. The place was an important centre of learning, as reflected in the beautiful pen-work of the Lindisfarne Gospels, which date from around 700.

On Holy Island: reached by car across a causeway that's closed when the tide is high.

Lindisfarne Priory's most famous feature is a slender ruined arch now popularly known as the Rainbow Arch.

Norham Castle stands on a cliff above the River Tweed, with Scotland just a stone's throw away across the water.

NORHAM CASTLE

English Heritage • ££ • Usual hours

This very imposing castle ruin is the most northerly in England (if you don't count Berwick-upon-Tweed, of which there's barely anything left). It stands on the bank of the River Tweed, which to all intents and purposes has been the border with Scotland since 1237, when Alexander II of Scotland signed the Treaty of York and effectively gave up Scottish claims to the English counties of Northumberland and Cumberland. Even today, Scotland still starts on the other bank of the river.

By far the most significant building of the castle is the keep, which looks pretty solid from the front but in fact is half-ruined. Despite its condition, it's still very impressive (the best half-ruined keep in England, in fact). It was built in two halves: the side furthest away from the entrance was first to be completed, in about 1121, while the other half wasn't constructed until about 1160. The vaulted basements (or 'undercrofts') of both halves are still intact, and by

comparing them, you can clearly see the different styles of construction used at different dates. The older half has what's known as a 'groin vault', with arches across it, while the more recent side is a 'barrel vault'.

The survival of these vaults also means that you can get up to first-floor level, where the hall would have been in the older part of the building, which is slightly larger. The whole of the western third of the keep – the side that you come up the stairs on – was rebuilt in the early 1400s, at which time a fourth floor (fifth, if you count the basement) was added. The spiral stair which runs from top to bottom is of this date.

The rest of the castle retains the original layout from the 1100s, with the inner ward separated from the lower outer ward by a large moat and curtain walls around both wards. Much of the actual stonework that you now see, however, dates from an extensive rebuilding in the early 1500s after the troubles of 1513, when the castle was battered by Scots artillery for two days and captured.

Within three weeks, the Scots had been defeated at Flodden (*see Etal Castle, opposite*) and Norham was back in the hands of its rightful owner, the Bishop of Durham, but the place clearly needed to be updated so that it could be defended by (as well as from) guns. Most of the curtain walls of the inner and outer wards were rebuilt with handy additions like gun-loops. The only earlier parts are a stretch of wall in the outer ward by the keep, which is from the 1100s, and the West Gate (the one at the bottom of the site, pointing towards the village). This was the original main gate of the castle and also dates from the 1100s, but it had a short barbican added in about 1408.

The castle's position meant that it suffered in the wars between England and Scotland, particularly in the early 1300s: it was besieged in 1318 for almost a year, in 1319 for seven months and again in 1322, and in 1327 it was briefly taken by the Scots.

Near Norham village: signposted from the A698 west of Berwick-upon-Tweed.

PRUDHOE CASTLE

English Heritage • ££ • Usual hours

This was a large and important castle, but it hasn't stood up well to later alterations. In the early 1800s a large house was built right across the middle of the castle, and at the same time most of what remained of the earlier buildings in the outer ward – including the great hall – was simply knocked down and carted away.
The result is that the castle retains its original layout (and still looks the part from the outside, where you can see

Prudhoe was the third castle on the Tyne, after Tynemouth and Newcastle. It guarded an important crossing-place.

the earlier curtain walls) but has the ambience of the later house.
The two main buildings are the keep, which is badly ruined, and the gate which is still the only point of access to the castle. This gate is easily the castle's most interesting feature. A long barbican leads up to the gatehouse itself, which is one of the earliest buildings, dating from the early 1100s. Upstairs, reached by an external stair, is a chapel, and over that is a later room added to provide secure storage for documents.

The site, on a rocky outcrop overlooking the Tyne, was a naturally strong one used as a defensive settlement even before the Normans arrived. The first Norman motte castle was built here about 1080, and the castle was rebuilt in stone in the 1100s. It was besieged by the Scots in 1173 and 1174, but was not taken.

Signposted off the A695 at Prudhoe.

ROUGHTIN LINN

ROCK CARVINGS

On privately owned land • Free • Open access at any reasonable time

A remarkable monument of the bronze age, this is the largest ancient carved stone in England. It has over 60 different carvings on it, the most obvious ones being 'cup' marks and sets of concentric circles. What it all meant, nobody knows. Personally, I'd be tempted to make comparisons with the sacred places of the aboriginal Australians, where similar rock outcrops are painted with decorations thousands of years old.

By the minor road from Kimmerston (near Ford) to the B6525 near Lowick. Where the track to Roughtin Linn Farm meets the road, walk a few yards further east and the path to the rock is to the north of the road.

Early English art: there are more than 60 carvings on this rock at Roughtin Linn, all as much as 4000 years old.

WARKWORTH CASTLE

English Heritage • ££ • Usual hours

Warkworth is probably the most enjoyable castle to visit in the whole of England. Everything about the place is just a little bit special, from the size and ingenious design of the keep to the remarkable carvings on a tower known as the Lion Tower.

The castle isn't the only thing to see, either. A short walk along the riverbank is the extraordinary Warkworth Hermitage, a chapel carved into a cave in the rock, which you can visit via a short boat trip in the summer months. In the village there's a fortified bridge from the late 1300s, another reminder of the precarious existence led by the people of this region in late medieval times, with the Scots raiding southwards and the English fighting back northwards.

It's hardly surprising that such a strong castle was built here, but Warkworth was not just a bulwark against the Scots: it was also an expression of the power and prestige of the Percy family, to whom it was

Warkworth's fantastic keep is great fun to explore – all the rooms seem to connect with all the other rooms.

granted in 1332 by Edward III. The Percys, who already had a great castle at Alnwick, were treated like kings in Northumberland and tended to get ideas above their station.

The great keep at Warkworth was built in the late 1300s by the fourth Henry de Percy, first Earl of Northumberland, whose political ambitions practically ruined the family. He helped depose King Richard II in 1399, then led a rebellion against Henry IV in 1403 during which his son, Henry Hotspur, was killed at Shrewsbury and Warkworth was battered into submission by the king's cannon.

The keep is probably the most advanced example of keep design in England: the last word in keeps, if you will. What makes it so special is its size and intricate layout, so that in exploring it you find yourself popping up and down staircases and in and out of surprising rooms all of which seem to link with one another by stairs or passageways. Right down the middle runs a light well, with an ingenious

system of rainwater collection which also enabled the drains of the toilets to be flushed out. There's a fantastic cutaway illustration in the guidebook (indispensable for its plans and diagrams) which shows this drainage system, complete with several tiny soldiers sitting on the toilet seats.

Apart from the keep, the best bit is the Lion Tower (left of the gatehouse as you come in) with its remarkable heraldic carvings. The lion was the symbol of the Percy family, and above it are two shields bearing other family emblems. All the carving would have been brightly painted. This was the official state entrance for visitors to the lord's hall that stood behind, and at the other end of the hall is another tower which gave private access to the hall and to the lord's chamber, the solar, on the first floor. There's not an awful lot left of any of this, but with the keep being such a huge treat, it hardly matters.

Clearly signposted at southern side of Warkworth village; large, free car park.

SEE ALSO...

BELLISTER PELE TOWER, *Bellister Estate, south of Haltwhistle* – Ruin of a defensive tower in the grounds of a large house, the estate of which is now owned by the National Trust.

BERWICK-UPON-TWEED CASTLE, *signposted in a park next to the railway station* – This was once the most important of the border castles, but there isn't a lot left because its remains were destroyed by the building of the railway. There is one interesting piece of wall which runs down a steep hill to the Water Tower by the river.

BERWICK-UPON-TWEED RAMPARTS AND BARRACKS, *all around the town* – Vast earthwork banks supported by stone walls form the remarkable Elizabethan town defences. The museum in the Barracks is very dull, unless you want to know about the last 400 years of soldiering, so content yourself with a good stroll round the impressive ramparts instead. (*English Heritage; Ramparts: free access at any time, Barracks: £££, usual hours.*)

BLACK MIDDENS BASTLE HOUSE, *on minor road near Gatehouse, north-west of Bellingham* – Good example of a 'bastle house', the most basic kind of fortified house found in the region (essentially it's just a thick-walled two-storey farmhouse). The countryside round these parts is fantastic. (*English Heritage, free, open access at any reasonable time.*)

BOTHAL CASTLE, *near Morpeth* – Modest castle of the mid-1300s with a fine gatehouse (not vastly different from the one at *Hylton Castle, County Durham*) which is restored and in use. Privately owned; not open to the public.

CHILLINGHAM CASTLE, *Chillingham, near Alnwick* – A square of walls with a tower at each corner (very like *Castle Bolton, Yorkshire*) dating basically from about 1350 but heavily updated as a house in the 1600s and afterwards. Famous for a herd of wild cattle that still wanders its grounds. (*Privately owned, £££, limited hours – May to September.*)

CHIPCHASE CASTLE, *near Wark* – The oldest part is a turreted tower of the 1300s (similar to the old keep at *Belsay Castle, page 241*) but a very ostentatious Jacobean mansion was added later (1621). Privately owned and not open to the public.

CORBRIDGE VICAR'S PELE, *by the church in Corbridge* – It is privately owned and you can only look at the outside, but all the same this is an interesting example of the most basic kind of pele tower – a tall, thin house with its main accommodation on the first floor. It looks very archaic and slightly grim.

DILSTON CASTLE, *near Corbridge* – This is a small tower-keep of the early 1400s which is now ruined. It stands in the grounds of the privately owned Dilston Hall.

DOD LAW ROCK CARVINGS, *scattered all over the moor to the east of the B6525 near Doddington* – The moor here is good, open walking country with lots of footpaths, and there are rock carvings to be found all over the place, as well as three iron age enclosures (one is a settlement with large huts inside, while the others might just be stock-pens).

FORD CASTLE, *Ford, near Etal* – There is a very grand house here built in the 1700s around the remains of an earlier castle (built in the mid-1300s, rebuilt in the mid-1500s). It is some kind of educational centre and is not normally open to visitors.

GREAVES ASH HUT CIRCLES & ENCLOSURE, *west of Ingram, near Linhope Spout waterfall* – Large group of fine circular stone huts, each about 6m (20ft) across with paved floors. They date from the iron age and were possibly still used into the Roman era.

HAGGERSTON CASTLE, *by the A1 south of Berwick* – A single tall tower of uncertain date remains from a large defended manor house; it is in the grounds of a caravan site.

KIELDER CASTLE, *near Kielder Water* – Not a castle at all, but a Gothick hunting lodge dating from 1775.

LANGLEY CASTLE, *near Haydon Bridge* – A large and very solid-looking tower house built in 1350. It was restored in the late 1800s, but it looks pretty good, and it is now in use as a hotel.

MITFORD CASTLE, *near Morpeth* – Rare (for Northumbria) early Norman motte castle, built round about 1100, with a later D-shaped enclosure on the mound, inside which stood a five-sided keep. It's all very ruinous now. (*Local council, free, open access at any reasonable time.*)

MORPETH CASTLE, *Morpeth* – There were two castles in the town, but all that is left is a gatehouse of the later one, and this was converted into a private house in the late 1800s.

THIRLWALL CASTLE, *Greenhead* – Ruin of yet another tower-house from the mid-1300s, rectangular with a tower at each corner. (*Local council, free, open access at any reasonable time.*)

AND...

CHEW GREEN ROMAN FORTLET & CAMPS, *by river Coquet, south of Brownlow Law* (permission to visit needed from duty officer at Redesdale Army camp ; there are four temporary camps built by troops heading north, the earliest about 80 AD for a full legion); FIVE BARROWS, *Holystone Common* (there are actually nine bronze age stone cairns here); FIVE KINGS STANDING STONES, *on Dues Hill, just south of previous entry* (actually there are four stones, one fallen); GREAT HETHA FORT and HETHA BURNS SETTLEMENTS, *south-west of Hethpool, west of Wooler* (also Hethpool stone circle); HUMBLETON HILL HILLFORT, *just west of Wooler* (a fine hillfort with walled enclosures and traces of huts); HIGH ROCHESTER ROMAN FORT (BREMENIUM), *just north of Rochester by the A68* (the middle of nowhere); LORDENSHAWS HILLFORT, near Hesleyhurst (also has marked stones); OLD BEWICK HILLFORT, on hill above river Breamish; RISINGHAM ROMAN FORT, *West Woodburn, west of the A68* (when the Romans abandoned it in the late 300s, they left a ton of coal in the bath-house); YEAVERING BELL HILLFORT, *Old Yeavering*.

Bibliography

These are some of the books I have found particularly useful or enjoyable while researching this book…

Besides the NATIONAL TRUST AND ENGLISH HERITAGE HANDBOOKS, published by the respective institutions and available free to members (or for a price to non-members through bookshops), there is one book which I have carried everywhere with me while researching this book and which I would thoroughly recommend to anyone who is developing an interest in archaeology.

It is THE SHELL GUIDE TO BRITISH ARCHAEOLOGY by Jacquetta Hawkes (with Paul Bahn, published by Michael Joseph in 1986). I believe it is now out of print, but it's well worth trying to get your hands on a copy. It's a nice, simple guide to all the most outstanding archaeological sites in Britain (many more than could be fitted into this book), and it covers Scotland and Wales too (though not Northern Ireland).

Another book you will inevitably find useful is a good, basic introduction to the history and architecture of castles, and here CASTLES OF ENGLAND, SCOTLAND AND WALES by Paul Johnson (published by Weidenfeld and Nicholson in a paperback edition in 1989, and still widely available in new editions) is in a class of its own. It isn't a guidebook, but it is a very good description of the history of castles, from Norman mottes to Victorian gothic fantasies. At times it can seem a little heavy, but persevere and it will reward you with lots of fascinating details. The book is well illustrated and represents good value.

Don't be without a serious (but not too heavy) introduction to archaeology in Britain. There are two good ones: both are rather more like textbooks than something you'd read for fun, but give them a chance and put some effort in, and you will certainly find them rewarding.

The more accessible of the two is ARCHAEOLOGY OF THE BRITISH ISLES by Andrew Hayes (published in 1993 by Batsford and English Heritage),

which is the ideal way of getting a good overview from the old stone age right up to Norman times. Rather more intense and specialised, but also very interesting, is PREHISTORIC BRITAIN by Timothy Darvill (first published in 1987 by Batsford) which starts with the ice ages and runs up to the Roman (therefore historic) era.

Not really books, but good fun, and also very useful… there are two historic maps published by the Ordnance Survey in association with the Royal Commission for Historic Monuments in England (RCHME) and its Welsh and Scottish counterparts. ANCIENT BRITAIN details many of the most important prehistoric sites, labelling them as neolithic, bronze age, iron age, Roman era or post-Roman. ROMAN BRITAIN features all the significant Roman sites in the country.

If you are developing an interest in the archaeology of your region, there is an excellent series published by Longman under the general title 'A Regional History of England'. Two volumes which I have found particularly enjoyable and enlightening (perhaps because they cover the most interesting areas of the country) are Barry Cunliffe's WESSEX TO AD 1000 and Malcolm Todd's THE SOUTH-WEST TO AD 1000, the latter covering the archaeology of Devon and Cornwall.

A handy tool for the serious student of local history who is keen to track down less well-known castle remains in his or her area (and one which I have found useful) is the comprehensive, scholarly CASTLES OF BRITAIN AND IRELAND by Plantagenet Somerset Fry (published by David & Charles in 1996). It's not light reading, and it's not a guidebook, but it is a very solid work of reference.

Also immensely useful for local historians are modest publications from locally based publishers: they tend to be cheap and informative, written by local enthusiasts. Cumbria and Cheshire are fortunate enough to be covered by books of this kind:

CASTLES IN CUMBRIA by Jean Cope (published by Cicerone Press of Milnthorpe) has lots of information in it that you won't find anywhere else, including interesting descriptions of the fortified houses known as 'pele towers', while CASTLES OF CHESHIRE by PW Cullen and R Hordern (from Crossbow Books) is a cheap and very comprehensive guide to many less well-known castles of the county (in particular, it's the only place to get a good idea of what Chester Castle was like in its heyday). There is a series of very inexpensive, very informative little volumes entitled NORTHUMBRIAN CASTLES written by Frank Graham (published by Butler Publishing of Thropton, Rothbury) which will add interest to a castle-hunter's visit to the north-east of England.

Two of the most interesting stories of twentieth-century archaeology are told in Penguin paperbacks neither of which is exactly up to date, but both of which are still of great value.

Colin Renfrew's BEFORE CIVILISATION tells the story of how radiocarbon dates were shown by newer techniques, such as tree-ring dating, to need lots of modification, which changed the whole picture of European history.

ARTHUR'S BRITAIN by Leslie Alcock (who excavated the hillfort at South Cadbury in Somerset) details the search for the historical truth behind the legendary King Arthur, and it remains fascinating even though the revised preface which the author added in 1987 acknowledges that there is no particularly good case for Arthur having been a real, historical figure.

Not only on a fascinating topic, but also written by one of the country's foremost archaeologists, THE ANCIENT CELTS by Barry Cunliffe (published by Oxford University Press in 1997) represents the very latest opinion on its subject. It is rather heavy and studious in places, but it presents a picture of the Celts which makes far more sense than anything that has gone before. Undoubtedly worth getting your hands on if you have a serious interest in the iron age.

Index

Entries in **bold type** are main listing entries, each of which is accompanied by a photograph.